Asymmetric Autonomy

and the Settlement of Ethnic Conflicts

NATIONAL AND ETHNIC CONFLICT
IN THE 21ST CENTURY

Brendan O'Leary, Series Editor

Asymmetric Autonomy

and the Settlement of Ethnic Conflicts

Edited by

Marc Weller and Katherine Nobbs

PENN

UNIVERSITY OF PENNSYLVANIA PRESS

PHILADELPHIA • OXFORD

Published by
University of Pennsylvania Press
Philadelphia, Pennsylvania 19104-4112

Printed in the United States of America on acid-free paper
10 9 8 7 6 5 4 3 2 1

A Cataloging-in-Publication Record is available from the Library of Congress
ISBN 978-0-8122-4230-0

Contents

Preface

This book is an outcome of a long-term research project supported by the Carnegie Corporation of New York. We are particularly grateful for this support and for the generous advice and guidance offered by Steve del Rosso of the Corporation.

The first phase of the project addressed the nature of self-determination conflicts and the deficiencies of international legal regulation in this respect. This work, previously appearing in scholarly articles and book chapters, is now embodied in a monograph (*Escaping the Self-Determination Trap*). During this phase, the principal collaborators of the project also addressed traditional mechanisms of ethnopolitical conflict settlement (*Autonomy, Self-Governance, and Conflict Resolution*).

The team then extended its investigation into an analysis of complex power sharing as a new means of addressing previously unresolvable conflicts. Over the 1990s in particular, major innovations had taken place in this area; we set out to analyze these while simultaneously refining the theoretical understanding of the meaning and complexity of the concept of power sharing (*Settling Self-Determination Conflicts*).

The emphasis on complex power sharing in international settlement practice has now been somewhat eclipsed by a return to autonomy settlements. However, this is by no means a simple reversion to previous practice. Instead, many of the most recent settlements, or projected settlements, are supported by power-sharing arrangements. These, along with more monodimensional autonomy settlements, share a strong focus on asymmetrical autonomy. It was thus deemed appropriate at this point to investigate the novel aspects of asymmetrical state design as a tool of ethnopolitical conflict settlement.

As this volume goes to press, the team is turning its attention to another aspect of the management of interethnic relations. Having devoted much time and energy to issues of the macroconstruction of ethnically diverse (or divided) states, we are now addressing solutions that can be adopted below the level of major constitutional revision. This work (*Political Participation of Minorities*) considers the institutions, mechanisms, and practices for fostering political participation of nondominant groups in the overall state, in relation to issues or regions of special importance to the respective communities.

We therefore see this volume as part of our ongoing investigation into ways and means of accommodating nondominant groups within existing states. We are particularly indebted to members of the global research team assembled for this project. Once again, the contributions we have received are original and reflective, and they significantly advance the agenda of this venture: to contribute to the stabilization of states placed at risk through ethnopolitical conflict.

Finally, we would like to extend our sincerest gratitude to Peter Agree and Alison Anderson their of the University of Pennsylvania Press for their support and patience during the editorial process.

Introduction

Marc Weller

Over the past two decades, there has been a profusion of settlements of self-determination and ethnic conflicts. In the majority of these cases, asymmetric autonomy has been used as the principal tool of settlement. What follows is an investigation of this novel practice.

The concept of autonomy conjures up a sense of separateness, of self-governance largely independent of a central state. Independence of governance from the center suggests a potential for separation by means of the centrifugal forces of disintegration. Nevertheless, autonomy solutions have been increasingly proposed as a remedy to separatist tendencies within states. In short, what appears at first sight to be a disintegrative solution is said to have an integrative effect. This book seeks to address this apparent paradox. The first of its three principal aims is to test the integrative power of the autonomy design.

Where autonomy is offered as a means of conflict settlement, it needs to be tailored specifically to the particular circumstances of the situation in question. This lack of generality adds to the difficulties encountered with autonomy as a solution to ethnoterritorial conflict. While the autonomy design has to be sufficiently specific to meet the exigencies of the case at hand, it must be incorporated within the existing structure of the overall state as, generally, the central authorities will not be willing to change the overall constitutional makeup of the state in order to accommodate separatist pressure emanating from just one or more of its segments. Hence, asymmetric settlements tend to ensue.

Asymmetric state designs bring with them certain problems and dilemmas of their own, beyond the difficult dimension of the ethnic conflict that may have led to their institution. The second principal aim of this book is to identify the challenges inherent in asymmetrical settlements and to establish whether and how they have been gradually overcome as experience in the design of such settlements has increased.

During the first wave of post-Cold War settlements of internal (and mainly ethnic) conflict, autonomy or self-governance solutions were deployed as part of a package: there were to be strong elements of complex power sharing, balancing the autonomy design. These would include internationally entrenched, and often internationally supervised, human rights mechanisms that stretched into the area of self-governance, provisions to ensure democratic practices and the rule of law, dispute settlement mechanisms, and consociationalist instruments (veto, grand coalitions, executive power sharing) (Weller and Metzger 2008). However, in addition to these more complex solutions, there have been a surprising number of achieved or attempted monodimensional autonomy settlements. Monodimensional settlements are where autonomy is simply granted, without much consideration of governance within the newly autonomous unit, of its relations with the center, or of the way the remaining powers of the center are to be exercised with respect to the unit. Accordingly, monodimensional settlements tend to permit a great deal of autonomy without balancing this freedom from central state control with integrationist or power-sharing tools. This is often the result of the nature of the conflict that has necessitated the settlement. The central government may be tempted to settle without having incorporated sufficient safeguards and balancing mechanisms, simply because it needs to terminate a long-running and costly conflict. There is no desire to sustain the fight, in the hope of achieving a more balanced settlement later. In instances of this kind, there may be insufficient provision for the involvement of the autonomous entity in the overall state or vice versa. Competences may be loosely defined or unrealistically assigned to the autonomy. Or, new minorities and vulnerable groups may be left without protection in the autonomous entity. Regional or local government structures may not have adequate tools at their disposal to permit smooth transition from "wartime" leadership to democracy. Human rights implementation in the autonomous unit may be neglected. The third principal aim of this book is thus to investigate whether the recent spate of asymmetric autonomy settlements has managed to avoid these pitfalls, and if so, how.

Working Definitions

Although there is no universally accepted definition of autonomy, there is nevertheless some consensus relating to its core features. First, there are three types of autonomy: personal, functional or cultural, and territorial.

Personal Autonomy

Personal autonomy guarantees a space for the exercise of preferences by the individual. While personal autonomy relates to cultural or religious preferences that may be shared by a group, it is left to the individual to make these choices on a personal basis. Of course, general human rights law protects individual choice through freedom of thought, religion, expression, and so on. Personal autonomy adds a further dimension to this cluster of rights; it is a special right that is available where a dominant culture, often one influenced by religious precepts, establishes patterns of conduct that permeate society and that may be enforced by public authorities. In such instances, personal autonomy permits the individual to opt out of this dominant pattern and to conform instead to a different set of cultural expectations and practices. Such personal autonomy has often been granted by Muslim-oriented states to non-Muslim inhabitants.

Personal autonomy has become particularly relevant where internal peace settlements result in the establishment of new territorial units of self-government. Often these units will have been established in order to acknowledge the desire of a territorially compact minority for self-government in areas where they constitute a local majority. This, in turn, means that new minorities emerge within these areas. Personal autonomy may then be offered to ensure that this group is not submerged within the dominant cultural practices of the new unit of self-government. For instance, the 1999 Rambouillet draft settlement for Kosovo would have offered ethnic Serb residents in Kosovo the opportunity to opt out of the system of local administration of family law and to apply Serbia's family law instead. The very complex set of settlements for Sudan generates personal autonomy for non-Muslims in certain areas, including the capital city of Khartoum.

Cultural and Functional (Nonterritorial) Autonomy

Cultural autonomy goes beyond the acknowledgment that members of minorities within society should not be required to conform to all practices that characterize the identity and culture of the majority.[1] Cultural autonomy recognizes the distinct identity of minorities, and their collective identity as a group, and seeks to foster the preservation and further development of that collective identity. Toward this end, minorities are invited to establish their own representative bodies. These may be empowered by the state to disburse public funds and to exercise certain public functions in relation to all members of the respective minority within the state concerned. These functions tend to relate to education, language, and culture. Where these functions go beyond what can be understood as cultural self-administration (or autonomy) by a minority, one may speak of functional autonomy. Cultural and functional autonomy normally apply in relation to all members of certain minorities that tend to be specifically enumerated in fundamental legislative texts, irrespective of their place of residence in the territory of the entire state. Where cultural or functional autonomy is applied only in specified territorial areas, the concept approaches that of territorial autonomy.

Territorial Autonomy

Territorial autonomy, in its most general sense, describes self-governance of a demographically distinct territorial unit within the state (Berhardt 1981; Dinstein 1981; Ghai 2000; Hannum 1996; Lapidoth 1997, 27, 57 ff.; Marko 1995, 262 ff.; Reynolds 2001; Suksi 1998). There is some divergence within attempts to define territorial autonomy, but the following elements would need to be present:

1. *Demographic distinctiveness.* The system of self-administration must be established to reflect the demographic (ethnic, cultural, linguistic, or religious) characteristics of the dominant group within the territory in question. This is what distinguishes autonomy from other forms of local or regional self-governance.
2. *Devolution, not decentralization.* Public power is exercised directly by the autonomous unit, as a result of full devolution to it of public authority. Where a territorial unit merely exercises public power on behalf of another, superior state agency, this involves a decentralized but fundamentally unitary state. The local unit essentially acts as an executive agency of the center, even if it has some freedom in determining how to implement directives from above.
3. *Legal entrenchment.* The autonomy must be established in the legal system of the state concerned. It is subject to debate whether it is sufficient to establish autonomy in ordinary legislation, or whether it must be constitutionally entrenched. Indeed, according to some, autonomy only exists where the autonomous status cannot be changed without the consent of the autonomous unit itself (formal constitutional entrenchment). In some instances, autonomy may also be entrenched in international agreements, or in internal peace settlements that may have been generated with international involvement.
4. *Legal supremacy.* It is clear that the autonomous entity, however advanced its powers, exists within the overall legal order of the state concerned. The granting of autonomy does not generate a right of external self-determination (secession), unless provisions for that aim are expressly provided for in the autonomy settlement.
5. *Statute-making powers.* Autonomy typically advances upon ordinary local or regional self-government inasmuch as the autonomous

unit will often be granted the power of establishing its own basic law, or statute. However, this statute must remain within the area of competence assigned to the autonomous unit by legislation or a constitutional settlement.

6. *Significant competences.* Autonomy will generally assign significant legislative and executive competences to the autonomous entity. Generally, this competence will be specifically defined in the autonomy law or settlement. At times, the overall state will enjoy residual authority, although there are a significant number of both recent and traditional asymmetric autonomy arrangements that reverse this expectation.

7. *Parallel action.* In genuine autonomy designs, both the autonomous unit and the central government can directly exercise public powers in relation to individuals within the autonomous territory. However, this parallel exercise of powers will not normally concern the same issue areas but will instead be related to the separate and distinctive competences of the autonomous unit and the center respectively.

8. *Limited external relations powers.* Autonomous entities will have either no power in foreign affairs or limited authority to engage in international contacts that correspond to the substantive competences that have been granted to them. This may include so-called "executive agreements" in relation to commercial or cultural issues. In some instances, there may be opportunities for the development of special links with neighboring states, or more likely, with regions in neighboring states through cross-border cooperation.

9. *Institutions.* Autonomy will generally provide for legislative, adjudicative, and executive institutions. Hence there will be a regional-local assembly, a regional-local government, regional/local courts, and executive agencies under regional-local control, including the police.

10. *Integrative mechanisms.* The powers of self-governance will typically be balanced with tools that ensure the continued and effective integration of the autonomous unit within the overall state. This includes the availability of a dispute settlement mechanism at the level of the constitutional court, arrangements for the transfer of resources between the center and the autonomous unit, and the guaranteed representation of the autonomous unit in the structures of national government. Where autonomy extends to federalism, one would expect to see more extensive provision for representation of the entity in the central organs of the overall state. This might involve establishment of a second parliamentary chamber.

The breadth and scope of territorial autonomy arrangements is highly diverse, and is contingent on the constitutional and political background of the case. At the most advanced level of self-governance, one may exclude state unions from the concept of autonomy. Such unions will generally preserve the separate international legal personality of the constituent entities. There may even be a right of possible separation.[2] Similarly, within confederations, the constituent units will also retain wide authority, transferring to the center only a narrow category of competences that can be best exercised jointly. For instance, initially, it appeared that Bosnia and Herzegovina had been constructed as a confederation of the Republika Srpska and the mainly Croat-Muslim Federation that had been arranged before the Dayton settlement of 1995. Gradually, that state may be undergoing transformation into a more integrated federation. Federal states can be considered as examples of autonomy settlements if self-government is adopted as a means of accommodating demographic diversity (Belgium, and in some respects Canada).[3]

As will be noted at greater length below, asymmetrical federal designs are sometimes adopted as a way of terminating secessionist disputes. These are solutions in which one or two entities are given a federal-type status, without transforming the entire state into a federation. Such a solution has been adopted, for instance, in relation to Southern Sudan, and is being explored in relation to Moldova/Transdniestria. Formerly in Georgia, South Ossetia and Abkhazia were candidates for such treatment. However, designation as an asymmetrical federation is being avoided in these instances and increasing reference is made instead to autonomy, disguising somewhat the very wide powers of self-governance that are sometimes foreseen.

At the lowest end of the spectrum, one may consider cases of local autonomy: enhanced local government of certain municipalities based on their demographic composition. An example is "enhanced" local self-government provided in the Ohrid settlement for Macedonia. While it was not felt politically prudent to designate the areas concerned as autonomous units, significant special provision was made in relation to them in view of their ethnic composition.

These settlements tend to be asymmetrical by definition, given the unique character of the one or more ethnic issues that require settlement. Such settlements may be obtained due to an agreed process of constitutional devolution (United Kingdom, Spain), as a result of a mainly internal peace process (Mali, Philippines, the attempted settlement for France/Corsica), of partly internationalized internal peace processes (Papua New Guinea/Bougainville), or on the basis of an international settlement (Aaland Islands, South Tyrol, Bosnia and Herzegovina).[4]

Asymmetric Settlements and Conflict Regulation

Asymmetric autonomy is not a new concept, as Chapter 1 in this volume demonstrates. However, asymmetry has nevertheless increased in popularity in international practice. In fact, at present asymmetrical autonomy solutions are being pursued in relation to most ethnic conflicts that are subject to active settlement attempts.

Asymmetrical state-building is a feature of the ongoing second wave of post-Cold War settlements to secessionist conflicts. The first wave, which occurred during the period from 1988 to about 2000, was characterized by one of two features. Both the dynamics and energy of the immediate post-Cold War environment helped the parties to grasp the opportunity for a settlement after prolonged stalemate (for instance, Northern Ireland), or new conflicts erupted with such intensity that they demanded decisive international action. The post-Cold War transition released a significant amount of already-conflicting energy in parts of the former Warsaw Pact region, and generated new conflicts as well. These were sufficiently violent to trigger international diplomatic or forcible intervention. This intervention terminated the conflicts and pressured the parties into a settlement (Bosnia, Rambouillet, Ohrid).

This left unresolved a number of cases where (a) a secessionist group effectively controlled territory, (b) the government was unable to displace it or to effect a decisive outcome, and (c) there was no willingness or capacity to force a settlement though international diplomatic or military intervention. Given the relatively strong position of the secessionist group (which benefits from the status quo at least in the short to mid-term), international mediation efforts were not able to focus on complex power sharing as a solution. Instead, the settlements focused on preserving the status of self-governance that was generated by the secessionist groups through force, rather than on a more complex power-sharing solution that would require a greater element of cooperation between the secessionists and the central authorities.

While asymmetric settlements appear to have proliferated, this area has not, as yet, attracted much academic attention.[5] There is one useful collection of essays on this subject (Agranoff 1999), which, however, was published prior to the latest wave of asymmetrical initiatives. Hence, it was deemed useful to revisit the concept at this juncture.

Just as the discussion of autonomy has spawned a very wide range of possible definitions, there are also varying approaches to the phenomenon of asymmetry. The principal distinction that may be drawn relates to de facto or de jure approaches. De facto approaches measure the "felt" degree of competence and power, in accordance with factors such as population size, economic and fiscal resources of the respective entities, and so on. However, the difficulty with this approach, as outlined by Brendan O'Leary in this volume, is that all situations are essentially asymmetrical if one focuses on the relative power or influence of the constituent units of a state in real terms. The de jure approach, by contrast, offers greater clarity. The existence or extent of asymmetry can be immediately identified through a study of the formal constitutional and legislative instruments establishing the state. On the other hand, that approach in itself may not be fully capable of encapsulating the administrative realities of the autonomy system. Hence, throughout this book, we consider the formal, de jure, aspects of asymmetrical designs without losing sight of the reality of their implementation.

Wide-ranging self-governance would ordinarily be accommodated in a federal state design. However, in many of these cases, full federalization is not seen as a possible alternative for the central government. This hesitation may be based on a fear of federalism being a first step toward independence, on great popular opposition to a federal settlement, or sometimes on ignorance in relation to the concept of federalism. Hence, the solution of choice that may appear acceptable to both sides is to grant a federal-type autonomy status only to the secessionist entity, without at the same time significantly changing the constitutional structure of the overall state.

One may distinguish a number of different types of asymmetrical settlement (Stevens 1977; Ghai 2001; McGarry 2005). First, there are designs whereby just one unit within an otherwise central state is granted a federal-type autonomy status. The overall state does not change its unitary character as a result (federacy). Instead, autonomy remains an anomaly (Zanzibar). In another case, the unitary state is maintained but more than one unit enjoys a federal-type status while the overall state still remains a unitary one. In fact, the autonomous units may differ in the extent of authority that is assigned to them (Transdniestria and Gagauzia in Moldova).

A third type of asymmetrical design consists of several autonomous units accommodated within a state that is constituted as fully devolved or as a formal federation. However, one or more of these might have a special or anomalous status of enhanced autonomy. This anomaly can take various forms. It might extend to greater powers of internal self-government, or in other words it might enjoy more competences than do other units. However, the asymmetry can also extend to enhanced external powers of representation in relation to the center. For instance, a blocking vote may be generated for a certain entity or class of entities, either generally or in relation to special types of decisions, including constitutional changes. Or there may be guaranteed governmental representation through reserved ministerial seats (Southern Sudan).

A fourth type of asymmetry may again provide for a fully federal-type state. However, in this model, asymmetry is regularized. As opposed to the standard definition of a federation, which would require equal status and competences for all federal subjects, there are different types or classes of federal subjects (complex asymmetrical federation) which share common powers and characteristics. This was the case, for instance, in the Socialist Federal Republic of Yugoslavia, or the Union of Socialist Federal Republics. The Russian Federation remains a highly complex asymmetrical federation.[6]

Recent settlements, and present negotiations in a number of cases, appear to be very much focused on the first type of asymmetrical settlement. The overall state retains a unitary and centralized character. However, the special circumstances of the separatist unit or units are to be accommodated by an exceptional federal or autonomy status that is made available to the respective entity or entities alone.

Cases for Consideration

A number of possible cases present themselves for analysis. These include instances of existing settlements and cases in which progress is being made toward a settlement.[7] While some of these settlements offer interesting complexity, others fall into the category of incomplete or fairly monodimensional solutions. It will be useful to address both to gain a comparative perspective.

The first chapter in this book considers "classical" instances of asymmetrical settlements, including in particular the Aaland Islands and South Tyrol. It asks whether these generally successful instances can serve as positive examples for later generations of settlement.

Perhaps one of the most interesting cases relates to the complexity evidenced in the Russian Federation. It is difficult to track the many different layers of competence that, at least in theory, appertain to the different classes of federal subjects. Of course, central powers have been reasserted to a considerable extent. Accordingly, it will be interesting to learn how resilient the complex asymmetrical autonomy structures have been to this recentralization.

While autonomy has been studied to a considerable extent in relation to Europe, there is a dearth of scholarship addressing cases in Africa. In part, this may be due to the reluctance of African governments to consider formal autonomy arrangements, fearing disintegration of the state if the fragile present system is disrupted. However, there are some attempts at generating autonomies, including asymmetrical ones. Chapter 4 addresses three of them: Tanzania, Mali, and South Africa.

In view of Quebec's occasionally secessionist tendencies, the Canadian Constitution is also of particular interest. It is interesting to investigate whether Quebec's unique position within the overall state in this respect is reflected in a special kind of asymmetry formally expressed, or whether the doctrine of equality makes such a settlement persistently difficult.

Hong Kong is also faced with a unique and difficult situation, as a result of its history and its relative dominance by the rest of China. Of course, China does claim to have established significant practice in relation to autonomy in other regions. The question is whether the unique history of Hong Kong, bound very tightly into the "sovereignty" of China while enjoying wide-ranging autonomy in its economic and judicial affairs, may inspire other regions. Where China itself is concerned, the possible value of Hong Kong's experience in relation to Taiwan is sometimes mentioned. Others point to Tibet and, indeed, other regions featuring indigenous populations that are seeking a stronger expression of their identity through enhanced autonomy.

Finally, the United Kingdom constitutes an important example of settlement. There, the issue of representation of the devolved regions in the center has given rise to particular interests and concerns. For while Scotland and Wales (and Northern Ireland) enjoy competences independent of the rest of the union in relation to a wide range of governance issues, England enjoys no corresponding autonomy as it has not constituted itself as a "region." Hence, its elected representatives do not have full authority in relation to the affairs of the devolved entities. Conversely, the Scottish, Welsh, and Northern Irish parliamentarians sit in the Westminster parliament and take part fully in decisions that principally, or exclusively, affect England. The diversity of settlement in relation to the three territories, each featuring a different level of asymmetrical autonomy, is also of particular interest.

Chapter 9 considers a case of "simple" asymmetrical settlement, the case of Gagauzia, whereby the Organization for Security and Cooperation in Europe obtained a wide-ranging settlement between Gagauzia and the central Moldovan government in 1994. However, the failure to provide for sufficient detail in the assignment of competences led to a risk of collapse of the agreement. The question therefore arises as to whether short, simple, and monodimensional settlements merely delay reignition of the conflict they were meant to address.

Another interesting forward-looking case is furnished by the Constitution of Iraq, which offers an innovative asymmetrical settlement design that provides for potential regionalization of the country. While only one region is presently designated as such, others may establish themselves under the current constitution. Therefore, asymmetry is variable, according to future developments that may ultimately lead to full federalization. This development is highly innovative and warrants careful consideration.

At present, a number of additional asymmetrical settlements are emerging in other parts of the globe, some of which also offer a variable geometry. In Sri Lanka, protracted efforts are being undertaken to relaunch an initiative that would give provinces wide-ranging powers of self-governance, starting with the northeast. In the past, insufficient emphasis has been placed on discussing the issue of governance within that proposed unit, including democracy and human and minority rights. A particularly difficult aspect of this case concerns the position of the mainly Muslim minority that would find itself in a virtually independent region dominated by a militant Tamil leadership (Edrisinha and Seymour 2005, 424). Moreover, it does not appear as if the central government is willing to accommodate genuine autonomy through the necessary constitutional changes. Hence, the latest settlement proposal, which would, in fact, avoid many of the pitfalls of previous monodimensional initiatives, is unlikely to be implemented.

The temptation of simple asymmetrical settlements is also evident in the so-called "frozen" conflicts of the Caucasus region. In Georgia, asymmetrical settlement options relating to Abkhazia and South Ossetia were on the table for over a decade. However, obstructions in negotiations on one side, and an unwillingness to consider the requisite broader constitutional changes necessary in Georgia on the other, led to protracted stalemate. Unfortunately, the situation has now been resolved through the use of force.

A final and interesting case is that of Puntland. As opposed to Somaliland, Puntland is willing to reintegrate with Somalia. However, it is demanding an asymmetric status that reflects the virtual independence it has enjoyed for some time. Somaliland, on the other hand, has managed to consolidate its de facto independence, remaining outside of the many attempts to resurrect Somalia as a fully functioning state. It is therefore interesting to compare the strategies and outcomes generated in relation to both these entities.

Notes

1. Most recently, see, e.g., Smith and Cordell 2008; Nimni 2007, 345.

2. For instance, the State Union of Serbia and Montenegro confirms the potential statehood of both Serbia and Montenegro, and provides modalities for potential dissolution. There are exceptional cases, however, where the terminology of union may be deployed to emphasize the extensive separate identity of the

constituent entities, while at the same time providing for an express safeguard against secession, e.g., the proposed "indissoluble" state union proposed for Cyprus under a UN-mediated peace plan in 2004.

3. One may include unusual constructions such as the constitution of Bosnia and Herzegovina in this category.

4. Italy has maintained that the arrangements for South Tyrol (the so-called "Package" and the "Operational Calendar") that led to the new Autonomy Statute of 1971–72 are not formally the result of international agreement. However, it is fair to say that that the arrangement has also been internationally entrenched, including through parallel decisions by the Italian and Austrian parliaments.

5. The concept was shaped by Charles D. Tarlton (1965, 861); more recent studies include Agranoff 1999; Ghai 2000, 2001; McGarry 2005; and Watts 2005, 2008.

6. For a more detailed examination of the Russian case, see Bowring, this volume.

7. See Ghai and Regan 2000. Another early instance from this "second wave" of settlements is Gagauzia; see Neukirch 2002.

References

Agranoff, R., ed. 1999. *Accommodating diversity: Asymmetry in federal states.* Baden-Baden: Nomos.

Berhardt, R. 1981. Federalism and autonomy. In *Models of autonomy*, ed. Y. Dinstein. New Brunswick, N.J.: Transaction Books.

Dinstein, Y., ed. 1981. *Models of autonomy.* New Brunswick, N.J.: Transaction Books.

Edrisinha, R., and L. Seymour. 2005. Adopting federalism: Sri Lanka and Sudan. In *Forum of federations: Handbook of federal countries.* Montreal: McGill-Queen's University Press.

Ghai, Y. 2001. Constitutional asymmetries: Communal representation, federalism and cultural autonomy. In *The architecture of democracy*, ed. A. Reynolds. Oxford: Oxford University Press.

———, ed. 2000. *Autonomy and ethnicity.* Cambridge: Cambridge University Press.

Ghai, Y., and A. Regan. 2000. Bougainville and the dialectics of ethnicity, autonomy and separation. In *Autonomy and ethnicity*, ed. Y. Ghai. Cambridge: Cambridge University Press. 242–65.

Hannum, H. 1996. *Autonomy, sovereignty, and self-determination: The accommodation of conflicting rights.* Rev. ed. Philadelphia: University of Pennsylvania Press.

Lapidoth, R. 1997. *Autonomy: Flexible solutions to ethnic conflicts.* Washington, D.C.: U.S. Institute of Peace.

Marko, J. 1995. *Autonomie und integration: Rechtsinstitute des Nationalitätenrechts im funktionalen Vergleich.* Vienna: Böhlau.

McGarry, J. 2005. *Asymmetrical federalism and the plurinational state.* Third International conference on federalism, Brussels, 30 March. Available from author at mcgarryj@post.queensu.ca.

Neukirch, K. 2002. Autonomy and conflict-transformation: The Gagauz territorial autonomy in the Republic of Moldova. In *Minority governance in Europe*, ed. K. Gal. Budapest: Local Government Initiative Books. 105–24.

Nimni, E. 2007. National cultural autonomy as an alternative to minority territorial nationalism. *Ethnopolitics* 6, 3: 345-64.

Reynolds, A., ed. 2001. *The architecture of democracy.* Oxford: Oxford University Press.

Smith, D. J., and K. Cordell. 2008. *Cultural autonomy in contemporary Europe.* London: Routledge.

Stevens, R. M. 1977. Asymmetrical federalism: The federal principle and the survival of the small republic. *Publius* 7, 4: 177–204.

Suksi, M., ed. 1998. *Autonomy: Applications and implications.* Dordrecht: Kluwer Law International.

Tarlton, C. D. 1965. Symmetry and asymmetry as elements of federalism: A theoretical speculation. *Journal of Politics* 27: 861.

Watts, R. L. 2008. *Comparing federal systems.* 3rd ed. Montreal: McGill-Queen's University Press.

———. 2005. A comparative perspective on asymmetry in federations. Asymmetric working paper 4. Kingston: IIGR School of Policy Studies, Queen's University.

Weller, M., and B. Metzger, eds. 2008. *Settling self-determination disputes.* Dordrecht: Nijhoff.

Part I
Asymmetrical Approaches to State Design

Chapter 1
Cases of Asymmetrical Territorial Autonomy

Stefan Wolff

Territorial autonomy is not an entirely new approach for resolving self-determination disputes, but its application has become far more widespread since the end of the Cold War. Prior to that, it was mostly cases in Europe (or overseas territories related to European states, such as the Netherlands Antilles) that benefited, with some success, from the application of territorial autonomy as a conflict resolution mechanism. This is not to say that there are no examples of territorial autonomy elsewhere in the world that predate the end of the Cold War, but few of them have proved viable conflict settlements. Eritrea was granted autonomy within a federal Ethiopia in 1952 on the basis of a UN General Assembly resolution, but within ten years this arrangement had failed, leading to Eritrea's annexation by Ethiopia in 1962 and the imposition of direct (military) rule five years later, triggering a long civil war that ended with Eritrea gaining independent statehood in 1993 (Hannum 1996, 337–41; Joireman 2004; Benedikter 2007, 29). In Asia, a prominent example of failed autonomy is that of Iraqi Kurdistan. An agreement between the Kurdish Democratic Party and Saddam Hussein's Baath Party in 1970 initially appeared to provide an acceptable arrangement, but the 1974 implementing law saw the government in Baghdad renege on a number of issues and delimit the territorial reach of autonomy to the areas in which the Kurds formed a majority of the population according to the 1957 census. Taken almost two decades earlier, the latter was clearly outdated and its use for demarcating the boundaries of the autonomous entity was rejected by the Kurds as it would not have included quite a number of areas they considered Kurdish. Moreover, not unlike the situation in Iraq in 2009, the 1974 implementing legislation failed to resolve the status of Kirkuk and ownership of its natural resources (cf. Hannum 1996, 190–94; Bengio 2005, 174). In all these cases, the governance arrangements established were asymmetrical in the sense defined by Marc

Weller in the Introduction to this volume. Within their own limitations, Eritrea and Iraqi Kurdistan both had status akin to a federacy arrangement, as did Northern Ireland until 1972 and again for a short period of time in 1974. In Italy (after 1948) and Spain (after 1979) arrangements emerged in which there was overall devolution, but which were asymmetric in the sense that different powers and different levels of power were devolved to the constituent regions of the two states.

Farther back in history, what we consider territorial autonomy today has some forerunners in the way empires managed their vast territories, partly in view also of avoiding dissent from peoples and communities subjugated to the ruling, or dominant, nation or ethnic group. Examples include a number of provinces of the Ottoman empire, most prominently in the Balkans, but extending to Egypt and Lebanon as well, the Austrian Kronländer, and, after the 1867 compromise, Hungary, in the Habsburg empire, and Finland in the Russian empire for most of the nineteenth century. These, too, were essentially asymmetric arrangements. In the German empire, after 1871, the Reichsland of Alsace-Lorraine is another instructive example of an asymmetric arrangement. Ceded by France to Germany at the end of the Franco-Prussian War, which led to the creation of the German empire, Alsace-Lorraine was not made a federal entity—as were all the other German kingdoms, principalities, city-states, and so on, that formed the Wilhelmine Reich—but placed under the direct rule of the emperor. Over time, this arrangement developed into a form of autonomy more limited than that of "proper" federal entities, but nonetheless with substantial powers of self-governance (see Wolff 2002, chap. 4).[1]

As a tool of statecraft, autonomy has thus been a familiar, albeit not excessively implemented, mechanism for at least the past two centuries, one that always resulted in asymmetrical state designs. Yet, its significance as a conflict preventing and conflict resolving arrangement increased only over the course of the twentieth century. This is arguably related to the rise of nationalism as an increasingly powerful political ideology and the realization that related aspirations for self-determination needed to be taken seriously and given institutional expression, if violent conflict and redrawing of international boundaries was to be avoided in ethnically plural states. While territorial autonomy is not automatically linked to forms of democratic governance, its success as a conflict settlement strategy has become increasingly connected to the management of ethnic or other forms of cultural diversity in democratic polities and is frequently prescribed as a governance model to countries struggling with diversity management. More often than not, the optimism to resolve self-determination conflicts qua autonomy is derived from two European "model" autonomies: South Tyrol and the Aaland Islands.[2] These two cases are at the center of this chapter and are analyzed extensively in the last section. Prior to these case studies, the next section deals with some more general conceptual and empirical issues related to asymmetric territorial autonomy arrangements in pre-1990 Europe to set the stage for the more detailed discussion. The chapter concludes with a brief exploration of the continued relevance of these historical cases of asymmetric territorial autonomy.

Defining Autonomy in Pre-1990 Europe: Conceptual and Empirical Issues

There are considerable conceptual and empirical problems with the definition of autonomy.[3] While Weller's Introduction presents a very useful way around some of the conceptual difficulties, it is nonetheless helpful to trace the "academic" history of the concept through the disciplines of both international law and political science. It is thus possible to illustrate how autonomy as a tool of statecraft and autonomy as a tool of conflict resolution, especially in self-determination conflicts, have become more and more intertwined, so that a definition such as Weller's can be based on empirical observation with significant analytical power as well.

Tim Potier (2001, 54) has noted that "international lawyers have failed to come to any agreement on a 'stable' workable definition for autonomy. . . . [I]t escapes definition because it is impossible to concretise its scope. It is a loose and disparate concept that contains many threads, but no single strand." This difficulty in pinning down and conceptualizing autonomy has also been recognized in political science. Two of the most eminent scholars in the field, Brendan O'Leary and John McGarry, observed in 1993 that "Overlapping cantonisation and federalisation there exists a grey area of territorial management of ethnic differences which is often found in conjunction with external arbitration. International agreements between states can entrench the territorial autonomy of certain ethnic communities, even though the 'host state' does not generally organise itself along either cantonist or federalist principles" (McGarry and O'Leary 1993, 32).

Despite this appreciation of definitional difficulties in the nature of autonomy, political scientists and international lawyers have not hesitated to propose a variety of definitions. Michael Hechter (2000, 114) describes political autonomy as "a state of affairs falling short of sovereignty." In Ted Robert Gurr's (1993, 292) understanding, "autonomy means that a minority has a collective power base, usually a regional one, in a plural society." Hurst Hannum and Richard Lillich (1980, 859) stated in their influential essay on the concept of autonomy in international law that: " 'autonomy' is understood to refer to independence of action on the internal or domestic level, as foreign affairs and defence normally are in the hands of the central or national government, but occasionally power to conclude international agreements concerning cultural or economic matters also may reside with the autonomous entity." In her extensive study on autonomy, Ruth Lapidoth draws a clear distinction between territorial political autonomy and personal autonomy.[4] To her, "Territorial autonomy is an arrangement aimed at granting a certain degree of self-identification to a group that differs from the majority of the population in the state, and yet constitutes the majority in a specific region. Autonomy involves a division of powers between the central authorities and the autonomous entity" (Lapidoth 1997, 174–75). In contrast to a territorial conception, "Personal autonomy applies to all members of a certain group within the state, irrespective of their place of residence. It is the right to preserve and promote the religious, linguistic, and cultural character of the group through institutions established by itself" (175).

Regardless of the scope and detail of the above definitions, their one common feature, direct or indirect, is the transfer of certain powers from a central government to that of the (thereby created) autonomous entity. In practice, autonomy arrangements incorporate executive, legislative, and judicial powers to varying degrees. In cases where it is used as an instrument for ethnic conflict prevention and settlement, autonomy ideally includes a mix of the three that enables the ethnic group in question to regulate independently the affairs central to the concerns of its members, which are usually easily identifiable as they manifest themselves in concrete claims. However, as autonomy falls short of full sovereignty, this often happens within the broader constitutional and legislative framework of the minority's host country and under the supervision of a central government or similar agencies ensuring the compliance of all actions of the autonomous institutions with the regulations set up for the execution of the autonomy. However, as Daftary (2000, 5) rightly asserts, autonomy means that "powers are not merely delegated but transferred; they may thus not be revoked without consulting with the autonomous entity. . . . [T]he central government may only interfere with the acts of the autonomous entity in extreme cases (for example when national security is threatened or its powers have been exceeded)." In similar terms, Wolff and Weller (2005, 13) define autonomy as "the legally entrenched power of ethnic or territorial communities to exercise public policy functions (legislative, executive and adjudicative) independently of other sources of authority in the state, but subject to the overall legal order of the state."

As a consequence of this wide range of definitions, there is little consensus over what forms of state construction actually qualify as "autonomies." Palley (1991, 5), for example, claims that "Political autonomy may range from devolution of power to small communities, through regionalism, to federal government," and cites as examples South Tyrol, Swedish-speakers in mainland Finland and the Aaland Islands, the German minority in Denmark, and the Danish minority in Germany, Belgium, Switzerland, and the Netherlands. Elazar, in the introduction to his *Federal Systems of the World: A Handbook of Federal, Confederal and Autonomy Arrangements*, identifies 91 "functioning examples of autonomy or self-rule, ranging from classic federation to various forms of cultural home-rule" in 52 different states (Elazar 1991), while Benedikter (2007) counts 58 regions across the world with territorial autonomy.

In the context of this chapter and volume, it is helpful to bear in mind that autonomy is seen here as a tool of statecraft and a mechanism for settling self-determination conflicts.[5] Not every form of autonomy—broadly in the sense of Wolff and Weller above—is relevant to this analysis. The German or Austrian federal states, for example, are less significant than the Swiss confederation; home rule in Northern Ireland and regionalization in France have greater relevance than the application of the subsidiarity principle to local municipalities in Finland or Ireland. If the concept of autonomy is limited in such a way that it applies only to cases in which this form of state construction was implemented as part of the settlement of a self-determination conflict, the number of potential cases diminishes. Moreover, if only territorial autonomies are considered, the number of relevant cases in pre-1990 Europe decreases further (see Table 1).[6]

Thus, nine countries in pre-1990 Europe included forms of territorial autonomy established in an effort to settle self-determination conflicts. Of these, Belgium has undergone further significant constitutional reforms since 1990 and found itself in a deep constitutional crisis regarding its federal consociational structure in the summer of 2008. Yugoslavia no longer exists following its bloody disintegration, a process that began in 1991 and of which Kosovo's independence in 2008 is the latest, hopefully last, chapter. Territorial autonomy in Northern Ireland was abrogated in 1972 with the institution of direct rule from Westminster and, despite several attempts to restore some form of self-governance, it took until 1998 and a further 2006 settlement before autonomy regained traction as a mechanism of conflict settlement (see McGarry below). Spain continues to see violence in one of its autonomous regions, the Basque country, and in Switzerland some violence preceded the establishment of the canton of Jura in 1979, similar to the violence in South Tyrol that started a process of reform leading to a much improved autonomy stat-

TABLE 1. Territorial Autonomies in Pre-1990 Europe

Metropolitan state	Autonomous territorial entity/entities (year of establishment)
Belgium	Flemish Region (1980), Walloon Region (1980), Brussels-Capital Region (1989)
Denmark	Faeroe Islands (1948), Greenland (1978)
Finland	Aaland Islands (1920)
Italy	Sicily (1948)
	Sardinia (1948)
	Trentino-Alto Adige/Sudtirol (1948)
	Friuli-Venezia Giulia (1948)
	Aosta Valley (1948)
Portugal	Azores (1976), Madeira (1976)
Spain	17 autonomous communities (established between 1979 and 1983)
Switzerland	23 cantons and 6 half-cantons[a]
United Kingdom	Northern Ireland (1921–72)
Yugoslavia	6 republics (Bosnia and Herzegovina, Croatia, Macedonia, Montenegro, Slovenia, Serbia), 2 autonomous provinces (Kosovo and Vojvodina, both part of Serbia)[b]

a. The 1999 revised constitution only mentions 26 equal cantons, removing the term *half-canton* from the constitutional dictionary. Two half-cantons, Obwalden and Nidwalden, have always existed in the Swiss Federation; the other four emerged from the split of the full cantons of Appenzell (1597) and Basel (1833). The 1979 separation of Jura from Bern resulted in Jura becoming a canton in its own right.
b. This refers to the Socialist Federal Republic of Yugoslavia established in 1946, not its forerunners the Kingdom of Serbs, Croats, and Slovenes (1918–29) or the Kingdom of Yugoslavia (1929–41).

ute in 1972. Territorial autonomies in Denmark, Finland, and Portugal have also seen significant reforms over the years.

This is, admittedly, a mixed picture of the success of autonomy in Europe before 1990. However, even the failures offer important insights. Among them is the perhaps trivial observation that all the successful autonomies have seen significant changes to their frameworks over time, highlighting the need to understand autonomy as a dynamic rather than static arrangement. More important, however, the successes and failures of the pre-1990 period also indicate that for autonomy to succeed in addressing self-determination conflicts, other mechanisms may need to be present. Territorial autonomy cannot be expected to be sufficient for sustainable conflict settlements in two principal types of situations, which will additionally require power sharing mechanisms.[7] If the self-governing territories are ethnically heterogeneous, arrangements have to be made to accommodate local population diversity. This can take

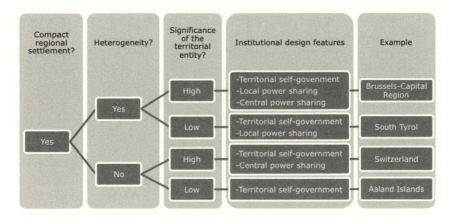

Figure 1. Context and institutional design for conflict settlement.

the form of a regional consociation, as in Brussels or South Tyrol.[8] If the significance of the territory in question relative to the rest of the state is high and necessitates power sharing at the center, the institutional outcome is a sovereign consociation, as in Belgium or Switzerland.[9]

The Belgian case also indicates that regional and sovereign consociations are not mutually exclusive but can occur together. Three key characteristics thus emerge as crucial in determining the precise nature of the institutional design of territorial autonomy for the settlement of self-determination conflicts (see Figure 1): the compactness of the settlement patterns of groups in a given state, the degree of ethnic heterogeneity in the territorial entities to which powers and competences of self-governance are to be assigned, and their significance relative to the rest of the state.

A fourth situational characteristic—transnational links—also shapes institutional design in a significant way. Such links are often determined by historical or ethnic relations between populations and territories divided by contemporary international boundaries.[10] In these instances, formal transnational institutions may be established or so-called paradiplomatic powers may be granted to territorial autonomies. However, there is another reason territorial autonomies should be invested with paradiplomatic powers: the ability to engage in the international arena is increasingly important to discharge their "other" powers effectively, for example, in relation to economic development and cultural-identity maintenance. Thus, establishment of formal transnational institutions or conferral of paradiplomatic powers to self-governing territorial entities need not happen only in cases in which historic, ethnic, or other transnational links necessitate it, but can become a feature of institutional design regardless of the existence of these links.[11]

How and Why Does Asymmetry Matter?

Academic discussion of autonomy to date has paid relatively little attention to the dimension of asymmetry that is inherent in many such conflict-settlement arrangements. Of the definitions of autonomy discussed above, only that of McGarry and O'Leary touches upon it. This is not to say that asymmetry is being ignored, but it is often taken as a given, so little further analysis is normally devoted to it. Yet, if territorial autonomy regimes are to provide lasting and stable settlements to self-determination conflicts, it is important to understand the precise impact asymmetry has on the nature and functioning of these regimes.

This is not the place for a lengthy discussion of asymmetry—important implications in relation to it have been usefully elaborated by Weller in the Introduction. A number of aspects, however, can and need to be specified in the context of the analysis of the two classical examples of asymmetric territorial autonomy regimes, the Aaland Islands and South Tyrol.

As noted by Weller, for states asymmetry offers an opportunity to maintain the overall state structure. For example, states can avoid the dreaded "f-word" federalization. Embracing asymmetry, moreover, endows institutional architects with a significant degree of flexibility to cater to the very specific situational characteristics that a conflict might bring with it and that need to be addressed in its settlement. Such an approach includes being able, from the state perspective, to minimize the control it cedes to each self-determination movement in the settlement process, and it allows for sequential, decoupled settlement processes, avoiding the potential need to "open" existing deals with each new settlement.

From the perspective of self-determination movements, asymmetry thus might also create a situation in which states are more willing to compromise, as concessions to one movement need not be replicated in other dispute settlements. This, essentially, assumes that both parties—state and self-determination movement—are motivated by a genuine desire to resolve their conflict within the boundaries of the existing state. It is important to note that such an assumption is not always realistic. Asymmetry, while clearly useful in many cases, is not a panacea for the resolution of territorial self-determination disputes. The application of asymmetry presupposes its utility to cater to the different needs of the state (maintaining sovereignty and territorial integrity) and the self-determination movement (gaining greater control over the destiny of the group it represents). At the same time, it implies that in the case of several self-determination disputes within the boundaries of the same state, asymmetry can accommodate different levels of demands by the various movements. The problem of sequential and decoupled settlement processes, noted as a potential advantage to the state, however, is just as likely to backfire: movements with initially lesser demands might be encouraged by a prior settlement to raise the stakes and ask for an equally advantageous deal; alternatively, subsequent settlements perceived as "better" may lead to reopening disputes that had already been settled. Asymmetry thus inevitably raises the specter of comparison, in itself a potential conflict causing factor (cf. Horowitz 1985).

Asymmetry is thus a double-edged sword whose application requires careful consideration of potential consequences. As the following two case studies illustrate, its benefits can clearly outweigh any possible costs, but only if asymmetry is embraced by all conflict parties as a solution to their dispute, if it is dynamically developed over time rather than conceived as a one-off static solution, and if it responds to real needs on the ground and can protect past achievements against subsequent erosion of the status and powers of autonomous entities.

Standard Bearers of Autonomy: Aaland Islands and South Tyrol

Of all the pre-1990 cases of territorial autonomy in Europe, two stand out in terms of their longevity and success—the Aaland Islands and South Tyrol. Established in 1920 and 1948 respectively, they are among the oldest such arrangements and are frequently referred to as model cases in academic and policy debates on territorial autonomy as a mechanism for settling self-determination conflicts. The detailed examination here of both autonomy arrangements serves a dual purpose. First, it gives an in-depth and up-to-date overview of the specifics of institutional design in two cases of asymmetric territorial autonomy in Europe whose origins lie in the pre-1990 period. Second, the two case studies will test the assumptions above, in particular, that specific situational characteristics determine the overall institutional design of territorial autonomies and the extent to which this involves asymmetric forms of state construction, that is, to which autonomy requires further tools, such as power sharing or paradiplomatic powers, to succeed in its objective of settling self-determination conflicts.

The Autonomy of the Aaland Islands Since 1920

The Aaland Islands are an archipelago of some 6,000 islands spread over almost 7,000 square kilometers off the Swedish coast. Ruled by Sweden for nearly seven hundred years and with a linguistically and culturally Swedish population, the islands fell to Russia in 1809 and made part of the Grand Duchy of Finland in the Russian empire. When, in 1917, Finland declared its independence in the wake of the collapse of the Tzarist empire, it seceded with all territory that was part of the former Grand Duchy, including the Aaland Islands. Yet, before Finland could formally establish its sovereignty over the islands, the Aalanders sought to exercise their right to self-determination as unification with Sweden, and rejected Finnish offers of autonomy. The dispute lasted several years until the Council of the League of Nations adopted a resolution annexing the islands to Finland with the proviso that they be granted autonomy within Finland.

The Establishment of the Autonomy Regime After 1920

The establishment of the autonomy regime for the Aaland Islands after the end of the First World War was the result of compromise between Finland and Sweden (Jansson 1998, 3), brokered by the League of Nations, without direct consultation of the Aalanders or their political representatives but essentially with clear benefits for them. From an international legal perspective, the status of the islands was unresolved following the secession of Finland from the Russian empire. As Finland had physical possession of the islands and demonstrated great resolve in holding onto them in the face of a Swedish-supported movement in Aaland seeking reunification with Sweden, the League of Nations Council awarded the islands to Finland but demanded additional Finnish guarantees beyond what Finland had already offered in the 1920 Aaland Autonomy Act. The final element of the compromise was the restoration of the demilitarization and neutrality regime of the Aaland Islands—a gesture toward Sweden (given the proximity of the islands to the Swedish coastline and the capital, Stockholm) and other great powers concerned about the strategic location of the islands in the Baltic Sea. The nature and substance of the guarantees required by the Council were negotiated directly between Finland and Sweden, and their final approved version included a provision that authorized the League of Nations Council to monitor application of the guarantees. This form of international legal entrenchment was exceptionally strong at the time, not least because it related to a guarantee of key elements of a territorial autonomy regime that went beyond most other minority provisions under the League regime.

The guarantees required by the Council and agreed between Sweden and Finland became part of domestic Finnish legislation as a separate act, alongside the existing 1920 Autonomy Act. Several provisions of the Guarantee Act have remained cornerstones of the autonomy of the

Aaland Islands ever since. They include restrictions on teaching Finnish in publicly funded schools (changed under the 1991 revised Autonomy Act), on sale of real estate to immigrants to Aaland, and on immigrants' ability to pursue commercial activity in the islands. Under the guarantee provisions, the right to domicile could be earned after five years of legal residence in the islands and included entitlement to vote and stand for election. A governor for the islands can only be appointed by the president of Finland with the agreement of the president of Aaland's legislative assembly.[12] Finally, a financial provision in the Guarantee Act enables the autonomous region to use 50 percent of all revenues from land tax at its own discretion.

From the outset, thus, elements of asymmetry were present in the Aaland autonomy regime. These related to the implementation of the demilitarization and neutrality regime, the special status of the islands with regard to applicability of Finnish legislation, the limitations on the ability of the Finnish government to exercise its functions in the Aaland Islands, and the guarantee of the islands' status in an international agreements and domestic legislation. The two international dimensions of the Aaland regime in particular must be seen in the context of the post-First World War approach to minority issues. International involvement was the norm rather than the exception, as illustrated in the arrangements adopted for the Saar territory (interim internationalized governance followed by a local referendum on the territory's status), of the Free City of Danzig (an autonomous city-state under League of Nations protection, separated from Germany and with special economic relations with Poland), and of the Memel territory (initially administered by a Council of Ambassadors on behalf of the League of Nations, but later annexed by Lithuania and granted autonomy)—to name but three. However imperfect, this notion of international involvement established, and to some extent protected, the asymmetrical status of these territories in relation to their metropolitan states.

The Revised Autonomy Act of 1951

At the end of the Second World War, the international legal situation of Aaland autonomy was rather unclear. The League of Nations system was effectively functioning by the late 1930s, and the League itself was replaced by the United Nations in 1946. Moreover, Finland was treated as a co-belligerent of Nazi Germany and its allies, and was politically highly dependent on the Soviet Union. Thus, the stability and sustainability of the Aaland autonomy regime was called into question. Sweden from the 1940s on had begun to maintain that the negotiations with Finland in 1921 on the League-stipulated guarantees constituted an international agreement that continued to oblige Finland to protect the Aaland autonomy regime; Finland did not officially accept this interpretation, yet neither did it officially dispute it. On the contrary, Finland committed itself to fulfilling its obligations toward Aaland and demonstrated this intention with the revision of the Aaland Autonomy Act of 1951,[13] which expanded Aaland's autonomy and introduced the notion of regional citizenship (the so-called right to domicile). Another novel element of the 1951 Act concerned the application of international treaties to the Aaland Islands. The new provision stipulated that any elements of such treaties found to be in contravention with existing regulations under the Autonomy Act would only be applied to Aaland subject to the consent of the regional assembly. Moreover, any changes to the 1951 Act required consent of both Aaland and Finnish parliaments, under procedures similar to amendment of the Finnish Constitution.

The 1951 revisions to the original Act on the Autonomy of the Aaland Islands were thus important in two ways from the perspective of autonomy as a conflict settlement mechanism. First, they enhanced the already existing autonomy regime. Second, they provided for strong domestic legal entrenchment, ensuring that the autonomous powers and status of the Aaland Islands cannot be changed in any way without the consent of the Aalanders themselves. The 1951 Act indeed underscored the commitment of the Finnish government to protect the autonomy Aaland had gained at the end of the Second World War, regardless of the state of affairs concerning the international supervisory mechanism in place through the 1920s and 1930s.[14] Conceptually, it is important to see this in the context of asymmetry: strengthening Aaland's autonomy went hand-in-hand with an increase in the degree of its asymmetry.

The 1991 Act on the Autonomy of the Aaland Islands

The Autonomy Act of 1920 devolved significant executive and legislative powers to the Aaland Islands and provided the structure of government for the autonomy with a locally elected assembly of thirty members (Lagting) and an executive (Landskapsstyrelse) supported by a civil service.[15] Revisions in 1951 and 1991 expanded the competences of the autonomy, while leaving the structure of government as such largely intact, including the fact that there remains to this day no separate judicial system for the Aaland Islands; justice is administered by and within the unitary judicial system of Finland (in a sense, the only symmetrical dimension of the governance arrangements). A third institution of quite unique character, affirmed by the 1991 Act, is the Aaland Delegation, a joint body of the autonomy and the central government.

According to the 1991 Act in force as of 2009, the law-making powers of the Aaland assembly and the Finnish parliament are divided into two separate lists, detailing individual areas of competence. The legislative competence of the Aaland assembly extends over 26 different areas, including the organization and duties of the Aaland assembly and government; the flag and coat of arms of Aaland; municipal boundaries, elections, and administration; additional taxes on income, trade, and amusement, and municipal taxes; public order and security; environment; social welfare, including health care; education and culture; agriculture, hunting, and fishing; postal service and the right to broadcast by radio or cable in Aaland. In all these areas, the Aaland government enjoys executive powers and is bound by the acts passed by the Aaland assembly. The competences of the autonomous parliament and government are delimited in the sense that the parliament in Helsinki retains competences in 41 separate areas, including: constitutional issues, fundamental rights and freedoms, foreign relations and foreign trade, shipping and aviation, citizenship, defense, and currency policy. The 1991 Act also foresees legislative supervision of the activities of the Aaland assembly. Thus, any act passed by the Aaland assembly must be notified to the Finnish Ministry of Justice and the Aaland Delegation. The Aaland Delegation is to issue an opinion on the legality of any such act (whether the act falls into the legislative competence of Aaland) before it is presented to the Finnish president for signature. The president can only annul an act in part or in full in accordance with a Supreme Court decision that the Aaland assembly has exceeded its legislative powers or that a specific act undermines the internal or external security of Finland. Any annulment has to occur within four months of the notification of the act to the Ministry of Justice.

The Aaland Delegation is constituted as a joint organ of the autonomous region and the Finnish state, with two members each elected by the Aaland assembly and the Finnish Council of State, and chaired by the governor of Aaland or another person appointed by the president of Finland with the agreement of the speaker of the Aaland parliament. The Delegation plays a role in vetting Aaland legislation (see above), in funding the Aaland autonomy according to the provisions on equalization (essentially, payment to Aaland of 0.45 percent of Finnish state revenue), tax retribution, extraordinary grants and advance payments, and in dispute resolution (see below).

Three other substantive issues are of interest in relation to the Aaland autonomy regime: the right to domicile, provisions for the use of language, and the relation between the autonomy regime and international treaties, especially EU legislation. All three issues also underscore the asymmetrical character of the governance arrangements pertaining to the Aaland Islands, especially in the way they apply to individuals' rights and increase the influence of the islands government on Finland's foreign, and especially European, policy.

The right to domicile is a unique form of regional citizenship available only to legal residents of the Aaland Islands. It was originally introduced in the 1951 Act, but proficiency in Swedish was made a formal requirement for obtaining regional citizenship only in the 1991 Act. The right of domicile is automatically granted to children of Finnish citizens resident in Aaland and with at least one parent who has the right. Citizens of Finland legally resident in Aaland for at least five years and proficient in Swedish can also obtain this regional citizenship on application. Regional citizenship implies the right to participate in elections and stand for office, acquire real estate, exercise a trade or profession in Aaland, and be exempt from conscription.

As far as the protection of the Swedish language is concerned, the 1991 Act confirms and enhances existing far-reaching provisions from earlier acts. The official language in the Aaland Islands is Swedish, used at all levels of administration and in the Aaland Delegation. Personal communication between individual citizens and the organs of the state in Aaland and the courts can also be conducted in Finnish. The language of instruction in all public schools is Swedish,[16] and graduates from Aaland educational institutions are exempt from the Finnish-language proficiency requirement for admission to and graduation from Swedish-language or bilingual Swedish-Finnish educational institutions in Finland. Furthermore, all state officials in the Aaland Islands need to be proficient in Swedish.[17]

Under the provisions of the 1991 Act, the islands are granted significant influence on negotiations of, and exemptions from application of, international and European treaties.[18] These include the right to propose negotiations on a treaty or other international obligation, the right to be informed of ongoing negotiations in any area relevant to competences assigned to the autonomy, and the right to participate in such negotiations. Any treaties or other obligations entered into by the Finnish government that affect an area of competence of the autonomy can only be applied to Aaland if the Aaland assembly consents. Any provisions contrary to the Act require a two-thirds majority in the Aaland assembly before they can be applied in the islands. As far as EU affairs are concerned, the Aaland government has the right to participate in formulating national Finnish positions in relation to all matters in, or affecting, Aaland's competences.[19] Wherever an EU decision concerns the application of a common policy in Aaland, the Aaland government has the right to formulate the Finnish position on its own. EU decisions are to be implemented by either the autonomy or the state if they relate to separate areas of competence, but in areas of joint competence the state takes priority subject to consultation with the Aaland government and potential dispute resolution through the Aaland Delegation (see below). Moreover, the Aaland government has the right to nominate one of the representatives of Finland to the Committee of the Regions of the European Community.

This particular form of participation in the international and European arenas must also be seen in connection with another dimension of the autonomy's paradiplomatic powers, its active participation in the institutions of Nordic cooperation,[20] the Nordic Council and the Nordic Council of Ministers, which, too, adds to the asymmetric character of the Aaland autonomy regime. Following a Danish initiative in 1980 and subsequent revisions to the Helsinki Agreement of 1962, the Aaland Islands (along with Greenland and the Faeroe Islands) were able to send two representatives each (elected from among members of their assemblies) to the Nordic Council (the parliamentary body of Nordic cooperation) and appoint their own delegations to the Nordic Council of Ministers, initially consisting of all Aaland government ministers but now primarily comprising officials whose portfolios cover aspects of Nordic cooperation. While this may seem a rather limited manifestation of paradiplomatic competences, it is quite unique in the sense that it affords autonomous entities parity with states in all matters of decision making, in sharp contrast, for example, to the (non-)status that autonomous entities have in other international organizations, such as the European Union or the United Nations. In addition, there are numerous arrangements for cross-border cooperation between the Aaland Islands and Sweden, especially in culture, education, and media.

From a procedural perspective, the relations between the autonomy and the Finnish state foresee both state supervision of the legislative activity of the Aaland assembly, but also a number of mechanisms to resolve disputes over legality and authority between the organs of the Aaland autonomy and the Finnish state. First, any Aaland government decree that conflicts with an act passed by the Aaland or Finnish parliaments automatically becomes invalid. Conflicts of authority on the execution of administrative functions between the autonomous and state governments are referred to the Supreme Court, which must consult with the Aaland Delegation and relevant officials of the Finnish state before issuing a verdict. Finally, the Aaland Delegation itself is competent to resolve disputes between the autonomy and the state when these concern matters of shipping lanes in Aaland or land acquisition by the state in Aaland. The Aaland Delegation may also issue recommendations on how to resolve disputes between the Aaland and Finnish governments over the application of EU policies in areas in which both the autonomy and the state claim competence.

The 1991 Act overall further enhances and consolidates the competences granted to the Aaland Islands and retains their solid entrenchment in Finnish law by continuing to require the consent of the Aaland assembly to any future changes in the Act. In particular, in relation to the application of European and international obligations of the Finnish state, it introduces a number of measures that seek to protect the autonomy from further erosion. However, as Nauclér (2005) points out, it remains to be seen to what extent it will be possible in the future to fully protect an arrangement that has grown organically for almost a century. It is important to note the genuine desire of both the Aaland and Finnish governments to immunize Aaland's autonomy as much as possible against unintended erosion. Ironically, the asymmetric status of the Aaland Islands within the Finnish polity requires extra protective measures such as those enshrined in the 1991 Act—measures that in themselves further increase the existing level of asymmetry.

The Evolution of South Tyrol's Autonomy 1948–2001

The conflict in South Tyrol arose from historical affinity of the German-speaking population of the area with the Habsburg Empire and later Austria, both in terms of ethnic identity and national belonging and the region's unwillingness to be incorporated into the Italian state after the end of the First World War.[21] While the conflict saw only sporadic and low-intensity violence, there was nonetheless a high level of political activism among South Tyrol's German-speakers in pursuit of conditions conducive to expression, maintenance, and preservation of their distinct identity. This manifested itself in campaigns against incorporation in Italy after 1919, including an unrecognized referendum in favor of continued membership in the emerging Austrian federation in 1920, for reincorporation into Austria after 1945, and eventually for substantive provincial autonomy within the Italian state.

The Autonomy Statute of 1948

The 1946 Paris Agreement between Austria and Italy, appended to the Allied Peace Treaty with Italy after the Second World War, obliged the Italian government to grant autonomy to South Tyrol. In drafting an autonomy statute on the basis of the Paris Agreement, the government needed to balance the political and economic interests of the two major ethnic groups in the area—Germans and Italians—against the interests of the Italian Republic and its international commitments. It had to fulfill the Paris Agreement by granting autonomy to South Tyrol and, at the same time protect the Italian population in South Tyrol and satisfy the aspirations of the inhabitants of the neighboring province of Trentino, with which South Tyrol was joined in the autonomous region Trentino-Alto Adige in 1947. In addition, the Italian government had to bear in mind the effect the autonomy statute for South Tyrol would have on similar minority situations elsewhere in the country—primarily the French-speaking minority in the Val d'Aosta and the Slovene-speaking minority in the Trieste area. It took almost two years, 29 January 1948, for the Constituent Assembly of Italy to approve the autonomy statute. A 31 January press declaration by the Austrian foreign minister characterized the statute as satisfactory and asked the German-speaking South Tyroleans to be loyal citizens of the Italian state (Stadlmayer 1965, 480).

This new autonomy statute, however, did not contribute to the settlement of the South Tyrol problem. On the contrary, the interpretations of the statute by the Germans in South Tyrol and by the Austrians gave rise to high expectations on the part of the German minority, expectations not subsequently met by the Italian interpretation and implementation of the statute. The view of the German-speaking population was that both the Paris Agreement and the 1948 autonomy statute were legal instruments that would strengthen the German position in South Tyrol in two ways: numerically, by the return of those who had left under the 1939 Option;[22] and economically and socially by a redistribution of employment according to ethnic proportions. The Italian interpretation was that with these two document, the state had finally been equipped with internationally recognized instruments to resist further German encroachment and maintain the existing degree of Italianization.

One of the biggest causes of German South Tyrolean resentment was the insufficient transfer of power from the region to the province laid down in Articles 13 and 14 of the autonomy statute. In other words, while South Tyrolean German-speakers had hoped for a highly asymmetric interpretation and implementation of the statute, the Italian government sought to minimize asymmetry by limiting the competences actually devolved to the province. The bitterness and disappointment of the South Tyrolean People's Party (SVP)—the predominant German party in the area—at the failure to achieve their economic and social objectives (control of the labor exchanges, immigration, language issues, ethnic proportions in the public sector) led them to suspend, in 1959, any cooperation at the regional level with the major Italian party at the time, the Christian Democrats (DC), which would have been essential for a more favorable Italian interpretation and administration of the autonomy statute.[23] Nevertheless, official negotiations between the SVP and the Italian government on autonomy were reopened in 1954 but failed to achieve anything. This led to growing opposition within the SVP against the party leadership, which was perceived by many rank-

and-file members as too moderate. The 1957 party congress saw an almost complete transformation of the SVP leadership. From then on, SVP policy aimed for a revision of the 1948 autonomy statute in favor of full provincial—instead of shared regional—autonomy and the mobilization of the German-speaking South Tyrolean population for this goal. In other words, the SVP recognized the territorial integrity of the Italian state but sought to establish a full-fledged autonomous unit of South Tyrol instead of a province subordinate to an Italian-dominated region. However, the new policy did not strengthen the SVP position vis-à-vis the Italian government; rather, its powerlessness became increasingly obvious, especially in the light of these ambitious objectives. Dissatisfaction among local party organizations increased and finally erupted in a brief campaign of violence in 1961 (initially confined to the toppling of power pylons as symbols of Italian domination), after several Austrian initiatives, including at UN level, had equally failed to achieve any changes in Italian policy toward South Tyrol.[24]

This violent escalation of the conflict was the clearest indication yet that the autonomy statute of 1948 had failed to provide an institutional framework within which both Italian and German interests could be accommodated in a mutually satisfactory manner. South Tyrolean aspirations for asymmetry were simply not matched by an equal level of Italian enthusiasm to employ asymmetry as a mechanism to settle the conflict. The reasons for this failure did not lie solely within South Tyrol or Italy, as there were also a number of external conditions that limited the chances of success for the 1948 statute from the outset, including Austria's insistence that Italy had not fulfilled the letter and spirit of the Paris Agreement, the failure of several rounds of negotiations between the two countries, and the ill-fated attempt to internationalize the South Tyrol question at the UN, which raised South Tyrolean hopes without delivering any substantive change in their situation. Similarly, European institutions, still in their infancy, failed to exert sufficient pressure on all parties involved to resolve contentious issues in the framework of the 1948 autonomy statute.

The Package Solution of 1969

Following a brief campaign of violence, which was swiftly contained by the Italian government, it took eight years of negotiations before an agreement was reached between Italy and Austria, which consisted of a substantial revision of the 1948 autonomy statute and a so-called operational calendar in which both governments committed themselves to a certain sequence of events which would eventually lead to the end of the dispute over South Tyrol.

This operational calendar outlined the procedures for the implementation of the package solution as well as steps to be taken by both governments to settle the dispute. No time frame was given as to when certain parts of the package had to be fulfilled and specific steps for the eventual settlement completed. The sequence of events, however, was explicitly stated as the settlement of the dispute requiring prior full implementation of the autonomy statute. Only then was an official settlement of the Austro-Italian dispute to go ahead. This official settlement consisted of two main parts. One included declarations of the heads of both governments before their parliaments about the settlement, parliamentary motions on the issue, official letters to the secretary general of the UN regarding the fulfillment of UN Resolution 1457 of 1960 and an Austrian declaration that the dispute had been settled. The other, more far-reaching part was a bilateral agreement between Austria and Italy that in case of any further disputes the International Court of Justice would be approached. The operational calendar strengthened the Austrian position vis-à-vis the Italian government, and with it that of the German-speaking population in South Tyrol (Zeller 1989, 84).[25]

The substantive part of the settlement on which the two governments agreed, and which found the approval of a marginal majority of 52.4 percent in the SVP at an extraordinary party congress in 1969, contained 137 single measures, 25 detailed provisions, and 31 rules of interpretation (Peterlini 1997, 115f.). Among the most important measures were the substantial changes and additions to the 1948 autonomy statute, which devolved more powers to the province, and the regulations that determined the equal status of the German language as a second official language in the province; the redrawing of constituency boundaries for senate elections, which assigned a third constituency to South Tyrol; and the establishment of a proportionality scheme for recruitment and appointment of staff according to ethnic proportions in the public sector and for distribution of public housing. The so-called "internal guarantee" of the new statute took the form of a standing commission at the office of the Italian prime minister, monitoring the implementation of the statute. This indicated a clear shift in Italian policy, now more fully embracing the idea of asymmetric governance arrangements in and for South Tyrol.

The new autonomy statute, the central part of the package, passed all parliamentary hurdles in Italy and came into force on 20 January 1972. As a territorial autonomy statute, however, it had the double character of an instrument regulating the decentralized self-government of the province of South Tyrol and the region of Trentino–South Tyrol and providing for the protection of the German- and Ladin-speaking minorities. Its official name—"Measures in Favor of the Population of South

Tyrol"—emphasized that minority protection was only part of a whole set of measures and regulations dealing with the distribution of powers between different levels of government and between the two ethnic groups, Germans and Italians. Only fifteen articles were specifically and exclusively aimed at the German-speaking population within the province (and thus, by extension, at interethnic relations), while the rest of the articles strengthened provincial autonomy vis-à-vis the region and the central government as a whole and introduced procedures to mediate between all ethnic groups in South Tyrol.

The substantive competences South Tyrol has enjoyed since the 1972 statute are wide-ranging, and include primary, secondary, and tertiary legislative powers. The areas of legislative competence are distinct in each of these areas, as are the specific boundaries within which they are to be exercised.

South Tyrol enjoys primary legislative competence in virtually all areas of education and culture, economy and economic development, environment, public housing, communication and transport including relevant infrastructure, tourism, welfare, and the provincial political and electoral structures. The most significant change introduced with the 2001 constitutional reforms was the provision that the province enjoy primary legislative competences in *all* areas not specifically reserved for the center or otherwise designated as secondary or tertiary competences. That is, in addition to the specific primary legislative domains named in the autonomy statute, primary legislative competences now include additional policy areas previously assigned to the center by default.

The province's secondary legislative competences include teaching arrangements in primary and secondary schools, establishment and oversight of employment agencies, public health, civil aviation, energy production and distribution, foreign trade and foreign and EU relations, and science and technology.

Tertiary legislation can be passed by the provincial assembly in some areas of transport and transport infrastructure, public health services, and pay structures in the education system. Apart from these policy areas that were traditionally the domain of central legislation, further competences were delegated to the province from the region, consisting primarily of administrative functions in relation to chambers of industry, trade, commerce, and agriculture, as well as oversight of financial institutions.

The distinction between these three levels of legislative competence has its source in the legal boundaries to which they are confined. The 2001 reforms (of both the autonomy statute and Constitutional Law No. 3) generally extended these boundaries, which is particularly obvious in relation to South Tyrol's primary legislative competences. These are now constrained only by the Italian Constitution and the country's EU and other international obligations, rather than by the previous more vague notions of "national interests" and "basic provisions of the social and economic reforms of the Republic." Secondary legislation, that is, legislation in areas of concurrent competences, is constrained by framework legislation in which the center determines the basic principles of legislation while the province makes the detailed arrangements as they are to apply in South Tyrol. Tertiary legislative competence is constrained in two ways. First, only in specifically "delegated" policy areas beyond the stipulations of the autonomy statute can such competence be exercised by the province. Second, provincial legislation must comply with a range of particular constraints specified in individual cases of delegated legislative competence, as well as with the more general constraints on primary and secondary competences.

At the heart of the reorganization of ethnic relations in the province and the region are formalized mechanisms of power sharing, which are unique in the Italian context and thus another dimension of the asymmetry of the South Tyrol autonomy arrangement.[26] Going far beyond the provisions of the 1948 autonomy statute, these mechanisms can be found in relation to three distinct dimensions at both regional and provincial levels: voting procedures in the two assemblies, rotation of high offices between the ethnic groups, and coalition government.

To begin with the latter, the government of South Tyrol must reflect the ethnic proportions of the provincial assembly. A simple majority of votes in the assembly is not sufficient to establish the government unless this majority consists of votes from both Italian and German representatives; in other words, the autonomy statute in practice requires a German-Italian coalition government. This "implicit" coalition requirement is complemented by a more explicit one deriving from the compulsory equitable distribution of the offices of the two vice-presidents of the provincial government between the German and Italian ethnic groups.

Another feature of power sharing in South Tyrol established by the 1972 autonomy statute is compulsory rotation of offices in the presidency of the provincial assembly. Elected by the assembly, the presidency consists of one president and one vice-president, as well as three deputies who act as secretaries. An elected representative of the German-speaking group must be chosen as president and an Italian as vice-president in the first half of every five-year legislative period; in the second half their roles reverse.

All legislation from the provincial assembly is prepared by legislative commissions. Their members are the president, vice-president, one of the presidency's secretaries, and four or five "ordinary" members chosen by government and opposition parties in the assembly, again reflecting ethnic proportions in the assembly.

At the regional level, and again unique in the Italian context, similar provisions were made to ensure adequate representation of the German and Italian ethnic groups, and thus, by extension, a functioning system of power sharing. The regional assembly, made up of the entire cohort of elected deputies from both provincial assemblies (South Tyrol and Trentino), operates on the same principle of rotating offices between president and vice-president; in addition, it also changes session location between Bozen/Bolzano (first half) and Trient/Trento (second half). As for the regional government, the same principles operate that are in force at the provincial level.

In order to give each ethnic group additional leverage and incentives to make the power-sharing arrangements work, specific voting procedures and other mechanisms for adoption of provincial laws were established. If any bills put before parliament are considered to affect the rights of a particular ethnic group in South Tyrol, a majority of the deputies of this ethnic group can request "separate voting," a determination of support for the specific bill among each ethnic group. If this request is denied, or if the bill is passed in spite of two-thirds of representatives from one ethnic group voting against it, the group opposing the bill can take the matter to the Italian constitutional court in Rome. Thus, there is no formal veto power in the arrangements. While defending democratic decision-making procedures against a blockade of the political process, nevertheless a mechanism exists that potentially offers legal redress outside the political process. Only in one respect has a more or less formal veto right been established: in relation to the provincial and regional budgets. Here, separate majorities are required from both ethnic groups. If this is not forthcoming, all chapters of the budget are voted on individually. Those failing to receive the required double majority are referred to a special commission of the assembly, and if no agreement is reached the administrative court in Bozen/Bolzano makes a final and binding decision. In this sense, power-sharing arrangements not only add a dimension of asymmetry per se but also affect the way other aspects of asymmetry (in this case legislative power) operate. This adds a further layer of complexity to the nature of the South Tyrol autonomy regime, and underscores the earlier conceptual point that asymmetry arises in response to situational specificity and contributes to the effectiveness of an autonomy arrangement as a conflict settlement mechanism if it is used in a flexible, responsive, responsible manner of state construction.

The focus on the German-Italian dichotomy with respect to power sharing and a number of other areas, where the principle of proportional rather than equal representation of ethnic groups was in force, clearly disadvantaged the Ladin-speaking group. Most of the traditional disadvantages experienced by the Ladins have been formally addressed during the implementation process of the 1972 Autonomy Statute, and more drastically in its 2001 reform.

Over the years, and in line with the implementation of the 1972 Autonomy Statute and Austria's accession to the European Union in 1995, South Tyrol's paradiplomatic competences increased and found firm institutional expressions in cross-border relations and other activities. Thus, South Tyrol/Italy has maintained very strong relations with Austria throughout the post-1945 period but is also particularly active in various EU-sponsored interregional cooperation programs. Moreover, since 1991 there have been strong interparliamentary ties between the regional assemblies of the Bundesland Tyrol in Austria and the two provinces of Trentino and South Tyrol in Italy, as well as cooperation at the executive level to address issues of regional concern, including environmental protection, economic development, and educational exchange. The three entities also have a joint office in Brussels to represent their individual and common interests at the EU level. Paradiplomacy in the case of South Tyrol thus fulfills a dual function, helping preserve identity-based links with Austria and enabling a more effective discharge of the functions of the autonomy, especially in relation to its economic consequences.

The 2001 Reform of the Autonomy Statute

The formal settlement of the South Tyrol conflict between Austria and Italy in 1992 according to the procedures set out in the operational calendar did not mean an end to the further dynamic development of the autonomy and power-sharing regulations. Led by the SVP, the provincial government sought to further improve and extend the regulations of the 1972 statute in order to increase the province's autonomy and to improve the quality of life for all three ethnic groups. From the mid-1990s on, the provincial government was granted an extension of its powers, among others, in the sectors of education, employment, transport, finance, privatization of state-owned properties, energy, and European integration.

As part of these and other significant changes, a reformed autonomy statute came into effect on 16 February 2001, marking the third autonomy statute for the province since the end of the Second World War. In it, the status and powers of the two provinces Trentino and South Tyrol were greatly enhanced to the extent that South Tyrol and Trentino no longer constituted subordinate units of the region of Trentino-South Tyrol and individually had more legislative and administrative powers than the region itself. In particular, the following new regulations increased the degree of autonomy enjoyed by both provinces.

- In contrast to the previous autonomy statute, the 2001 version explicitly recognized the internationally guaranteed nature of South Tyrol's autonomy. By virtue of its being a constitutional law, the new autonomy statute gave an even firmer guarantee of the inviolability of South Tyrol's autonomous status.
- All legislation in relation to elections became the competence of the provinces, allowing them to determine, for example, whether the president of the provincial government should be directly elected. Respective legislation no longer required approval by the government commissioner.
- In the future, amendments to the autonomy statute could also be developed by the two provinces, without involvement of the region.
- If the Italian parliament intended to change or amend the current statute, it had to consult representatives of the province, as opposed to representatives of the region as was previously the case.
- Members of the provincial government could be appointed with a two-thirds majority in the provincial assembly without having to be its members.
- Representation of the Ladins in the presidency of the regional and provincial assemblies and in the regional government was now part of the power-sharing arrangement, and members of the Ladin ethnic group could be coopted into the South Tyrol provincial government.

In addition, for the first time ever, the term "South Tyrol" was officially incorporated in its German version into the Italian Constitution as part of the Constitutional Law on Federalism, adopted in March 2001.

What this revision of the autonomy statute shows, together with developments since 1972 in general, is that the real strength of the South Tyrol arrangements derives from the flexibility of its implementation process. The particular combination of territorial autonomy and power sharing has also facilitated the increasing identification of all ethnic groups with the arrangements as they have developed over time. With the enhanced and formalized participation of the Ladin ethnic group in the political process in South Tyrol, the 2001 reforms also indicate that the province has moved beyond the traditional Italian-German dichotomy and that institutions are now more than ever fully representative of the ethnic demography of the province while at the same time serving the interests of the population as a whole rather than the particular interests of one or another individual ethnic group. In this sense, asymmetry has provided a basis for the emergence of a cross-communal identity focused on the particularity of the status of South Tyrol as a distinct territorial entity in Italy and transcends the ethnic identity of individual residents. This

important integrative benefit of asymmetry at the local level has significantly contributed to mitigating local interethnic tensions and has thus
made the overall asymmetric settlement more viable.

The Continued Relevance of "Historical" Cases
of Territorial Autonomy

Historical cases though they may be, the settlements for the Aaland Islands and South Tyrol should certainly not be consigned to the dustbin
of history, nor are they merely a footnote in the history of asymmetric
state construction. First of all, they remain important reference points
for the wider debate on autonomy as a conflict settlement mechanism
because they are among the oldest and most successful examples of such
arrangements, and thus are often cited as illustrations when it comes to
discussing possible solutions for similar conflicts elsewhere in the world.
While this does not mean that either or both can simply be taken as blue-
prints for state construction elsewhere, they do offer important insights
into the specificities generated by asymmetry and how to manage them.
The Aaland Delegation and the South Tyrol Standing Commission in the
office of the Italian prime minister have certainly proved their worth in
dealing with issues related to the implementation and operation of these
two autonomy arrangements. Moreover, concrete provisions in the case
of the Aaland Islands regarding the right of the autonomous entity to be
involved in international negotiations and limitations on the application
of resultant obligations are useful mechanisms to protect autonomy arrangements from being undermined by globalization and Europeaniza-
tion. Proper legal entrenchment has, in both cases, also strengthened
the autonomy against undue interference by the central state, contributing another feature to protect asymmetric arrangements from "equal-
izing" tendencies on the part of the central state.

A comparison between the Aaland Islands and South Tyrol is also instructive when it comes to the issue of monodimensional versus complex asymmetry. Aaland is clearly a case of monodimensional asymmetry,
with the islands being the only autonomous entity in Finland, whereas
South Tyrol has been one among five entities with a special autonomy
statute in Italy since 1948, first in a regionalizing state and since 2001 in
a federalizing one. The acceptance of complex asymmetry, in the case of
South Tyrol, has been highly beneficial to the autonomy. Not only has it
allowed for an unprecedented number of powers to be devolved to the
region but it has also made it possible to establish governance arrangements that are unique among all other Italian regions. On the one hand,
the region itself no longer plays a significant role, and the two provinces
(Trentino and South Tyrol) are the main loci of power. On the other

hand, South Tyrol is a case of a nested consociation: there is effective executive and legislative power sharing both at the level of South Tyrol as a province and at the level of the region of Trentino-South Tyrol. The stability of these arrangements demonstrates two things. First, in line with the earlier assumptions about the influence of situational characteristics on the institutional design of territorial autonomies, autonomy, as granted in the 1948 statute, was in itself insufficient to deal with the conflict in South Tyrol. Second, no matter how situation-specific the characteristics of one particular conflict are, they can be accommodated in an asymmetric settlement, alongside other situations with similar or dissimilar characteristics, without affecting the overall construction of the central state.[27]

Related to this is also the observation that incorporated in both autonomies are mechanisms that allow the two entities to play a limited role in the international arena. These reflect the identity dimension of the conflict that territorial autonomy was meant to address, as well as the functional dimension of the two autonomies being able to effectively discharge their powers. Close cooperation between the Aaland Islands and Sweden in the context of Nordic cooperation addresses the identity dimension, while Nordic cooperation and the role of the Aaland authorities in negotiation and implementation of European and other international treaties and obligations reflects the more functional dimension. For South Tyrol, the formal role of the autonomy in relation to European integration is more limited, but there are similarly comprehensive arrangements in place to enable regional, cross-border cooperation between South Tyrol and Austria and in the broader regional context of the Alpine mountains.

In sum, therefore, the territorial autonomy arrangements adopted and developed in the cases of the Aaland Islands and South Tyrol will continue to be relevant in the future. At the time of their original negotiation and implementation they may rightly have been considered as highly unique, if not idiosyncratic. With the benefit of hindsight, however, and especially in light of the growing political and wider academic interest in territorial autonomy as a mechanism to settle self-determination conflicts, their architects may well be considered unusually long-sighted. The Aaland Islands and South Tyrol are important examples of the successful settlement of self-determination conflicts qua territorial autonomy, they offer a range of specific mechanisms as part of two distinct complex institutional designs, and they highlight the need for, and possibility of, constant evolution in the face of changing contextual circumstances. In other words, the Aaland Islands and South Tyrol validate the *principle* of resolving self-determination conflicts qua asymmetric territorial autonomy but caution against its static and unimaginative application.

Notes

1. Another historical example worth noting is Irish Home Rule; cf. McGarry, this volume.

2. A former U.S. diplomat put it to me this way: "When we were dealing with Nagorno Karabakh in the early 1990s, we looked for examples. South Tyrol was the only one we found. So we tried to sell that to them." Northern Ireland, post-2006, stands a good chance of being added to this short list.

3. There have been a number of attempts to conceptualize "territorial solutions" for ethnic conflicts, especially the use of autonomy arrangements. These include especially Benedikter 2007; Coakley 2003; Dinstein 1981; Ghai 2000; Hannum 1996; Lapidoth 1997; Nordquist 1998; Wehengama 2000; Weller and Wolff 2005 .

4. This distinction is made by a number of scholars, including Heintze 1997, 37–46; 1998, 18–24; Hechter 2000, 72 ff.; Potier 2001, 55–56, 59–60.

5. For broader comparative assessments of the institutional designs of territorial autonomy as a mechanism of conflict settlement, see also Suksi 1998; Wolff 2004b, 2008. O'Leary 2005 is an excellent theoretical treatment with application to Iraq. Nordquist uses the term "seized autonomies" to identify cases in which autonomy was "seized by arms and/or other threats to internal or international security" and counts a total of eleven cases between 1920 and 1995 (Nordquist 1998, 64, 74–77).

6. Table 1 excludes territorial autonomy arrangements in the former Soviet bloc: Czechoslovakia (Czech Socialist Republic and Slovak Socialist Republic, both established in 1969) and Soviet Union (15 Republics, 16 if one counts the short-lived Karelo-Finnish Socialist Soviet Republic that existed from 1940 to 1956 when it was incorporated into the Russian SFSR as the Karelian Autonomous Soviet Socialist Republic, as well as numerous lower-level autonomous republics and districts within them).

7. Power sharing is a form of governance whereby representatives of different groups make decisions jointly in one or more branches of government. Power-sharing can occur as a result of guaranteed arrangements, e.g., particular parliamentary election (reserved seats, quotas) and/or government appointment procedures (d'Hondt mechanism, guaranteed posts for members of particular groups) in combination with specific decision-making procedures in relevant branches of the government (qualified or concurrent majorities) or emerge as a result of the electoral process as part of coalition formation. I am primarily interested in the former, guaranteed type of power sharing, but will note voluntary power-sharing coalitions where appropriate.

8. For an extensive comparison of regional consociations, see Wolff 2004b.

9. For states, territory possesses certain value in and of itself, including natural resources, the goods and services produced there and the tax revenue generated from them, and military or strategic advantages in terms of natural boundaries, access to the open sea, and control over transport routes and waterways. Additionally, for ethnic groups, territory very often is also important in a different way—as a crucial component of their identity. Territory is then conceptualized

more appropriately as place, bearing significance in relation to the group's history, collective memories, and "character." Yet for ethnic groups, too, territory is, or can become, a valuable commodity as it provides resources and a potential power base. Sovereign consociations are of course also possible without provisions for territorial self-governance. The key example is Lebanon, but it too underlines the importance of self-governance (or segmental/group autonomy), in this case nonterritorial, or cultural/personal autonomy extending to individuals as members of a group rather than living in a specific territory.

10. In a broader sense, transnational links need not be just with immediately neighboring countries, but can, as a consequence of past intra-empire migration or emigration, connect population groups across greater distances (consider existing links between Germany and the descendents of ethnic German minorities in central and eastern Europe and the former Soviet Union, as far as Kazakhstan; or the relations between Hungary and ethnic Hungarian minorities in central and eastern europe, the Balkans, and parts of the former Soviet Union, as well as among those communities and the Hungarian diaspora in the United States).

11. More generally on the potential contribution of paradiplomacy to conflict resolution, see Wolff 2007. The notion also ties in well with Weller's criterion viii of "limited external relations powers." For the European context, see Danspeckgruber 2002, 2005.

12. Traditionally, the nominee for governor of the Aaland Islands is selected from the largest party in the legislative assembly, the Lagting. Failing agreement between the president of Finland and the president of the Aaland assembly, a list of five nominees is drawn up by the local parliament and submitted to the Finnish president, who can request further nominations if none of the submitted candidates are considered suitable.

13. According to Hannikainen 1997, 62) Finland even offered to have fulfillment of its obligations monitored by an international supervisory system, but this was prevented by the Soviet Union.

14. It should also be noted that there was no single occasion on which the Aaland Islands felt it necessary to refer any matter to the League Council.

15. A very detailed analysis of the 1991 Act is Palmgren 1998.

16. This confirms earlier provisions, but the 1991 Act introduces the possibility of an Act of Aaland introducing further legislation to allow Finnish as language of instruction.

17. This is a new provision on the 1991 Act.

18. Finland joined the EU in 1995.

19. For a more detailed discussion of the impact of EU membership on Aaland autonomy, see Nauclér 2005.

20. For a detailed discussion of the participation of the Aaland Islands in Nordic cooperation, see Nauclér 2005.

21. When South Tyrol was annexed to Italy in 1919, pursuant to the London Agreement of 1915 between the Entente and Italy, the Italian government of the day promised the German-speaking population of the area wide-ranging autonomy. However, a program of rapid Italianization was introduced immediately after the fascist takeover of 29 October 1922.

22. Hitler and Mussolini had agreed in 1938 that Germans in South Tyrol would be given a choice to accept Italianization or emigrate to Germany (which by then had already annexed Austria). While a large number of South Tyrolean Germans opted for emigration, a considerably smaller number actually executed

their choice. On numbers voting for emigration and numbers of émigrés, see Alcock 1970; Cole and Wolf 1974; and cf. Wolff 2002.

23. On the provincial level, this SVP-DC coalition held until the electoral demise of the DC in the early 1990s.

24. At the end of the 1960 UN session, a resolution was adopted on 31 October that called for bilateral negotiations between Austria and Italy to resolve the South Tyrol question. In case these would not be successful, it was recommended that the dispute should be referred to other international organizations, including the International Court of Justice. The UN session of 1961 returned to the issue, but merely referred the parties back to the resolution adopted a year earlier.

25. There are two reasons for this. The calendar qualifies the Paket as a "later practice" of the fulfillment of the Paris Agreement, but it denies the Italian interpretation of the Paket as part of voluntary inner-Italian legislation and places all legislative measures in connection with implementation in the context of the fulfillment of the Paris Agreement (Zeyer 1993, 54).

26. Detailed discussions in Pallaver 2008; Wolff 2002, chap. 6; 2004a, b.

27. In this context, note McGarry's 2007 important argument that the necessity for asymmetric arrangements arises, in part, from the limits of symmetric ones.

References

Alcock, A. E. 1970. *The history of the South Tyrol question.* London: Michael Joseph.

Benedikter, T. 2007. *The world's working regional autonomies: An introduction and comparative analysis.* London: Anthem Press.

Bengio, O. 2005. Autonomy in Kurdistan in historical perspective. In *The future of Kurdistan in Iraq,* ed. B. O'Leary, J. McGarry, and K. Salih. Philadelphia: University of Pennsylvania Press.

Coakley, J., ed. 2003. *The territorial management of ethnic conflict.* 2nd ed. London: Frank Cass.

Cole, J. and E. R. Wolf. 1974. *The hidden frontier: Ecology and ethnicity in an Alpine valley.* New York: Academic Press.

Daftary, F. 2000. *Insular autonomy: A framework for conflict settlement: A comparative study of Corsica and the Åland Islands.* Flensburg: European Centre for Minority Issues.

Danspeckgruber, W. 2005. Self-governance plus regional integration: A possible solution to self-determination conflicts. In *Autonomy, self-governance and conflict resolution: Innovative approaches to institutional design in divided societies,* ed. M. Weller and S. Wolff. London: Routledge.

———. 2002. Self-determination and regionalisation in contemporary Europe. In *The self-determination of peoples: Community, nation, and state in an interdependent world,* ed. W. Danspeckgruber. Boulder, Colo.: Lynne Rienner.

Dinstein, Y. ed. 1981. *Models of autonomy.* New Brunswick, N.J.: Transaction.

Elazar, D. J. 1991. Introduction. In *Federal systems of the world: A handbook of federal, confederal and autonomy arrangements,* ed. D. J. Elazar. London: Cartermill.

Ghai, Y. 2000. *Autonomy and ethnicity: Negotiating competing claims in multiethnic states.* Cambridge: Cambridge University Press.

Gurr, T. R. 1993. *Minorities at risk.* Washington, D.C.: U.S. Institute of Peace Press.

Hannikainen, L. 1997. The international legal basis of the autonomy and Swedish character of the Åland Islands. In *Autonomy and demilitarisation in international law: The Åland Islands in a changing Europe*, ed. L. Hannikainen and F. Horn. The Hague: Kluwer Law International.

Hannum, H. 1996. *Autonomy, sovereignty, and self-determination: The accommodation of conflicting rights*. Rev. ed. Philadelphia: University of Pennsylvania Press.

Hannum, H., and R. B. Lillich. 1980. The concept of autonomy in international law. *American Journal of International Law* 74: 858–89.

Hechter, M. 2000. *Containing nationalism*. Oxford: Oxford University Press.

Heintze, H.-J. 1998. On the legal understanding of autonomy. In *Autonomy: applications and implications*, ed. M. Sukksi. The Hague: Kluwer Law International.

———. 1997. *Wege zur Verwirklichung des Selbstbestimmungsrechts der Völker innerhalb bestehender Staaten*. In *Selbstbestimmungsrecht der Völker: Herausforderung der Staatenwelt*, ed. H.-J. Heintze. Bonn: Dietz.

Horowitz, D. L. 1985. *Ethnic groups in conflict*. Berkeley: University of California Press.

Jansson, G. 1998. Introduction. In *Autonomy and demilitarization in international law: The Åland Islands in a changing Europe*, ed. L. Hannikainen and F. Horn. The Hague: Kluwer Law International.

Joireman, S. 2004. Secession and its aftermath: Eritrea. In *Managing and settling ethnic conflicts: Perspectives on successes and failures in Europe, Africa, and Asia*, ed. U. Schneckener and S. Wolff. London: Hurst.

Lapidoth, R. 1997. *Autonomy: Flexible solutions to ethnic conflicts*. Washington, D.C.: U.S. Institute of Peace Press.

McGarry, J. 2007. Asymmetry in federations, federacies, and unitary states. *Ethnopolitics* 6, 1: 105–16.

McGarry, J., and B. O'Leary. 1993. Introduction: The macro-political regulation of ethnic conflict. In *The politics of ethnic conflict regulation*, ed. J. McGarry and B. O'Leary. London: Routledge.

Nauclér, E. 2005. Autonomy and multi-level governance: Innovation or anomaly? In *Autonomy, self-governance and conflict resolution: Innovative approaches to institutional design in divided societies*, ed. M. Weller and S. Wolff. London: Routledge.

Nordquist, K.-Å. 1998. Autonomy as a conflict-solving mechanism: An overview. In *Autonomy: Applications and implications*, ed. M. Sukksi. The Hague: Kluwer Law International.

O'Leary, B. 2005. Power sharing, pluralist federation, and federacy. In *The future of Kurdistan in Iraq*, ed. B. O'Leary, J. McGarry, and K. Salih. Philadelphia: University of Pennsylvania Press.

Pallaver, G. 2008. South Tyrol's consociational democracy: Between political claim and social reality. In *Tolerance through law: Self-governance and group rights in South Tyrol*, ed. J. Woelk, F. Palermo, and J. Marko. Leiden: Nijhoff.

Palley, C. 1991. Introduction. In *Minorities and autonomy in Western Europe*. London: Minority Rights Group.

Palmgren, S. 1998. The autonomy of the Åland Islands in the constitutional law of Finland. In *Autonomy and demilitarisation in international law: The Åland Islands in a changing Europe*, ed. L. Hannikainen and F. Horn. The Hague: Kluwer Law International.

Peterlini, O. 1997. *Autonomie und Minderheitenschutz in Trentino-Südtirol*. Vienna: Braumüller.

Potier, T. 2001. *Conflict in Nagorno-Karabakh, Abkhazia and South Ossetia: A legal appraisal.* The Hague: Kluwer Law International.

Stadlmayer, V. 1965. Die Südtirolpolitik Österreichs seit Abschluß des Pariser Abkommen. In *Südtirol: Eine Frage des europäischen Gewissens,* ed. F. Huter. Vienna: Verlag für Geschichte und Politik.

Suksi, M. 1998. The constitutional setting of the Åland Islands compared. In *Autonomy and demilitarisation in international law: The Åland Islands in a changing Europe,* ed. L. Hannikainen and F. Horn. The Hague: Kluwer Law International.

Wehengama, G. 2000. *Minority claims: from autonomy to secession.* Aldershot: Ashgate.

Weller, M., and S. Wolff, eds. 2005. *Autonomy, self-governance and conflict resolution: Innovative approaches to institutional design in divided societies.* London: Routledge.

Wolff, S. 2008. Complex power sharing as conflict resolution: South Tyrol in comparative perspective. In *Tolerance through law: Self-governance and group rights in South Tyrol,* ed. J. Woelk, F. Palermo, and J. Marko. Leiden: Nijhoff.

———. 2007. Paradiplomacy: scope, opportunities and challenges. *Bologna Center Journal of International Affairs* 10: 141–50.

———. 2004a. Settling an ethnic conflict through power sharing: South Tyrol. In *Managing and settling ethnic conflicts: Perspectives on successes and failures in Europe, Africa and Asia,* ed. U. Schneckener and S. Wolff. London: Hurst.

———. 2004b. The institutional structure of regional consociations in Brussels, Northern Ireland, and South Tyrol. *Nationalism and Ethnic Politics* 10, no. 3: 387–414.

———. 2002. *Disputed territories: The transnational dynamics of ethnic conflict settlement.* New York: Berghahn.

Wolff, S., and M. Weller. 2005. Self-determination and autonomy: A conceptual introduction. In *Autonomy, self-governance and conflict resolution: Innovative approaches to institutional design in divided societies,* ed. M. Weller and S. Wolff. London: Routledge, 1–25.

Zeller, K. 1989. *Das Problem der völkerrechtlichen Verankerung des Südtirolpakets und die Zuständigkeit des Internationalen Gerichtshofes.* Vienna: Braumüller.

Zeyer, C. 1993. *Der völkerrechtliche und europarechtliche Status von Südtirol.* Frankfurt am Main: Peter Lang.

Chapter 2

The Russian Constitutional System: Complexity and Asymmetry

Bill Bowring

The Paradoxes of Russian Federalism

The Russian Federation (RF) is the largest and most complex in the world. In 2000, it was composed of no fewer than 89 "subjects of the Federation." As of 1 March 2008, it had 83. The reason for this surprising "shrinkage" are explored below. It is plain that since 2004 there has been a premeditated assault on the foundations of Russian federalism, with profound consequences for potential for ethnic conflict.

In this chapter, I start with an analysis of the five types of subjects of the Russian Federation. Next, I point out some competing if not contradictory principles of the 1993 Russian Constitution. Third, I explore a contemporary Russian assessment of asymmetry in the Russian context. Fourth, I trace the complex history of Russian federalism from its roots in Tsarist and Soviet Russian history. I argue that the apparently confusing and fragmented character of contemporary Russian federalism is in fact the outcome of a long historical development, in which at least some of the aspirations of Russia's many ethnonational minorities have been accommodated. I then turn to some recent developments, which threaten to destroy this structure for artificial and ulterior motives. I analyze in detail the developments during Putin's presidency: abolition of direct elections for presidents and governors, and finally, and most recently, a number of contentious mergers.

The Russian Federation and Its Subjects

According to the 1993 Constitution, there are two equally correct names for the territory under discussion: "Russia," and "the Russian Federation." It should be noted first that the phrase Rossiiskaya Federatsiya

(Russian Federation) cannot be directly translated into English. The Russian language has two words translated into English as "Russian." The first, "russkii," means "ethnic Russian"; the second, "rossiiskii," "civic Russian." The federation is the "Rossiiskaya" not the "Russkaya" federation—the country not of ethnic but of civic Russians, that is, of bearers of citizenship under the Constitution.

The subjects are as follows. First, and most important for our purposes, Russia has 21 ethnic republics, the successors of the "autonomous republics" of the USSR, named after their "titular" people, with their own presidents, constitutions, and, in many cases, constitutional courts. There has been no reduction in the number of ethnic republics, not least because of the potential strength of their resistance.

Next, there are nine enormous *krais*, a word often translated as "region," with their own appointed governors. In 2000 there were six, with elected governors.

The most numerous subjects of the Federation are the 46 *oblasts*, territorial formations inhabited primarily by ethnic Russians, also with governors. There were 49 *oblasts* in 2000.

The four autonomous *okrugs* (AO), also ethnic formations, reflect a relative concentration of the indigenous peoples that give them their name. There were ten of these in 2000; the six that have disappeared have been "united" with larger neighbors, often in very controversial circumstances. For all their formal constitutional equality under the 1993 Constitution, they were for the most part located *within* other formations (*krais* and *oblasts*), with consequences that will be explored later in this chapter.

There is a Jewish autonomous *oblast*, located in the Russian Far East.[1]

Finally, two "cities of federal significance," Moscow and St. Petersburg, are also subjects of the Federation.

It is important to remember that of at least 150 nationalities in the Russian Federation, only 32 had their own territorial units (Kempton 1996, 609). This number has shrunk.

The diversity and respective powers of subjects of the Federation, as set out in the 1993 Constitution, are shown in Table 1. This extraordinary ramification reflects both the Soviet nationalities policy, and the multiethnic character of the Tsarist empire, themes which will be explored in this chapter.

The Contradictory Legal Basis of Russian Federalism

In her classic monograph, Irina Umnova observes that the legal foundations of the Russian Federation are to be found in a number of documents. These are the Constitution of the Russian Federation of 1993, the Federal Treaty, the federal constitutional and federal laws, treaties

TABLE 1. Types of Subject of the Russian Federation

21 ethnoterritorial Republics, named after their "titular" people, e.g., Bashkortostan (Bashkirs), Chechnya (Chechens), Khakassiya (Khakas), Marii-El (Mari), Tatarstan (Tatars)[a]	•are characterized by the 1993 Constitution as "states"—Art. 5(2) •have their own constitutions—Art. 5(2) cannot become part of other subjects of the RF—Art. 66(4) •cannot include other subjects of the RF—Art. 66(4) •have the right to determine their own state languages—Art. 68(2)
9 *krais* and 46 *oblasts*, territorial administrative units with majority ethnic Russian population	•have their own charters—Art. 5(2) •cannot become part of other subjects of the RF—Art. 66(4) •may include autonomous *okrugs*—Art. 66(4)
2 "cities of federal significance," Moscow and St. Petersburg	•have their own charters—Art. 5 (2) •may not become part of other subjects of the RF—Art. 66(4) •may not include other subjects of the RF—Art. 66(4)
(Jewish) autonomous *oblast*	•has its own charter—Art. 5 (2) •is part of the RF as a unique entity—Art. 5(1) •may be subject to a federal law on autonomous *oblast*—Art. 66(3) •may not become part of other subjects of the RF—Art. 66(4) •may not include other subjects of the RF—Art. 66(4)

a. The full list: Adygeya; Bashkortostan; Buryatiya; Chukotka; Dagestan; Ingushetiya; Kabardino-Balkariya; Kalmykiya; Karachaevo-Cherkessiya; Kareliya; Khakassiya; Komi; Marii El; Mordoviya; Severnaya Osetiya; Tatarstan; Tyva; Udmurtiya; Chechnya; Chuvashiya; Sakha (Yakutiya).

between organs of state power of the Russian Federation and the organs of state power of the subjects of the Federation, and last, the constitutions (charters) of the subjects themselves (Umnova 1998, 44; see also Salikov 2004).

Thus, there are two levels of federal relations. First, there are direct relations of state power between the Federation and its subjects as such. Second, there are relations between unmediated bearers of state power of the Federation and its subjects. These include the "people" of the RF (its citizens, who by Article 3 of the Constitution make up its political community), and organs of state power. It follows that a series of complex relations are possible: the people of the RF and the people of a subject; the people of the RF and organs of state power of a subject;

TABLE 2. Contradictory Principles of the Russian Federation

Unity, integrity, and equality of the Federation	Principles tending to decentralization and asymmetry
Reach of RF sovereignty to all its territory—Art. 4(1); integrity and inviolability of its territory—Art. 4(3)	Self-determination of the peoples of the RF—preamble, Art. 5(3); plenitude of power of subjects of the RF outside the limits of competence of the RF for matters of joint competence of the RF and its subjects—Art. 73; recognition of (ethnic) republics within the RF and the existence of their rights to external state attributes—constitution, state language—Art. 5(2) and 68(2)
Supremacy of RF Constitution and federal laws on whole of its territory—Art. 4(2), 15; unity of legal and economic space—Art. 6(2), 8(1), 74, 75	Possibility of treaty-based delimitation of matters of competence and jurisdiction between organs of state power of the RF and those of its subjects—Art. 11(3); right of subjects to establish their own legal regulation on matters outside the competence of the RF, and outside joint competence—Art. 76(4), (6)
Unity of system of state power—Art. 5(3), 77(2), 78	Right of subjects of the RF independently to establish their own system of organs of state power in accordance with the fundamental constitutional system of the RF and the general principles of the organization of executive and legislative organs of state power provided by law—Art. 77(1)
Equal rights of subjects of the RF—Art. 5(1), (4)	Asymmetrical nature of the RF, and differentiated constitutional and legal status of its subjects—Art. 5(1), 65(1), 66, 68(2)

organs of federal state power and the people of a subject. However, Umnova points out that according to Article 66(2) of the RF Constitution, the constitution (charter) of a subject is adopted by its legislative organ; adoption by a referendum is precluded. This, in her view, is an undemocratic exclusion of the unmediated bearer of state power (the people of the subject) (Umnova 1998, 50).

Varlamova has also pointed out a number of competing, if not contradictory, principles at work in the Russian Constitution (Varlamova 2001, 13); see Table 2. She adds that there are no insurmountable contradictions between these principles, only that the future federal character of Russia depends on their interpretation: the broadening of the authority of central power or its decentralization (14).

Asymmetric Federations: A Russian View

Russia is frequently chosen by Western scholars as a case study in federalism. McGarry states that "Russia created an asymmetrical federation in the immediate years after the fall of the Soviet Union, although the Putin government has since sought to roll this back" (2005, 1). De Figueiredo and Weingast assert that "an appropriately structured federal system seems well suited for a country as large and diverse as Russia" (2002, 19). However, they consider that actual federalism in Russia displays a range of pathologies. First, they point to the "striking lack of cooperation between center and regions" (20). For Obydenkova, "asymmetry, as a result of 'federal bargaining' and the flexibility of institutions, is unavoidable, especially in the process of regime change accompanied by miscalculation of multi-level reforms and mistakes" (2004, 3). Does it help to avoid conflict? She examines the Russian case, taking the republics of Bashkortostan, Tatarstan, and Sakha-Yakutiya against three parameters: geopolitical, economic, and ethnic. Her conclusion is that while these factors have an impact on center-periphery relations, they do not determine the intensity of conflict or the scope of demands (Obydenkova 2004, 38). While size, population, natural resources, and the ethnic factor do stimulate a subject of the Federation to bargain for more independence, the intensity of conflict is also influenced by fiscal arrangements, and by the nature and interpersonal relations of the elite.

Umnova provided what remains, in my view, the strongest Russian analysis and prognosis of the genesis and fundamental features of Russia's unique brand of federalism. She starts from two types of federalism, delegated (where states join together in a union), and decentralized (where power is transferred from the center) (1998, 29). The principle of a noncentralized state is subsidiarity (31), as in the United States. She argues that Russian political practice often mixes the principle of subsidiarity and the principle of delegation. For this she quotes the speaker (in 1993) of the Supreme Council of Tatarstan, F. Kh. Mekhametshin, who insisted that a federation must be formed on the principle of subsidiarity, that is, from bottom to top on the basis of delegation (33).

Umnova describes three types of federation: symmetrical, asymmetrical, and symmetrical with aspects of asymmetry. The first, with subjects which are identical in nature and equal in status, is the ideal but exists nowhere. The second is the least successful and, as in the case of the Tanzanian Constitution of 1977, brings together two utterly dissimilar entities—Tanganika and Zanzibar. She distinguishes three types of state in which the national factor has been brought into play. The first group are states that have undergone collapse and either disappeared or been reorganized—the USSR, Yugoslavia, Czechoslovakia, Nigeria. The second are states retaining their integrity but undergoing internal cataclysms in the form of local ethnic conflicts inspired by separatism—India, Canada, the Russian Federation. The third group consists of stable and relatively peaceful federations—Belgium and Switzerland (Unmova 1998, 43). In her view, the existence of this group shows that the combination of territorial and ethnic (national) factors in structuring a federation is possible. This will only succeed, however, if the following conditions are met: statehood is preserved; the rights and freedoms of the person and citizen are not violated, nor the equal rights of nations and their right to self-determination; and the development of nationalism is not stimulated.

The History of the Formation of Russian Federalism

This can be divided into three phases (see also Kossikov 1996, 1). First, however, a brief mention of the Tsarist and Soviet history is in order.

The Russian empire was organized on administrative principles, although there is a long history of varying degrees of autonomy, the Grand Duchy of Finland being the extreme example (Kutafin 2006). Peter the Great created eight *guberniyas* (provinces) in 1708, in the wake of his victories against Sweden in the Great Northern War, and Catherine I increased their number to 14. In 1775, Catherine the Great, with Prince Potemkin's immense conquests, established 44 provinces and 2 regions with provincial status. By 1914, the Empire consisted of 81 provinces and 20 regions (Teague 2008).

Despite the fact that in reality the USSR functioned as a state with strongly centralized power, under the control of the Communist Party with its principle of "democratic centralism," the formal, constitutional position was different—and quite different from the Tsarist empire. The USSR presented itself as a confederation, a union of sovereign republics with the right of secession; and the Russian Socialist Federation of Soviet Republics (RSFSR) as a unitary state with strong elements of territorial autonomy (Khazanov 1997). Of course, the ethnic populations which did not receive their "own" territory, especially the indigenous peoples of the north, lost out in this competition. The goal of leaders of the "titular" nationality in a particular territory was to preserve as much as possible of its ethnic character and territorial integrity. Dowley observed as follows:

> Elites in the ethnic autonomous republics and national level republics were
> appointed to represent the ethnic group interests in the larger state, and

> thus, their natural political base of support was supposed to be the ethnic group. Other political appointments in these regions were made on the basis of ethnicity, a Soviet form of affirmative action for the formally, institutionally, recognised ethnic groups referred to in the early years of the Soviet Union as *korenizatsiya* or nativisation. (1998, 363)

The chairmen of the Supreme Soviets of Tatarstan and Bashkortostan, both of which aspired to the status of "union republics," were always members of the Presidium of the Supreme Soviet of the USSR, along with those of the Union Republics—the only two "autonomous republics" so represented (Shaimiev 1996, 1). By the end of the 1970s, more than half of the professional cadre in half of the Union Republics and 11 of the 21 autonomous republics in the RSFSR were composed of the titular ethnic group. Social mobility of ethnic groups was higher than that of Russians (Drobizheva 1996, 2). As the Soviet Union weakened and finally collapsed, in December 1991, it is hardly surprising that the same leaders sought to turn symbolic authority into real power, and had a strong base for doing so.

The first document of constitutional significance of the late Soviet period was the Declaration on State Sovereignty of the RSFSR of 12 June 1990, adopted by the Congress of People's Deputies.[2] The basic idea of the Declaration was the establishment of Russia as a sovereign democratic rule of law state on the basis of people's power, separation of powers, and federalism. It also called for greater rights for the autonomous republics, autonomous *oblasts* and autonomous *okrugs*, as well as administrative *krais* and *oblasts*. But at this stage Russia was only formally speaking a federation. According to Umnova, there was the parallel emergence of two contradictory developments: ensuring the statehood of Russia on the one hand, and its disintegration on the other (Umnova 1998, 57).

The process of "sovereignization" of the subjects of the RSFSR was also exemplified in laws that followed the declaration: the Laws of the USSR "On the foundations of economic relations of the USSR, and union and autonomous republics" (10 April 1990), and "On delimitation of competences between the USSR and subjects of the federation" (26 April 1990).[3] These laws raised the autonomous republics in the RSFSR to a significant extent to the level of subjects of the USSR, equal to the union republics in their interconnections with the USSR.

The First Phase of Russian Federalism

The first step was the period of the collapse of the USSR and the adoption of the Russian Declaration of State Sovereignty, the second was the signature of the Federal Treaty and the enactment of necessary amendments to the Russian Constitution of 1978, and the third was the adoption of the Russian Constitution of 1993.

TABLE 3. Declarations of State Sovereignty

Subject of the Federation	Declaration of state sovereignty
1990	
Russian SFSR	12 June
R. of Severnaya Osetiya	20 July
R. of Kareliya	9 August
R. of Khakassiya	15 August
Abkhaziya (a breakaway from Georgia)	25 August
R. of Komi	29 August
R. of Tatarstan	30 August
R. of Udmurtiya	20 September
Yuzhnaya Osetiya (breakaway from Georgia)	20 September
R. of Yakutiya	27 September
R. of Chukotka	29 September
R. of Buryatiya	8 October
Koryakskii Autonomous Okrug	9 October
Komi-Permyatskii Autonomous Okrug	11 October
R. of Bashkortostan	11 October
R. of Kalmykiya	18 October
Yamalo-Nenetskii Autonomous Okrug	18 October
R. of Mari El	22 October
R. of Chuvashiya	24 October
R. of Gorniy Altai	25 October
R. of Tyva	1 November
R. of Karachaevo-Cherkessiya	17 November
Chechen-Ingush Republic	27 November
R. of Mordoviya	8 December
1991	
R. of Kabardino-Balkariya	31 January
R. of Dagestan	15 May
R. of Adygeya	2 July

The period between 1990 and March 1992, has been described as the "parade of sovereignties." The abortive coup d'état of 18 August 1991 swiftly led to the demise of the USSR. The Minsk Agreement of 8 December 1991 and the Alma-Ata Declaration of 21 December 1991[4] laid the USSR to rest. During this period an extraordinary process began. From July to November 1990 the majority of the "ethnic" autonomous republics attempted to throw off their autonomous status, and to take on sovereign statehood. They did this by way of a series of declarations.[5]

Mikhailov (2004, 106) has shown graphically how a large number of subjects of the Federation declared state sovereignty even before the collapse of the USSR in December 1991; see Table 3. These territories—two of them located in Georgia, soon to become an independent state—

wanted to become full-fledged members of the USSR and to enter into treaty relations with the RSFSR. And some of the autonomous *okrugs* unilaterally decided to become autonomous republics. Such decisions were taken in 1990 by the legislatures of the Chukotka and Yamalo-Nenets autonomous *okrugs*. Chukotka successfully left the Magadan *oblast* to become a subject of the RF, according to the judgment of the Constitutional Court of the RF of 11 May 1993.[6]

Both Boris Yeltsin and Mintimer Shaimiev were democratically elected on 12 June 1991—the former as the first president of the RSFSR, the latter as the first president of Tatarstan (Shaimiev 1996a, 2). One of the factors which precipitated the abortive putsch of August 1991 was the real threat of ethnic separatism. The putsch leaders, who were leading officials of the Communist Party of the Soviet Union, believed they were saving the Union.

The real threat of the transformation of Russia into a confederation provided the direct impetus for a draft Federative Treaty. On 31 March 1992 the RSFSR and most of the subjects signed the Federative Treaty, setting out the division of powers. The Treaty was incorporated into the 1978 Constitution of the RSFSR, going into effect 10 December 1992. In the view of Umnova, Russia turned from a unitary state into a half-federation or quasi-federal state (1998, 63). She also considers that for the regions other than the ethnic republics, the Treaty "won" a status of autonomy similar to the regions of unitary decentralized states, such as Italy and Spain (both since the 1980s). One of the most important guarantees of autonomy was the principle, to be found in Art. 84 of the Treaty and Art. 84(9) of the amended 1978 Constitution, that the territories of these formations could not be changed without their agreement.

It is notable that not all the subjects of the RSFSR agreed with the provisions of the Federative Treaty. Neither Tatarstan nor the Chechen-Ingush Republic signed it. On 21 March 1992 Tatarstan, despite the decision of the Russian Constitutional Court of 13 March 1992,[7] held a referendum confirming the status of Tatarstan as an independent republic and subject of international law, with its own relations with the RF and other republics and also with foreign states on the basis of treaties and legal equality.

The status of the Chechen-Ingush Republic was not at all clear; practically speaking, it escaped from the control of the federal authorities (Umnova 1998, 72). The Republic of Bashkortostan also had a special relation to the Treaty. The process of "republicanization" at this point began to transgress the limits of legality. On 27 October 1993 Sverdlovsk *oblast* adopted a Constitution of the Urals Republic. This republic was proclaimed unilaterally.[8] On 9 November 1993 President Yeltsin issued his decree "On stopping the activities of the Sverdlovsk Oblast deputies," and declared that the actions of the Soviet in adopting its decisions of

1 July 1993 on the status of Sverdlovsk Oblast within the RF and of 27 October 1993 on the Constitution of the Urals Republic were null and void from the moment of their enactment (see also Easter 1997, as to the attempt to create a new Urals Republic).[9]

We may note the very different trajectories of Chechnya and Tatarstan since then (see Derlugyan 2002). The history of Chechnya is an exception which proves the rule. The Chechen Republic was and is one of the most ethnically homogeneous of all the Russian republics, with Chechens, unusually, in an absolute majority. The Chechens defied the Russian empire until 1864. They suffered the brutal deportation by Stalin of their whole population in 1944. On 9 June 1991 the Chechen Republic, arbitrarily carved out of the Chechno-Ingush Republic, decided to secede from the USSR and RSFSR. This did not automatically mean the use of armed force by Russia, but there was no possibility of compromise. This was not least because of the gross injustices suffered by Chechens in this and past centuries (Pain and Popov 1999). Conflict followed almost as a matter of course, and lasted from 1994 to 1997.

Russia acceded to the Council of Europe in 1996, and ratified the European Convention on Human Rights in 1998. Russia has, on a large number of occasions, been condemned by the European Court of Human Rights for serious violations of the human rights of Chechens.[10] On 23 March 2003 a new Constitution of the Chechen Republic was adopted by referendum.[11] That constitution was drafted by Putin's supporter Akhmad Kadyrov, who was assassinated on 9 May 2004.[12] His son Ramzan Kadyrov then ruled Chechnya, with the assistance of the "Kadyrovtsy," fighters who until very recently had been fighting the Russians. The journalist Anna Politkovskaya, a fierce critic of Kadyrov, was murdered in Moscow on 7 October 2006, while carrying out an investigation of his autocratic rule.[13] On 5 April 2007 Ramzan Kadyrov was installed as president,[14] having reached the necessary age of thirty, under President Putin's new rules, discussed below. Kadyrov was nominated by Putin and confirmed the following day by 56 of 58 possible votes in the Chechen legislature.[15] He has now asserted a greater degree of autonomy even than was sought in 1991–92, and has been described as the "Warrior King" of Chechnya (Osborn 2007).

The trajectory of Tatarstan has been quite different. I have noted above Tatarstan's Declaration of State Sovereignty, in which state sovereignty was declared as the "realisation of the inalienable right of the Tatar nation, of all people of the republic to self-determination" (Tishkov 1997, 56). President Shaimiev stresses the fact that the "people of Tatarstan" were not divided into ethnic groups (1996a, 5). In a referendum of that time, no less than 62 percent of its population, Tatars and Russians, supported sovereignty. Tatarstan, like Chechnya, refused to sign the Federative Treaty in March 1992, but, unlike the Chechen leadership, Shaimiev entered into lengthy negotiations with the Russian government.

The Second Phase: The 1993 Constitution of the Russian Federation

During 1993, a so-called "budget and finance war" developed between the federation and its subjects, and turned into a full-fledged crisis in September 1993. This crisis was only resolved by the adoption of the new constitution on 12 December 1993. However, the new constitution itself bore all the hallmarks of a compromise document. Art. 76 provided that like the republics all subjects of the federation could enact their own laws and independently decide on their own executive system.

Moreover, in seven of the ethnic republics (Bashkortostan, Mordoviya, Chuvashiya, Adygeya, Dagestan, Karachaevo-Cherkessiya, Tyva) as well as in ten *oblasts* the majority of voters voted against the new constitution. In two republics, Tatarstan and Chechnya, referenda did not take place at all. Unofficial sources suggest that 13 of the 21 republics voted against the new constitution, and altogether 31 subjects voted against. Thus the new constitution suffered a deficit of legitimacy from the outset.

The constitutions of a number of republics to the Russian Federation also vary sharply: three groups may be distinguished (Mikhailov 2004, 409). First, the constitutions of Tatarstan and Chechnya lacked any reference to the fact that they were part of the Russian Federation, or to the supremacy of its constitution and laws. Second, the constitutions of Bashkortostan, Ingushetiya, Tyva, and Sakha (Yakutiya) recognized membership of the federation but said nothing about the supremacy of the federal constitution or laws. Third, all the others recognized both membership and supremacy.

The Third Phase: Post-1993 Russian Federalism

Varlamova has identified three stages in the evolution of Russian federalism from 1993 (2001, 25). She terms the first stage, 1994–1995, "subject treaty-based." During this period priority was given to individual regulation (at the level of the constitution or charter of the subject and bilateral agreements with the federal center), and a growing tendency to asymmetry in the Federation and even movement toward confederation. Two leading commentators, Constitutional Court Judge B. S. Ebzeev and Professor L. M. Karapetyan (Ebzeev and Karapetyan 1995) took the view that Russia as a constitutional state could not be treaty-based. Umnova strongly disagreed (1998, 78), and she must be right. Thus, Art. 70 of the Constitution of the Republic of Bashkortostan declares that its relation with the RF is based on treaties. By its Constitution, it retains the whole gamut of state power with the exception of those powers voluntarily ceded by it to the RF.

Many republics did not recognize any change to their status under the Federative Treaty as the result of the 1993 Constitution. Article 8 of the Constitution of Sakha (Yakutiya) declared that it is a subject of the RF on the basis of the Treaty. Article 1 of the Constitution of the Republic of Tyva recognized its inclusion in the RF on the basis of this and other treaties. Art. 68 of the Constitution of the Republic of Buryatiya provided that it had the right to delegate voluntarily defined competences for defined periods to the RF (Umnova 1998, 79–80).

Most extraordinary and probably unique to the RF, however, was the number of bilateral treaties entered into between the federation and its subjects. Very many of these treaties contradicted the express provisions of the 1993 Constitution. Thus, on 15 February 1994, Tatarstan signed the treaty "On the Demarcation of Competences Between the Government of the Russian Federation and the Government of the Republic of Tatarstan" and twelve agreements with Moscow, affirming its constitution and presidency, republican citizenship, a significant degree of sovereignty over oil and other natural resources, special provisions for military service, and other rights and powers (Tishkov 1997, 243). Further examples are the treaties with Kabardino-Balkariya (June 1994), Bashkortostan (August 1994), Udmurtiya (October 1995), and Omsk Oblast (May 1996) (see Shulzhenko 1998, 68; Lysenko 1998, 2). As of June 1998, more than half the regions had concluded some 46 similar treaties (Alekseyev et al. 1998a, 334). Frommeyer considered that this process "could lead to the disintegration of the Russian Federation" (1999, 53). Varlamova also points out that the Constitutional Court was rarely called on to decide issues arising between the federation and its subjects; these were for the most part resolved through informal and political means (2001, 26).

In the second stage identified by Varlamova (2001, 29), the RF sought unify the legal situation of subjects of the federation, and guarantee the supremacy of the federal constitution. Thus, the presidential decree of 12 March 1996[16] made it clear that treaties must not change the constitutional status of a subject of the federation. However, treaties concluded between 1996 and 1998 continued to contain provisions violating the federal constitution, if not so obviously (Ivanov 1999). For this reason, laws were enacted in June and October with detailed rules for the organization subjects of the RF.[17] The enactment of these laws gave rise to a series of judgments and decisions of the Constitutional Court of the Russian Federation, at the request of regional bodies and private citizens, seeking authoritative adjudication of the powers and duties of subjects of the RF (Varlamova 2001, 30).

The year 1996 also saw the beginning of Russia's experiment in "national-cultural autonomy," that is, nonterritorial autonomy, about which Aleksandr Ossipov and I have written extensively (Ossipov 2004; Bowring 2002, 2005, 2007, 2008), and which may be coming to an end.

Dismantling Sovereignty After 2000: Putin's Policies

The third stage identified by Varlamova was the "strengthening of the 'vertikal' of power" (2001, 73). This had three main objectives:

- bringing the legislation of the subjects into line with the law of the RF,
- weakening the influence (formal and informal) of leaders of the regions on the activities of federal organs of power, and
- strengthening responsibility toward federal power.

Following his election in 2000 President Putin on several occasions declared his strong opposition to the bilateral treaties and his determination to bring them to an end. According to Hyde, writing at the beginning of this process, "Putin's reforms may represent only a brief departure from previous practices, only a temporary swing of the pendulum in favor of central power" (2001, 738). This was to underestimate Putin's determination (see Hahn 2001), exemplified by the Presidential Decree of May 2000,[18] which, without amending the RF Constitution, created seven federal districts, each comprising six to eighteen subjects of the RF, headed by plenipotentiary representatives, mostly drawn from the military and FSB, and supported by senior representatives of the prosecutors, FSB, police, and other federal organs. A federal register of all normative acts enacted by the subjects of the RF was created, to be held at the Ministry of Justice, and copies of all normative acts were required to be sent within seven days of their enactment in the regions.[19] In February 2001 Deputy General Prosecutor Yu. S. Biryukov announced that in the previous six months 3,273 unlawful normative acts had been discovered, of which 2,544 had either been repealed or brought into line.[20]

In the view of V. E. Chirkin, the creation of the seven federal districts was a first step toward the strengthening and unifying of subjects of the RF with a view to a future federation, not, of course, of seven subjects, but of twenty-five to thirty (2000, 48–49). However Varlamova argues, in my view correctly, that given the historical roots of the present structure, a quick and artificial solution should be avoided in favor of a more cautious, step-by-step approach, even if this takes a number of years (2001, 91).

At last, the RF Constitutional Court issued a fundamental Judgment on 7 June 2000,[21] followed by a Clarification on 27 June 2000,[22] in response to a group of Duma deputies requesting investigation of a number of provisions of the constitutions of Altai in the first case, and of the (ethnic) republics of Adygeya, Bashkortostan, Ingushetiya, Komi, Severnaya Osetiya-Alaniya (known as North Ossetia) and Tatarstan in the second. The Court held the following to be incompatible with the Constitution of the RF:

- state sovereignty of the republics as subjects of the RF;
- the assumption of the republics of supreme power within their territories;
- recognizing the people of the republic as the bearers of sovereignty and unique source of power;
- asserting, following from the principle of sovereignty, the supremacy of the republic's constitution and laws;
- suspending the effect of legal acts of the RF in its territory;
- asserting the treaty-based character of the status of the republic as a subject of the RF, and the fact of its inclusion or remaining in the RF at all;
- asserting the status of the republic as a subject of international law; and
- declaring the rules governing property relations with regard to natural resources.

Varlamova asks why it took seven years for the republics' assertion of sovereignty to be challenged. The answer to that question is simple, she says: the deputies were instructed to do so by the new president, Vladimir Putin. She does not know, however, why only six of twenty-one republics were challenged (2001, 79).

Varlamova also points out that the reaction of the republics can be characterized as "deaf dissatisfaction" (79). In Bashkortostan there were serious problems with publication of the decision.[23] Only Severnaya Osetiya-Alaniya (known as North Ossetia) made the necessary amendments to its Constitution. Adygeya, Altai, Ingushetiya, and Tatarstan retained the provisions the Constitutional Court had found to be unconstitutional. There are very similar provisions in the Constitution of Bashkortostan adopted in November 2000.[24] In the opinion of the general prosecutor the old constitution had 44 articles that contradicted federal law; the new one 51.

Nevertheless, an amending law of July 2000 introduced strict mechanisms for responsibility, including individual criminal liability.[25] In the view of Varlamova, the main problem of this law is that it contradicts the RF Constitution, since it purports to give to the parliament and president of the RF powers they do not have (2001, 96).

Finally, the Federal Law of 5 August 2000 provided that the Council of the Federation was to be composed, not, as previously, of the presidents and the governors of the subjects of the Federation, but by elected representatives of the legislatures of the subjects and appointed representatives of the president or governor.[26] On the one hand, this could be said to increase the likelihood that members would focus on the business of the Council. On the other hand, however, in Varlamova's view, the Council's status as an independent and influential body, able to act as part of a system of checks and balances, was radically reduced (Varlamova 2001, 103).

At the same time, President Putin continued to take measures to eliminate treaty-based relations within the RF. By 2003 some 30 of the 42 treaties had been abrogated (Sharlet 2003, 338). And on 9 February 2007 the Russian State Duma ratified a new power-sharing agreement "giving Tatarstan a degree of economic and political autonomy that no other region enjoys." This development directly contradicts Putin's policy of centralization, and has been seen as a serious defeat for the *siloviki*, the "party of power" (Smirnov 2007). On 11 July 2007 the Federation Council, having first rejected the law in February, voted 122 to 4 in favor of the new treaty (Arnold 2007). President Shamaiev said in an interview: "First of all, I want to say that although this agreement is shorter in length, it is very significant, particularly from a political perspective, because the 1994 agreement was prepared under very difficult conditions." He explained that the original power-sharing treaty between Tatarstan and Russia dealt mostly with property issues, while the new treaty bears a mostly political significance and gives Tatarstan more autonomy than other Russian Federation subjects. Most important, Shaimiev said, it marks a first in Russian history (Gilfanov 2007). The treaty inter alia obliges the Tatar president to speak the Tatar language in addition to Russian, and allows regional authorities to issue "internal passports" with an insert in the Tatar language.

Putin's Eradication of Directly Elected Presidents and Governors

From 2000 on Putin used administrative and judicial pressure to keep politically inconvenient governors and other leaders from seeking reelection. Hashim adds, "Only a few defiant regional leaders, like Republican presidents of donor and ethnic regions such as Tatarstan and Bashkortostan, have maintained sufficient autonomy in spite of increased federal intervention in order to strengthen the power *vertikal*" (Hashim 2005, 36). In the view of Yuri Filippov, the basic idea was to "remove excessive politicisation . . . and to replace politicians with managers and bureaucrats" (Yu Filippov 2004).

The 3 September 2004 massacre at the Beslan school provided Putin with the motive for replacing direct election of presidents and governors.[27]

As Lemaître put it, "The Kremlin wants us to believe that Beslan was possible because the vertical of power was imperfect and there was still too little managed democracy in Russia. We disagree. . . . It had become clear, well before September 2004, that the Kremlin was more concerned with consolidating its grip on power than with the rule of law" (2006, 410).

On 13 September, at a session of the Government of the Russian Federation with participation of the heads of the subjects of the federation—the presidents and governors—Putin simply announced that henceforward, as part of the response to terrorism, the heads of the subjects would no longer be directly elected but rather the president would nominate a candidate to be elected, formally, by the subject's legislature.

The opposition politician Irina Khakamada described this as nothing short of a coup d'état, and unconstitutional.[28] But most governors did not protest.[29] The requisite federal law was signed by Putin on 12 December 2004—ironically, on Constitution Day.[30] Under the new law, if the president's candidate is rejected twice by the subject, he can dissolve the legislature and impose his own choice as acting governor (Bransten 2004; McFaul and Stoner-Weiss 2008).

The Asymmetric Federation Under Threat? "Forced" Mergers

Has the Kremlin been looking to dissolve the ethnic republics altogether? Yasmann (2006) notes the series of mergers that were taking place as of 2006, which have led to the "shrinkage" of the number of subjects of the Russian Federation with which I started this chapter. In his view, "there are many signs that political considerations are behind the merger efforts, and that the Kremlin's real goal is effectively to dissolve the troublesome ethnic republics in the North Caucasus and Volga region."

As I noted above, the regions concerned are the autonomous *okrugs*, precisely those ethnic autonomies created in the Soviet period. One reform plan published in 2006 envisaged 28, instead of 83, subjects of the RF, merging all ethnic republics with neighboring Slav administrative areas to form new provinces, eliminating any reference to ethnicity in their names (see Yasmann 2006). The proposed mergers would be

- The Republic of Tatarstan with Ulyanovsk Oblast to create Volgo-Kama Province
- The Republic of Bashkortostan with Orenburg Oblast to create Yuzno-Ural Province
- The Republic of Udmurtiya with Perm Krai to create Zapadno-Ural Province
- The Republics of Marii El and Chuvashiya with Kirov Oblast to create Volgo-Vyatka Province

- The Republic of Kalmykiya with Astrakhan, Volgograd, and Rostov *oblasts* to create Volgo-Don Province
- The Republics of Chechnya, Ingushetiya, Dagestan, Kabardino-Balkariya, and Severnaya Osetiya with Stavropol Krai to create North Caucasus Province
- The Republics of Adygeya and Karachayevo-Cherkessiya with Krasnodar Krai to create Prichenornormskaya Province

This process has been named "the parade of mergers" by Pimenov (2005), echoing Yeltsin's "parade of sovereignties." Bazhenov (2007) argues that Russia should be composed ideally of 35–50 regions, which all should be named *krai* rather than the czarist *guberniya*, in keeping with Russian history. Table 4 lists the mergers that have taken place so far, starting at the end of 2003, just before Putin's election to a second term. The process has, without doubt, been driven by the Kremlin.

As Dmitriyev (2007) observes, the apparently large votes in favor of each merger conceal considerable opposition to the merger process. For example, protests by the Buryat intelligentsia, led by historians Nikolai Tsyrempilov and Shirap Chimitdorzhiyev, have been ignored. They demand the restoration of the borders of the Buryat-Mongol Autonomous Soviet Socialist Republic, which was abolished by Stalin in 1937 and divided into three parts, following allegations of "pan-Mongolism" and irredentism—seeking to leave the USSR. The Moscow Helsinki Group has published a detailed report (2006), on gross irregularities committed during the 16 April 2006 referendum on the Irkutsk merger. They point out that the proportion of those voting in Irkutsk was barely 50 percent in the March 2004 presidential elections, and the minimum turnout for local elections is only 20 percent. More than 50 percent was required for the referendum. The "result" was a vote in favor of 99.51 percent in the Ust-Ordynski Buryat AO—reminiscent of the extraordinary "turnout" in the 2007 and 2008 parliamentary and presidential elections—and 68.98 percent in Irkutsk. I noted above that the Transbaikal (Zabaikalskii) *krai* came into existence on 1 March 2008, eliminating another of the "fragments" of the Buryat-Mongol autonomy. In an interview, the governor of Chita, Ravil Geniatulin, was quite clear as to the rationale behind merger: "the strengthening of the state as a whole" (Trunov 2007). He had nothing to say concerning the fate of the Buryat people.

Conclusion

As I indicated at the start of the chapter, the complex, contradictory, but ultimately rather effective Russian form of asymmetric federalism has helped Russia to maintain its territorial integrity, and, with the excep-

TABLE 4. Mergers, 2003–2007

Date of referendum	Merger	Date in force
7 December 2003	Perm *oblast* and the Komi-Permyanskii autonomous *okrug*, creating the Perm *krai*. The proposal on merger was approved by "an overwhelming majority." It is said that the ethnic Komi of the AO would have preferred a merger with the Republic of Komi.	1 December 2005
17 April 2005	Taimyr (with a population of 37,000) and Evenkiiski (population less than 18,000) autonomous *okrugs* into the Krasnoyarsk *krai* (population 3 million). The proposal on merger was "approved by an overwhelming majority." The Evenskii AO is now a "municipal district."	1 January 2007
23 October 2005	Kamchatka *oblast* and the Koryakskii autonomous *okrug* to create the Kamchatka *krai*. The proposal on merger was approved by an overwhelming majority (see Bigg 2005).	1 July 2007
April 2006	A majority of voters approved a merger between Irkutsk *oblast* and the Ust-Ordyn Buryat autonomous *oblast*, now home to about 15 percent of Russia's 400,000 ethnic Buryats (see Boykewych 2005).	1 January 2008
11 March 2007	Merger between Chita *oblast* and the Aginskii Buryat autonomous *okrug* to form a united Zabaikalskii *krai* (meaning "the other side of Lake Baikal"). The proposal on merger was approved by "an overwhelming majority" (Trunov 2007). Preparatory work has begun on the merger of Arkhangelsk *oblast* and the Nenets autonomous *oblast*. The process on merger is frozen. The problem is that Arkhangelsk is poor, while the Nenets AO is rich.[a]	1 March 2008

a. On merger with Komi, see Web site in Russian at http://www.perm.ru (accessed 20 August 2008); on Evenskii AO see http://www.evenkya.ru (accessed 20 August 2008); on the Kamchatka *krai* see Legislative Assembly Web site, containing a history, http://www. zaksobr.kamchatka.ru/common/3.html (accessed 20 August 2008); on Irkutsk *oblast*, http://www.govirk.ru (accessed 20 August 2008); on the AO, its Web site is still in existence, http://www.aginskoe.ru (accessed 20 August 2008); also see http://www.chita.ru (accessed 20 August 2008), the site for Zabaikalskii *krai*; on Arkhangelsk and Nenets see Vetrov and Tirmaste (2008).

T<small>ABLE</small> 5. "National" (Ethnic) Populations of Russia by Self-Description, 2002 Census

	People (millions)		2002 % of 1989	Percentage of total	
	1989	2002		1989	2002
Total	147.02	145.16	98.7	100	100
Russians	119.87	115.87	96.7	81.5	79.8
Tatars	5.52	5.56	100.7	3.8	3.8
Ukrainians	4.36	2.94	67.5	3.0	2.0
Bashkirs	1.35	1.67	124.4	0.9	1.2
Chuvash	1.77	1.64	92.3	1.2	1.1
Chechens	0.90	1.36	by 1.5	0.6	0.9
Armenians	0.53	1.13	by 2.1	0.4	0.8
Mordovians	1.07	0.84	78.7	0.7	0.6
Belarusians	1.21	0.81	67.5	0.8	0.6
Avars	0.54	0.76	139.2	0.4	0.5
Kazakhs	0.64	0.66	103.0	0.4	0.5
Udmurts	0.71	0.64	89.1	0.5	0.4
Azerbaijanis	0.34	0.62	by 1.9	0.2	0.4
Mari	0.64	0.60	94.0	0.4	0.4
Germans	0.84	0.60	70.9	0.6	0.4
Kabardians	0.39	0.52	134.7	0.3	0.4
Ossetians	0.40	0.51	128.0	0.3	0.4
Dargins	0.35	0.51	144.4	0.2	0.4
Buryats	0.42	0.45	106.7	0.3	0.3
Yakuts	0.38	0.44	116.8	0.3	0.3
Kumyks	0.28	0.42	by 1.5	0.2	0.3
Ingushes	0.22	0.41	by 1.9	0.1	0.3
Lezgins	0.26	0.41	by 1.6	0.2	0.3

tion of Chechnya, to avoid ethnonational conflict. I have shown how recent "reforms," ostensibly designed to strengthen the Russian state and its unity, have the potential for reopening past conflict and creating new ones. Writing in 2007, Oversloot observed: "That V. V. Putin has, thus far, not attempted to change the text of the 1993 Constitution, and that he has not tried to remove the limits which the 1993 Constitution also sets upon presidential power, is, nevertheless, considered to be of great importance" (2007, 64). However, more recently he concluded that "A reduction in the number of subjects to merely a few dozen . . . may prove to be much more difficult, and even politically risky" (2009, 134). The presidency of Dmitry Medvedev will be sorely tested by the challenges which will surely now emerge, and he has indicated that he will be cautious. Speaking about a possible merger of the Novgorod,

Leningrad and other regions, Medvedev emphasized that he had always thought that "these processes may not be imposed" from above. "Such processes must be initiated by people and decided in a referendum."[31] Recent research shows that "the economic rationale of keeping the republic's wealth motivates both Russians and titulars to support separatism" in republics such as Tatarstan (Hagendoorn, Poppe, and Minescu 2008, 370; and see Badretdin 1997). Whatever the desire of the Kremlin for administrative logic, the desire of the ethnic republics for greater autonomy will persist and may grow stronger.

Notes

1. Its Web site—with Hebrew-style Cyrillic—is http://www.eao.ru (accessed 9 August 2009).

2. Vedomosti of the Congress of People's Deputies RSFSR and Supreme Soviet RSFSR, 1990, No. 2, Art. 22.

3. Vedomosti of the Congress of People's Deputies of the USSR and the Supreme Soviet of the USSR, 1990, No. 16, Art. 270; No. 19, Art. 329.

4. *Rossiisskaya Gazeta,* 10 December, 24 December 1991.

5. *Deklaratsii o suverenitete soyuznikh i avtonomnikh respublikh,* Moscow, 1991.

6. Vestnik of the Constitutional Court of the RF 1994 No. 2–3, 53–59.

7. Vestnik of the Constitutional Court of the RF 1993 No. 1, 40–52.

8. *Yekaterinburgskii Vedomosti,* 30 October 1993.

9. Collection of the acts of the president and government of the RF 1993 No. 46, Art. 4447.

10. In 2002, the author founded the European Human Rights Advocacy Centre (EHRAC), which has now taken some 50 cases to the European Court of Human Rights on behalf of Chechens against the Russian Federation; there have already been significant victories.

11. *BBC News,* 24 March 2003 "Chechnya backs new constitution," http://news.bbc.co.uk/1/hi/world/europe/2879383.stm (accessed 9 August 2009).

12. Charles Gurin, Akhmad Kadyrov is assassinated, *Eurasia Daily Monitor* 6, 1, 9 May 2004
http://www.jamestown.org/single/?no_cache=1&tx_ttnews[tt_news]=26479 (accessed 9August 2009).

13. Editorial: Murder in Moscow: The Putin era of brutality claims a victim of rare courage, Washington Post, 8 October 2006.
http://www.washingtonpost.com/wp-dyn/content/article/2006/10/07/AR2006100700718.html (accessed 9 August 2009).

14. Ramzan Kadyrov, Chechnya strongman, installed as president, *New York Times* 5 April 2007, http://www.nytimes.com/2007/04/05/world/europe/05iht-web0405-chech.5161439.html (accessed 9 August 2009).

15. Kadyrov becomes Chechnya president, *Al Jazeera English,* 3 March 2007, http://english.aljazeera.net/NR/exeres/C7155E33-A492-4590-919D-89ABD-4BAE155.htm (accessed 9 August 2009).

16. No. 370, Sobraniye zakonodatelstvo RF 1996 No. 12, 1058.

17. Law of 24 June 1999, "On principles and procedure for delimitation of matters of powers and competences between organs of state power of the RF, and organs of state power of subjects of the RF." No. 119-FZ *Sobraniye zakonodatelstvo*

RF 1999 No. 26, 3176. Law of 6 October 1999, "On general principles of the organization of legislative (representative) and executive organs of state power of subjects of the RF" No. 184-FZ *Sobraniye zakonodatelstvo* RF 1999 No. 43, 5005; 2000 No. 31, 3205; 2001 No. 7, 608.

18. Decree of 13 May 2000, "On the plenipotentiary representatives of the President of the RF in the federal districts" No. 849 *Sobraniye zakonodatelstvo* RF 2000 No. 20, 2112.

19. Decree of 10 August 2000, "On supplementary measures for guaranteeing the unity of the legal space of the RF," No.1486 Sobraniye zakonodatelstvo RF 2000 No. 33, 3356.

20. Yu. S. Biryukov "*Prokuratura bystrovo reagirovaniya* (Quick response prosecution service)," *Nezavisimaya Gazeta,* 28 February 2001.

21. No. 10-P.

22. No. 92-O.

23. *Na net i publikatsii net: Kto pryachet ot zhitelei Bashkortotstana resheiye Constitutsionnovo Suda Rossii* (No publication whatsoever: Who is hiding the decision of the Constitutional Court of Russia from the inhabitants of Baskortostan), *Rossiiskaya Gazeta,* 2 September 2000.

24. *Vedomosti Gosudarstvennovo Sobraniya, Presidenta i Kabineta Ministrov Respubliki Bashkortostan* (Gazette of the State Council, President and Cabinet of Ministers of the Republic of Bashkortostan) 2000, No. 17, 1255.

25. No. 106-FZ, Sobraniye zakonodatelstvo RF 2000, No. 31, 3205.

26. "On the procedure for composition of the Council of the Federation (Upper House) of the Federal Assembly (Parliament) of the RF," No. 113-FZ, Sobraniye zakonodatelstvo RF 2000, No. 32, 3336.

27. On the massacre: The Beslan school tragedy, *The Guardian,* www.guardian.co.uk/world/beslan, (accessed 9 August 2009); on Putin's action: Website of the President of Russia, 4 September 2004, http://president.kremlin.ru/appears/2004/09/04/1752_type63374type82634_76320.shtml. (accessed 9 August 2009).

28. Inititsiativy po izmeneniyu sistemy gosudarstvennovo ustroistva—"eto fakticheski perevorot"—Irina Khakamada, Regnum.ru information agency, 14 September 2004, http://www.regnum.ru/news/324418.html (accessed 9 August 2009)

29. See, e.g., *Rossisskaya Gazeta,* 15 September 2004, printing responses of a number of heads, http://www.rg.ru/2004/09/15/gubernatory.html (accessed 9 August 2009).

30. No. 160-FZ, http://document.kremlin.ru/doc.asp?ID=025563 (accessed 9 August 2009); http://www.rg.ru/2004/12/15/gubernatory-dok.html (accessed 9 August 2009).

31. Dmitry Medvedev says direct gubernatorial elections unrealistic, 18 November 2008, *Administrative Reform in Russia,* http://ar.gov.ru/en/main_menu_en/news-events/index.php?m2=all&np2=195&ps2=10&q2=corruption&sp2=1&sy2=1&ul2=http://ar.gov.ru/&wf2=2221&wm2=sub&from4=24&id4=602 (accessed 9 August 2009)

References

Alekseyev, S., et al. 1998. *Ideologicheskiye orientiry Rossii* (Russia's ideological orientation). Vol. 1. Moscow: Kniga i Biznes.

Alexander, J. 2004. Federal reforms in Russia: Putin's challenge to the repub-

lics. *Demokratizatsiya* 12, 2. http://findarticles.com/p/articles/mi_qa3996/
is_200404/ai_n9376563/pg_2/ (accessed 9 August 2009).

Arnold, C. 2007. Russia: Federation Council backs Tatarstan power-sharing bill.
Radio Free Europe/Radio Liberty, 11 July. http://www.rferl.org/content/arti-
cle/1077565.html (accessed 9 August 2009).

Badretdin, S. 1997. Russia's future breakup and Tatarstan's independence.
Turkistan-Newsletter 97 (25 July): 1–27. http://www.euronet.nl/users/sota/
TN9727.htm (accessed 9 August 2009).

Bazhenov, Yu. 2007. *Krai dalyokii, krai rodnoi* (Distant *krai,* my own *krai*), 24
April. Pravaya.ru (pravoslavno-analiticheskii sait) http://www.pravaya.ru/
look/11987?print=1 (accessed 9 August 2009).

Bigg, C. 2005. Russia: Regions continue to merge. *Radio Free Europe/Radio Liberty,*
11 August. http://www.rferl.org/content/article/1062375.html (accessed 9
August 2009).

Bowring, B. 2008. Legal and Policy Developments in the Russian Federation in
2007 with regard to the Protection of Minorities." In vol. 6, 2006/7 *European
Yearbook of Minority Issues*.Leiden: Martinus Nijhoff, 2008. 529–43.

———. 2007. The Tatars of the Russian Federation and national cultural autonomy: A contradiction in terms? Ethnopolitics 6, 3: 417–35.

———. 2005. Burial and resurrection: Karl Renner's controversial influence on
the "national question" in Russia. In *National-cultural autonomy and its contemporary critics,* ed. E. Nimni. Abingdon: Routledge. 191–206.

———. 2003. Postcolonial transitions on the southern borders of the former
Soviet Union: The return of Eurasianism? In *Tracking the Postcolonial in Law,
Griffith Law Review* special issue 12, 2: 238–62.

———. 2002. Austro-Marxism's last laugh? The struggle for recognition of national-cultural autonomy for Rossians and Russians. *Europe-Asia Studies* 54, 2:
229–50.

———. 2000. Ancient peoples and new nations in the Russian Federation: Questions of theory and practice. In *Accommodating national identity: New approaches
in international and domestic law,* ed. S. Tierney. The Hague: Kluwer Law International. 211-230

Boykewich, S. 2005. Planned merger worries Buryats. *Moscow Times,* 13 November. http://www.buryat-mongolia.info/?p=303&language=en (accessed 9 August 2009).

Bransten, J. 2005. Russia: Kremlin approves regions' decision to merge. *Radio Free
Europe/Radio Liberty,* 19 April, http://www.rferl.org/content/article/1058551.
html (accessed 9 August 2009).

———. 2004. Russia: Putin signs bill eliminating direct elections of governors.
Radio Free Europe/Radio Liberty, 13 December. http://www.cdi.org/russia/john-
son/8497-10.cfm (accessed 9 August 2009).

Chirkin, V. E. 2000. *Novii rossiisskii federalizm: Strategiya i taktika* (The new Russian
federalism: Strategy and tactics). *Pravo i politika* 12: 45–63.

Dagbaev, E. 2008. *Politicheskiye strategii aktorov v protsesse ukrupleniya regionov* (The
political strategy of actors in the process of enlarging regions). In *Regionalis-
tika i etnopolitologiya* (Regional studies and ethno-politics), ed. R. F. Turovski.
Moscow: ROSSPEN (Russian Political Encyclopedia). 45–69.

Derlugyan, G. 2002. *Mir na slome epoch: Chechnya i Tatarstan v perspective vsemirnoi istorii* (The world at the scrapping of the epoch: Chechnya and Tatarstan from the
perspective of world history.) *Druzhba Narodov* 3 (Peoples' Friendship). http://
magazines.russ.ru/druzhba/2002/3/del.html (accessed 9 August 2009).

Dmitriyev, I. 2007. Federal misalliance robbing Peter to pay Paul. *Moscow News,* 10 December. http://english.mn.ru/english/issue.php?2007-12-10 (accessed 9 August 2009).

Dowley, K. 1998. Striking the federal balance in Russia: comparative regional government strategies. *Communist and Post-Communist Studies* 31: 359–80.

Drobizheva, L. 1997. *Natsionalizm v respublikakh Rossiiskoi Federatsii: ideologiya elity i massovoye coznaniye* (Nationalism in the republics of the Russian Federation: Ideology of the elite and mass consciousness). *Panorama-Forum* 9, "Eurasianism: For and Against" http://www.kcn.ru/tat_ru/politics/pan/tom9/t86. zip (accessed 9 August 2009)

———. 1998. Power sharing in the Russian Federation: The view from the center and from the republics. In *Preventing deadly conflict: Strategies and institution: Proceedings of a conference in Moscow,* ed. G. W. Lapidus with S. Tsalik. New York: Carnegie Corporation. Easter, G. 1997. Redefining centre-regional relations in the Russian Federation: Sverdlovsk *oblast. Europe-Asia Studies* 49: 617–35. Report to the Carnegie Commission on Preventing Deadly Conflict, Institut vseobshchei istorii (Rossiiskaia akademiya nauk). Stanford University. Center for International Security and Arms Control. New York: Carnegie Corporation. http://www.wilsoncenter.org/subsites/ccpdc/pubs/moscow/mosfr.htm (accessed 9 August 2009).

Ebzeev, B. S., and L. M. Karapetyan. 1995. *Rossisskii federalism: Ravnopraviye i assimetriya konstitutsionnovo statusa subyektov* (The Russian federation: Equal rights and asymmetry of the constitutional status of its subjects). *Gosudarstvo i Pravo* (State and Law) 11, 3: 8–12.

de Figueiredo, R., and B. Weingast. 2002. Pathologies of federalism, Russian style: Political institutions and economic transition. Paper for the conference Fiscal Federalism in the Russian Federation: Problems and Prospects for Reform, Higher School of Economics, Moscow, 29–30 January 2001, rev. March 2002. http://faculty.haas.berkeley.edu/rui/mpfrussia.pdf (accessed 9 August 2009).

Filippov, V. 1998. *Natsionalno-kulturnaya avtonomiya: Problemy i suzhdeniya* (National-cultural autonomy: Problems and assessment). Moscow: Ethnosphere Centre.

Filippov, Yu. 2004. State duma ponders Russia's future. *RIA-Novostii,* 29 October, http://www.cdi.org/russia/328-8.cfm (accessed 9 August 2009).

Frommeyer, T. 1999. Power sharing treaties in Russia's federal system. *Loyola of Los Angeles International and Comparative Law Journal* 21, 1: 1–53.

Gilfanov, R. 2007. Tatarstan: President following democracy "in the best interests of our people." Interview with President Mintimer Shamaiev. *Radio Free Europe/Radio Liberty,* 3 August. http://www.rferl.org/content/article/1077969. html (accessed 9 August 2009).

Giuliano, E. 2006. Do grievances matter in nationalist mobilization? Evidence from Russia. Working draft, mrgec.mcgill.ca/Giuliano%20paper%20on%20 grievances%20in%20Russia.doc (accessed 9 August 2009).

———. 2000. Who determines the self in the politics of self-determination? Ethnicity and preference formation in Tatarstan's nationalist mobilisation. *Comparative Politics* 32, 3: 295–316.

Gorenburg, D. 1999. Regional separatism in Russia: Ethnic mobilisation or power grab? *Europe-Asia Studies* 51: 245–74.

Hagendoorn, L, E. Poppe, and A. Minescu. 2008. Support for separatism in ethnic republics of the Russian Federation. *Europe-Asia Studies* 60, 3: 353–73.

Hahn, G. 2001. Putin's federal reforms: Reintegrating Russia's legal space or up-setting the metastability of Russia's asymmetrical federalism. *Demokratizatsiya* 9, 4. http://findarticles.com/p/articles/mi_qa3996/is_200110/ai_n9001194/ (accessed 9 August 2009).

Hashim, S. M. 2005. Putin's *Etatization* project and limits to democratic reforms in Russia. *Communist and Post-Communist Studies* 38: 25–48.

Hutcheson, D. 2005. Review of *The Dynamics of Russian Politics: Putin's Reform of Federal-Regional Relations* vol. 1, ed. P. Reddaway and R. Orttung (Lanham, Md.: Rowman and Littlefield, 2004). *Slavic Review* 64, 1: 209–10.

Hyde, M. 2001. Putin's federal reforms and their implications for presidential power in Russia. *Europe-Asia Studies* 53, 5: 719–43.

Ivanov, V. 1999. *Vnutrifederalniye dogovory 1998 god: Noviye shagi v storonu indivi-ualizatsiii federativnikh otnoshenii* (Intrafederal treaties in 1998: Further steps toward individualization of federative relations). *Konstitutsionnoye pravo: Vostochnoevropeiskoye obozreniye* 2, 27: 47–57.

Kempton, D. R. 1996. The republic of Sakha (Yakutia): The evolution of cen-tre-periphery relations in the Russian Federation. *Europe-Asia Studies* 48: 587–613.

Khakimov, R. S. 2005. The Tatars: An afterword. *Anthropology and Archeology of Eurasia* 43: 345–61.

Khazanov, A. 1997. Ethnic nationalism in the Russian Federation. *Daedalus* 126: 121–42.

Khenkin, S. 1997. *Separatizm v Rossii—pozady ili vperedi?* (Separatism in Russia—backward or forward?). *Pro et Contra* 2.2. http://uisrussia.msu.ru/docs/nov/pec/1997/2/ProEtContra_1997_2_01.htm (accessed 9 August 2009).

Kossikov, I. 1996. Federalism and regionalism in contemporary Russia. Speech delivered September 1996 at thirteenth International Seminar European Union, http://www.google.co.uk/url?sa=t&source=web&ct=res&cd=4&url=http%3A%2F%2Fwww.helsinki.fi%2Faleksanteri%2Fmaisterikoulu%2Fopinto-opas%2Fluentokurssit%2Foppimateriaali%2Frussia_beyond%2FShortened%2520version%2520of%2520readings.doc&ei=YjJ_SumCF8WfjAe-jMnwAQ&usg=AFQjCNEIAod0NRoHaefhy-7J25xb9EDFEw&sig2=M63saXTpPkDvHWSyjHLCYg (accessed 9 August 2009).

Kutafin, O. E. 2006. *Rossiiskaya avtonomiya* (Russian autonomy). Moscow: Pros-pektr.

Lemaître, R. 2006. The rollback of democracy in Russia after Beslan. *Review of Central and East European Law* 31: 369–411.

Lysenko, V. N. 1998. Distribution of power: The experience of the Russian Fed-eration. In *Preventing deadly conflict: Strategies and institutions; Proceedings of a conference in Moscow*, ed. G. W. Lapidus with S. Tsalik. Report to Carnegie Com-mission on Preventing Deadly Conflict, Institut vseobshchei istorii (Rossiiskaia akademiya nauk); Stanford University. Center for International Security and Arms Control. New York: Carnegie Corporation, 1998. http://www.wilsoncen-ter.org/subsites/ccpdc/pubs/moscow/mosfr.htm (accessed 9 August 2009)

Malik, H. 2000. Introduction to *Russian-American relations: Islamic and Turkic di-mensions in the Volga-Ural Basin*, ed. H. Malik. London: Palgrave: 1–25. Also available at Palgrave site, http://www.palgrave.com/pdfs/0333733894.pdf (accessed 9 August 2009).

———. 1994. Tatarstan's treaty with Russia: Autonomy or independence? *Jour-nal of South Asian and Middle Eastern Studies* 18, 1. http://www.tatar.ru/index.php?wrap=84&page=5& node_id=1379&full=638 (accessed 9 August 2009).

Martin, T. 2001. *The affirmative action empire: nations and nationalism in the Soviet Union, 1923–1939.* Ithaca, N.Y.: Cornell University Press.

McFaul, M. 2004. The Putin paradox, Center for American Progress, 24 June. http://www.americanprogress.org/issues/2004/06/b99061.html (accessed 9 August 2009).

McFaul, M., and K. Stoner-Weiss. 2008. The myth of the authoritarian model: How Putin's crackdown holds Russia back. *Foreign Affairs* 87, 1. http://www.foreignaffairs.com/articles/63047/michael-mcfaul-and-kathryn-stoner-weiss/the-myth-of-the-authoritarian-model (accessed 9 August 2009).

McGarry, J. 2007. Asymmetrical autonomy and conflict regulation: A response to Adeney, Conversi, Hechter and Rezvani. *Ethnopolitics* 6, 1: 133–36.

———. 2005. *Asymmetrical federalism and the plurinational state.* Position paper for Third International Conference on Federalism, Brussels, 3–5 March.

Mikhailov, V. V. 2004. *Respublika Tatarstan: demokratiya ili suverenitet?* (The Republic of Tatarstan: Democracy or sovereignty?). Moscow: Institute of Africa, Russian Academy of Science.

Moscow Helsinki Group. 2006. On violations committed in the course of organising and carrying out referendum on merging Irkutsk region and Ust-Ordynski Buryatskyi Autonomous District. Report, http://www.mhg.ru/files/Report062.doc (accessed 9 August 2009).

Obydenkova, A. 2004. The role of asymmetrical federalism in ethnic-territorial conflicts in the era of democratisation: The RF as a case study. European University Institute Working Papers SPS no. 2004/16. Badia Fiesolana: EUI.

Osborn, A. 2007. Ramzan Kadyrov: The Warrior King of Chechnya. *The Independent*, 4 January. http://www.independent.co.uk/news/people/ramzan-kadyrov-the-warrior-king-of-chechnya-430738.html (accessed 20 August 2008).

Ossipov, A. 2004. *Natsionalno-kulturnaya avtonomiya: Idei, resheniya, instituty* (National-cultural autonomy: Ideas, decisions, institutions). St. Petersburg: Centre for Independent Sociological Research.

Oversloot, A. 2009. The merger of federal subjects of the Russian Federation during Putin's presidency and after. *Review of Central and East European Law* 34: 119–35.

Oversloot, H. 2007. Reordering the state (without changing the Constitution): Russia under Putin's rule, 2000–2008. *Review of Central and East European Law* 32: 41–64.

Pain, E. A. 1999a. Russia: The ethnic dimension. *Russia.* http://www.russia-all.ru/society_general.htm (accessed 20 August 2008).

Pain E. A., and A. A. Popov. 1999. Chechnya—from past to present. Amina (Chechen Republic Online).http://www.amina.com/article/history.html (accessed 9 August 2009).

Pimenov, S. 2005. *Parad obyedinenii* (The parade of mergers), 17 June. Polit-NN.ru (Polit in Nizhniii Novgorod) http://www.polit-nn.ru/?pt=analytics&view=single&id=3 (accessed 9 August 2009).

Reddaway, P., and R. Orttung, eds. 2004. *The dynamics of Russian politics: Putin's reform of federal-regional relations.* Vol. 1. Lanham, Md.: Rowman and Littlefield.

Salikov, M. 2004. The Russian federal system: Sub-national and local levels. Paper delivered at conference Subnational Constitutions and Federalism: Design and Reform, 22–27 March. Center for State Constitutional Studies at Rutgers-Camden, camlaw.rutgers.edu/statecon/subpapers/salikov.pdf (accessed 20 August 2008).

Shaimiev, M. 2006. *My vsegda byli za federalism, no podlinniy, a ne na slovakh* (We were always for federalism, but authentic, not in words only. Interview with Rosbalt, 28 March http://president.tatar.ru/pub/view/1022 and http://www. rosbalt.ru/print/248514.html (accessed 9 August 2009)

―――. 2002. *Krepit yedinstvo naroda, dvigatsya vperyod, ne otgorazhibayas ot ostalnovo mira* (To strengthen the unity of the people, to move forward, not isolating ourselves from the rest of the world). Welcome of the president of Tatarstan to the Third World Congress of Tatars, 29 August at http://president.tatar.ru/ pub/view/567 (accessed 9 August 2009)

―――. 1996a. Conflict prevention and management: The significance of Tatarstan's experience. In *Preventing deadly conflict: Strategies and institutions; Proceedings of a conference in Moscow*, ed. G. W. Lapidus with S. Tsalik. Report to the Carnegie Commission on Preventing Deadly Conflict, Institut vseobshchei istorii (Rossiiskaia akademiya nauk); Stanford University. Center for International Security and Arms Control. New York : Carnegie Corp., 1998. http:// www.wilsoncenter.org/subsites/ccpdc/pubs/moscow/mosfr.htm (accessed 9 August 2009)

―――. 1996b. *Opyt vzaimootnoshenii Tatarstana i Rossii* (Experience of the interrelations of Tatarstan and Russia). *Panorama-Forum* 6.

Sharlet, R. 2003. Resisting Putin's federal reforms on the legal front. *Demkratizatsiya* 11, 3: 335–42.

Shulzhenko, Yu. 1998. *Institut konstitutsionnovo nadzora v Rossiskoi Federatsii* (The institution of constitutional review in the Russian Federation). Moscow: Institute of State and Law.

Smirnov, A. 2007. Tatar treaty suggests dissent inside Kremlin on regional policy. *Eurasia Daily Monitor* 4, 33. http://www.jamestown.org/single/?no_cache=1&tx_ttnews[tt_news]=32494 (accessed 9 August 2009).

Sokolova Z. P, N. I. Novikova, and N. V. Sorin-Chaikov. 1995. *Etnographi pishut zakon: Kontekst i problemy* (Ethnographers write a law: Context and problems). *Etnographicheskoye obozreniye* 1: 74–88.

Teague, E. 2008. Regional mergers in the Russian Federation. Paper presented to Association for the Study of Nationalities 2007 World Convention, New York. Copy with author.

Tishkov, V. 1997. *Ethnicity, nationalism and conflict in and after the Soviet Union: The mind aflame.* London: Sage.

Trunov, R. 2007. Chita region governor discusses merger in Russian Federation. *Moscow News*, 24 May, http://www.mnweekly.ru/national/20070524/55251167. html (accessed 9 August 2009)

Umnova, I. 1998. *Konstitutsionni osnovy sovremennovo possiiskovo federalizma* (The constitutional foundations of contemporary Russian federalism). Moscow: Dyelo.

Varlamova, N. 2001. *Sovremenniy Rossiisskii federalizm: konstitutsionnaya model i politico-pravovaya dinamika* (Contemporary Russian federalism: Constitutional model and political-legal dynamic). Moscow, Institute of Law and Public Policy.

Vetrov, P., and M.-L. Tirmaste. 2008. V Nenetskom okruge ne znayut, chevo zhdat ot Arkhangelskovo gubernatora (In the Nenets *okrug* they do not know what to expect from the Arkhangel governor). *Kommersant* 45, 3862, 20 March, http:// www.kommersant.ru/doc.aspx?DocsID=869006 (accessed 9 August 2009).

Vishnyakov, V. G. 1998. *Konstitutsionnoye regulirovaniye federativnikh otnoshenii* (The constitutional regulation of federal relations). *Gosudarstvo i Pravo* (State and Law) 12: 20–29.

Wertheim, S. 2003. Language ideologies and the "purification" of post-Soviet Tatar. *Ab Imperio* 1: 347–69.

Yasmann, V. 2006. Analysis: The future of Russia's "ethnic republics." Radio Free Europe/Radio Liberty, 21 April. http://www.rferl.org/articleprint-view/1067861.html (accessed 9 August 2009).

Ziyatdinova, F. 1995. Historical memory of the Tatar ethnic group. *International Affairs* (January 1995). http://www.tatar.ru/index.php?wrap=84&page=5&node_id=1379&full=793 (accessed 9 August 2009).

Zverev, A. 2002. The patience of a nation is measured in centuries: National revival in Tatarstan historiography. In *Secession, History and the Social Sciences*, ed. B. Coppieters and M. Huysseune. Brussels: VUB University Press. 69–87.

Chapter 3
Partial Asymmetry and Federal Construction: Accommodating Diversity in the Canadian Constitution

Raffaele Iacovino

In a cursory overview of asymmetrical federations, the Canadian case stands out in several respects. First, although a strong secessionist movement exists in Quebec, there has been little recourse to violence that would necessitate international mediation. Second, a recent "pact" or settlement that addresses the secessionist movement has not been instituted—indeed, the most recent constitutional rounds ended in 1992 with the failure of the Charlottetown Accord, and the subsequent rejection of independence in the Quebec referendum closed the case. What remains is the persistent claim that the status quo contains within it the necessary institutional mechanisms to alleviate such pressures. Indeed, the recent history of intergovernmental relations and constitutionalism in Canada is marked by a curious measure of indifference for one of the most powerful secessionist movements in the world. Third, with regard to cultural and territorial autonomy, Canada is marked by "diversity of diversities" that often undercut one another in the country's attempt to find an agreement that satisfies all of its constituent partners. Nation building in Canada has thus been characterized in part by various attempts to recognize the country's politically salient identities, often resulting in clashing visions that are metaconstitutional in nature (Cairns 1992). Finally, with regard to the place of nation building activities and attempts to consolidate national identity as the basis for citizenship and representation, Canada is caught between formal procedural markers of identification that apply uniformly across the country and a constant challenge from Quebec, which has undertaken a coherent nation-building strategy of its own since the "Quiet Revolution" in the 1960s.

Moreover, one is struck by the extent to which asymmetry in Canada is at once as viscerally rejected as it is embraced. This has resulted in a situation where theorists and scholars have for the most part vaunted its merits and its "inevitable" foray into Canada's institutional landscape, while at the same time garnering much negative reaction from federal legislators, in part due to a large body of literature documenting its unpopular status among the general population (Seidle and Bishop 2005). As such, in Canada there exists a curious relationship with asymmetry. Its capacity to accommodate diversity has produced a seemingly unending body of thought that includes considerations about: its role in structuring relations between constituent units in the country's history as a well-acknowledged "fact" (see Milne 1991; Watts 1999); the fact that it has over time nourished debates that range from attempts to shed light on the country's actual founding principles to a novel way forward in a global world (see, for example, Kelly and Laforest 2004); its status as the most likely candidate to address Canada's persistent constitutional impasse;[1] as the best way forward in addressing the policy interdependence between federal and provincial governments, particularly in terms of fiscal arrangements; as the logical consequence of deep-seated sociological differences in relation to the existence of Quebec (McRoberts 1997; Webber 1994), with a majority Francophone population, as well as in the case of Aboriginal peoples;[2] and generally, as a vehicle for infusing Canadian federalism with a measure of flexibility that allows for constant adaptation to changing international and domestic circumstances. Indeed, Canada is something of a beacon for discourses on asymmetry, challenging singular understandings of political community and producing what some have called a "Canadian school" over questions of diversity, or a unique "Canadian conversation" (Kernerman 2006) that at once appeals to creative tensions about belonging and serves to keep the question of diversity alive.

At the same time, asymmetrical federalism has also served as a catalyst for debates about what is "wrong" with Canadian federalism. In this sense, it is taken as symptomatic of a failure to consolidate a sense of overarching national identity in the country through nation-building efforts at the center and as a strategy of appeasement in responding to what is a perceived as an illegitimate countervailing and competing *projet de société* in Quebec.

As a result, asymmetry in Canada is often approached indirectly, presented as a consequence of differential policy choices or administrative dealings between governments; as the outcome of intergovernmental practices and functional requirements in order to accommodate disparate needs of constituent units, and so on, rather than as a defining principle that reflects, fundamentally, the meaning and purpose of Canadian federalism. It is this narrative—one of an institutional and structuring principle that exists in the shadows, appearing now and again, eliciting tensions old and new, and strong reactions that touch upon sentiments of allegiance as well as notions of fairness—that will be recounted in this chapter. Kenneth McRoberts (2000, 25) captures this dynamic succinctly: "Canada more than ever is a multi-national state in terms of its underlying social and cultural reality. Yet, it's also more than ever a nation-state in its dominant discourse and political institutions." The disjuncture between practice and discourse is clear in Canada, and it in part nourishes the notion that asymmetrical solutions can only be partially enacted—as an outgrowth of effective governance.

A further note must be considered in introducing asymmetrical federalism in Canada. Since calls for asymmetry are based on prescriptive measures for federalism, normative concerns cannot be sidestepped in contemporary debates. One must avoid proceeding with analysis by looking only at the structure of society, as this neglects the nation-building efforts undertaken over the years by both Canada and Quebec. To look only at the state, however, would be to miss out on some underlying reasons for asymmetry and the "federal spirit"—the idea that difference is one of the underlying purposes of federalism rather than a stumbling block to achieving unity. As such, this chapter will straddle these two approaches, looking at the interplay between the norm of asymmetry in Canada and actual attempts to institutionalize or accept it in fact. Asymmetry in Canada invokes existential questions related to self-identification. It should not merely be approached as a pragmatic institutional device meant to lessen conflict.

Moreover, this chapter will demonstrate that the constitutional politics of difference and asymmetrical federalism as an institutional corollary is the Canadian contribution to political science that dare not speak its name. Diversity management in Canada has taken an eerily uniform bent, leaving the country with what I argue is largely a myth about its commitment to recognizing diversity, largely propagated due to its formal adherence to sociocultural diversity (multiculturalism) and personal bilingualism while shunning serious efforts at instituting formal asymmetry as the logical outcome of the recognition of national pluralism.[3] As such, asymmetry in Canada is only partly in force because it must constantly contend with a powerful nation-building project that defines the country through the equality of individuals and provinces, multiculturalism, and bilingualism from coast to coast.

The "Morality" of Federalism in Canada and Quebec as a Catalyst for Asymmetry

The Morality of Federalism as a Structuring Principle

The debate in Canada is animated by a moral imperative that sees in asymmetry a way of "being true" to the federal spirit (Rocher 2006). Michael Burgess (2000) aptly compares the source of this debate to shortcomings in the study of political science more generally—to what extent are moral principles necessary to supplement, legitimize, or strengthen formal or legal provisions in ascertaining political outcomes? A comparative volume on asymmetry seems like an unlikely place to introduce the issue of moral federalism, but one cannot grasp the institutionalization of asymmetry in Canada without reference to this particularly salient point.

As early as 1962, James Corry, a noted constitutional scholar, witnessed a trend whereby the nine other provinces offered little resistance on a principled front to the notion that the federal government might act to consolidate certain policy areas within provincial jurisdictions. Elsewhere, Corry (1978) has described the requirement to accept nonformal guiding principles for federalism as a "constitutional morality." For Burgess, this morality was none other than an attempt to infuse the meaning of Canadian federalism with a persistent concern for Quebec's difference. Burgess offers a particularly poignant quotation by Corry:

> Aside from the strict constitutional law, there is in every country a constitutional morality which must be observed if a tolerant and democratic polity is to survive. . . . If we speak of constitutional morality as distinct from constitutional law, I would be the first to say we need a new constitutional morality. . . . Quebec's objections . . . have not been primarily the distribution of powers under sections 91 and 92 but rather the stamp of English-Canadian preferences and outlook on most of what the federal government does. This is why English-Canadians have to think more sympathetically about what it would be like to stand in Quebecers' shoes, and try to modify their preferences and outlook to take account of the preferences and outlook of Quebecers in a wide range of matters. Here indeed we do need a new and more scrupulous constitutional morality. (Corry 1978, 2–10; cited in Burgess 2000, 29)

Canada is presently caught in a tug of war between those advocating principled asymmetry and those that seek to limit asymmetry as a tool to better infuse Canadian federalism with some measure of flexibility. The divide here boils down to the relevance of attributing causal salience to the *idea* of asymmetry as an important principle in and of itself in defining the contours of the Canadian associative community.

Burgess notes that the difficulty that political scientists encounter is that they cannot quantify morality-based demands, while the case for asymmetry is often captured best by such appeals. Canada was to be a country where "French and English agreed both to live apart and to live together" (LaSelva 1996, 25). This is the ideal that for Quebecers has nourished the purpose and meaning of the country since its inception. Charles Taylor aptly describes the unchanging basis of this position. Quebec "needs an independent political instrument in order to ensure participation in economic direction, a role in technology design and the like either because of the overwhelming force of the neighboring Anglo-Saxon culture of 250 million, the richest and strongest economy in the world, or because of the greater political clout that the English-Canadian majority inevitably exercises in Canada; or for both reasons" (Taylor 1993, 42).

Taylor's claims for the explicit recognition of Quebec specificity within the Canadian federal system, elsewhere referred to as a respect for "deep diversity," has been echoed forcefully over the years by many observers as the only logical "fit" for the reconciliation of national pluralism and federalism—or to remain faithful to the perceived "purposes" of federation from Quebec's perspective.

Asymmetry and Quebec: The Catalyst or the Problem?

It is clear that the accommodation of Quebec's specificity—homeland to a large French-speaking population that considers itself a civic nation—has been the central issue relating to the discourse and practice of asymmetry in Canadian federalism. For those who view asymmetry as a logical outgrowth of Quebec's place in the federation, Canada is assumed to consist of, and be the result of, a compact between at least two nations, two collectivities, two majorities, two host societies, two founding peoples, and so on. Indeed, Kenneth McRoberts has argued that the presence of Quebec in Canada, as a consolidated minority nation with developed institutions that command allegiance from its citizens, is in itself a category of asymmetry if one allows for sociopolitical asymmetries based on national identification or allegiance. As such, the response by central state nationalists can go in one of two directions: accommodate this asymmetry in national identification by structuring institutions along such boundaries; or deny the existence of a separate minority nation altogether, and commit resources to strengthening a uniform and centrally defined nation that sees a federation "normalize" toward a classic nation-state model. These are the primary dynamics at play when considering Quebec as a catalyst for asymmetry in Canada (McRoberts 2006).[4]

Hamish Telford has argued rather forcefully that the difficulty in instituting formal asymmetry in Canada lies not simply with a vision of symmetrical federalism that prevails in English Canada, but is due primarily to ambivalence with regard to the purposes of federalism altogether.

Telford contends that the prevailing vision in the rest of Canada is that federalism represents a hindrance to national unity, while Quebec, since the country's founding debates, has always sought "more federalism." As such, "Asymmetrical federalism has emerged as the two solitudes have pushed federalism in opposite directions. It is not clear though if asymmetrical federalism serves either solitude well" (Telford 2005, 1).

Telford recounts a similar story of attempts by the federal government throughout the twentieth century to increase centralization and Quebec's refusal to accept this supposed imperative of a modern state. From the postwar federal government involvement in establishing a comprehensive welfare state, to Quebec's refusal to assent to the Constitution of 1982 that included a centralizing Charter of Rights and Freedoms, to the more recent Social Union Framework Agreement (SUFA), Quebec governments of all stripes have refused to waver. The usual picture of Quebec demanding asymmetry as a measure of its distinct status may be misplaced—the real catalyst for asymmetry is English Canada's reluctance to embrace classical federalism.

For Telford, asymmetry represents an uneasy modus vivendi with which Quebecers are willing to live, since outright sovereignty is a course fraught with various costs and uncertainties. At the same time, federalism as a value is weak in English Canada. Telford aptly captures this dynamic, where asymmetry is not a principled response to the accommodation of diversity but a default position:

> So, as things stand, asymmetrical federalism in Canada assumes an all against one character. English-speaking Canadians see Quebec standing alone and tend to view the province as an obstacle to unity, while Quebecers believe they have to fight tooth and nail for what rightfully belongs to the province— indeed all the provinces—under the constitution. Asymmetrical federalism positions Quebec as the family outcast, forced to eat in the kitchen while the rest of the family eats together in the dining room. This is one way to ensure that the family continues to live under the same roof, but it does not establish a spirit of unity nor is it a celebration of diversity. (Telford 2005, 5–6)

John McGarry (2005a) has noted that Canada follows a general pattern in which state nationalists are more likely to reject asymmetry if it is taken as a mechanism for accommodating the existence and claims of minority nations. Asymmetry is resisted in Canada because, first, it is viewed as potentially challenging to national unity, representing a slippery slope toward Quebec secession. We can call this a matter of "state logic" that confronts all central states that are charged with responding to issues about territorial integrity and stability. Second, asymmetry is seen as threatening the core principles of liberty and equality,[5] thus touching upon conceptions of justice. This view appeals to uniform conceptions of equality that translate into several concrete concerns: concerns about the possibility that Quebec will enjoy more powers than other member-states, challenging the idea of equal citizenship from coast to coast; concerns with the manner in which Quebec might treat its minorities—particularly the Anglophone community; concerns associated with representation in central institutions, which have already prompted much criticism from Western provinces; and generally, an uneasy feeling about a province that has threatened secession throughout the past forty years having those demands validated through the granting of differentiated powers.

Although not readily apparent and largely an empirical question, the assumption that the demands of minority groups for more powers are more likely to result in human rights violations is a particularly powerful sentiment with much historical credence.[6] However, it is clear that this is simply the normative extension of a certain state logic. The basis of these views is that the minority nationalist movement is sectarian and therefore less inclusive than the wider society, which is in a better position to accommodate difference. Indeed, as we will see below, this perception might explain Canada's preference for formal "symmetrical" decentralization over asymmetry.

A Brief Account of Federalism and Asymmetry in Canada

Asymmetry in Practice

In standard accounts, asymmetrical federalism refers to an institutional arrangement in which one or more of the federated member-states enjoys distinct forms of autonomy relative to the others. This can be the result of constitutional entrenchment—variable distribution of powers among different orders of government—or it may be an outcome of fiscal arrangements and general bilateral or multilateral administrative agreements between the central government and one or more constituent units. Ronald Watts has argued that asymmetry is usually assumed to constitute a departure from some norm of federations, probably due to the strong influence of American federalism. He cites the classic study undertaken by Charles D. Tarlton (1965), where it is argued that once we look beyond formal legal-constitutional provisions, "it is clear that cultural, economic, social and political factors in combination have in all federations produced asymmetrical variations in the power and influence of different constituent units, and that these affect the degree of harmony or disunity within federal systems" (Watts 2005, 2).

For over three decades of megaconstitutional politics, Canada has flirted with various institutional forms of federal asymmetry with varying intensity. Throughout this period of constant introspection—numerous

Royal Commissions, parliamentary committees, and public consultations, two failed constitutional rounds, repatriation of the constitution from the United Kingdom, and two referendums in Quebec—a chorus of voices in the background have called for the formal recognition of Canada as a multination state and for the logical adherence to asymmetry that follows from such a structuring principle. Reg Whitaker captures the basic thrust behind the call for asymmetry in Canada: "The case for asymmetrical federalism would be that everyone wins and no one loses while the rest of Canada gains an effective national government that is not rejected by Quebec" (Whitaker 1993, 108).

Canadian federalism is simultaneously characterized as asymmetrical in practice while symmetrical in its self-conception. David Milne (1994) shows that asymmetry inevitably emerges from the variable influence exercised by member-states and the unequal distribution of resources at their disposal. Milne's conclusions stem from outcomes of intergovernmental processes and the diverse legislation inherent in a federal system. This inventory of attributes of member-states however, clashes with other approaches that seek to institutionalize asymmetry as a device that explicitly recognizes differentiated powers due to territorial claims for national self-determination. One view sees equal governments producing different outcomes to meet disparate circumstances, while the other acknowledges some unchanging nature of political communities that mandates formal recognition of asymmetry. In the former, diversity is taken as the outcome of federalism rather than as the justification for its implementation.

Watts (2005) has also contributed a useful conceptual distinction between de jure and de facto asymmetry.[7] Stated simply, de jure asymmetry refers to differential powers attributed to constituent units that have a basis in law, or in the constitution. De facto asymmetry, in contrast, refers to reversible agreements among particular constituent units and the central government that belong more specifically to the realm of public policy. These agreements generally correspond to practical considerations or are the result of intergovernmental negotiations in specific policy sectors. While several asymmetrical formulas have been adopted in the Canadian Constitution over the years, none are so great as to warrant the label of "special status" for any one province. Most such provisions indicate a certain flexibility to account for local circumstances, and remain largely faithful to a uniform reading of equality while expressing difference in terms of degree rather than principle (see Hogg 2002; Milne 1994).

Elsewhere, Watts provides a list of asymmetries that highlight some variability in the scope of provincial autonomy: the exemption of Quebec from section 94,[8] in which the federal government may make uniform laws for the common law provinces, with their consent, in the areas of civil and property rights, as well as in court procedure; section 129's stipulation that allows for civil law only in Quebec; section 109, which did not grant Alberta, Manitoba, and Saskatchewan the power to control their public lands (until 1930); and a provision of differentiated subsidies accorded to the provinces under sections 118 and 119.

For central institutions, linguistic rights and minority education rights, Watts notes the unequal application of the provinces in the interest of regional balance in section 22 (Quebec and Ontario are treated independently while other provinces are lumped together as "regions" for the purposes of representation in the Senate) and in section 23, which makes provisions for different qualifications for the selection of senators from Quebec (based on electoral districts); in sections 133 and 93 (2) and for Manitoba in sections 22 and 23 in the Manitoba Act, 1870, variations concerning language use and minority education rights for Quebec; and in section 93 of the Constitution Act, 1867, different denominational education rights subsequently applied for Alberta, Newfoundland, and Saskatchewan. We can add to this list section 33 of the Constitution Act, 1982, which allows governments to enact legislation in a given area notwithstanding the provisions set out in the Canadian Charter of Rights and Freedoms, potentially resulting in an unequal application of Charter rights across provincial jurisdictions.[9]

In terms of asymmetries not available to all provinces, yet "acceptable" to the extent that they flow from uncontroversial local circumstances, Milne lists the fact that only Quebec and New Brunswick are formally represented in *la francophonie* (recent proposals by the federal government have offered Quebec a seat at UNESCO), and the existence of variable shared-cost programs, for example, in the forestry sector (the funding split with Newfoundland is 90-10, while it is at 60-40 with British Columbia).

In asymmetries that are the result of provisions available to all provinces with only some availing themselves of this option, Milne includes the series of agreements on immigration over the years between the central government and Quebec;[10] the fact that only Quebec, Alberta and Ontario collect corporate income tax, while Quebec also collects personal income tax; and finally, that Quebec has opted out of various shared-cost programs with compensation, including but not limited to special welfare programs, youth allowance, and so on.

Such studies reveal that contrary to those theorists that view Canada as uniform in its discourse on federalism, the country is actually a highly decentralized federation with much adaptation to local circumstances.

It emerges as a "free-for-all," showing that federal programs are rarely applied evenly.

A Brief History of the Politics of Asymmetry

The golden era of soft asymmetry to accommodate Quebec took place during the period of the "Quiet Revolution." Liberal Prime Minister Lester B. Pearson signed various bilateral agreements that allowed Quebec to assume full responsibility in areas that were either partly or fully funded by the federal government (McRoberts 1997). Three key developments characterized Pearson's approach. First, tax points were granted to Quebec as compensation for opting out in areas such as hospital insurance, education, and welfare, where national programs had already been instituted. Second, with regard to new programs, Quebec was funded at the same level as other provinces while administering some programs alone, such as student loan initiatives and youth allowances. Third, in 1965 all of the provinces except Quebec made use of a 1951 constitutional amendment that provided concurrency of jurisdiction for old-age pensions (with provincial paramountcy) by establishing the federally administered Canada Pension Plan. Quebec was allowed to develop its own pension plan.

Pearson's successor, Pierre Trudeau, did not share this approach to recognizing Quebec's specificity, and sought to undermine such arrangements if not eliminate them altogether. Indeed, Trudeau entered politics in part to construct an alternative project that would undercut nationalist tendencies and thus the push for special status in Quebec. From the Official Languages Act, to the Canadian Charter of Rights and Freedoms protection for linguistic minorities and emphasis on uniform individual rights, to the policy of multiculturalism—Trudeau sought to institutionalize a vision of Canada in which Quebec's historic claim to dualism would have no place. In cases where the Trudeau government negotiated bilateral deals with Quebec—the 1978 Cullen-Couture agreement on immigration for example—the central government actively prodded other provincial governments to enter into similar agreements, in order to prevent the appearance that Quebec was enjoying a particular status (McRoberts 1997, 153).

In the late 1980s, the Meech Lake Accord, an attempt to get Quebec to assent to the 1982 Constitution Act, included a clause stipulating that the Charter of Rights and Freedoms was to be interpreted "in a manner consistent with . . . the recognition that Quebec constitutes within Canada a distinct society." This was the high point for the recognition of special status for Quebec, and when Meech was not ratified by all ten provincial legislatures by the imposed deadline (in part due to Trudeau's timely intervention), the idea of granting Quebec special status was invoked as one of its primary shortcomings, The potential for its reappearance has waned ever since. During the Charlottetown round of negotiations that followed, the term "asymmetrical federalism" rarely came to the forefront. Nevertheless, the accord would have frozen Quebec's seats in the House of Commons at 25 percent regardless of its relative population, and proposed a reformed Senate in which Francophone senators would have direct responsibility in matters related to the French language and culture. Overall, the accord failed after a referendum across all Canadian jurisdictions. In Quebec, it was seen as a net loss in relation to Meech, and in the rest of Canada it was perceived as another attempt to placate Quebec through an unjustified recourse to special status.

The Calgary Declaration of 1997, a statement of principle by governments in the rest of Canada, signaled the nail in the coffin for asymmetry along the lines of Quebec specificity. Subsequent relations would be implicitly governed by these principles. The most revealing clause read that "the unique character of Quebec society, including its French-speaking majority, its culture and its tradition of civil law, is fundamental to the well-being of Canada. . . . [I]f any future constitutional amendment confers powers to one province, these powers must be available to all provinces." This view took hold, and these are the parameters through which debates on asymmetry were to proceed.[11]

A Revival of Asymmetrical Federalism in Canada?

Following the failed Quebec referendum of 1995, Prime Minister Jean Chrétien took a hard-line approach toward Quebec (Plan B), including a moratorium on constitutional reform. Intergovernmental relations in Canada would henceforth be addressed in an incremental, ad hoc fashion, and "nonconstitutional renewal" became the buzz phrase of that period. Moreover, the central government asked for a Supreme Court reference on the legality of the unilateral secession of Quebec. Briefly, the judgment stated that while this action by Quebec could not be undertaken under present constitutional provisions, the larger constitutional order in Canada allowed Quebec to initiate constitutional change if the province received a popular mandate based on a clear question and through a clear majority,[12] and that the rest of Canada would be obliged to negotiate in good faith. The issue of what constitutes a clear majority and clear question was left to the determination of political actors. While both Ottawa and Quebec viewed the ruling as validating their claims about the legitimacy of secession, the federal government's response was the Clarity Act, which allowed Parliament to determine whether a majority or question was acceptable prior to a future referendum in order to trigger its obligation to negotiate in the event of a positive result in Quebec.

With Paul Martin replacing Chrétien as Liberal leader, and a particularly damaging scandal in which the Liberal Party was found to be diverting back into party coffers funds earmarked for increasing the visibility of Canada in Quebec, the hard-line approach of the Chrétien era was somewhat hampered. In September 2004, Martin and the ten provincial governments signed a First Ministers Accord on Health Care. Along with the March 2005 agreement between the federal government and Quebec regarding the use of employment insurance funds for parental leave, the period has been widely hailed as a resurrection of asymmetrical federalism.

The deal covering health care funding is paramount, however, due to its explicit mention of the term "asymmetrical federalism" in a separate appendix addressing Quebec, entitled "Asymmetrical Federalism That Respects Quebec's Jurisdiction." [13] The document explicitly refers to the capacity for asymmetry to instill some flexibility into intergovernmental relations in Canada. The preamble to the specific provisions relating to Quebec reads as follows:

> Recognizing the Government of Quebec's desire to exercise its own responsibilities with respect to planning, organizing and managing health services within its territory, and noting that its commitment with regard to the underlying principles of its public health system—universality, portability, comprehensiveness, accessibility and public administration—coincides with that of all governments in Canada, and resting on asymmetrical federalism, that is, flexible federalism that notably allows for the existence of specific agreements and arrangements adapted to Quebec's specificity, the Prime Minister of Canada and the Premier of Quebec have agreed that Quebec's support for the joint communiqué following the federal-provincial-territorial first ministers' meeting is to be interpreted and implemented as follows . . .

In substantive terms, very little demarcated the expectations placed on Quebec relative to the other provinces other than the fact that Quebec would establish its own wait-reduction plan; it would report to Quebecers on its progress; and health funding transferred from Ottawa was to be used by Quebec at its own discretion. Indeed, federal cash transfers to the provinces through this agreement are strictly symmetrical on a per capita basis. The document ends with an explicit acknowledgment that the agreement does nothing to abrogate from Quebec's full jurisdiction over the provision of health care. In short, Quebec accepts the general tenor of the accord but is allowed to set standards and monitor developments on its own. The agreement was hailed by Benoît Pelletier, Quebec's intergovernmental affairs minister, as the "only efficient way to endorse and promote the true values of federalism" (Pelletier 2004; see also 2007). Pelletier also commended the limited nature of the accord—regarding the fact that it does not require constitutional amendment in that it does not attempt to alter the division of powers.

It is important to note that, notwithstanding the explicit reference to asymmetrical federalism, the agreement follows Canadian precedent in which Quebec exercises the opt-out provision while other provinces do not. Health is a provincial jurisdiction—ideally, the federal government would simply cede this to the provinces and fiscal adjustments would follow. It is no wonder, then, that the opt-out is seen as an acceptable compromise—allowing provinces not to be locked into policy choices that shut out the federal government because of Quebec's particular preferences to run programs on its own. Again, the multination emerges in spite of itself as a natural outgrowth of particular preferences rather than through wholesale recognition.

The chorus of opposition to such developments, however, came swiftly. Senator Serge Joyal, a Trudeau loyalist, responded with a scathing critique of this new approach: "The project known as asymmetrical federalism contains within itself a confusing trap. It gives birth to the hope that stripping the federal government of its powers would ultimately strengthen the capacity of Quebecers to develop in accordance with their own particular genius. The dynamic created may hold attractions for some, but is no less pernicious for that. It gives legitimacy to the thesis that Quebec cannot be well served in Canada" (Joyal 2004, D8).

The debate is nicely encapsulated here. Creative approaches to the accommodation of Quebec are always confronted with the fear that national unity will be the victim. The unity imperative remains the single most effective tool at the disposal of centralists in preventing any talk of constitutional reform that would entrench asymmetry in principle. Allan Gregg, a noted pollster and pundit in Canada, has also criticized this emerging tendency toward asymmetry as a manifestation of what he calls "Frankenstein federalism" (Gregg 2005, 61), liable to undercut the principle of symmetry that lies beneath the equality of provinces doctrine. Again, the debate inevitably comes down to normative concerns about the very bases of the Canadian associative community—where asymmetry is usually caught in the middle of debates about the relative merits of centralization versus decentralization and their effects on national unity.

In a larger perspective, such measures are rather limited in scope, and fail to address the kind of asymmetries that would respond to an overhaul of the country's internalization of national diversity. Indeed, the stars may be as perfectly aligned as they are apt to get. Under Jean Charest, the Liberal Party of Quebec (Parti libéral du Québec; PLQ) has assumed a soft nationalist position, keen to demonstrate that federalism "works" for Quebec, in a somewhat pragmatic yet mildly principled fashion. Moreover, Benoît Pelletier has undertaken a coherent campaign to return to asymmetrical federalism by framing it as a natural outcome of the federal ideal as it has developed historically in Canada. This position in Quebec, combined with more receptive audience in the form of consecutive minority governments in Ottawa, has resulted in a more pronounced call for creative solutions to deal with Quebec's demands with regard to the fiscal imbalance and the resulting federal spending power;[14] for a more predictable structure of federal funding with compensation for policies within Quebec's jurisdiction; for respect for the principle of provincial autonomy; and for greater voice in international affairs for Quebec as an extension of its powers.

Indeed, this conciliatory yet firm approach by Quebec has been bolstered by the election of a Conservative government in Ottawa, led by Prime Minister Stephen Harper, which announced in its campaign platform that it largely accepted this approach in its relations with Quebec. Under the banner of "open federalism," Harper promised Quebec that the fiscal imbalance would be addressed, the federal spending power would be restrained, and Quebec would get an independent seat at UNESCO. The strategy worked, as the Conservative Party's electoral support in Quebec jumped from about 10 percent in late December 2005 to about 24 percent about a month later.[15] At the same time, reaction to Harper's overture to Quebec in the rest of Canada was muted due to the fact that questions of identity and historical redress were not touched on.

In recent years, provinces have collaborated, through the Council of the Federation, in order to try and get some leverage and predictability over federal funding, while Quebec has steadfastly remained firm in its opposition to the federal spending power. As a key architect of the revival of asymmetry, Pelletier has argued that the Council of the Federation as a platform for the development of provincial interests is more than a forum for exchange—it has internalized the respect for diversity in Canadian federalism as a key component of its mandate. Pelletier stresses that Quebec has taken steps to affirm its asymmetrical status in the federation, not just to increase international representation and address fiscal concerns, but to be a leader in areas associated with Quebec's specificity—safeguarding and contributing to the flourishing of the Francophone community across Canada, for example (Pelletier 2006, 538).

Pelletier's ideas merit further consideration. Apart from his advocacy on behalf of de facto asymmetry, he has proposed a way toward embracing asymmetry that is rooted in constitutional law, not uniquely in intergovernmental processes and administrative agreements. Pelletier points to section 94 of the Constitution, an obscure and little-used provision,[16] as a means by which to bridge the divide between bilateral deals centered on the opt-out scenario on the one hand, and actually reopening constitutional talks and venturing into the perceived "dangerous game" of constitutional amendment on the other. It nevertheless stems from a legal and irreversible legal process rather than intergovernmental practice. It is also hailed as a key to limiting the federal government's spending powers and a justificatory provision for provincial opting in of programs directed by the central government (Brock 2007).

To reiterate, section 94 stipulates that Quebec, as a civil-law province, is exempt from a provision allowing for uniformity of laws among common law provinces whereby the federal Parliament, with the consent of the provincial legislatures, may standardize laws on property and civil rights, as well as court procedure, and continue to legislate in these fields of jurisdiction. The centralization that is potentially generated in this provision has never been contemplated. Whether or not section 94 signals more "powers" for Quebec is debatable. Some argue that it indicates special status for Quebec, while others such as Jennifer Smith make the opposite claim, as an option that is not available to Quebec therefore may be interpreted as signaling less power for the province (Smith 2005, 2). For Pelletier, section 94 provides a clear constitutional basis for the justification of Quebec's special status, paving the way for asymmetry. Traditionally, other provinces have exhibited less opposition to federal government encroachment. In short, "Section 94 is eloquent proof that there exists in Canada constitutional rules which permit the development of asymmetrical federalism. This provision allows us to make the demonstration that asymmetrical outcomes are in conformity with the vision of the founding fathers. It forces us to stop perceiving asymmetry as an obstacle to a healthy federalism especially when it allows Quebec to do things differently" (Brock 2007, 7).

Marc-Antoine Adam (2007) contends that section 94 reveals that further integration among common law provinces was anticipated by the founders, thus representing explicit recognition that Quebec sought to maintain its specificity. A slight difference in his argument is that while Pelletier sees this as justifying special status, Adam approaches its usefulness in terms of its capacity to serve as a constitutional basis for an opt-in formula. Nevertheless, the key is that section 94 on the surface seems consistent with a two-nation view of the federation long held by Quebec. It forms the legal basis for Quebec to demand fiscal compensation from the federal government for any new programs it develops with the other provinces.

Kathy Brock views such interpretations as misplaced and sees a more fruitful approach in open and principled federalism. One of the problems she identifies is that provinces are not as eager to integrate as Pelletier and Adam imply; thus section 94 actually empowers the provinces.

The story is not one of resignation in the presence of a powerful centripetal force. In the end, it simply gives all provinces the same powers that Quebec has in preventing Ottawa from unwanted intrusion, reinforcing the norm of provincial equality. For Brock, the federal government must strive to accommodate the different conditions in each province—and this does not deny that Quebec is different, it simply acknowledges that Quebec is one of many different provinces. Section 94 is thus taken as a device to equalize provincial status vis-à-vis the central government *because* of Quebec's status as a civil-law province. Brock points to "principled federalism" as a more fruitful alternative—with the central government vacating provincial jurisdictions unless a strong national demand exists (Brock 2007, 17–20).

While such debates proceed, Prime Minister Stephen Harper has embraced incremental asymmetry as a potential way forward, although he expresses it as one element of his doctrine of "open federalism." In a December 2005 speech in Quebec City and a January 2006 letter to the chair of the Council of the Federation (Banting 2006, 82), Harper outlined his vision that included asymmetrical provisions directed at Quebec. Broadly, Harper stressed a respect for the division of powers, a renewed push to work collaboratively with provincial and territorial governments, and most important for the purposes of this analysis, an acknowledgment of the special institutional and cultural role for the Quebec government. Concretely, the proposals called for limiting the use of the federal spending power, initiating a process with provincial governments in order to eliminate the vertical fiscal imbalance, and creating new outlets for the Quebec state in international affairs.[17]

According to Alain Noël, the success of "open federalism" in the party's electoral showing in Quebec reveals deep-seated and fundamental preoccupations among Francophone Quebecers regarding the place of Quebec in the federation—even though so little was conceded by Ottawa in these promises (Noël 2006, 26). In his words, "The Quebec objectives that I have associated with open federalism—recognition and autonomy—are not the objectives of a party, and not even the objectives of Quebec federalists. They have guided all Quebec governments, sovereignists and federalists alike, for more than fifty years. Seeking recognition and autonomy within the Canadian federation is something like the foreign policy of Quebec. It has staying power, no matter who governs" (34).

Noël goes on to demonstrate the simplicity with which open federalism was presented to Quebec—placing Quebec "at the heart of Canada," evoking the memory of René Levesque in promising improved accountability and trust in federal politics, and so on. For Noël, these overtures tapped into a dual understanding of Canada which continues to hold sway in Quebec. In other words, all it took was a small sprinkle of "moral federalism," without rocking the boat of constitutional politics or alienating the rest of Canada with the formal recognition of Quebec as a loosely defined "distinct society." Quebec was taken as both an autonomous province that could make common cause with other provinces and a national state that seeks recognition from its negotiating partners.

The hard part, however, will be to ascertain whether these "one shot deals" can go further to institutionalize Quebec's specificity. This would require, at the very least, some explicit recognition of Quebec's national character. The language of nationhood is consolidated in Quebec. Indeed, even the federal Parliament passed a motion stating that "this House recognizes that the Québécois form a nation within a united Canada."[18] This goes much further than terms such a "distinct society" or "unique language and culture." In terms of autonomy, the Conservative government is well-positioned to tackle this dossier because its platform is much more open to provincial autonomy and thus in addressing issues such as the federal spending power and fiscal imbalance. It remains to be seen, however, if the commitment to autonomy will result in real limitations on the federal spending power—the complete removal of conditions on federal block transfers and the utmost restraint in direct spending in areas of exclusive provincial jurisdiction.

Conclusion

Recent discourse on asymmetry seems to indicate a sense that "the time has come." Moreover, de facto asymmetry serves to quell the perceived dangers of identity politics while still accounting for the primary cleavages of Canadian political life. Nevertheless, it remains an incremental approach that seeks to avoid blowing the whole house open, and embracing multinational federalism as a logical conclusion would require much more formal asymmetry than is currently contemplated.

We have seen a slight revival of the idea of "moral federalism," federal ideals, normative bases, the language of covenant, federalism as an independent variable, and so on in some responses to recent developments. Reconciling different conceptions of the political salience of identity with the reasons for community remains the defining feature of the Canadian experiment. This is the background narrative of asymmetry in Canada. Those who reject its attributes fear that identity as a structuring variable in Canadian federalism will lead to a clash with the unity imperative. The result is a somewhat petty game in which asymmetry crops up in side deals and administrative arrangements that do not portend to reflect fundamental founding principles. We are thus left with flexible devolution as something of a "third way" between untrammeled identity politics that would restructure the federation and the prevalence of uniformity as a corollary of the unity imperative.

Regardless how asymmetry is defined, there exists a large measure of consensus that it is broadly associated with the existence of Quebec. Many new issues have arisen to challenge the structure, purpose, and meaning of Canadian federalism, including Aboriginal rights and claims for self-government; the new demands from cities as economic hubs that require increasing revenues; the very specific issue of federal-provincial fiscal arrangements; and the increasingly coherent and powerful provincial demands made in concert through the Council of the Federation. Through all such developments, however, asymmetry has demonstrated remarkable staying power as an option that can potentially treat the ills of the Canadian federal system.

Is Canada coming out of its amnesia? Indeed, if the so-called federal spirit must be persistently pursued if it is to be kept alive, as Michael Burgess indicates, this is a difficult task when it only comes from the initiatives of a minority and is at best "tolerated" by the majority. What does emerge as incontrovertible is that two obstacles continue to stand in the way of its full symbolic implementation. First, asymmetry touches on strong sentiments about the national political community, particularly outside Quebec, in which it is viewed with suspicion as the potential precursor to the slippery slope of secession. Second, and related to the first, it is rejected on the grounds that it is inherently contrary to powerful notions of equality among provinces and/or individuals. Moreover, with most provinces enacting legislation that requires provincial referendums for future constitutional change, it is even less likely that formal recognition of a distinct status for Quebec as a central aspect of Canadian federalism will come to fruition. Indeed, as McGarry has shown, the irony is that powerful central governments can more easily institute this form of asymmetry than is the case in decentralized federations such as Canada, which have many more institutional obstacles to overcome. Perhaps decentralization as a response to national pluralism paradoxically works against formal recognition of asymmetry, and Quebec will have to resign itself to the fact that Canada will not be reconstituted in the future.

Notes

The author would like to acknowledge the support of the Skelton-Clark Memorial Fund, Queen's University.

1. The list here is seemingly exhaustive. For a sample of some of the more classic works, see LaSelva 1996; Kymlicka 1995; Gibbins and Laforest 1998; Tully 1995; Taylor 1993.

2. This chapter will not assess Aboriginal claims to self-government as an

emergent manifestation of asymmetrical federalism in Canada. These claims stem from a distinct status in the Canadian Constitution as well as a long history of treaty rights. Moreover, in recent years, both the federal and provincial governments have signed various power-sharing agreements with particular First nations. The scope and nature of such agreements is complex and cannot be treated with justice in a chapter of this magnitude. This chapter will limit its analysis to the discourse and practice of asymmetry as it relates to federal and provincial governments.

3. See McRoberts 2004 for a review of the distinction between personal and territorial bilingualism and its implications for federalism in Canada.

4. Without delving too deeply into the links between appeals for "equality" and the structure of the federation, it must be noted that Quebec's perspective has been to adhere to the principle that regardless of developments in the rest of Canada. As such, for Quebec the idea of equality has always rested on the maintenance of its status as a "majority group," a founding constituent of the federal pact, or an equal partner—with corresponding institutional protections. The idea here is that Quebec's National Assembly ought to have the appropriate tools to govern a national majority, and that treating Quebec as but another province reduces Quebec to the status of a permanent minority, unable to meet its particular needs and thus in a position of structural inequality vis-à-vis the majority group. For western provinces, in contrast, equality implies that Quebec's potential status as a "special" member of the federation is inherently unjust since it ought to be taken as a province, equal in status to the others. The principle of equality is invoked here to counter the perceived preponderance of Quebec's influence in the federal government. Symmetry is thus the preferred course, since its underlying aim is to ensure the formal equality of representation for member-states regardless of particular sociopolitical contingencies.

5. For a rebuttal to this general concern, see Gagnon 2001. Also, Will Kymlicka (1995) has contributed much to dispel this notion in his influential argument that the capacity for minority nations to provide a secure "societal culture" to its members, and thus a context of choice for the flourishing of personal autonomy is actually consistent with liberal principles.

6. See Keating 2001; Moore 2001; McGarry 2005a for ways to lessen the likelihood of such developments.

7. Peter Russell (2004) has also made this distinction, referring to hard/direct versus soft/indirect asymmetries.

8. Section 94A (added in 1966), however, is not consistent with de jure asymmetry. While it grants the federal government jurisdiction over old-age pensions and supplementary benefits, it nevertheless gives all provinces the capacity to opt out.

9. While the Notwithstanding Clause was seen as a means to ensure some balance between the legislative and judicial branches, its use is largely seen as illegitimate. Quebec applied it to all relevant legislation in 1982 as a form of protest against the repatriated constitution, but did not renew it in 1987. It was employed by Quebec in 1988 over its sign laws, but later removed when the law was rewritten. Many have pointed out that the visceral rejection of the option to invoke the clause reveals the power of the charter as a definitive statement of Canadian citizenship.

10. The most recent and comprehensive is the MacDougall-Tremblay agreement of 1991, which grants Quebec extensive powers over selection and integration.

11. For more on this period of Canada's constitutional history, including a discussion of Trudeau's vision, see Gagnon and Iacovino 2007.

12. In its opinion, the Supreme Court identified four broad principles as the bases of the Canadian constitution: democracy, constitutionalism and the rule of law, federalism, and protection of minorities. It must be noted that the Supreme Court's ruling applied to all the provinces.

13. For the full text of the First Ministers Accord on Health Care, see www.hc-sc. gc.ca/hcs-sss/delivery-prestation/fptcollab/2004-fmm-rpm/bg-fi_quebec_e. html (accessed 1 September 2008).

14. In basic terms, the fiscal imbalance refers to a situation where the provinces do not have enough revenues to fulfill their responsibilities under the constitution, due to structural imbalances with regard to the revenue-raising capacities of the respective orders of government. As such, this vertical imbalance allows the central government to employ conditional transfers to shape provincial policies (spending power), while leaving provinces particularly susceptible to federal cutbacks or priorities. See Council of the Federation, www. councilofthefederation.ca.

15. In the 2008 election, the Conservative Party retained ten seats in Quebec, while popular support dipped slightly to 21 percent. While a detailed analysis of this drop in popular support cannot be undertaken here, the Conservatives did nevertheless maintain their new foothold in Quebec, and a widely publicized campaign denouncing a proposed cut in arts funding by the Conservative government is usually credited with explaining the loss in support.

16. It has only been used twice, in 1869 and 1902.

17. As of 5 May 2006, Quebec enjoys the status of an associate member of the organization, alongside the Canadian parliamentary delegation. Quebec's external relations in areas that lie within its jurisdictions have been a long-standing demand by Quebec governments since the founding of the Gérin-Lajoie doctrine in the mid-1960s (see Paquin 2006).

18. Debates about the meaning of the term "Québecois" dominated subsequent discourse, leading some commentators to lessen the impact of the motion by claiming the Francophone Quebec residents form a nation in the cultural/ sociological sense, and that this does not apply to the territory of Quebec—a much more acceptable formulation for an audience that does not recognize the role of the Quebec state as a representative of a national minority.

References

Adam, M.-A. 2007. Federalism and the spending power: Section 94 to the rescue. *Policy Options*: 30–34.

Banting, K. 2006. Open federalism and Canada's economic and social union: Back to the future? In Open federalism: Interpretations, significance, ed. K. Banting. Kingston: IIRG, Queen's University.

Brock, K. L. 2007. Open federalism, section 94 and principled federalism. Paper prepared for the annual meeting of the Canadian Political Science Association, University of Saskatchewan, 29 May–1 June.

Burgess, M. 2000. The federal spirit as a moral basis to Canadian federalism. *International Journal of Canadian Studies* 22: 13–35.

Cairns, A. 1992. *Charter versus federalism: The dilemmas of constitutional reform.* Montreal: McGill-Queen's University Press.

Corry, J. 1978. The uses of a constitution. In *The Constitution and the future of*

Canada. Special Lectures of the Law Society of Upper Canada. Toronto: Richard De Boo. 1–15.

———. 1962. Constitutional trends and federalism. In *Politics: Canada,* ed. P. Fox. Toronto: McGraw-Hill.

Gagnon, A.-G. 2001. The moral foundations of asymmetrical federalism: A normative exploration of the case of Quebec and Canada. In *Multinational democracies,* ed. A.-G. Gagnon and J. Tully. Cambridge: Cambridge University Press. 319–37.

Gagnon, A.-G., and R. Iacovino. 2007. *Federalism, citizenship and Quebec: Debating multinationalism.* Toronto: University of Toronto Press.

Gibbins, R., and G. Laforest, eds. 1998. *Beyond the impasse: Toward reconciliation.* Montreal: IRPP.

Gregg, A. 2005. Quebec's final victory. *Walrus,* February.

Hogg, P. 2002. *Constitutional law in Canada.* Student ed. Toronto: Carswell.

Joyal, S. 2004. What kind of a country do we want? *Montreal Gazette,* 31 October.

Keating, M. 2001. *Plurinational democracy: Stateless nations in a post-sovereignty era.* Oxford: Oxford University Press.

Kelly, S., and G. Laforest. 2004. *Débats sur la foundation du Canada* (Debates over the foundation of Canada). Quebec: Presses de l'Université Laval.

Kernerman, G. 2006. *Multicultural nationalism: Civilizing difference, constituting community.* Vancouver: University of British Columbia Press.

Kymlicka, W. 1995. *Multicultural citizenship: A liberal theory of minority rights.* Oxford: Clarendon.

LaSelva, S. 1996. *The moral foundations of Canadian federalism.* London: McGill-Queen's University Press.

McGarry, J. 2005a. Canadian lessons for Iraq. In *The future of Kurdistan in Iraq,* ed. B. O'Leary, J. McGarry, and K. Salih. Philadelphia: University of Pennsylvania Press. 92-115.

———. 2005b. Asymmetrical federalism and the plurinational state. Working draft paper for the Third International Conference on Federalism, Brussels, 3–5 March.

McRoberts, K. 2006. Les modèles asymétriques au Canada et en Espagne. In *Le fédéralisme canadien contemporain: Fondements, traditions, institutions,* ed. A.-G. Gagnon. Montreal: Presses de l'Université de Montréal.

———. 2004. Struggling against territory: Language politics in Canada. In *The politics of language: Language, nation and state,* ed. T. Judt and D. Lacorne. New York: Palgrave.

———. 2000. Cultures, language, and nations: Conceptions and misconceptions. Paper presented to the Sixteenth Annual London Conference for Canadian Studies. Birkbeck College, University of London, 26 February. www.mri.gouv.qc.ca/london/en/pdf/discours/ McRoberts.pdf (accessed 1 September 2000).

———. 1997. *Misconceiving Canada: The struggle for national unity.* Oxford: Oxford University Press.

Milne, D. 1994. Exposed to the glare: Constitutional camouflage and the fate of Canada's federation. In *Seeking a new Canadian partnership: Asymmetrical and confederal options,* ed. L. Seidle. Montreal: IRPP.

———. 1991. Equality or asymmetry: Why choose? In *Options for a new Canada,* ed. R. L. Watts and D. M. Brown. Toronto: University of Toronto Press. 285–307.

Moore, M. 2001. *The ethics of nationalism.* Oxford: Oxford University Press.

Noël, A. 2006. Il suffisait de presque rien: Promises and pitfalls of open federalism. In Open federalism: Interpretations, significance, ed. K. Banting. Kingston: IIGR, Queen's University.

Paquin, S., ed. 2006. *Le prolongement externe des compétences internes: Les relations internationales du Québec depuis la doctrine Gérin-Lajoie*. Quebec: Presses de l'Université Laval.

Pelletier, B. 2007. Federal asymmetry: Let us unleash its potential. In *Constructing tomorrow's federalism: New perspectives on Canadian governance*, ed. I. Peach. Winnipeg: University of Manitoba Press.-

———. 2006. L'avenir du Québec au sein de la fédération canadienne. In *Le fédéralisme canadien contemporain: Fondements, traditions, institutions*, ed. A.-G. Gagnon. Montreal: Presses de l'Université de Montréal.-

———. 2004. We stand on guard for asymmetry. Globe and Mail, 8 November.

Rocher, F. 2006. Le dynamique Québec-Canada ou le refus de l'idéal fédéral. In *Le fédéralisme canadien contemporain: Fondements, traditions, institutions*, ed. A.-G. Gagnon. Montreal: Presses de l'Université de Montréal.-

Russell, P. 2004. *Constitutional odyssey: Can Canadians become a sovereign people?* 3rd ed. Toronto: University of Toronto Press.

Seidle, L., and G. Bishop. 2005. Public opinion on asymmetrical federalism: Growing openness or continuing ambiguity. IIGR Working Papers, Asymmetry Series. Kingston: IIRG, Queen's University.

Smith, J. 2005. The case for asymmetry in Canadian federalism. IIGR Working Papers, Asymmetry Series. Kingston: IIRG, Queen's University.

Tarlton, C. D. 1965. Symmetry and asymmetry as elements of federalism. *Journal of Politics* 27: 861–74.

Taylor, C. 1993. *Reconciling the solitudes: Essays on Canadian federalism and nationalism*. Ed. G. Forest. Montreal: McGill-Queen's University Press.

Telford, H. 2005. Survivance versus ambivalence: The federal dilemma. IIGR Working Papers, Asymmetry Series. Kingston: IIRG, Queen's University.

Tully, J. 1995. S*trange multiplicity: Constitutionalism in an age of diversity*. Cambridge: Cambridge University Press.

Watts, R. L. 2005. A comparative perspective on asymmetry in federations. IIGR Working Papers, Asymmetry Series. Kingston: IIRG, Queen's University.

———. 1999. The Canadian experience with asymmetrical federalism. In *Accommodating diversity: Asymmetry in federal states*, ed. R. Agranoff. Baden Baden: Nomos. 118–36.

Webber, J. 1994. *Reimagining Canada*. Montreal: McGill-Queen's University Press.

Whitaker, R. 1993. The dog that never barked: Who killed asymmetrical federalism? In *The Charlottetown Accord, the referendum, and the future of Canada*, ed. D. K. McRoberts and P. Monahan: Toronto: University of Toronto Press, 1993. 107–16.

Chapter 4
Elusive Autonomy in Sub-Saharan Africa

Coel Kirkby and Christina Murray

Many conflicts in sub-Saharan Africa are framed as "ethnic" or "tribal." In such situations, it is increasingly common to attempt to accommodate diversity through power-sharing arrangements and, particularly, autonomy (Ghai 2005; Haysom 2002). But few African rulers are prepared to contemplate regional or local autonomy in response to domestic conflicts. Colonial powers created highly centralized states and only in the run-up to independence did they consider federal solutions to hold together their fractious creations. Every federal and consociational experiment—Cameroon, Ethiopia (and Eritrea), Federation of Rhodesia and Nyasaland, the Mali Federation, Nigeria and others—either fell apart or was held together by violence (Currie 1964).

Most postindependence rulers have put considerable effort into further consolidating power and securing their states, frequently in the context of artificial boundaries, first drawn at the Berlin Conference of 1884–85, that split ethnic and linguistic groups. Rulers often maintain control by limiting access to scarce resources to family or "tribe," and by dispensing state monopolies through vast patronage networks. But excluding groups of people from governance (and even a decent livelihood) has done little to build strong national identities. Given this particular history, African states have proven especially prone to having communities demand autonomy, threaten secession, or even take up arms to forge their own states. It is thus unsurprising that African rulers have remained committed to the 1964 Organization of African Unity resolution "to respect the frontiers existing on their achievement of national independence,"[1] and have resisted any proposals that might weaken them (Herbst 2000). In the wave of constitution-making and multiparty reforms in the 1990s, asymmetrical arrangements granting autonomy to subnational groups continued to be as unpopular as ever (Prempeh 2007).

Accordingly, none of the three countries examined in this chapter, Tanzania, Mali, and South Africa, constitute a textbook example of asymmetrical arrangements adopted to resolve ethnic conflict.[2] Tanzania is usually considered an example of an asymmetrical federation (or federacy, as McGarry 2007 would label it), but its asymmetry is an accident of hasty union rather than a cure for ethnic division. Mali has confronted persistent demands for autonomy from its northern Tuareg population by choosing symmetrical devolution rather than fulfilling an earlier promise of "special status" for the Tuareg regions.[3] In South Africa, the formally symmetrical Constitution anticipates that provinces and municipalities may have unequal responsibilities, but such arrangements have proven politically impossible.

This chapter uses these three examples for the modest purpose of highlighting some of the particular problems with territorial asymmetry as a solution to ethnic conflict in sub-Saharan Africa. While personal and cultural autonomy are important forms of asymmetrical political arrangements and are common in the plural legal orders of Africa, this chapter focuses on the elusiveness of asymmetry in territorial arrangements.[4]

The United Republic of Tanzania

The peculiar union of Tanzania is best described, following McGarry, as a federacy, where a small, autonomous unit exists within an otherwise unitary state (McGarry 2007; Stevens 1977). The mainland, Tanganyika, is the silent partner that has almost 40 times the population and 570 times the area of autonomous Zanzibar, which is composed of two main islands, Unguja and Pemba, lying fifteen miles east of the coast. The current Union Constitution gives Zanzibar the right to govern over all but twenty-two matters reserved for the Union government, as well as certain powers, such as electing its own president and legislature. These can be amended only by a super majority in both the Union and Zanzibar legislatures.[5] In short, the Tanzanian federacy is a unique arrangement with both federal and unitary features.

The peoples of Zanzibar and the mainland have long had an interdependent relationship symbolized by the shared Kiswahili language—the language of people on Zanzibar and the coast, and the de facto language of everyday affairs and government in Tanzania. They also share a colonial past under the British, who, however, undid much of Kiswahili's unifying power by dividing these people into races and tribes. In 1948, the British took a census of East Africa that forced Zanzibar's population to divide itself into predetermined categories: Shirazi (so-called mixed African-Persian), Arab, Indian, and various African tribes. By the 1950s, newspapers on Zanzibar battled each other to forge strong "African" and

"Arab" identities (Glassman 2000). In so doing they created ethnicized identities that would coalesce around two principal political parties, the "African" Afro Shirazi Party (ASP) and the "Arab" Zanzibar Nationalist Party (ZNP). This division would have serious repercussions for both Zanzibar and the mainland.

Before Zanzibar's independence in 1963, elections to the local legislative council under ultimate British authority resulted in a near even split between "African" ASP and "Arab" ZNP factions (AEDa n.d.). While the ASP won a slim majority of votes, the first-past-the-post electoral system resulted in a legislative majority for the ZNP. Shortly after independence under the hereditary "Arab" sultan and a ZNP-controlled legislature, a small, armed group of 300 militants led by an ASP Youth leader took advantage of an atmosphere of a frustrated majority and polarized identities to storm the sultan's palace in a surprise coup. The sultan fled, but over 15,000 Zanzibaris, mostly those identified as Arabs, out of a total population of 300,000, were killed.

The ASP's success, and its bloody repercussions, surprised even itself. Sheikh Abeid Karume, the ASP leader, feared a countercoup by supporters of the deposed sultan or even his own radicals (Bakari 2000). Moreover, British and American agents were pushing him to unite with Tanganyika to avert the possibility of Zanzibar falling under communist sway. Julius Nyerere, president of Tanganyika, had sent a small, but crucial, contingent of 300 policemen to Zanzibar to keep order after the massacres. Nyerere favored a union to promote Pan-Africanism and cement cultural and trade ties, and, more pragmatically, as a way of preventing the revolution from spreading to the thus-far peaceful mainland. In short, the perception of danger was crucial in pushing Karume and Nyerere toward eventual union (Bailey 1973, 35).

On 22 April 1964, mere months after the coup, Karume and Nyerere signed the Articles of Union,[6] an agreement to form "one Sovereign Republic" named the United Republic of Tanzania (Art. 1). The announcement took at least some political elites and most ordinary people in both countries by surprise (Bakari 2000, 136). The Union arrangements were unorthodox. As Bakari says, "one of the obvious, awkward features of the Tanzanian union was the existence of three jurisdictions under two governments" (138). The Articles created a distinct executive and legislature for Zanzibar to deal with non-Union matters (Art. 3 (a)). No similar body was to exist for the rest of the territory of Tanzania, the erstwhile Tanganyika. Zanzibar would be represented in the Union government through a reserved vice-presidency and disproportionately high representation in the National Assembly (Art. 3 (b)–(c)). The Union government was allocated eleven areas of competence, the rest were to be exercised for the mainland by the Union government and by the Zanzibar government for the isles (Art. 3 (iv)). The Articles of Union were intended as an interim measure until a Union constitution was drafted— which would not happen until 1977. Yet the only protection the Articles seemed to offer to Zanzibar's autonomous powers was the implicit requirement that Zanzibari representatives to the Constituent Assembly agree to adopt a final Union constitution (Arts. 2 and 7 (b)).

A year after the Union, Tanzania took a step toward becoming a one-party state when the governing parties on the mainland and Zanzibar, Tanganyika Africa National Union (TANU) and Zanzibar's ASP, became the sole legal parties in their respective areas. Nyerere's dominance was entrenched in 1977 when ASP merged with TANU to form Chama Cha Mapinduzi (CCM) and then the new Constitution declared CCM the sole party of Tanzania (Bailey 1973, 39). The 1977 Constitution also listed ten new Union matters, including, critically, industrial licensing, higher education, oil, registering political parties, and a Court of Appeal of the United Republic. This doubling of enumerated Union powers did not go down well in some parts of Zanzibar and would form the basis of later grievances (Bakari 2000, 139–40).

The 1977 Constitution makes special provisions for the representation of Zanzibar in all three branches of government. The vice-president is to be nominated on the "principle" that when the president comes from "one part of the United Republic," then the vice-president will come from "the other part" (Art. 47(3)). (This principle supplements a CCM practice of rotating its leadership between individuals from Tanganyika and Zanzibar that ended with the 2005 election of Kikwete from Tanganyika.) The National Assembly has exclusive legislative powers over "all Union matters and also in relation to all other matters, concerning Mainland Tanzania" (Art. 64(1)). The awkward phrasing is meant to give the National Assembly legislative power over Tanganyika without invoking that silent partner's name.

Zanzibar retains its own executive and legislature. The president of the Revolutionary Government of Zanzibar has significant powers (Art. 103) and is automatically a member of the Union Cabinet (Art. 54 (1)). The House of Representatives consists of both elected and appointed members (Art. 106), and may legislate over all non-Union matters on the islands (Art. 64 (2)). In addition to National Assembly members directly elected from island constituencies, Zanzibar's House of Representative may elect five of its own members to sit as special representatives. While Zanzibar's representation in the Union government is out of proportion to its population, its influence is small since its few extra representatives are lost in the 324-member National Assembly.[7]

The Union kept the two distinct court systems of Tanganyika and Zanzibar (Bierwagen and Peter 1989, 407–8). The 1977 Constitution

continued the High Court of the United Republic, which had wide jurisdiction. But it also permitted a High Court of Zanzibar with concurrent
jurisdiction, and specific review power over "laws applicable in Zanzibar"
(Arts. 114–15). Zanzibar also retained *kadhi's* courts with limited jurisdiction over family matters between professed Muslims (Bierwagen and
Peter 1989, 407). The Court of Appeal for East Africa heard final appeals
from both systems until the East African Community (EAC) collapsed
in 1977.[8] Since then, the new Court of Appeal for Tanzania has heard
final appeals on Union matters. It holds regular sessions in Zanzibar.
The 1977 Constitution also introduced the Special Constitutional Court
of the United Republic to hear disputes between the Union and Zanzibar governments regarding Union matters (Arts. 125–28). However, it
has never been constituted.

In 1991, President Mwinyi created the "Presidential Commission on
Single Party or Multiparty System in Tanzania" to consider whether Tanzania should return to multiparty status (Peter 2006). The Commission
did not find much support for multiple political parties, but nevertheless endorsed permitting other parties. The Union government duly
amended the Constitution to declare Tanzania, "a democratic and socialist state which adheres to multiparty democracy" (Arts. 3). By permitting
political pluralism, the CCM seemed to willingly relinquish its thirty-year
hegemony. This apparent surrender of power did not happen, however,
as CCM won 62 percent and 59 percent of presidential and parliamentary votes, respectively, in the first multiparty Tanzanian elections in 1995
(AEDb n.d). Subsequently the CCM has consolidated its lead, and in
2005 won 80 percent of the presidential vote and 70 percent of the parliamentary vote. Yet CCM's total dominance on the mainland is not mir-
rored in Zanzibar.

Zanzibar's 1995 elections were contested by two parties: the CCM led
by Salim Amour, and the Civic United Front (CUF) led by Seif Shariff
Hamad.[9] The 1995 elections replayed the split voting of the early 1960s.
Amour won and became president of Zanzibar by a margin of just 0.8
percent. In the House of Representatives elections, CCM won 26 seats
to CUFs 24. The CUF's narrow defeat masked a crushing loss since the
president was all-powerful in the practice of Zanzibari politics. To further add to the loss, the House of Representatives had an additional ten
reserved seats for women, ten presidential appointees, five regional com-
missioners, and the attorney general; twenty-six in all. Thus the CCM
took 47 of 75 seats (Bakari 2001, 249–51).

Post-1995 politics in Tanzania is thus fractured in at least two ways. At
the Union level, the CCM has consolidated its dominant position as a
party, holding periodic elections with less and less participation and increasing margins of victory (AEDb n.d.). But on Zanzibar, political sup-

port is split nearly evenly between the nationally dominant CCM and the local CUF. This fractious divide led to predictable electoral violence in 2000 and 2005 when the CCM won again by greater margins, but with international condemnation for the elections as both unfree and unfair.[10] The CUF platform remains popular with many as they campaigned on a promise to push for a "3-tiered" system with a new, explicit government for Tanganyika in addition to the Union and Zanzibar governments (Chirambo 2000). While CUF refused to participate fully in the Zanzibari House of Representatives, its popularity created pressure on Amour's CCM to assert Zanzibari autonomy from the mainland CCM party and Union government.

The CUF and Zanzibari CCM share two basic complaints against the mainland-dominated Union. First, Zanzibar surrendered its sovereignty in 1964, but believes it has benefited less from the arrangement than the mainland. For instance, Zanzibari representatives in the National Assembly have complained that insufficient international donor monies make their way to the islands (Nyanje 2003). Second, they claim that Zanzibar's economy is marginalized since it (1) has no control over macroeconomic policy or banking institutions, (2) is not meaningfully consulted on Union budget or policies, and (3) subsidizes governance of Tanganyika because the Union government fulfills that role (Bakari 2000, 142–43; Bakary 2006). The shared complaints both center on Zanzibar's marginal role in the Tanzanian Union.

The CUF makes a third and yet more contentious claim that Zanzibar deserves greater autonomy, even sovereignty. The CCM has sought to manage this claim by pushing for greater autonomy but always within the Union. Since 2004 Zanzibar's flag has flown over the islands (BBC 2004). Amani Abeid Karume, Amour's successor as president and CCM leader, has tried unsuccessfully to have Zanzibar's soccer team a member of FIFA (Fédération Internationale de Football Association) (Nuhu 2001). Zanzibar has also pushed for independent membership in the new East African Community (PSTZ 2001; Swedi 2003; Yussuf 2005; *East African* 2006). This is an especially delicate demand since Zanzibar's main industry, exporting cloves, has suffered from large-scale smuggling. Karume's government has sought to fight this by taking over customs powers from the Union. For example, Karume dubbed the navy the Anti-Smuggling Force (KMKM) and tasked it with catching those evading Zanzibari customs (Bakari 2001, 134). Tanzanian officials have made it clear, however, that customs is a Union matter that they are unwilling to part with (1977 Constitution, Art. 10, First Schedule; Tomric Agency 2001).

People from the mainland are more sanguine about the Union, but do have at least two ready complaints. First, many are annoyed by Zanzibar's assertions of sovereignty. Not only are they counter to the spirit (if not the letter) of the Articles of Union, they are embarrassing to the Union government. Second, Zanzibar complains of economic marginalization in the Union but consistently stymies attempts to harmonize its economy with the mainland. Zanzibar claims it does not benefit from the Central Bank, for example, but refuses to place its accounts there (Bakari 2000, 143). Besides these complaints, one might also point to the enormous *political* energy that mainland politicians expend on placating relatively tiny Zanzibar. In the lopsided Union, Zanzibar gets disproportionate attention—good, bad, or (actively) indifferent.

In 1999, the Union government convened the Kisanga Commission to consider the Union Constitution. The Commission's final report made the controversial recommendation to create a three-government structure—Union, mainland (Tanganyika), and Zanzibar—while decreasing the Union president's powers.[11] But this recommendation, like many others, has not been implemented. Unsurprisingly, the Union government also refuses to recognize Zanzibar as a sovereign state (*Daily News* 2007), a position confirmed by the Court of Appeal in *S.M.Z. v. Machano Khamis Ali*, which held that "Zanzibar . . . is neither a state nor is it sovereign." [12]

The CCM-CUF stalemate on the islands exacerbates the strained relations between the mainland and Zanzibar. Union institutions appear particularly ill-suited for resolving disputes between the two governments.[13] In early 2002, for instance, exerting its power over immigration and customs, the Union government told Zanzibar to stop collecting visa fees charged for visiting the isles (PSTZ 2003). The issue has become a stalemate. Another dispute arose in 2006 when the Zanzibar government refused to let the new Commission on Human Rights and Good Governance (CHRGG), established by the Union government, work on the islands. The Zanzibar government demanded that it have greater say in both appointing the head commissioner and the final report (Rwambali and Edwin 2006). The Union government capitulated and the CHRGG has begun its work on the islands (Stephen 2006; Sapu-AFR 2005).

The Union of the United Republic of Tanzania is clearly under multiple stresses within the islands, and between Zanzibar and the mainland. In 2001 the CCM and CUF negotiated the *Muafaka*, a power-sharing deal.[14] On 9 March 2001, six months after contested elections, both parties on Zanzibar agreed to end animosity and abuse of state institutions for partisan purposes and to build a democratic government. A later report by a review committee recommended a series of changes, including a government of national (Zanzibari) unity, transparency, and greater tolerance (Yussuf 2004). In 2008 the CCM and CUF moved toward this goal by agreeing to permit a formal power-sharing arrangement on the islands. But this agreement has not been implemented and the referendum planned to manage the new standoff had not been held by mid-2009. As Haroub Othman has warned: "Experience has shown us that the present arrangement where the winner with a slight majority takes it all is the source of the political crisis in Zanzibar" (quoted in BBC 2008).

The long-standing, polarized politics of Zanzibar has returned with multiparty elections. This has forced the Zanzibar CCM to shore up its slim majority by taking a stronger (and popular) rhetorical stance against its fellow party members in control of the Union government. Certainly, over the first decade of the twenty-first century, institutions and procedures for dealing with intergovernmental disputes have been better developed. Responsibility for managing relations between Zanzibar and the mainland now lies primarily with the Union prime minister and the chief minister of Zanzibar, and not with the two presidents. This arrangement appears intended to facilitate a less partisan approach to disputes. It is also hoped that proper use of the Joint Finance Commission, established in the 1977 Constitution, will ease some of the tensions concerning public finance (Oloka-Onyango and Nassali 2003, 42). Nevertheless, both governments tend to respond to issues on an ad hoc basis. This is likely to be the case as long as the CCM retains control of Zanzibar.

Despite the rhetoric of sovereignty there seems to be general support for retaining the Union that is now over forty years old (Oloka-Onyango and Nassali 2003, 42). The questions for Zanzibaris and Tanzanians now are how to accommodate Zanzibar's aspirations within the Union and strengthen the Union's mediating role on the divided islands.

Mali

Mali's territory is defined by two borders, one natural and the other man-made.[15] The natural border is the Niger River, which divides the relatively lusher grasslands of the south from neighboring Guinea, Côte d'Ivoire, and Burkina Faso. The man-made border runs in long straight lines drawn by the French to separate Mali from Mauritania, Algeria, and Niger. In so doing this border also separates the nomadic Tuaregs and Moors of the sandy north and northeast from their relatives in those bordering countries. These groups together represent no more than 10 percent of Mali's twelve million people. Most Malians share more with West African culture and live near the Niger River's shores far away in the southwest. With a population density of only ten people per square kilometer, Mali is one of the least densely populated nations on earth and a novel solution was needed to govern the diverse people bound and divided by its borders.

The term Tuareg in Mali refers to the people descended from Berbers and Arabs who crossed the Sahara about 500 years ago (Randall 2005,

296). While Tuareg men famously wear a distinctive veil that covers their faces (Murphy 1964), there is no sharp racial or cultural distinction between the Tuareg and the Songhai, their immediate neighbors along the Niger's northern reaches.[16] Tuaregs are also Sunni Islam co-religionists with 90 percent of Mali's population. Instead, Tuareg animosity is directed toward the Malian state and is not so much "ethnic" as it is political. The first Tuareg rebellion from 1962 to 1964 aimed at creating an Organisation Commune des Régions Sahariennes, a transfrontier community of Saharan peoples (Tuareg, as well as Berbers and Moors) (Poulton and Youssouf 1998, 25). The revolt was quickly and brutally suppressed by the Malian army, but the idea of an autonomous polity would return in times of acute state repression.

Malians began their independence from French colonial rule with an ill-fated experiment in federalism.[17] The Mali Federation united two former French colonies, Senegal and Soudan (present-day Mali), in early 1959. The federation collapsed before its second anniversary because, as Foltz argues, Léopold Senghor, the federalist Senegalese leader, chose to abandon this project rather than risk his precarious domestic political base (Foltz 1965, 187). After the collapse of the Mali Federation, Soudanese leaders declared the first Free Republic of Mali. The Constitution of September 1960 continued the three-tiered colonial administrative structures below the central government, of regions, encompassing circles (*cercles*), with districts (*arrondissements*) as the smallest unit (Seely 2001, 508). These subnational units (*collectivités territoriales*) were to be "freely administered" by local elected leaders. But their limited autonomy was quickly undone when the government replaced devolved canton chiefs with civil servants delegated from the central public service.[18]

After a military coup in 1968, Lieutenant Moussa Traoré further centralized power in the southern capital of Bamako. His regime made a half-hearted attempt to decentralize some powers in 1977, which in practice amounted to little more than symmetrical deconcentration (Seely 2001, 509). During the mid-1970s, droughts ravaged northern and eastern Mali along the Saharan frontier. The Tuareg suffered the worst and escaped the drought by drifting down to the more populous, "African" south. Here they rubbed up against the sedentary population (506). This event sharpened Tuareg identities as a clash of lifestyles between the "blue" people and southerners led to communal tensions, exacerbated by Malian officials skimming off a large portion of the international aid meant to alleviate the Tuareg situation.

Drought hit the Malian Sahara hard again in 1983–84 and again the Tuareg faced similar southern migrations and poor reception. After the drought, they moved north and organized with Tuareg groups in Algeria and Niger to defend themselves against perceived and real persecution by officials in their respective states. Malian Tuareg became increasingly politicized during this traumatic time and began to forge an exclusive Tuareg identity for the first time (Randall 2005, 316–17). From 1990, various Tuareg rebel factions raided the northern-most Malian towns. Traoré's army responded with military repression. By 1991 there was a full-fledged rebellion in the northeast, as well as popular demonstrations in the capital, Bamako, seeking to oust the Traoré dictatorship.

The Tamanrasset Accord of 6 January 1991, between Traoré and two Tuareg factions, was more a ceasefire agreement than a comprehensive plan for local Tuareg autonomy.[19] While the rebels demanded more development money and the replacement of southern administrators with local representatives, Traoré responded by promising some local autonomy for the three northern regions with substantial Tuareg populations: Timbuktu, Gao, and Kidal. The accords would create "constituency councils" composed of two elected members for every one representative from local economic and social organs (Randall 2005, 506). Traoré's proposed compromise, however, proved unpopular in the populous south since his opponents resented the army's perceived surrender to Tuareg rebels and the threat of "autonomy" to Mali's integrity (Lode 2002).

Before Traoré could implement the Tamanrasset Accord he was deposed in a coup. Amadou Touré, Mali's new ruler, established a transitional council (Comité de Transition pour le Salut du Peuple) that promised to hand over power to a civilian government within the year. Representatives from various Malian interest groups, including two from Tuareg separatist groups, came together for two weeks in a national conference to write a new, democratic constitution and a multiparty electoral law (Seely 2001, 510). The delegates debated a special status for the northern region, but ultimately left it out of the final constitution that passed with over 90 percent of the popular vote in a January 1992 referendum.

In April, after the referendum but before the elections, General Touré signed the "National Pact" with the Azawad Tuareg rebel factions.[20] At a total of 86 articles, the peace agreement is far more comprehensive than the brief Tamanrasset Accord. The north was to be demilitarized and select Tuareg soldiers to be integrated into the Malian national army (Art. 7(a)).[21] In exchange, the Tuareg signatories agreed that there should be no armed forces other than the Malian army. The Pact promises to repatriate refugees into their villages (Art. 11). The greater goal was to integrate northern and southern economies. The Pact also created a more detailed administrative structure for three northern regions. Most important for reconciliation (and its limited success) are Articles 15–17, which created a Special Statute for the North of Mali (Statut particulier du nord du Mali). Under it, new elected assemblies were created at the communal, regional, and interregional levels. Art. 15(b) listed nearly twenty competencies to be transferred to these assemblies, including agriculture, farming, environment, ecosystem preservation, transport, health, education, culture, and the research and promotion of local languages. The Pact was compatible with the newly adopted Constitution of the Third Malian Republic, which provided for future laws entrenching elected subnational units with "free administration" (Arts. 97–98) in short and broadly defined provisions,[22] leaving room for interpretation consistent with an asymmetrical grant of power to the Tuareg regions.

Two months later Alpha Oumar Konaré was elected as first president of the Third Republic and promised to implement the National Pact in the framework of the new Constitution.[23] Konaré honored the Pact, but extended its decentralized promise equally to every region in Mali. This move walked a fine line between appeasing Tuareg rebels with self-governance and forestalling "a loss of support . . . in the heavily populated south" (Seely 2001, 516).

In June 1992 Konaré created a Decentralization Mission to determine how to implement symmetrical decentralization. The Mission visited villages throughout Mali for three years to let them "self-select" their borders, finally settling on eight regions (plus Bamako), 49 circles, and 20 urban and 684 rural communes.[24] Each commune has an elected council.[25] Deconcentrated (and eventually devolved) civil servants monitor "national interests" while implementing the council's decisions.[26] Commune councillors elect representatives to the circles from among their members, who in turn elect representatives to the regions. The subnational units' main responsibilities are for education and health (Kassibo 1997; Seely 2001, 513–14). Regions deal with schools for professions, and the administration of hospitals and public health, while circles handle secondary schools and communes deal with pre- and primary schooling and literacy programs. The subnational units also have potential shared competency over "waterworks, energy, transportation, roads, communication, local markets, sporting and cultural events, and tourism" (Seely 2001, 514), but these powers must be devolved by national legislation.

The 1992 Constitution also creates a new institution, the High Council of the Communities (Haut Conseil des Collectivités), to integrate regional governments into the national government. It is responsible for advising the national government on all local and regional development concerns, but its advisory role is limited to making proposals to the national cabinet concerning either environmental protection or improving the quality of life for its constituents (1992 Constitution, Art. 99). National councillors are elected indirectly by the subnational units for five-year terms, and they in turn elect a president of the HCC (Arts. 102–3). As of 2009 there are 75 councillors, 8 for each region and

Bamako, as well as 3 representatives for Malians living abroad.[27] The HCC is so far more like a consultative body for subnational governments than a second national legislative chamber.

While the HCC has very limited powers, it is now a functioning institution within the governance hierarchy in Mali. Unlike the National Assembly, the HCC may not be dissolved by the president (Art. 100). It sits twice a year for no more than thirty days as convened by the president and may meet once more with the National Assembly to deliberate on regional and local issues (Arts. 103, 105; Kassibo 1997; Seely 2001, 513–14). The HCC president has three other important powers: the president must consult with him or her before taking exceptional measures to deal with a state emergency (Art. 50), and he or she may request the Constitutional Court to review both an organic law before it is promulgated (Art. 90) and an international treaty before it is ratified (Art. 88). In sum, the HCC has significant powers that integrate local governments into the constitutional structure of Mali.

The HCC only began operating in April 2002 (Doumbia 2004). Even two years later, its capacity to do meaningful work was unclear. In May 2004, the HCC reviewed the national government's Decree 02-313 of 2002 that would transfer education competences to the subnational units (Badiaga 2006). In this case, the HCC president complained that the law included only nine of twenty transferable powers under the Constitution. Nevertheless, the 57-member council approved the law unanimously. The HCC appeared to have little sway over the central government. Moreover, it relies heavily on the UNDP and assorted NGOs for institutional support for its functions, and its intensive program on decentralization and human rights for its councillors (Diallo 2004; UNDP n.d.). It appears that the promise of the HCC to represent regional and local (especially Tuareg) interests in the national government has yet to materialize.

By 1999, 682 communes had an elected council and mayor. Yet the first elections did not go smoothly. After the 1997 elections fiasco where opposition parties boycotted a rerun of the National Assembly vote,[28] the first subnational government elections were postponed and finally held on staggered dates in urban, southern rural, and northern rural communes. Konaré's Alliance for Democracy in Mali (ADEMA) party won all urban communes and 59 percent of rural seats. While at least 30 parties contested the elections, voter apathy at the national level seemed to afflict these elections too. The next elections in 2004 saw a 43 percent nationwide voter turnout and higher turnout in two of the three regions with a substantial Tuareg population: Timbuktu (53.6 percent) and Goa (49.3 percent).[29] Interestingly, ADEMA, the party of the new president (and former army general), Touré, won an even greater share of the seats in these three regions than the national average.[30] What this means for the Tuareg situation is uncertain. There is no regionally based, Tuareg-interest party. Most Tuareg appear to vote for the dominant ADEMA party—or not at all. Either way, it is not at all clear how decentralized, democratic governance is helping the Tuareg engage the Malian state by either controlling their own local affairs through communal councils or representing their regional interests through national councillors elected to the HCC.

Devolution in Mali is best seen as an attempt by the central government to avoid promised asymmetric autonomy to the Tuareg minority, while maximizing the purported benefit of local governance across the country. As Seely explains, Konaré pursued this risky reform even though he had (1) a new and fragile peace with the Tuareg, (2) divided political support, (3) strict financial targets from the World Bank's structural adjustment plan, and (4) a history of failed "decentralization" reforms (Seely 2001, 504–5). By June 1995, all main Tuareg factions had joined the peace and agreed to "freely administered" subnational units (a carefully chosen phrase to avoid the word "decentralization," which in the past equated to Tuareg repression). Southerners were also placated since the north did not receive a special status. International sponsors, from the World Bank to the UNDP, supported the reforms that correspond to the latest "good governance" doctrine stressing the principle of subsidiarity (Kassibo 1997). Malians themselves support symmetrical decentralization but implementing the reforms has been difficult in practice and, most important, they have not brought an end to the violence.

On the night of 23 May 2006, a small band of Tuareg attacked two army bases in the Kidal region (Dick and Touré 2006). The rogue attacks, perhaps intentionally, were exactly two years to the day after the original date for the second communal elections (Doumbia 2006). The president quickly negotiated yet another pact, the so-called "Algiers Accords," which reaffirmed the decentralization reforms initiated over a decade earlier (*Le Républicain* 2006). In an earlier interview, Hassan Fagaga, a purported Tuareg rebel leader, justified the use of violence as an appropriate response to the government's continued discrimination against Tuaregs in the newly integrated national army, and a general failure to develop the region (Ben Ali 2006). Asked if he wanted independence, Fagaga replied, "No, we want an autonomy that permits us to take control of our own affairs within the Malian state."

In summary, faced with a demand for self-government within the Malian state, successive Malian leaders have promised autonomy but failed to deliver it in practice. Decentralized, locally elected governance is slowly becoming a reality in Mali but has failed so far to satisfy some Tuaregs. The peculiar territory of the Malian state, a colonial whim, has sharpened this tension by pitting increased Tuareg autonomy against the state's territorial integrity. In this sense, Mali's situation is similar to that of many other postcolonial African states that ensnared different peoples within an arbitrary national border drawn by departing colonial powers.[31]

South Africa

Apartheid South Africa was a classic example of a divided society with a racist white minority governing a disenfranchised black majority. Accordingly, when, in the late 1980s, the possibility of a transition to democracy emerged, many foreign observers argued that power sharing would be a necessary ingredient of any settlement. Some form of power sharing was assumed to be the only way in which the apartheid regime could be enticed to give up power. Moreover, and with particular relevance to the concerns of this volume, some influential commentators, notably Arendt Lijphart, argued specifically that substantial autonomy should be given to different groups, whether by way of federalism or by other means (Murray and Simeon 2007). The thinking was that, once the white government lost power and black people were no longer united by a common oppressor, ethnicity would assert itself as a political force.

Certainly, South Africa is diverse by almost any measure. The national census, Statistics South Africa, classifies the population by racial group (SSA 2005). "Africans" make up 79.4 percent of the total; "whites" 9.3 percent; "colored" 8.8 percent; and people of Indian and Asian descent just 2.5 percent of the population. Language, a surrogate for ethnicity, provides another measure of diversity in South Africa. No group dominates here. IsiZulu is the most widely spoken home language (23.8 percent), followed closely by isiXhosa. Afrikaans, spoken both by many whites and much of the "colored" population, ranks third, followed by English. Other languages are spoken by far fewer people.[32]

But South Africans embraced a form of power sharing in a government of national unity for a short time only and, despite some federal elements in the 1996 Constitution, most are reluctant federalists. They do not describe the country as a federation and there is little enthusiasm for encouraging the new provinces to use their constitutional powers. Moreover, the federal elements of the new Constitution do not seek to protect ethnic groups or encourage them to develop regional ethnic, cultural, or linguistic identities. Instead, it is specifically designed to diffuse ethnic minority nationalism. While the preamble celebrates South Africans as "united in our diversity," the enforceable Bill of Rights emphasizes individual rights.[33]

The opposition of most South Africans to the institutionalization of racial or ethnic identity and their ambivalent attitude to the devolution of power to provinces is a direct consequence of the country's history (Sparks 1990). In 1910, South Africa was created through the union of two British colonies and two erstwhile "Boer" republics which had been conquered by the British at the turn of the century. A policy of racial segregation was perpetuated in the new country which, when the Afrikaans-based National Party came to power in 1948, became the rigorously implemented policy of *apartheid* ("separateness") for which South Africa was notorious. At its height, apartheid led to the labeling of all South Africans according to racial groupings determined by the white government. Each label led to distinct treatment: whites enjoyed immense privilege while Africans were assigned to newly created "homelands" (called Bantustans) that correlated to a supposedly distinct tribe. The apartheid government intended to create ten new independent states out of these territories but only four were granted "independence" and the international community did not ever extend recognition to them.

Thus South Africa's transition to democratic, nonracial rule took place against a background of deeply entrenched racial oppression, ethnic identity imposed by the apartheid state, and the attempted balkanization of the country into Bantustans. Transitional negotiations were dominated by the African National Congress (ANC), led by Nelson Mandela, and the governing National Party. But the maverick Inkatha Freedom Party (IFP), a Zulu-nationalist party based in KwaZulu-Natal, also had substantial influence as its cooperation was needed to end ongoing violence there. The three principal parties differed sharply on a number of issues, including federalism. The ANC aversion to a consociational or federal system in which different ethnic groups could secure political power at subnational level is easily explained. Not only would ethnically delineated subnational units perpetuate the apartheid Bantustans, but the weakened central government would be hampered in its ability to transform and redistribute wealth. Moreover, claims for regional autonomy barely masked the desire of the apartheid government and the IFP to retain enclaves of power in the provinces of the Western Cape and KwaZulu-Natal respectively. On the other hand, the former apartheid government and the IFP insisted on some devolution of power to prevent a central government (presumably ANC) monopoly on power. The IFP claims were the most aggressive and for a short while carried with them a threat of succession. These claims succeeded to such a degree that a full twelve of the thirty-four "Constitutional Principles" at the heart of the settlement concerned federal or multilevel government.[34] These were also among the most detailed of the principles, leaving little to the yet-to-be-elected Constitutional Assembly, with its inevitable black, pro-ANC majority. The form of devolution of power to which the parties agreed was a compromise with weak provinces along the German cooperative federal model rather than the stronger, more competitive model of the United States or Canada.

The 1996 Constitution entrenches only limited exclusive powers for provinces. A large number of powers are to be exercised concurrently by the national and provincial governments (Schedules 4 and 5) and the controlling hand of the national government is ever present. The national government may set norms and standards for provincial governments in significant development areas such as health, welfare, education, and the environment (Sec. 146 (2)); it may intervene in provinces that fail to fulfill their functions (Sec. 101 (1)); and it may even legislate on small number of matters on the "exclusive" provincial list when that is in the interests of the national economy, security, and so on (Sec. 44 (2)). Provinces have negligible power to raise taxes. Instead, the Constitution secures for them an unconditional "equitable share" of revenue raised nationally, which amounted to over 80 percent of provincial revenues in 2007 (DNTSA 2007). Provinces may not veto national laws. Instead they have a say in national lawmaking through the National Council of Provinces, a regionally based second chamber modeled on the German Bundesrat. Provinces may adopt constitutions, but the scope for innovation in provincial constitutions is narrow (Secs. 142–45).

Drawing provincial boundaries is where one might have expected ethnic identity to be most salient. Although a number of provinces have clear linguistic majorities, there was no deliberate attempt to constitute provinces as linguistically or culturally homogeneous (Fox 1995; Muthien and Khosa 1995). Instead, the boundaries approximate those developed in the 1980s for the purposes of industrialization and development.

Neither outside observers nor South African negotiators considered entrenching asymmetry in the distribution of powers to the new provinces. To most South Africans, the idea of disparate powers among regions raised the specter of impoverished and underdeveloped Bantustans. Had more attention been paid to the needs of a developing state and regional inequalities in wealth and the capacity to govern in South Africa, more careful thought may have been given to an incremental and initially asymmetrical approach to the regions. Nevertheless, the implications of regional disparities were not entirely overlooked by the negotiators. This is reflected both in the initial arrangements for establishing the provinces set out in the 1993 Interim Constitution and in a provision in the 1996 constitution concerning the executive authority of provinces.

The Interim Constitution did not automatically confer powers on the newly established provinces. Instead, provinces were to be assigned powers only at the request of the premier and only if the province had the administrative capacity to exercise them (Interim Constitution, Sec.

235(8a)). This provision reflects an awareness of the complexity of dismantling the apartheid state and establishing brand new governments. However, its implicit word of caution went unheeded. The nine new provincial premiers demanded the full range of powers immediately and it was politically impossible not to treat them equally. The national government could not assign greater powers to the wealthy and relatively well-administered Western Cape province, where the erstwhile apartheid governing party had won power in the elections, than to the administratively weak, traditionally underserviced, and now ANC-controlled Limpopo and North West provinces. An asymmetrical process of devolving power would have been seen to reinforce the apartheid geography of enclaves of privilege amid large areas of neglect. In short, asymmetry would have granted power to the old, white bureaucrats who still ran the administratively stronger provinces, not to the predominantly black administrations in North West, Mpumalanga, Limpopo, and Eastern Cape.[35] Accordingly, powers were rapidly and equally devolved to all provinces—quashing any expectation that South Africa might follow Spain in gradually assigning increased powers to regions as they developed adequate capacity.

Nevertheless, the 1996 Constitution included a provision intended to address the problem of disparate provincial capacity. Section 125 (3) confers the power to implement national legislation on a province "only to the extent that the province has the administrative capacity to assume effective responsibility." The significance of this provision becomes apparent when it is read within the overall framework of provincial powers in South Africa. In the all-important concurrent areas of national and provincial competence, there are very few provincial laws. Most concurrent matters are governed by national laws that are implemented by provinces. Thus, in stipulating that a province may not implement national laws if it does not have the capacity to do so, Sec. 125 (3) potentially deprives provinces of their most important function—implementing key national laws in the areas of education, health, agriculture, welfare, and so on.

In the context of huge problems with administrative capacity in many provinces, this provision anticipates significant, if temporary, asymmetry. But again, in practice asymmetry has proved politically impossible and, despite the fact that some provinces cannot fulfill even their most basic responsibilities, this provision has not been used. Indeed, rather than permit the unequal distribution of powers among provinces, the national government has pulled some functions—most notably social grants—up to the center.

Of course, as in all federations, there is considerable asymmetry in practice among South African provinces. The constitutional framework formalizes this process by relieving provinces of the responsibility of adopting their own laws by allowing them to choose to implement national laws instead. Those provinces with the capacity to develop the sophisticated legal framework necessary to manage the onerous matters that fall within their jurisdiction can replace the national legal regime with their own. This has happened infrequently thus far. Yet if provincial lawmaking were to become more common, the statute books of different provinces might vary considerably. Some would probably remain small. But those provinces with relatively sophisticated legal and administrative capacity might have laws tailored to their needs replacing, to some extent, the current one-size-fits-all national laws.

The 1996 Constitution also provides for traditional leadership. In particular, it permits provinces to "provide for . . . the institution, role, authority and status of a traditional monarch" in provincial constitutions. This creates the opportunity for diverse political arrangements in provinces (1996 Constitution, Sec. 143(1b), 211–12). Moreover, the reference to a traditional monarch is well understood to refer to KwaZulu-Natal alone—the other six provinces with traditional leadership have more than one monarch (Murray 2004)! But, again, these opportunities are available to all provinces and do not reflect formal asymmetry in provincial powers.

South Africa foreswore asymmetry during its transition from apartheid and has thus far avoided it in practice. Yet the 1996 Constitution offers assertive provinces the opportunity to exercise powers that their less assertive neighbors do not use. At the moment it is unlikely that any of the eight ANC controlled provinces will break from the pack as the ANC is generally averse to any assertions of even limited autonomy.[36] The only exception is the Western Cape, where the national official opposition party, the Democratic Alliance won power in April 2009. But even here, strong political pressure from the ANC-led national government means that there is relatively little deviation from national policies. Significantly, though, in South Africa, unlike the rest of Africa, aversion to territorial autonomy and, in particular, asymmetrical arrangements, is based, not on a fear that increased autonomy will lead to the disintegration of the state, but on the assertion that only the central government can manage the transformation from apartheid properly and on a psychological resistance to the arrangements that were imposed on the majority in the negotiated settlement of 1993.

Conclusion

These three studies cannot do justice to nearly fifty states embracing the better part of a continent. They were chosen because they seem to illustrate contrasting aspects of asymmetrical territorial arrangements.

Tanzania is a relatively stable union of two sovereign states, challenged by the need to manage tense relations between its two components and the problem of minorities within a minority. Mali has resisted claims for autonomy in favor of a symmetrical program of decentralization and its tardy process (perhaps caused by limited administrative capacity, perhaps by lack of political will) prompts allegations that it is inadequate and, sometimes, precipitates violence. South Africans simply recognized the political risks in devolving powers asymmetrically and thus further entrenching long-standing privilege, and have instead struggled with a symmetrical distribution of powers to regions with greatly differing administrative capacity.

Claims for territorial autonomy in Africa are invariably perceived as challenges to the very existence of the state (Rothchild and Olorunsola 1983, 1 ff.). But each of the very different cases considered here reflects further concerns, illustrating the administrative and political difficulties of managing asymmetry noted by Ghai (2000, 13). Weak intergovernmental-relations institutions (Tanzania); mistrust and resentment caused by mutual perceptions of unfair treatment (and undue benefits) among regions (Tanzania and Mali); and a lack of administrative capacity at every level (Tanzania, Mali, and South Africa) make asymmetry an unpopular and risky choice in these African states.

Notes

1. OAU Resolution on Border Disputes, 1964, quoted in Herbst 2000, 104.

2. Almost no African state has adopted asymmetry as a tool of ethnic conflict settlement. Today in sub-Saharan Africa, only 6 of the 48 even have federal elements: the Comoros, Ethiopia, and Nigeria are self-proclaimed federations, while the Democratic Republic of Congo and South Africa have federal structures. Only Tanzania, a peculiar federacy, is asymmetric in practice.

3. Cameroon, Ethiopia, Nigeria, Senegal, and Uganda have followed Mali's example of resisting asymmetry by instead conceding some autonomy to all its regions (Kirkby and Fessha 2008).

4. Personal autonomy refers to a special right for a minority to withdraw from the dominant culture for specific purpose, such as religion. In Nigeria, for example, the current debate of *shari'a* in the north has raised question of whether it would apply to everyone, or might religious minorities be excluded (An-Na'im 2005). Cultural, or functional, autonomy refers to a distinct (though not territorially defined) community with special rights recognized by the state. In sub-Saharan Africa, customary law is often ascribed to particular groups to govern private law matters. Members of these groups may choose to have disputes settled in terms of either customary laws or the received European legal system—a choice of law not available to other citizens (Hooker 1975; Woodman 1996; Vanderlinden 1998).

5. Sec. 98(1b), Constitution of the United Republic of Tanzania, 1977.

6. Articles of Union between the Republic of Tanganyika and the People's Republic of Zanzibar, 12 April 1964.

7. There are 232 elected district representatives, 75 seats reserved for women, 10 appointed by the president, and 2 ex officio members. The women's reserved seats are "allocated in direct proportion to the number of seats a political party wins" and filled by the parties (Meena 2003).

8. See the 1977 Constitution, Sec. 108. For a history of the Court of Appeal, see Bierwagen and Peter 1989, 409–12.

9. Some CUF members have called for a return of the sultanate and the imposition of *shari'a* law (Warigi 2001).

10. After the CUF challenged the 2000 election results, its supporters took to the streets in protest. In January 2001, protests turned especially bloody on Pemba island as police opened fire, killing 35 and injuring more than 300 (AFP 2001; HRW 2001).

11. Jamhuri ya Muungano wa Tanzania, Kamati ya Kuratibu Maoni Kuhusu Katiba, Ripoti ya Kamati, Kitabu cha Kwanza, Mpiga Chapa wa Serekali (Dar es Salaam, 1999), cited in Makaramba 2001.

12. Criminal Application No. 8 of 2000, [2000] TZCA 1 (21 November 2000) (Court of Appeal of Tanzania at Zanzibar).

13. In a 1992 land reform act, for example, the Zanzibar government tried to oust the Court of Appeal's jurisdiction to hear appeal from a special land tribunal (Jones 1996, 31).

14. Joint Presidential Supervisory Commission Act 10 of 2001, http://www.kituochakatiba.co.ug/muafaka.htm (accessed 1 September 2008).

15. Map at http://www.lib.utexas.edu/maps/africa/mali_pol94.jpg (accessed 1 September 2008).

16. If anything, it is language that informs Tuareg identity. Kel Tamacheq, as the Tuareg refer to themselves, means "those who speak the Tamacheq language" (Poulton and Youssouf 1998, 1–4).

17. This experiment arose from a desire to create a strong African union in the aftermath of French colonial rule. The "federalists" argued successfully for a unified economy and Pan-Africanist prestige. The federalist victory was short-lived as Leopold Senghor, the Senegalese leader, withdrew from the Federation and declared an independent state on 26 September 1960 (Poulton and Youssouf 1998, 100, 117–18, 160).

18. The chiefs, first imposed by the French, had gathered some legitimacy in most people's eyes by the 1960s, and certainly more than the central government bureaucrats based in Bamako (Seely 2001, 508–9).

19. Of the 13 brief sections in the Accord, 8 deal with military restraint and three set up a mediation forum (Accord de Tamanrasset, 6 January 1991).

20. *Azawad* is a Tuareg word for the northern Malian regions of Timbuktu, Gao, and Kidar that stretch into the Sahel and Sahara (Pacte national conclu entre le gouvernement de la République du Mali et les mouvements et fronts unifiés de l'Azawad consacrant le statut particulier du nord du Mali, Bamako, Mali, April 1992).

21. Military integration faltered and would arise later as a continued grievance of some Tuareg rebels (Poulton 1996).

22. The constitution was promulgated by Decree No. 92-0731 P-CTSP, 12 January 1992, after it was approved in the 12 January 1992 referendum and appeal No. 2 of the Supreme Court, 14 February 1992 [1992 Constitution of Mali].

23. For a detailed analysis of the democratic transition, see Vengroff 1993.

24. Haut Conseil des Collectivités Territoriales, "Les Communes," Haut

Conseil des Collectivités du Mali, http://www.hccmali.org (accessed 1 September 2008).

25. Law No. 96-059 of 4 November 1996, cited in Kassibo 1997.

26. Law No. 95-022 of 20 March 1995, cited in Kassibo 1997; see also Seely 2001, 513.

27. Supra note 25.

28. The main opposition parties boycotted presidential and legislative elections that saw turnouts of only 28.4 and 21.6 percent respectively (AEDc n.d.).

29. The subnational elections also had marginally better voter turnouts than either the presidential or legislative elections of 2002.

30. Goa, 203 of 474 seats (43 percent); Timbuktu, 311 of 722 seats (43 percent); and Kidal, 77 of 133 seats (58 percent). The total national vote won by ADEMA was 3,332 of 10,777 seats (31 percent) (AEDc n.d).

31. Senegal, for example, has tried to implement decentralized reform to placate a secessionist movement without resorting to an explicit asymmetric solution (Ndegwa and Levy 2003).

32. Most South Africans speak at least two and usually three or four languages. Moreover, although Afrikaans was identified with the white apartheid government, it is spoken as a second or third language by many Africans.

33. Constitution of the Republic of South Africa, Act 108 of 1996, Preamble and chap. 2.

34. The negotiations took place in two stages. The first was before the elections were held. It resulted in agreement on an Interim Constitution. The Interim Constitution was accompanied by a set of "Constitutional Principles" that would have to be included in the country's "final" constitution, drafted in the second stage (Ebrahim 1998).

35. The legacy of homeland politics meant that bureaucracies in a number of provinces comprised administrators from the notoriously poorly run Bantustans.

36. It is worth noting here that on 16 December 2008 the breakaway Congress of the People Party was formed by former members of the ANC.

References

Africa Elections Database (AEDa). N.d. Elections in Zanzibar. AED, http://africanelections.tripod.com/zanzibar.html (accessed 1 September 2008).

————. b. N.d. Elections in Tanzania. AED, http://africanelections.tripod.com/tz.html (accessed 1 September 2008).

————. c. N.d. Elections in Mali. AED, http://africanelections.tripod.com/ml.html (accessed 1 September 2008).

Agence France Presse (AFP). 2001. Opposition blamed, police praised after Zanzibar bloodbath. 29 January.

An-Na'im, A. A. 2005. The future of *Shari'ah* and the debate in northern Nigeria. In *Comparative perspectives on Shari'ah in Nigeria*, ed. P. Ostien, J. M. Nasir, and F. Kogelmann. Ibadan: Spectrum Books. 327–57.

Badiaga, S. 2006. HCCT: oui, mais . . . *L'Essor Quotidien*, 23 May.

Bailey, M. 1973. *The union of Tanganyika and Zanzibar: A study in political integration.* Syracuse, N.Y.: Program of Eastern African Studies, Syracuse University.

Bakari, M. A. 2001. *The democratic process in Zanzibar: A retarded transition.* Hamburg: Institute of African Affairs.

————. 2000. The union between Tanganyika and Zanzibar revisited. In *Tanzania revisited: Political stability, aid dependency and development constraints*, ed.

U. Engel, G. Erdmann, and A. Mehler. Hamburg: Institute of African Affairs. 133–50.

Bakary, A. K. 2006. The Union and the Zanzibar constitutions. In *Zanzibar and the Union question*, ed. C. M. Peter and H. Othman. Zanzibar: Zanzibar Legal Services Centre. 1–33.

BBC News. 2008. Power-sharing deal for Zanzibar. 18 March.

———. 2004. Zanzibar to raise its flag again. 12 October.

———. 2001. Zanzibar rivals sign peace pact. 10 October.

Ben Ali, A. 2006. Hassan Fagaga. *Jeune Afrique*, 28 May.

Bierwagen, R. M., and C. M. Peter. 1989. Administration of justice in Tanzania and Zanzibar: A comparison of two judicial systems in one country. *International and Comparative Law Quarterly* 38: 394–412.

Chirambo, K. 2000. Tanzania opposition wants "equal status" for Zanzibar. Southern African Research and Documentation Center, 26 October.

Currie, D. P., ed. 1964. *Federalism and the new nations of Africa*. Chicago: University of Chicago Press.

Daily News. 2007. Union must stay. January 26.

Department of National Treasury of South Africa (DNTSA). 2007. Provincial budgets and expenditure review: 2003/04-2009/10. DNTSA Web site, www.treasury.gov.za/ publications/igfr/2007/prov/default.aspx (accessed 1 September 2008).

Diallo, M. Y. 2004. HCCT: Au coeur des enjeux du developpement local. *L'Essor Quotidien*, 18 August.

Dick, G. A., and M. N. Touré. 2006. Attaque des camps militaires de Kidal: LE CHOC. *L'Essor Quotidien*, 24 May.

Doumbia, S. 2006. La CND lance la mobilisation. *L'Essor Quotidien*, 9 March.

———. 2004. Session du HCCT: Un moment-charnière. *L'Essor Quotidien*, 4 May.

East African. 2006. Zanzibar wants a voice in the new EA federation. 14 August.

Ebrahim, H. 1998. *The soul of a nation: Constitution-making in South Africa*. Cape Town: Oxford University Press.

Foltz, W. J. 1965. *From French West Africa to the Mali Federation*. New Haven, Conn.: Yale University Press.

Fox, R. 1995. Regional proposals: their constitutional and geographical significance. In *The geography of change in South Africa*, ed. A. Lemon. New York: Wiley. 19–41.

French, H. W. 1997. Mali's slip reflects stumbling African democracy. *New York Times*, 7 September.

Ghai, Y. 2005. A journey around constitutions: Reflections on contemporary constitutions. *South African Law Journal* 122: 804–31.

———. 2000. Ethnicity and autonomy: A framework for analysis. In *Autonomy and ethnicity: Negotiating competing claims in multi-ethnic states*, ed. Y. Ghai. Cambridge: Cambridge University Press. 1-28.

Glassman, J. 2000. Sorting out the tribes: The creation of racial identities in colonial Zanzibar's newspaper wars. *Journal of African History* 41: 395–428.

Haysom, N. 2002. Constitution making and nation building. In *Federalism in a changing world: Learning from each other*, ed. R. Blindenbacher and A. Koller. Montreal: McGill-Queen's University Press: 216–39. 216–39.

Herbst, J. 2000. *States and power in Africa*. Princeton, N.J.: Princeton University Press.

Hooker, M. B. 1975. *Legal pluralism: An introduction to colonial and neo-colonial laws* Oxford: Clarendon.

Human Rights Watch (HRW). 2001. "The bullets were raining": The January 2001 attack on peaceful demonstrators in Zanzibar. 14 April. http://www.hrw.org/legacy/reports/2002/tanzania/zanz0402.pdf

Jones, C. 1996. Plus ça change, plus ça reste le même? The new Zanzibar land law project. *Journal of African Law* 40: 19–42.

Kassibo, B. 1997. La décentralisation au Mali: État des lieux. Bulletin de l'APAD 14. http://apad.revues.org/document579.html (accessed 1 September 2008).

Kirkby, C., and Y. Fessha. 2008. A critical survey of subnational autonomy in African states. *Publius* 38: 248–71.

Le Républicain. 2006. Du pacte national aux négotiations d'Algers: Les accords au crible. 7 July.

Lode, K. 2002. *Mali's peace process: Context, analysis and evaluation.* London: Conciliation Resources.

Makaramba, R. V. 2001. The state of constitutional development in Tanzania, 2001. Kampala: Kituo Cha Katiba, East African Centre for Constitutional Development. www.kituochakatiba.co.ug/Constm%202001%20Makaramba%20TZ.pdf (accessed 1 September 2008).

McGarry, J. 2007. Asymmetry in federations, federacies and unitary states. *Ethnopolitics* 6: 105–16.

Meena, R. 2003. The politics of quotas in Tanzania. Paper presented International Institute for Democracy and Electoral Assistance and Electoral Institute of Southern Africa and Southern African Development Community (SADC) Parliamentary Forum Conference. Pretoria, South Africa, 11–12 November.

Murphy, R. F. 1964. Social distance and the veil. *American Anthropologist* 66, 6: 1257–73.

Murray, C. 2004. *South Africa's troubled royalty: Traditional leaders after democracy.* Canberra: Federations Press.

Murray, C., and R. Simeon. 2007. Recognition without empowerment: Minorities in a democratic South Africa. *International Journal of Constitutional Law* 5: 699–729.

Muthien, Y. G., and M. M. Khosa. 1995. The kingdom, the *volkstaat*, and the New South Africa: Drawing South Africa's new regional boundaries. *Journal of Southern African Studies* 21: 303–22.

Ndegwa, S. N., and B. Levy. 2003. *The politics of decentralization in Africa: A comparative analysis.* Washington, D.C.: World Bank.

Nuhu, A. 2001. Zanzibar seeks FIFA membership. Panafrican News Agency, 14 April.

Nyanje, P. 2003. Sumaye intervenes in union/Z'bar funds debate. *Zanzibar News,* 3 February.

Oloka-Onyango, J., and M. Nassali, eds. 2003. *Constitutionalism and political stability in Zanzibar: The search for a new vision: A report of the fact finding mission organised under the auspices of Kituo Cha Katiba.* Dar es Salaam: Friedrich Ebert.

Peter, C. M. 2006. Constitution making process in Tanzania: The role of civil society organisations. In *Civil society and democratic development in Tanzania,* ed. A. S. Kiondo and J. E. Nyang'oro. Harare: MWENGO. 89–103.

Poulton, R. E. 1996. Après cinq ans de guerre: Vers la réintégration des Touaregs au Mali. *Le Monde Diplomatique,* November.

Poulton, R.-E., and I. ag Youssouf. 1998. *A peace of Timbuktu: Democratic governance, development and African peacemaking.* Geneva: United Nations.

Prempeh, H. K. 2007. Africa's "constitutionalism revival": False start or new dawn? *International Journal of Constitutional Law* 5: 469–506.

PST Zanzibar (PSTZ). 2003. Union, Zanzibar governments collide over visa money. 9 January.

———. 2001. Isles should have joined EAC separately, says AG. 21 May.

Randall, S. 2005. The demographic consequences of conflict, exile and repatriation: A case study of Malian Tuareg. *European Journal of Population* 21: 291–320.

Rothchild, D., and V. A. Olorunsola. 1983. Managing competing state and ethnic claims. In *State v. ethnic claims: African policy dilemmas*, ed. D. Rothchild and V. A. Olorunsola. Boulder, Colo.: Westview Press. 1–24.

Rwambali, F., and W. Edwin. 2006. Zanzibar: Clash over rights body. *East African*, 29 March.

Sadallah, M. 2001. CCM, CUF sign accord to bury hatchet. *PST Zanzibar*, 10 March.

Sapu-AFR. 2005. Zanzibar Bars Tanzania from Seeking Oil. 26 January. http://www.zanzibarhistory.org/2005_news.htm

Seely, J. C. 2001. A political analysis of decentralization: Coopting the Tuareg threat in Mali. *Journal of Modern African Studies* 39: 499–524.

Simeon, R., and C. Murray. 2008. 'Promises unmet: Multilevel government in South Africa' to be published by Cambridge University Press (India) in a volume in honour of MP Singh, edited by Rekha Saxena.

Sparks, A. 1990. *The mind of South Africa: The story of the rise and fall of apartheid.* London: Heinemann.

Statistics South Africa (SSA). 2005. Mid-year estimates for South Africa by population group and sex. SSA, www.statssa.gov.za/PublicationsHTML/P03022005/html/P03022005.html (accessed 1 September 2008).

Stephen, D. 2006. Team to review union revenue, aid sharing. *Daily News*, 23 May.

Stevens, R. M. 1977. Asymmetrical federalism: The federal principle and the survival of the small republic. *Publius* 7: 188–89.

Steytler, N., and J. Mettler. 2001. Federal arrangements as a peacemaking device during South Africa's transition. 31 *Publius* 4: 93–106.

Swedi, H. 2003. Zanzibar wants bigger role in EA community. *East African*, 3 February.

Tomric Agency. 2001. Why independent customs department for Zanzibar uncalled. 31 January. http://www.zanzibarhistory.org.

UNDP n.d. Haut Conseil des Collectivitiés du Mali. www.hccmali.org (accessed 1 September 2008).

Vanderlinden, J. 1998. Villes africaines et pluralisme juridique. *Journal of Legal Pluralism and Unofficial Law* 42: 245–74.

Vengroff, R. 1993. Governance and the transition to democracy: Political parties and the party system in Mali. *Journal of Modern African studies* 31: 541–62.

Warigi, G. 2001. Isn't it time Zanzibar rethought its union? *The Nation*, 4 February.

Woodman, G. R. 1996. Legal pluralism and the search for justice. *Journal of African Law* 40, 2: 152–67.

Yussuf, I. 2005. Zanzibar deserves EAC autonomous representation. *Guardian*, 2 February.

———. 2004. "Conference calls for govt of national unity in Zanzibar." *Zanzibar History.org.*, 20 September, www.zanzibarhistory.org/2004_news.htm (accessed 1 September 2008).

Chapter 5
Asymmetry in the Face of Heavily Disproportionate Power Relations: Hong Kong

Johannes Chan

On 1 July 1997, Hong Kong, the last major British Dependent Territory, became a Special Administrative Region (HKSAR) of the People's Republic of China (PRC) under the principle of "One Country, Two Systems." It is a most remarkable marriage, as the two systems are dramatically different. On one side of the border there is a small but sophisticated international financial center that adopts a market economy and that is governed by the rule of law with a high degree of freedom. On the other side there is a huge country that believes in central planning and socialist ideology, that emerged recently from almost complete lawlessness but is undergoing phenomenal economic growth and transformation and rapidly gaining an increasingly important place in world politics and economy. The two systems were to be married under the rubric of an almost idiosyncratic pursuit of sovereignty. Their union is also unique in that while one party enjoys virtually all political powers, the other enjoys an almost unprecedented extent of autonomous powers, analogous to that enjoyed by many independent states. Yet by and large the autonomy arrangement has led to strong integration with little demand for separation or disintegration. How does it work?

Historical Background

Situated at the southern border of China, Hong Kong was a remote fishing port in the nineteenth century. It has a size of only about a thousand square kilometers, and comprises three main parts: Hong Kong Island, Kowloon Peninsula, and New Territories. Hong Kong Island and Kowloon Peninsula were ceded to Britain in perpetuity respectively under the Treaty of Nanking (1842), and the Convention of Peking (1960), it being considered "obviously necessary and desirable that British subjects should have some port whereat they may careen and refit their ships when required, and keep stores for that purpose." [1]

The New Territories, which comprised about 80 percent of the land of Hong Kong and formed the immediate hinterland of Kowloon, was leased to Britain under the Convention of Peking (1898), for a period of 99 years commencing 1 July 1898.[2] The exact reason why a lease rather than a treaty of cession was adopted is unclear. At that time, a 99-year lease might well have been considered as good as indefinite. Another reason was that China was carved up by the foreign powers (including Japan) at that time, and since the other European powers were content with leases, it would have been problematic for Britain to demand a treaty of cession under the circumstances.[3] The lease expired on 30 June 1997.

As far as China was concerned, these three treaties were unequal, had been forced upon it, and thus had no legal effect. This position was adopted by both the Kuomintang (KMT) government and the Communist government, and is important in understanding the eventual solution adopted for Hong Kong. On the other hand, despite its view on the legality of these treaties, China adopted a pragmatic and tolerant approach and preferred to settle the matter by friendly diplomatic negotiation "when conditions were ripe." [4]

The different constitutional basis for the New Territories from the rest of Hong Kong has a profound impact on its land system. Apart from some insignificant exceptions, all land in Hong Kong is held on government leases. While the leases in Hong Kong Island and Kowloon Peninsula could last for a period as long as 999 years, the government had no power to grant leases in the New Territories longer than the lease the government itself held. Hence, all leases in the New Territories expired on 27 June 1997, three days before the expiry of the Convention of Peking. By the late 1970s, in light of the impending expiry of the Peking Convention, there were widespread concerns about the inability of the government to grant leases straddling 1997, particularly in relation to major infrastructural projects in the New Territories, the difficulty of raising long-term loans from the banking sectors, as well as the efficacy of property as a security for mortgage repayment. In March 1979, these considerations prompted the then Governor Sir Murray MacLehose to raise with Deng Xiaoping, the supreme Chinese leader, the issue of a possible extension of the leases beyond 1997, thereby precipitating the ensuing negotiations over the future of Hong Kong.

In the early 1980s, Hong Kong was already a major international financial center. Its population has grown from a mere 5,650 in 1841 to about 5 million in the early 1980s. A large majority of the population are of Chinese race. Indeed, about half the population are migrants from Mainland China who left the Mainland to avoid successive civil wars and political unrest (particularly after 1949) or to seek better economic opportunities in Hong Kong. Many of them regarded Hong Kong as a "borrowed place for a borrowed period of time," with a view to returning to China one day. Many maintained strong family ties with the Mainland. These migrants brought entrepreneurship to the Hong Kong financial capital, as well as a flow of cheap labor from which Hong Kong has fully benefited. Its economy took off soon after the Second World War, and it was gradually transformed into an international financial center in the 1970s.[5] In the late 1970s, Hong Kong alone contributed to almost 90 percent of Chinese foreign income.

Politically, under the temporary sojourn mentality, coupled with a colonial education policy, there was a strong sense of political apathy among Hong Kong residents. As long as the people were left alone to pursue their own lives, they were not interested in becoming involved in Hong Kong's political life or its social development. They were industrious, hard-working, enduring and content, and made virtually no demands for democracy or even a stronger participation in the governance of Hong Kong. This refugee mentality suited the colonial government, as it meant that there was little challenge to its governance or legitimacy. The government could afford to be benign, knowing full well that it could easily resort to an array of draconian legislative powers should such action become necessary.[6] With few people challenging its legitimacy, the colonial government could focus on improving economy and livelihood. The politically apathetic attitude was further reinforced by a low tax rate, the virtual absence of any social welfare (which meant people had to work hard), an extensive low-cost public-housing program that was introduced in 1953, and a relatively fair common law system. At the same time, the government was careful to avoid issues of national identity, history, culture, civic rights, and participation in the education system.[7] The riot in 1967, which was a spillover from the Cultural Revolution across the border, led to the adoption of a more inclusive governance policy. In the early 1970s, the government decided to adopt Chinese as an official language of Hong Kong, in addition to English.[8] It also introduced an extensive consultative system to bring the new generation of social and political elites into the governance, a process known as "administrative absorption." Thus, Hong Kong became a dream for any colonial regime—a place with high economic success and a contented and industrious population who readily identified themselves with the colonial government.

As a result of the changing international political scene and the rapid pace of decolonization in the 1960s, it became obvious by the late 1970s that the days of British occupation of Hong Kong were numbered. China had just emerged from the Cultural Revolution and was ready to adopt an "open door" policy. Britain was eager to take advantage of China's opening up to the outside world, and Hong Kong was a thorny issue standing in the way. It was also an opportune moment, as Deng Xiaoping appeared to be a more robust and pragmatic national leader. For Britain, the best-case scenario was to resolve the issue of sovereignty by an agreement allowing some form of continued British administration in Hong Kong, thereby enabling it to continue to reap Hong Kong's economic success and to seize the commercial opportunities arising from the opening up of China.

Thus, while the acquisition of Hong Kong was rooted in commercial considerations, its resolution was likewise underpinned by commercial reasons. A more charitable view would suggest that Britain wished to ensure the orderly and honorable transfer of sovereignty of its last major colony, while a more cynical take would indicate that Britain was eager to avoid a situation whereby people from Hong Kong would attempt to land at Heathrow for settlement in large numbers.[9]

The response of the Beijing leaders was firm and resolute: the time was ripe for a formal negotiation to settle the problem of Hong Kong. For the Beijing leaders, nothing was more important than bringing to an end decades of profound resentment and national humiliation over these unequal treaties. Reunification of Hong Kong with the motherland was a matter of national pride, historical mission, and personal glory. This was of particular importance to Deng Xiaoping, the Chinese leader who had just emerged to top leadership for the third time in his life and who was keen to consolidate his power over left-wing rivals. Thus, right at the beginning of the Sino-British negotiation, the Chinese leaders resolutely rejected any possibility of continued British administration over Hong Kong beyond 1997. Sovereignty was non-negotiable.

For the people of Hong Kong, the negotiation was an irony. Many were migrants from Mainland China who had fled to Hong Kong to avoid the communist regime. For the postwar generations that were born in Hong Kong, many of them readily identified themselves with the benign British regime, its Western culture and the rule of law. Indeed, at the early stage of the Sino-British negotiation over the future of Hong Kong, some local political elites tried hard to lobby for some form of continued British presence in Hong Kong after 1997. In this sense, Hong Kong differs from many other autonomous regions. There was never any serious issue of religious, cultural, or minority conflict. There was no strong resentment of the colonial regime. While there was relatively strong affinity or identification with the Chinese culture, many people had strong resentment toward, or recent bad memories of, the communist regime in

China. At the same time, there was only feeble affinity with Hong Kong, which was regarded as a borrowed place. Self-determination has never taken root in Hong Kong. This is partly the result of colonial education, and partly the result of political pragmatism. Unlike Taiwan, Hong Kong is dependent on the Mainland for water and food supplies. The inhabitants of Hong know full well that their bargaining power, if any, lies in their economic success and not in any threat of becoming independent. Those who found the return of Hong Kong to China unpalatable voted with their feet. Those who could not afford to go anywhere just resigned themselves to their fate. This sense of political helplessness was most strongly felt when China insisted on the exclusion of any representative from Hong Kong in the Sino-British negotiation over the future of the territory.

One Country, Two Systems

The Sino-British negotiation took place between 1982 and 1984. The result of the negotiation, the Sino-British Joint Declaration, comprises a short agreement, three annexes, and two exchanges of memoranda. It provides for the resumption of sovereignty by China on 1 July 1997 and the establishment of the HKSAR under the principle of "one country, two systems." It then sets out in 14 sections of Annex 1 detailed elaboration of the basic principles to be adopted by China regarding Hong Kong. The HKSAR is to enjoy a high degree of autonomy, except in foreign affairs and defense. The range of autonomous powers is remarkable. It has its own legislative, executive, and judicial power, including the power of final adjudication. The basic social, economic, and legal system and lifestyles will remain unchanged; socialist and Maoist policies will not apply to the HKSAR. Hong Kong may decide on its own financial and fiscal policies, as well as policies in the fields of culture, education, science, and technology, including its education system and its administration. It even enjoys the power to issue its own currency. It is to remain a free port and continue a free-trade policy, and can decide on its own disposal of its financial resources and manage its own system for shipping and civil aviation. Religious and community institutions may retain their autonomy. Previous laws in Hong Kong will remain basically unchanged. The court can continue to refer to common law jurisprudence after 1997, and judges before the changeover, including expatriate judges, will remain in their positions on the same terms of service. All public servants, including the police and expatriate civil servants, can remain in employment and continue their service on no less favorable terms than before. Fundamental human rights are guaranteed, and the two international bills of rights as applied to Hong Kong will remain in force. The extent of autonomous power is probably more extensive than most autonomous arrangements in the world. These policies are entrenched in the Basic Law of the HKSAR and will remain unchanged for fifty years.[10]

A major promise associated with the "one country, two systems" model is that Hong Kong people will govern Hong Kong. This assurance was made to allay fears that Hong Kong would be ruled by nominees appointed by Beijing. This assurance was reinforced in two ways in the Basic Law. First, certain key positions, including chief executive (Art. 44), president of the Legislative Council (Art. 71), Chief Justice (Art. 90), Chief Judge of the High Court (Art. 90), and principal officials of the government as defined in the Basic Law (Art. 101), are to be held only by Hong Kong permanent residents who are Chinese citizens with no right of abode in any foreign country. Second, the Basic Law severely restricts immigration from China to Hong Kong to avoid Hong Kong being swamped by Mainlanders. In this regard, Hong Kong is given the autonomy to impose immigration control over its borders and create its own "quasi-citizenship," Hong Kong permanent residency (Art. 22).

The Joint Declaration was recommended by the British government to the people of Hong Kong on the basis that it was a good agreement and that the alternative would be no agreement at all. That was the extent of self-determination. The Joint Declaration received general support and came into effect on ratification by the two governments on 25 May 1985. The following twelve years saw the drafting of the Basic Law, which was promulgated in 1990 and came into effect on 1 July 1997, and witnessed a highly sophisticated process on the part of Hong Kong to prepare its legal and constitutional system for the changeover, including the complicated process of preserving rights and obligations under international treaties that apply to Hong Kong.[11]

Sovereignty and Autonomy

Two major factors shaped the final outcome of the Hong Kong autonomy model. The first was the reunification of Taiwan. China has always maintained the view that Taiwan is part of China, only temporarily administered by a de facto usurper KMT government. Over the years, China has adopted confrontational, diplomatic, economic, and persuasive strategies to resolve the Taiwan issue without much success. The Hong Kong model is thus intended as a showcase for Taiwan. Indeed, Article 31 of the PRC Constitution, on which the legality of the Hong Kong model rests, was originally introduced with Taiwan in mind.[12] As far as the Chinese leaders are concerned, they are determined not only to conclude the model of "one country, two systems," but equally to ensure that it is a success, as a matter of national pride and as part of a greater process of Chinese reunification. Failure is not an option, and this is a key factor in contributing to the success of the autonomy model, measured by stability and prosperity in Hong Kong. In this sense, economic prosperity in Hong Kong is not only a financial and economic concern but part of the wider project of reunification. Thus, China has adopted a number of preferential measures in favor of Hong Kong to ensure its prosperity, such as exemption of residents from military service and taxes by the central government, great autonomy on the HKSAR government in monetary and financial policy and disposing of revenue from land sales, as well as considerable autonomy in the conduct of foreign relations. When Hong Kong was hit by the Asian financial crisis, the SARS epidemic, and the 2008 global financial tsunami, China again adopted various measures to boost the Hong Kong economy.[13] This required skillful statesmanship on the part of the Chinese leaders, as they had to maintain a delicate balance between Hong Kong and other parts of China (particularly the rapidly developing economies in the coastal region) that made similar claims for preferential treatment.[14]

In this regard, it should be noted that China is a huge and far from homogeneous country, of which Hong Kong is only a small, albeit important part. Formally, Hong Kong elected its own representatives to the National People's Congress, and various prominent people in Hong Kong were appointed to the influential National Committee of the Chinese People's Political Consultative Conference. Yet, in reality, Hong Kong has had little formal influence over national policies. Macau is another Special Administrative Region, but its social, economic, and political situation is very different from that of Hong Kong, and there is little alliance between the two regions to attempt to influence national affairs. On the other hand, the distinct legal system, management, and successful experience of Hong Kong provide much aspiration for the economic reform and modernization of China; in this sense, Hong Kong has exerted far more informal influence on China, although the exact extent of its impact is difficult to gauge.

The second factor, closely related to the first, is the mission of achieving reunification of Hong Kong with the Mainland. To China, this is a sacred historical mission that is far more important than any economic gain. Thus, while Hong Kong was economically important to China, the latter was prepared to adopt an uncompromising approach on sovereignty, even if that meant plunging the stock market to its lowest point during the Sino-British negotiation. China was equally adamant in insisting on stationing the People's Liberation Army in Hong Kong and extending the PRC Nationality Act to Hong Kong as these are symbols of sovereignty. On the other hand, once the issue of sovereignty was out of the way, China was prepared to be very accommodating of Hong Kong's autonomy, even to the extent of excluding state ideology (like socialist policies) and endorsing the retention of the bourgeois capitalist system and way of life for fifty years.

However, China was also eager to ensure that "one country, two systems" would not become a secessionist force or "counterrevolutionary basis" by according wide political and legal powers to Hong Kong. The central government retains responsibility for foreign affairs and defense.[15] Laws enacted by the legislature of the HKSAR are to be reported to the Standing Committee of the National People's Congress (NPCSC) for the record. The NPCSC may return such legislation to the HKSAR legislature with amendment if it considers that such legislation exceeds the autonomy of the HKSAR or is not in conformity with the provisions of the Basic Law governing the relationship between the central government and the HKSAR (Art. 17). Any law returned by the NPCSC is immediately invalidated.[16] The NPCSC also retains the power to amend the list of national laws that apply to the HKSAR, provided that these laws are related to defense and foreign affairs or "other matters outside the limits of the autonomy of the HKSAR," the precise scope of which is undefined.[17] It also retains the power to apply any national law to Hong Kong when a declaration of war or state of emergency in Hong Kong is made.[18] More controversially, the NPCSC retains the power of final interpretation and amendment of the Basic Law, although the State Council and the HKSAR may also propose bills for amendments to the Basic Law. The Central People's Government further retains the power of appointment of the chief executive of the HKSAR.

The exercise of these powers is, however, subject to some restraints. Thus, although the central government is responsible for foreign affairs, it also confers wide powers on the HKSAR to conduct external affairs on its own in the name of Hong Kong, China. This is in recognition of the fact that, as an international metropolitan city, Hong Kong has entered into agreements and has developed extensive relations with many countries and regions, particularly in the area of trade. The NPCSC power to return legislation to the HKSAR does not include the power to make amendments, are to be done only by the HKSAR legislature. In exercising the power of returning legislation to the HKSAR, applying national laws to the HKSAR, and interpreting the Basic Law, the NPCSC must consult a Basic Law Committee, which comprises an equal number of members from Hong Kong and the Mainland. More important, any amendment to the Basic Law cannot contravene the basic policies of China toward Hong Kong as contained in the Joint Declaration.

The design of the Basic Law reaffirms a central principle: Hong Kong is to be an autonomous region, not an independent political entity. The high degree of autonomy conferred on the HKSAR is to be exercised only in the framework of a unified country, and the central government retains all essential powers over the operation of the HKSAR. Sovereignty is sacred and secession is not to be tolerated. This has been a consistent theme since the beginning of the Sino-British negotiations over the future of Hong Kong. The sovereign power of China is largely unchallenged, but expectations regarding the extent of autonomy are very different on the two sides of the border. It is by no means clear when "one country" ends and "two systems" begins. Nor is it clear whether the model will ultimately (or within 50 years) lead to the merger or the retention of "two systems."

Thus tension is inevitable, which is not uncommon in many autonomous models or federal systems. Such conflict is usually resolved by an external mechanism or by an internal system such as a Supreme Court or a Constitutional Court.[19] No such mechanism exists in Hong Kong. There is no enforcement mechanism under the Joint Declaration[20] or at the international level.[21] The Basic Law Committee could serve as a venue for resolution of conflicts between the central government and the HKSAR. It comprises twelve members, six from the Mainland and six from Hong Kong. They include eminent law professors and legal practitioners from both sides. It is mandatory for the central government to consult the Committee in relation to its exercise of certain powers in the Basic Law, notably interpretation of the Law. While there was some initial expectation in Hong Kong that the Basic Law Committee could be developed into some kind of constitutional court, it seems that this was never China's true intention. The Committee is a working committee of the NPCSC. On a number of occasions when the Committee met to tender advice to the NPCSC on interpretation of the Basic Law, the meeting was convened at short notice. The agenda and working papers were distributed only at the last minute. The proceedings were confidential, and the impression was that the Committee was merely asked to endorse what has already been decided. The impartiality of the Committee was further called into question when its members readily engaged in local constitutional debates, and sometimes even became part of the controversy, well before the Committee was asked to give advice. A decade after the establishment of the HKSAR, the Basic Law Committee is still generally perceived as nothing more than a rubber stamp.

Thus, on the whole, despite various restraints on the exercise of its power, the autonomy design is highly asymmetrical in favor of the central government. The autonomy is largely confined to economic and social affairs rather than political and constitutional development. However, this does not mean that there has been no attempt on the part of Hong

Kong to expand the scope of autonomy. The next section will discuss one such futile attempt.

Exploring the Limits: Conflict Between the Two Systems

The most glaring conflict between the two systems lies in the legal system. The common law system is based on separation of powers, respect for individual liberty, and the prime importance of due process. The power of legal interpretation rests solely with an independent judiciary, and the interpretation process is for fine-tuning or incremental advancement of law. Certainty and predictability are fundamental to the system of rule of law. In this context, a constitution is the supreme law, the meaning of which is derived from judicial interpretation within a broadly liberal context. By contrast, the socialist system of law is based on democratic centralization, with all the powers concentrated in the NPC. Law is regarded as an instrument for achieving higher political goals and policies, and certainty or predictability is not the major concern. A constitution is a political promise that is not even judicially enforceable. Interpretation of laws is a political process dictated by policy considerations, and there is only a fine distinction between interpretation and amendment of laws. The power of interpretation is vested in the political organ, the NPCSC, and not in an independent judiciary.

The tension between the two legal systems is strongest when it comes to interpretation of the Basic Law. This tension arose squarely in *Ng Ka Ling v. Director of Immigration*.[22] The issue in this case was whether children born to Hong Kong permanent residents in the Mainland enjoyed a right of abode in Hong Kong after 1997 by virtue of Article 24 of the Basic Law when they did not enjoy such a right before 1997. A plain reading of Article 24 would suggest that they did. As the number of claimants rose to 5,000 within the first ten days of resumption of sovereignty over Hong Kong, the government pushed through emergency legislation to introduce a certificate of entitlement scheme. Under this scheme, all claimants for a right of abode in Hong Kong must produce a certificate of entitlement, which could only be applied for outside Hong Kong and would not be issued unless the applicant was granted an exit visa to leave the Mainland by the Mainland security authority. It was argued that the certificate of entitlement scheme was an unconstitutional restriction on the right of abode as defined in Article 24. The emergency legislation was enacted by a Provisional Legislative Council, which was not provided for in the Basic Law and was introduced and appointed by China when the original plan of the last colonial legislature, also serving as the first HKSAR legislature, fell through.[23] Thus, a supplementary argument was that the resolution of the NPCSC establishing the Provisional Legislative

Council was contrary to the Basic Law and hence its emergency legislation was of no effect. This constitutional argument directly challenged NPCSC authority.

The Court of Final Appeal first held that in exercising its judicial jurisdiction it had a duty to enforce and interpret the Basic Law. It thus had a legal obligation to examine whether any executive and legislative act of Hong Kong was consistent with the Basic Law. This jurisdiction was derived, not just from the Basic Law, but also from Article 31 of the PRC Constitution. The Basic Law was a piece of national legislation that applied to the whole of China and bound national institutions, including the NPCSC. Accordingly, the Court had jurisdiction to determine whether an NPCSC act was consistent with the Basic Law.[24] In so doing, it rejected the colonial position that a colonial court could not question the constitutionality of a legislative act of the United Kingdom Parliament on the ground that the Basic Law had introduced a new constitutional order.

To China, this was a startling proposition. The Court of Final Appeal was perceived to be usurping a power that even the People's Supreme Court did not enjoy. Great pressure was brought to bear on the Court of Final Appeal, which found it necessary to issue a rather ambiguous clarification that the Court did not and could not question the authority of the NPC or NPCSC "to do any act which is in accordance with the provisions of the Basic Law."[25] Although the clarification did not really clarify anything, it was generally perceived as a concession from the Court to back down from the very strong statement in its judgment. In an interpretation issued six months later, the NPCSC categorically decided that the interpretation adopted by the Court of Final Appeal was inconsistent with the legislative intent of the Basic Law, and reversed the judgment of the court regarding the interpretation of Article 24.[26] The legal community reacted strongly to the interpretation, regarding it as blatant interference with the rule of law and judicial independence in Hong Kong. For the first time in Hong Kong history, lawyers organized a silent protest march, on the eve of the third anniversary of the resumption of sovereignty.

This is a classic case of competing jurisdictions in an autonomous arrangement. The basic framework of the arrangement is that Hong Kong enjoys a high degree of autonomy save in foreign affairs and defense, and anything not within the autonomy of the HKSAR. Yet the ambit of what is outside that autonomy is only vaguely defined. As a result, the power of interpretation of the Basic Law is crucial in determining the scope of the autonomy. *Ng Ka Ling* can be seen as an attempt by the judiciary to push the outer limits of the autonomy as far as possible, first by asserting the power of final interpretation, and, second by expanding the scope of review to national organs. This was probably an ambitious move and, unsurprisingly, the NPCSC steadfastly rejected any such attempt and asserted its own equally unqualified power of interpretation over the Basic Law. According to the NPCSC, this power could be exercised at any time with or without judicial reference. The message was clear: it was for the central government and not the local court to determine the boundaries of sovereign power. In a politically asymmetrical arrangement, Hong Kong has no option but to accept this. Thus, in the subsequent case of *Lau Kong Yung v. Director of Immigration*, the Court of Final Appeal confirmed that the NPCSC has a general and unqualified power to interpret the Basic Law at any time, and that the Court had made no attempt to challenge the authority of the NPCSC in interpreting the Basic Law.[27]

The difficulty is how to reconcile the NPCSC power of interpretation with the common law system, under which the power can only be exercised in the process of judicial adjudication, and the interpretation has to be based on carefully reasoned analysis after hearing the full arguments from all parties in the course of litigation. By contrast, in the Chinese legal system, the interpretation is an essentially political statement by a political organ to deal with a political problem. There is no consultation or open debate. Interpretation of law is never a judicial process as such. While it is a legitimate exercise of power under the PRC legal system, the mere possibility of overturning a judicial decision by a political organ through a closed-door political process poses a great threat to judicial independence in the common law system. Thus, much of the controversy arising from this NPCSC interpretation is rooted in the very different nature of the two legal systems. Unfortunately, there is no mechanism for reconciling this difference, and in an asymmetrical model the system of the sovereign power prevails.

Two years later, the Court of Final Appeal attempted to reconcile the two systems without sacrificing the rule of law and judicial independence. In *Chong Fong Yuen v. Director of Immigration*, the Court held that it was a mistake to treat the NPCSC interpretation as a judicial act.[28] It was a legislative act. Under the common law system, a legislature would have the power to override a judicial decision, and the NPCSC interpretation should be regarded in the same light. However, until an interpretation was made, the Court, in exercising its judicial function, should not take into account the possible or even likely reaction of the legislature. Likewise, in its interpretation of the Basic Law, the Court should only approach the task by adopting common law principles, and should not speculate or be influenced by how the NPCSC is likely to respond to its decisions. Only in this way could the Court protect the integrity of the common law system. Accordingly, it rejected the relevance of a report by the Preparatory Committee, regarded by the NPCSC as evincing the intention of the drafters of the Basic Law, on the ground that the report, which came into existence well after the promulgation of the Basic Law, would be inadmissible evidence for interpretation under the common law system.[29] Since then the courts have repeatedly asserted that the Basic Law can only be construed according to the common law approach and principles of legislative interpretation.

In one sense this is a feeble attempt to resolve an inherent conflict between the two systems, which carves out an area where the Court would still have exclusive control but accepts the ultimate power of the sovereign. However, given that there will be very few cases which involve sensitive issue of sovereignty, this acceptance of sovereign power may ironically provide the best possible means of salvaging the integrity of the common law system.[30] This might appear precarious, but it seems to be the only pragmatic solution.[31]

One Country, Two Economic Systems?

While Hong Kong is given considerable autonomy in economic affairs, the autonomy is more restricted in areas of political affairs and democratic development. The Joint Declaration provides that the chief executive will be selected by election or through consultations held locally and appointed by the Central People's Government, and that the legislature will be constituted by elections. This general and vague formulation is in sharp contrast to the very detailed and elaborated provisions on the economic system. This vagueness also paved the way for disputes over constitutional development over the coming few decades.

Despite Hong Kong's great economic success, its governance was typically colonial up until the early 1980s. The governor was appointed by the British monarch. The Legislative Council comprised official members and unofficial members appointed by the governor. As soon as the Sino-British negotiations began, Britain, consistent with its project of decolonization, began to introduce some form of representative government. Election by functional constituencies was introduced in 1985. Seats in the Legislative Council were given to certain professional and business groups, entrenching their dominant influence within the political system. This system was originally intended to be transitional, to ensure the presence of necessary expertise in the Legislative Council. However, it soon became an almost permanent feature of Hong Kong's political landscape. Half the current members of the Legislative Council are still chosen by functional constituencies. In some constituencies, the electors comprise wholly or partly corporate voters, and this has exposed the system to manipulation, particularly by influential business tycoons through control of various corporate vehicles. This system suits China well, as members from functional constituencies tend to be more susceptible to Chinese or central government influence, or at least more sympathetic to those interests, serving as a useful countervailing force against the democratic faction in the Legislature.

Direct election by universal franchise on the basis of geographical constituencies was introduced to the Legislative Council for the first time in 1991.[32] Only 18 of 60 seats were then filled by direct election. While the Basic Law provides that the ultimate aim is to elect all members of the Legislative Council by universal suffrage, moves toward that aim are to be governed by the "actual situation in Hong Kong and the principle of gradual and orderly progress."[33] The Basic Law then defines the composition of the first three terms of the Legislative Council, which will eventually lead to an equal number of members chosen by direct election and functional constituencies, and prescribes a procedure for amending the method of forming the Council and its voting procedures after 2007, "if there is a need to do so."[34] It turned out that it was for the NPCSC to determine whether there was "a need" to change the system. In 2004, the NPCSC interpretation of the relevant provisions of the Basic Law provided that there was no need to change the electoral system for the 2008 election.[35] As a result, the review process could not even begin.

The colonial executive-led system does not accord with the changing aspirations for democracy in Hong Kong that have been evident since the 1980s. The chief executive, elected by a Selection Committee of 800 members,[36] does not have a popular mandate. The executive, without any vote in the Legislative Council, cannot confidently secure the passage of a bill it considers important. As a result, it forms loose alliances with pro-government political parties and business sectors and marginalizes the democratic camp. The influence of elected members of the Legislative Council is further weakened by a separate voting system under which any private member bill or motion that is not proposed by the executive can only be carried by majority support in both the functional-constituency and direct election sector. On the other hand, the Democratic Party has consistently secured over 60 percent of the votes in successive geographical elections. It has the mandate of the people, but not the corresponding political power. This disproportionate power as a result of the contrived political system has led to frustration and disillusion on both sides, which imposes a further strain on the relationship between the legislature and the executive.[37]

Ironically, a fragmented legislature actually suits the interests of the central government and conforms better to its notion of "executive-led government." It is also a means of ensuring that Hong Kong will not go out of its way to become a political power base that can influence democratic demands on the Mainland. For the central government, the overriding concern is stability and prosperity. Stability is to be achieved through strong local government and weak political opposition. A representative government with strong political parties is not regarded as conducive to the maintenance of stability. This explains the central government's preference for an "executive-led government" as the principal philosophy of governance. Prosperity is to be achieved by consolidating the capitalist system, and this is translated into the provision of a privileged and preferential status for the business sector. The development of a representative government should not be undertaken at the expense of diminishing the role of the business sector, to which the economic success of Hong Kong is attributed. Moreover, it is perceived that a democratic government will lead to a welfare state and the emergence of populism, affecting the operation of the capitalist system.

Two points emerge. The first is that the design of "one country, two systems" is not intended to create a separate power base. Neither the chief executive nor the local legislature (and less so the judiciary) should form an alternative power source to the central government. It was never the intention of the autonomy scheme to nurture a strong local autonomous political entity. Second, the high degree of autonomy is a means of entrenching the successful economic system. Influenced by both the colonial model before the changeover and the Singaporean model, the Chinese leaders believe that the economy of Hong Kong will somehow continue to thrive as long as it is left to run by the capitalist system with no interference. Rightly or wrongly, the central government believes that a market economy can be separated from the political system. Hence, the Joint Declaration and the Basic Law contain elaborate provisions for preserving the economic system but few regarding the political system. In short, "one country, two systems" is really about "one country, two economic systems." The prevailing discourse is one of "stability and prosperity." Hong Kong is portrayed as an economic entity, and aspirations for democracy are dismissed by the central government as a more or less emotional response to economic failures.[38]

On the other hand, the regular deadlock between the legislature and the executive has developed to a point that it is hampering the efficiency of the government. In the summer of 2005, half a million people took to the street to express their anger at the government's stubborn attempt to push through the national security bill.[39] This protest successfully forced the government to withdraw the controversial bill and eventually led to the downfall of the chief executive. While it is true that the large turnout was partly due to poor economy at that time, it did convey a clear warning sign in relation to governance. The chief executive tendered his resignation a few months later on "health" grounds. While his resignation was attributed to the success of popular power, it would not have been possible without agreement from Beijing. This is of great significance, as the chief executive is known to be an extremely loyal patriot who enjoys the blessing of the central government. While the Communist government is known to disavow a disloyal member, it is rare to disavow a loyal but incompetent member. Its consent to remove the chief executive displayed an unusually high degree of pragmatism in its handling of the affairs of Hong Kong. It also marks a subtle change in its approach to the democratic movement.

When the NPCSC rendered its interpretation in April 2004, dismissing any hope of direct elections for both the Legislative Council and the chief executive in 2007, it hoped this would bring an end to the debate surrounding democratic development, which had been ongoing for more than a decade but had never resulted in concrete action. It did not. The Chinese government gradually realized that unless this matter was resolved, it would continue to haunt Hong Kong. In December 2007, the NPCSC again ruled out direct election for the legislative council and the chief executive in 2011 and 2012 respectively, but it agreed that there could be direct election for the chief executive in 2017 and direct election for the Legislative Council, with the earliest possible time being 2021. However, there are still many details to be worked out. While the timetable for universal franchise comes as a disappointment to many people, it marks another significant pragmatic decision on the part of the Chinese leaders. It remains to be seen whether the election will be genuine or whether it will be a contrived affair marked by all kinds of hurdles relating to nomination and election procedures. If the promise is genuinely realized, it will raise the existing high degree of autonomy to a new level.

Human Rights and Judicial Review

While the central government exerts strong control over the appointment of the chief executive and the democratic development in Hong Kong, it has imparted considerable autonomy to the judiciary. This is partly an explicit recognition that the legal system is fundamental to the economic success of Hong Kong, and that the court plays a crucial role in the common law system. Thus, under the Joint Declaration and the Basic Law, apart from the abolition of appeals to the Privy Council and the establishment of the Court of Final Appeal, there is virtually no change in the judicial system (Arts. 19, 81). The chief justice and the chief judge of the High Court must be Hong Kong permanent residents of Chinese nationality with no right of abode in any foreign country (Art. 90), but there is no similar restriction for other judges, including judges of the Court of Final Appeal. Indeed, it is expressly provided that judges may be recruited from other common law jurisdictions on the basis of their judicial and professional qualities (Art. 92), and serving judges before the changeover remain in employment and retain their seniority on terms no less favorable than before (Art. 93). Judges are appointed on the recommendation of an independent commission composed of a majority of local judges and representatives of the legal profession (Art. 88). There are also provisions to protect the tenure of judges (Art. 89). The power of final adjudication is vested in the Court of Final Appeal, which may invite judges from other common law jurisdictions to sit on the Court as required.

The establishment of the Court of Final Appeal in Hong Kong has created a kind of self-identity. It is to succeed the Privy Council, one of the finest courts in the common law world. It has to maintain the same high degree of respectability. From the outset, the chief justice has been determined to establish a fine international reputation for the court. Thus, he has invited a panel of very distinguished overseas judges to serve on the Court of Final Appeal and has introduced a practice that in all substantive hearings there will always be an overseas judge. Not only has this brought eminence and great respect to the Court, but it also ensures that Hong Kong is continuously linked to the common law world. As the final arbiter of the common law, the Court has assumed a strong mission to uphold the rule of law and the basic values of the common law. The Basic Law presented great challenges and opportunities to the Court of Final Appeal in this regard. This sense of mission is explicit in the judgment of *Ng Ka Ling.* An earlier section described how the Court of Final Appeal attempted to extend its jurisdiction to cover resolutions and decisions of the NPCSC. Setbacks in this area have not deterred the Court from assuming a major constitutional role in the domestic system. It has been very receptive to international and comparative jurisprudence from all over the world in adjudicating cases, and has successfully established its reputation as a fine, liberal constitutional court that is reasonably vigorous in upholding fundamental human rights and the rule of law. The approach of the Court is best summarized in its leading judgment of *Leung Kwok Hung v. HKSAR*, where Li CJ stated

It is well established in our jurisprudence that the courts must give such a fundamental right [right to peaceful assembly] a generous interpretation so as to give individuals its full measure. On the other hand, restrictions on such a fundamental right must be narrowly interpreted. Plainly, the burden is on the Government to justify any restriction. This approach to constitutional review involving fundamental rights, which has been adopted by the Court, is consistent with that followed in many jurisdictions. Needless to say, in a society governed by the rule of law, the courts must be vigilant in the protection of fundamental rights and must rigorously examine any restriction that may be placed on them.[40]

The central government is content to leave the Court to develop this line of liberal jurisprudence so long as the subject matter falls within the domestic autonomy of the HKSAR. It is, of course, not easy to determine the exact boundaries. In *HKSAR v. Ng Kung Siu*, the Court had to determine whether the criminal offense of desecrating the national flag was consistent with the guarantee of freedom of expression.[41] Having surveyed legislative materials from a large number of countries that have statutory protection for national flags, the court adopted the rather cautious approach of upholding the validity of the criminal offense on the basis that it restricted only a particular mode of expression, not the content of the expression. The judgment has been subject to severe criticism.[42] On the other hand, this decision was rendered only six months after the NPCSC interpretation, when the relationship between the court and the NPCSC was still strained. While the Court could have easily gone the other way, it is obvious that another NPCSC interpretation would strike a fatal blow to the Hong Kong legal system. The Court had to balance upholding a strong notion of freedom of expression, which was at least controversial in the particular circumstances of the case, against endangering the integrity of the common law system. It thus decided to proceed very cautiously in its search for a new balance between adopting a strong libertarian approach and respecting the sovereignty of the central government.

The Court became more confident after the *Chong Fung Yuen* case, when it firmly established that, in interpreting the Basic Law, the common law approach should prevail in the absence of any relevant NPCSC interpretation. In *Yeung May Wan v. HKSAR*, sixteen demonstrators were charged with the offense of obstructing a public place and obstructing the police in the execution of their duty. These demonstrators belonged to a religious sect known as Falun Gong, which has been declared unlawful in Mainland China. The incident that gave rise to the criminal charges resulted from a demonstration outside the Liaison Office of the central government in Hong Kong. In marked contrast to its approach in *Ng Kung Siu*, the Court handed down a landmark judgment affirming the primacy of fundamental rights and striking down the criminal charges: "The freedom to demonstrate is a constitutional right. It is closely associated with the freedom of speech. These freedoms of course involve the freedom to express views which may be found to be disagreeable or even offensive to others or which may be critical of persons in authority."[43]

While *Yeung May Wan* might be explained as a case involving only domestic law and order, the next case is of great significance. In *Chen Li Hung v. Ting Lei Miao*,[44] the Court of Final Appeal had to address whether a bankruptcy order issued by a Taiwan Court would be recognized by the Hong Kong court, given that Taiwan was not recognized as a sovereign body by the PRC government. Notwithstanding the highly political context the Court, in a careful judgment, addressed the issue as a purely technical question of private international law and decided to give effect to the Taiwan Court's judgment. The judgment of Lord Cooke is a remarkably fine exposition of the delicate balance between law and politics, and autonomy and sovereignty, and is worth quoting here in extenso:

> As Godfrey JA points out in his judgment in the Court of Appeal, the Preamble to the Constitution of the People's Republic of China declares that Taiwan is a part of the sacred territory of the People's Republic of China and that it is the lofty duty of the entire Chinese people, including the compatriots in Taiwan, to accomplish the great task of reunifying the motherland. I think that reunification will tend to be promoted rather than impeded if people resident in Taiwan, one part of China, are able to enforce in Hong Kong, another part of China, bankruptcy orders made in Taiwan. . . . Viewing the case from a different perspective, the issue is essentially between the Taiwan creditors on the one hand and Mr Ting, Madam Chen and Mr Chan on the other. It is not an issue with which national politics have any natural connection. They should not be allowed to obtrude into or overshadow a question of the private rights and day-to-day affairs of ordinary people. The ordinary principles of private international law should be applied without importing extraneous high-level public controversy.[45]

This judgment again highlights the very delicate task with which the Hong Kong court is faced whenever the issue of sovereignty arises. Interestingly, this judgment has not attracted any criticism from the central government.

Conclusion

Hong Kong provides a unique autonomy arrangement which seems to defy the conventional wisdom relating to factors that contribute to a successful autonomy model.[46] It enjoys a remarkable degree of autonomy, including some powers normally reserved for an independent state. Despite the wide range of autonomous powers, the autonomy arrangement has not led to any disintegration. What is singularly significant in the case of Hong Kong is the absence of any ethnic, racial, or religious conflict. It is a relatively homogeneous society with the majority readily identifying themselves with China and Chinese culture. If they have been evident at all, demands for secession or independence have never taken root in Hong Kong before or after the handover. At the same time, Hong Kong was a highly developed economy even before the handover. It enjoys great economic success and is a fairly affluent society. It has an efficient government that is relatively free from corruption. It has a well-established system of rule of law and an effective legal system. These factors distinguish Hong Kong from many other autonomous models where the arrangement faces constant challenge from a strong demand for a separate identity arising from cultural, racial, ethnic, religious, or minority conflicts, or where peaceful coexistence is difficult to maintain due to an inefficient or corrupt regional or central government where human rights and rule of law do not prevail.

The autonomous model is regarded by China as a means for achieving sovereignty over the territory. It is not intended as a form of power sharing, and anything perceived as a threat to sovereignty will not be tolerated. The primacy of sovereignty in the autonomous design results from the rejection of any formal external monitoring system. It also leads to a highly asymmetrical autonomous model that lacks an effective dispute resolution mechanism. Any dispute is to be finally resolved by the central government; the Special Administrative Region is not really in a position to negotiate or bargain with the central government. The Basic Law Committee, which had the potential to develop into an effective dispute resolution mechanism, is only consultative and today is regarded as nothing more than a rubber stamping body. Influenced by the same notion of sovereignty, China is equally concerned with the democratic movement in Hong Kong, as strong democratic movements can easily lead to demands for greater self-governance, and with more equitable wealth distribution which is not considered to be conducive to the maintenance of a capitalist system. This leads to the more fundamental issue of the nature and purpose of "one country, two systems." To China, "one country, two systems" is really about "one country, two economic systems." Democratic development is only tolerated insofar as it is perceived as a necessary condition for economic growth, stability, and prosperity. If there is a conflict (or a perceived conflict) between entrenching the capitalist system and autonomy, entrenchment of economic interests always prevails. However, this view is not shared by many people in Hong Kong, and it remains a great challenge for China to manage the democratic aspirations of these forces in Hong Kong.

At the same time, Hong Kong continues to thrive as a capitalist jewel and an international financial center. The central government has exercised great self-restraint in not interfering with the domestic affairs of Hong Kong. Indeed, it has provided Hong Kong with a good deal of support by adopting various preferential policies to ensure its economic vitality and competitiveness. As China has itself experienced rapid economic growth over the last two decades, the autonomy arrangement has been mutually beneficial to both Hong Kong and China,[47] between which there is strong economic interaction. Hong Kong remains an important center for raising capital for China, and the successful experience of managing a complex market economy in Hong Kong has inspired China in its economic reforms and modernization programs.

Thus, the close economic tie between Hong Kong and the Mainland, the strong cultural identification with China, the absence of any separatist forces, the preservation of a civil society, and the overwhelming concern for unity and sovereignty in the autonomy design, have all contributed to the integration of Hong Kong with the Mainland.

Meanwhile, in such a highly asymmetrical autonomy, the arrangement is rather precarious, depending largely on tolerance by the central government. While the autonomous model is entrenched in the Basic Law, amendment and interpretation of the Law is vested solely in the central government. There is no enforcement mechanism under the Joint Declaration. Hong Kong itself has no means of defending itself. Being just a small part of China, it has little voice in China as a whole, not only in national affairs but in issues affecting Hong Kong.

Macau is another autonomous region in China. While the Basic Law in Macau is modeled closely on that of Hong Kong, Macau is in a very different social, economic, and political situation. Unlike many federal arrangements, the autonomous regions could hardly "gang up" to create a balance between the regions and the central government. For China, there is Tibet, on the one hand, which has been quite successful in gearing up international pressure on China in its demand for autonomy, and Shanghai and other special economic zones on the other, which are demanding preferential treatment similar to that accorded to Hong Kong. China must carefully balance these conflicting demands. Its great challenge is to manage this asymmetrical model and to strike a delicate balance between autonomy, economic success, and sovereignty. China would not be prepared to take any risks that would endanger the delicate design of distribution of powers in the Hong Kong autonomous model. China is careful to respect its high degree of autonomy and has exercised great self-restraint in relation to its economic and social development, giving as much support as necessary to sustain its economic vitality. It has also allowed the judiciary a relatively free space in which to operate, at times even when the boundary of autonomy is not entirely clear. At the same time, the central government has no hesitation to show that it is in control when it comes to Hong Kong's political and democratic development, although it also seems to be realizing that economic development cannot take place without simultaneous democratic development.

The current autonomous arrangement is to last until 2047. The position after 2047 is unclear. No doubt a lot will depend on China's economic and political development. However, if the experience of the 1970s is to provide a lesson, it is that the future of Hong Kong beyond 2047 will have to be resolved much earlier than 2047. There are three major forces that will sustain the autonomous arrangement. The first is the Taiwan factor. As long as the problem of Taiwan remains unresolved, there is strong incentive for the central government to maintain the status quo and the high degree of autonomy for Hong Kong, provided nothing in Hong Kong would be perceived as a challenge to its sovereignty. The second factor is the economic development of Hong Kong. It is in China's economic interests to maintain Hong Kong's position as a thriving international financial center. Ironically, the stronger the economy of Hong Kong, the stronger becomes the guarantee of the autonomous arrangement. The challenge for Hong Kong is to capitalize on the beneficial economic arrangement, maintain a good relationship with competing neighbors within China, and continue to maintain the efficiency and integrity of its own system when corruption is prevalent across the border. The third factor is the development of the rule of law and democracy in China, which has made considerable progress in this regard since the 1980s. It is a huge country with a huge population and subject to great regional disparity. In less than three decades, law and order have been restored. There are now few aspects of governance that are not covered by some laws, although their enforcement remains a major problem. By and large, governance is characterized by greater transparency, stability, responsiveness, and rationality. The gradual entrenchment of civil society in China may perhaps provide the best guarantee for "one country, two systems." Indeed, "one country, two systems" is best assured by Hong Kong continuing to maintain its separate identity, particularly in terms of its rule of law and its aspirations for democracy, and to inspire China as to how economic success, democracy, and human rights can coexist and reinforce one another without threatening sovereignty. In this regard, it is perhaps paradoxical that a conscious policy to remain distinct from the rest of China—including upholding the democratic movement in Hong Kong, retaining its distinctiveness, and advancing the rule of law—will provide the best guarantee for the autonomous arrangement.

Notes

1. Art. 3, Convention of Nanking (1842), reproduced in Parry 1969–81, 96: 465.

2. Convention Between the United Kingdom and China Respecting an Extension of Hong Kong Territory (1898), reproduced in Parry 1969–81, 186: 310. Ratifications were exchanged at London on 6 August 1898.

3. Britain has also acquired a lease in Weihaiwei to counter Russian influence (see Ghai 1999, 5).

4. There were plenty of opportunities when China could have demanded the return of Hong Kong and Macau. In 1972, China demanded successfully from the United Nations that Hong Kong and Macau be deleted from the list of colonies covered by the Declaration on the Granting of Independence to Colonial

People, asserting that Hong Kong and Macau were always part of China and their settlement was entirely within China's sovereign right. In 1974, China even turned down Portugal's offer to return Macau after the Portuguese military revolution (see Ghai 1999, 37–38).

5. In the 1950s, entrepreneurs from Shanghai arrived in Hong Kong with capital and experience, and helped set up the manufacturing, garments, and textiles industry. In the following two decades, Hong Kong moved into other light industries (plastic goods, toys, watches, electronics) and took advantage of its strategic geographical position in developing into an entrepôt. During this period, immigrants from the Mainland provided a continual cheap labor supply in a labor-intensive economy that enabled Hong Kong to keep its product cost low and be competitive in the global market. By the 1980s, Hong Kong had gone through another economic metamorphosis and moved into finances and services, soon emerging as a leading world financial center.

6. For a more detailed discussion, see Chan 2003, chap. 1.

7. For a long time, study of Chinese history in the secondary school curriculum ended in 1949. There was virtually nothing about what had happened in China since then. Nor did the school curriculum teach Potunghua until after the resumption of sovereignty.

8. Under the 1974 Official Languages Ordinance, Chinese became an official language except for law, where English remained the only official language. This was due partly to the common law system and partly to the difficulty of translating English legislation into Chinese. Equally authentic bilingual legislation was introduced only in 1989 by the 1987 Official Languages (Amendment) Ordinance, prompted by the 1984 Sino-British Joint Declaration. For a good discussion, see Cheung 1997.

9. For a more detailed discussion see Ghai 1999, chap. 1; Chan 2003, chap. 1.

10. In reaching the agreement, both sides were prepared to adopt a pragmatic approach, particularly on sensitive and difficult issues on which they could not agree. Thus, while clause 1 of the Joint Declaration says that China will "*resume* the exercise of sovereignty over Hong Kong," clause 2 says that the United Kingdom will "*restore*" Hong Kong to the People's Republic of China." The two sides were also unable to agree on the nature of passport that would continue to be held by British Dependent Territories citizens in Hong Kong after 1997. The United Kingdom described it in a memorandum as a "passport" that would entitle the holder to British consular services and protection *in a third country*, whereas China in a separate memorandum described it as a "travel document" that could be used for traveling to other states and regions but would not entitle holders to British consular protection in Hong Kong or China, without mentioning the position in a third country. Likewise, the Chinese government was concerned that the British government might dispose of the premium income arising from the sale of land before 1997. Hence, Annex 3 of the Joint Declaration set out principles governing land leases. It restricted the amount of new grants of land to not more than 50 hectares a year, and mandated an equal sharing of premium income from land transactions between the British Hong Kong government and the future HKSAR government. A Land Commission was set up to oversee the implementation of these policies.

11. As a major international financial center, Hong Kong has entered into numerous international treaties, some through the auspices of the United Kingdom, others in its own right. In contrast, having suffered successive civil wars and having been isolated from the rest of the world for almost a decade during

the Cultural Revolution, China has only entered into a handful of international treaties. Preserving the rights and obligations under these international treaties presented some of the most intriguing international law issues. For details see Chan 1996, 2001; Chen 1999; Mushkat 1997; Yu 1999.

12. See Preamble and Art. 11, Basic Law. Art. 31 of the PRC Constitution stipulates that "the state may establish special administrative regions when necessary. The systems to be instituted in special administrative regions shall be prescribed by law enacted by the National People's Congress in the light of the specific conditions."

13. These measures include relaxation of restrictions of Mainland residents to visit Hong Kong as tourists, facilitation of state enterprises to list in the Hong Kong stock market, and entering into a Closer Economic Partnership Agreement to allow specific industries and professionals in Hong Kong to offer their services in China.

14. This kind of tension was indeed foreseen at the time of concluding the Basic Law. While the Basic Law serves as a constitution for the HKSAR, it is itself a piece of national law promulgated by the National People's Congress and is binding on HKSAR government as well as other provincial and state organs. Thus, for instance, Art. 22 of the Basic Law stipulates that for entry into the HKSAR, people from other parts of China must apply for approval, and the number of persons who enter the HKSAR for the purpose of settlement shall be determined by the Central People's Government after consulting the HKSAR government.

15. See chapter 7 of the Basic Law.

16. This power has not been exercised.

17. Art. 18, Basic Law. The current list comprises 12 pieces of national laws, most of them uncontroversial in nature. The only two substantive pieces of national laws are the PRC Nationality Law and the PRC Garrison Law; the latter governs the conduct of the People's Liberation Army stationed in Hong Kong.

18. Art. 18, Basic Law. The Central Government shall only declare a state of emergency in Hong Kong by reason of turmoil within the HKSAR that endangers nationality unity or security and is beyond the control of the HKSAR government.

19. As an example of an external mechanism, see the case of Aaland, which was guaranteed by the League of Nations and underwritten by an agreement between Sweden and Finland (Ghai 2005, 36; Wolff, this volume).

20. Since 1997, the British government has submitted a half-yearly report to Parliament on the implementation of the Joint Declaration. There were a few occasions when the British government expressed concern of compliance with the Joint Declaration in relation to the democratic development in Hong Kong. The Chinese response is always that this is a domestic matter on which foreign governments have no say. Her view seems to be that once the HKSAR has been established, detailed implementation of the policies of the Chinese government regarding HKSAR is solely a matter of domestic affairs.

21. Under the 1992 U.S. Hong Kong Policy Act, 22 USC 5731, the U.S. may withdraw special treatment or status it has accorded Hong Kong on Chinese assurances of autonomy under the Joint Declaration. This is, however, a unilateral measure on the part of the United States and the power has never been exercised. Nor is its exercise likely to be well received by China.

22. [1999] 1 HKC 315.

23. Chris Patten, the last governor, exploited the gray area in the Basic Law by introducing into the 1995 Legislative Council 9 new functional constituencies

that covered virtually everyone except housewives and students, and an election committee that comprised all the elected members of the District Boards. China regarded this amendment as introducing disguised direct election and a contravention of the Basic Law. Negotiations over the constitutional reform failed, and China decided not to recognize the 1995 Legislative Council as the first Legislative Council of the HKSAR. As Patten could not form the first Legislative Council during British administration, she appointed a Provisional Legislative Council which lasted for 18 months, pending the formation of the first Legislative Council of the HKSAR.

24. [1999] 1 HKC 315 at 322.

25. [1999] 1 HKLRD 577.

26. Interpretation adopted by the NPCSC at its tenth session on 26 June 1999, reproduced in Chan, Fu, and Ghai (2000), 478–80.

27. [1999] 3 HKLRD 778.

28. [2001] 2 HKLRD 533.

29. It has been queried whether the Court could adopt one part of the NPCSC interpretation and reject another if the interpretation is akin to legislation (Yap 2007; for a reply, see Chan 2007).

30. It leaves open the situation where the NPCSC interprets the Basic Law on judicial referral. It would be difficult to conclude that the NPCSC would still be exercising a legislative function when the question of interpretation arises in the course of arguments before the Court of Final Appeal (Chan 2007).

31. See discussions on the cases on Falun Gong (*Yeung May Wan v. HKSAR* [2005] 2 HKLRD 212) and recognition of a judgment of the Taiwan District Court (*Chen Li Hung v. Ting Lei Miao* [2000] 1 HKC 461), below.

32. There were strong public demands for introduction of direct election in 1988, but it was postponed to 1991 largely due to objection from China. It was suggested that direct election could not be introduced before China had adopted the Basic Law so that it would not be seen as something bestowed by the British Hong Kong government but by virtue of the Basic Law.

33. Article 68, Basic Law. It was subsequently suggested that two other principles would be relevant, namely, balanced participation and conducive to the maintenance of the capitalist system. For a more detailed discussion, see Chan and Harris 2005.

34. Annex 2 to the Basic Law. Any amendment could only be made with the endorsement of a two-thirds majority of all the members of the Legislative Council and the consent of the chief executive, and it shall be reported to the NPCSC for the record. It is unlikely that any amendment that does not receive the support of the Central People's Government would be able to get the consent of the chief executive.

35. Decision of the NPCSC.

36. The chief executive is "elected" by an Election Committee which comprises initially 400 and subsequently 800 members to be elected from four major sectors and appointed by the Central People's Government, which has stressed that it is a substantive and not formal power. The sectors largely mirror the functional constituency system, and hence the Committee is exposed to considerable influence by the local and central government.

37. For instance, in the debates on the Covert Surveillance Bill, more than 300 amendments proposed by the pan-democratic camp were defeated irrespective of their merits. Likewise, about 80 amendments proposed by the Democratic

Party on the Race Discrimination Bill were voted down even when some were entirely neutral in nature.

38. Thus, when half a million people protested in June 2003 to express their dissatisfaction with the governance, the official response was that they took to the street for many different reasons, principally slow economic recovery and pains of economic restructuring (Hualing, Petersen, and Young 2005, chap. 1, 49–50).

39. For a full account, see ibid.

40. [2005] 3 HKLRD 164 at 178, para. 16; notes omitted.

41. [1999] 3 HKLRD 907.

42. See Wacks 2000, 3.

43. [2005] 2 HKLRD 212 at 216.

44. [2000] 1 HKLRD 252.

45. Ibid., at 264.

46. For useful discussion, see Lapidoth 1994; Ghai 2000, chap. 1; Ghai 2007, chap. 6.

47. A mutually beneficial arrangement is an important positive factor that would enhance the chances of success of an autonomy arrangement (Lapidoth 1994, 287).

References

Chan, J. 2007. Basic law and constitutional review: The first ten years. *Hong Kong Law Journal* 37: 407–47.

———, ed. 2003. *Immigration law and policy in Hong Kong: An inter-disciplinary study.* Hong Kong: Sweet and Maxwell.

———. 2001. Human rights in the Hong Kong Special Administrative Region: The first four years. *Kobe University Law Review* 35: 75–101.

———. 1996. State succession to human rights treaties: Hong Kong and the International Covenant on Civil and Political Rights. *International and Comparative Law Quarterly* 45: 928–46.

Chan, J., and L. Harris. 2005. The Constitutional Journey: The Way Forward. In *Hong Kong's constitutional debates*, ed. J. Chan and L. Harris. Hong Kong: Hong Kong Law Journal. 143–69.

Chan, J., H. Fu, and Y. Ghai, eds. 2000. *Hong Kong's constitutional debate: Conflict over interpretation.* Hong Kong: Hong Kong University Press.

Chen, A. 1999. Continuity and change in the legal system. In *The other Hong Kong report 1998*, ed. L. Chow and Y.-K. Fan. Hong Kong: Chinese University Press. 29–48.

Cheung, A. 1997. Towards a bilingual legal system: The development of Chinese legal language. *Loyola of Los Angeles International and Comparative Law Journal* 19: 315–36.

Dinstein, Y., ed, 1981, *Models of Autonomy*. New Brunswick, N.J.: Transaction Books

Hualing, F., C. Petersen, and S. Young, eds. 2005. *National security and fundamental freedoms: Hong Kong's Article 23 under scrutiny.* Hong Kong: Hong Kong University Press.

Ghai, Y. 2007. Constitutional asymmetries: Communal representation, federalism, and cultural autonomy. In *The Architecture of Democracy*, ed. A. Reynolds. Oxford: Oxford University Press.

———. 2005. The imperatives of autonomy: Contradictions of the Basic Law. In

Hong Kong's constitutional debates, ed. J. Chan and L. Harris. Hong Kong: Hong Kong Law Journal. 29-44.

_____. 2000. Ethnicity and autonomy: A framework for analysis. In *Autonomy and ethnicity: Negotiating competing claims in multi-ethnic states*, ed. Y. Ghai. Cambridge: Cambridge University Press.

_____. 1999. *Hong Kong's new constitutional order: The resumption of Chinese sovereignty and the basic law*. 2nd ed. Hong Kong: Hong Kong University Press.

Hannum, H. and R. B. Lillich. 1980. The concept of autonomy in international law. *American Journal of International Law* 77: 858–89.

Lapidoth, R. 1994. Autonomy: Potential and limitations. *International Journal on Group Rights* 1: 269–90.

Mushkat, R. 1997. Hong Kong and succession of treaties. *International and Comparative Law Quarterly* 46: 181–201.

Parry, C. ed. 1969–1981. *The Consolidated Treaty Series, 1648–1919*. Dobbs Ferry, N.Y.: Oceana.

Wacks, R. 2000. Our flagging rights. *Hong Kong Law Journal* 30: 1.

Wesley-Smith, P. 1994. *Constitutional and administrative law in Hong Kong*. Hong Kong: Longman Asia.

Yap, P. J. 2007. Ten years of the Basic Law: The rise, retreat and resurgence of judicial power in Hong Kong. *Common Law World Review* 36, 2: 166–91.

Yu, P. 1999. Succession by estoppel: Hong Kong's succession to the ICCPR. *Pepperdine Law Review* 27: 57–58.

Chapter 6
Asymmetric Autonomy in the United Kingdom

John McGarry

Asymmetric autonomy usually refers to an institutional arrangement in which different parts of a state enjoy different levels of autonomy. It arises in federations, when certain federal regions have more (or fewer) powers than others, or in unitary states, when some regions enjoy autonomy, including different levels of autonomy, while other regions are governed from the center. This is one of a number of kinds of asymmetry, as regions may also differ in their populations and resources, the representation that they have in the state's central or federal institutions, and in the design of their own internal (regional) institutions.

Asymmetric autonomy arises for different reasons. China, a unitary state, has allowed Hong Kong more autonomy than is enjoyed by the rest of the state because it eased its reabsorption and brought clear economic benefits (see Chan, this volume). In most cases, however, asymmetry is a response to pressures for autonomy, or more autonomy, from mobilized national communities, or when an independent entity is granted special self-governing privileges in return for joining a state. Examples of asymmetric autonomy include the Aaland Islands, Southern Sudan, South Tyrol, and Zanzibar. Asymmetric autonomy is also mooted as a possible solution to several current conflicts and standoffs, including in Moldova (Transdniestria) Sri Lanka (Tamil Eelam), and Sudan (Darfur).

The United Kingdom has one of the most complex examples of asymmetric autonomy. Before 1998, it was a tightly centralized state, although a "union" state rather than, as is often supposed, a strictly unitary state. Since 1998, it has granted different degrees of autonomy to its so-called "Celtic periphery" of Scotland, Wales, and Northern Ireland, but continues to govern England, representing 85 percent of its population, from the center at Westminster.

The United Kingdom's willingness to create asymmetric autonomous institutions is arguably related to its background as a union state.

Its decision to do so was a response to several different challenges. In Great Britain, the UK government faced differential aspirations for self-government. The Scots wanted far-reaching autonomy, the Welsh were more ambivalent, while the English remained content to be governed from Westminster. In Northern Ireland, London faced demands from Irish nationalists, both militantly and constitutionally expressed, for closer linkages with the Republic of Ireland, and for recognition of the Irish people's right to self-determination. Any institutions for Northern Ireland also had to accommodate the region's internal divisions. These multiple challenges, and the UK government response, make its experience relevant to several of the other cases covered in this volume. Few of them combine the challenges faced in the UK, but most face some of them.

This chapter discusses the appropriateness of the asymmetric UK arrangements for its particular (complex) situation. It discusses the background to the adoption of asymmetric autonomy and describes the new institutions. It argues that an asymmetry of institutional design across the regions is a fair response to asymmetric aspirations. The UK experience, it is argued, reveals the flexibility of asymmetric institutional design, which can cope not just with differential desires for autonomy but also with different levels of division within regions. The chapter then discusses criticisms of these arrangements, and concludes by drawing some comparative lessons from the UK experience with asymmetric autonomy.

Asymmetry in the United Kingdom

Prior to the 1990s, the UK was generally referred to in political science textbooks and elsewhere as a unitary state much like France or Japan. This was inaccurate. The British were not Jacobins, intent on destroying all particularisms and constructing a monistic national identity. The UK, as suggested by its name, was what Rokkan and Urwin call a "union" state (Rokkan and Urwin 1982). It recognized the distinctiveness of the historic nationalities and their boundaries in a range of different, that is, asymmetric, ways. Scotland, after the Acts of Union, retained its own established church, a separate legal system, and separate systems for education and local government. While Scotland's government, at least from the nineteenth century, came under the control of central institutions, a series of steps were taken to accommodate the Scots within these. From 1885, Scotland was given its own secretary of state, a position that was given full cabinet rank from 1926. Around this there evolved the Scottish Office, a branch of the British civil service, but largely housed in Edinburgh, which was given the task of lobbying for Scotland at the center, and adapting UK policies to Scottish conditions. Much Scottish legislation was passed separately at Westminster, and the committee stage of Scottish bills was heard before the Scottish Grand Committee, in which Scottish members of parliament (MPs) usually predominated. These were *territorial* provisions but they took place within a context of political centralization, which is why the UK was often seen as "unitary": the secretary of state, though by convention a Scot, was a representative of the UK government, and Scottish legislation depended, in the final instance, on majority support among all the UK MPs.

The treatment of Wales was much less distinctive—and less accommodating, reflecting its longer integration with England and the terms on which it was integrated. Its established church, until the early twentieth century, was the Church of England, which was not supported by most people in Wales. There was administrative decentralization, though less so than in Scotland, beginning with the Welsh Department of the Board of Education in 1907, and gradually expanding until it embraced seventeen departments by the 1950s. These were then taken under the umbrella of the Secretary of State for Wales and the Welsh Office, created in 1964. As with Scotland, the Welsh secretary of state was a member of the British cabinet. By contrast with Scotland, Wales was treated as part of England for legislative purposes, although the Welsh Office was able to make regulations flowing from this legislation.

Ireland was treated at least as distinctively as Scotland, but much less benignly. Ireland retained its own legal system and statute book, but, like Scotland, its legislation came, often separately, from Westminster. Its established church, until 1870, was the Anglican "Church of Ireland," which was rejected by most of its overwhelmingly Catholic population. It was governed by distinctive officials, primarily the chief secretary for Ireland, a UK cabinet minister, who, throughout the period from 1801 to 1921, never came from Ireland or represented an Irish constituency. Many of the boards and agencies that he presided over were not accountable to the UK parliament let alone Irish MPs. Through much of the nineteenth century Ireland was governed by emergency legislation, the only part of the UK to have this dubious distinction. Its regime was arguably closer to Britain's nonwhite colonies than to Scotland's, although its elected representatives, who before 1829 could not be Catholic, sat in the Westminster parliament.

Prior to 1998, then, the UK combined political centralization with an asymmetric system of administrative decentralization. The exception to this pattern was Northern Ireland, which, between 1921 and 1972, had its own regional legislature and a government responsible to it. This was part of a strategy that envisaged analogous institutional arrangements for Southern Ireland, but these were never established, and Southern Ireland seceded from the UK in 1921. Northern Ireland's parliament operated on the basis of the Westminster model of government, that is, it was majoritarian and executive-centered. As unionists were in a majority and the region was polarized between them and nationalists, this meant government by unionists of nationalists, or what O'Leary and I describe elsewhere as a regime of hegemonic control (O'Leary and McGarry 1996). Control broke down in the late 1960s, and the parliament was abolished in 1972, after three years of violent unrest. Between then and 1998, with the exception of a failed attempt at devolution on a power-sharing basis for five months in 1974, Northern Ireland was ruled directly from Westminster, in much the same way that all of Ireland had been ruled prior to 1921—by British ministers who did not represent Northern Irish constituencies, by a "Northern Ireland Office" that was separate from British departments, and by a legislative regime that relied on emergency laws and "orders in council" rather than, as in the case of England, Wales, and Scotland, ordinary legislation debated in the normal way at Westminster.

The asymmetric autonomy changes of the late 1990s do not mark a break from a symmetric past. The break is, rather, with the exception of Northern Ireland between 1921 and 1972, and briefly in 1974, from a centralized past, in which ultimate decisions were made at Westminster, by the UK parliament and/or a UK government responsible to it. In Northern Ireland's case, the Good Friday Agreement reached in 1998 renewed its autonomy, but this time, unlike 1921–72, on terms that were acceptable to both nationalists and unionists. The asymmetric nature of the changes adopted in 1998 are related to the preexisting asymmetries that have just been described—with the more integrated region of Wales receiving much less autonomy than Scotland or Northern Ireland (Jeffery and Wincott 2006). Arguably, the UK union-state legacy, and the different manifestations it took in the peripheral regions, also helped to maintain and shape the identity of the nationalities and their aspirations.

The autonomy arrangements adopted in 1998 are asymmetric in two main senses. First, not all regions of the state enjoy autonomy. England, which possesses around 85 percent of the UK population, has neither a parliament nor an assembly. The English regions do not enjoy self-government, although many of them are at least as populous as Scotland, Wales, or Northern Ireland. The practice outside London is what has been called "functional regionalism," to distinguish it from political autonomy (Keating 2006). This is based on a three-prong strategy, originating in the early 1990s, which combined the regional organization of central government departments, regional development authorities (RDAs), and nonstatutory regional chambers comprised of representatives from business, voluntary associations, and local governments (Sandford 2006). It has resulted in what Jeffery and Wincott describe as "little more than an improved capacity for centralized policymaking" (Jeffery and Wincott 2006, 8). The Greater London area has had, since 2000, a Greater London Authority, which replaced the Greater London Council abolished by the Thatcher government in 1986. It comprises a directly elected assembly and a directly elected mayor, but its powers are modest and much closer to those of an upper-tier local authority than those of an autonomous assembly.[1]

The lack of autonomy for England and the English regions reflects satisfaction among the English with the political status quo. Survey data shows that only a small minority of the English want their own parliament, no more than 19 percent between 1999 and 2003, and that the English are much more likely to trust the UK government to look after their interests than either the Scottish or Welsh (Curtice 2006, 121, 133).[2] The reason is straightforward: the UK parliament has 529 English MPs out of a total of 646 (83 percent) and, as the Scots are well aware, already operates as a reasonable facsimile of an English parliament. This also explains why the English are much more likely than any of the nationalities to identify with the whole state.[3] Indeed the dominant English view is that the UK is an English state, with the peripheral bits seen as optional add-ons. No serious political party supports an English parliament, and although the former leader of the Conservative Party, William Hague, briefly flirted with the idea in 1999, he quickly abandoned it.[4]

Support for English regional assemblies is similarly low, around 15 to 24 percent according to survey data (Curtice 2006, 122; Bogdanor 1999, 271). Even in the northeast of England, where support for regional devolution is relatively strong, it is still weak in absolute terms. When the government held a referendum in the northeast on a regional assembly in November 2004, its proposals were defeated by 78 to 22 percent on a 48 percent turnout.[5] Some supporters of regional assemblies argued subsequently that the government's proposals were rejected because they were not radical enough (Stevens 2004; Hazell 2006b, 231–32). However, supporters of radical autonomy, as in Scotland, Wales, and Northern Ireland, more typically support modest autonomy as something to build on, rather than reject it in favor of a centralized status quo.[6] There is low support for regional autonomy in England because the English regions do not have separate national identities. What desire for autonomy exists is based on functional needs only, and there are functional arguments for and against decentralization.

The absence of support for an English parliament or English regional assemblies means that a symmetric federation is not an option for the United Kingdom. This makes its situation analogous to the many states, such as Moldova or Sri Lanka, in which nationalities seek autonomy but the dominant people do not. The fact that the English do not seek symmetric devolution, or a symmetric federation, with England as a single region is, on balance, a good thing. A "region" based on England would be ten times larger than the next largest region, Scotland, and five times larger than all three peripheral regions (Scotland, Wales, and Northern Ireland) combined. This would make the English parliament a serious rival of the UK parliament, well placed to win out in any competition for resources between it and its Scottish, Welsh, and Northern Irish counterparts, particularly as nearly 90 percent of the central or federal parliament's MPs would be English. In a recent comparative study of the pathology of pluralist federations, Henry Hale argues that a leading cause of failure is the existence of a "dual power-structure," that is, when one of the federation's units is strong enough to rival the federal authorities (Hale 2004). A dual core-structure exists, in Hale's view, when a "core ethnic region" possesses at least 50 percent of the state's population, or 20 percent more than the second largest region. Hale shows how this imbalance destabilized the Soviet Union and the first Nigerian republic, and currently destabilizes Pakistan. England would represent a "core ethnic region" much more dominant than those in any of Hale's examples. A four-unit United Kingdom, dominated by England, would not provide for the multiple balance of power and shifting coalitions that are generally seen as conducive to federal stability, as England would not need to make alliances. A likely result would be that England would be constantly ranged against the periphery, making the UK analogous to a two-unit federation, which is generally regarded as unstable (Watts 1999). As its supporters argue, symmetric institutions based on the English regions would not have these difficulties.[7] This would create a federation similar to that of Canada, in which the English-speaking majority is divided among several regions, giving rise to a multiple balance of power in which coalitions have crosscut national boundaries. However, any autonomy arrangements that put the English regions on a par with Scotland, or even with Wales, would have to be imposed from the top, and would involve giving the English regions more autonomy than any of them want, or the nationalities less.

Second, the three parts of the UK that have been given autonomy—Scotland, Wales, and Northern Ireland—enjoy different forms of it. Scotland has been given a parliament with wide-ranging primary legislative powers in most fields of domestic policy.[8] It is the only region in the UK that has been given fiscal discretion, in its case the ability to vary UK taxation up or down by 3 percent, although it has not yet used this power. The Scotland Act spells out powers that have been reserved to Westminster, leaving the Scottish parliament in charge of residuary matters. As Weller observes in this book's Introduction, because it is usually the center that enjoys residual authority in contexts of regional autonomy, these arrangements are unusual. However, as Scotland's self-government is a case of devolution and not federation, the UK parliament at Westminster retains ultimate authority to legislate for Scotland in all matters, including those that are devolved. Since 1999 Westminster has legislated for Scotland in devolved fields on many occasions, although with the approval of the Scottish Parliament.

Scotland's relatively extensive autonomy is related to pre-devolution arrangements, and broadly involved transferring responsibility for governing and legislating for Scotland from the UK government's Scottish Office and Westminster to institutions that were accountable to the Scottish people. The level of autonomy is also in line with popular opinion, as measured by survey data and by support for political parties that back autonomy. In the 1997 UK election which preceded devolution, parties backing a Scottish *parliament*, meaning legislative devolution, won all of Scotland's 71 seats in the UK parliament. In the 1997 prelegislative referendum in Scotland, which had a 60.4 percent turnout, 74.3 percent of Scots voted in favor of a Scottish parliament, while 63 percent supported giving it "tax-varying" powers. As Scots First Minister Donald Dewar put it, legislative devolution appeared to represent the "settled will of the Scottish people," and post-devolution survey data suggests this remains the case.[9]

Wales has been given an assembly, with essentially the functions that had belonged to the secretary of state for Wales and the Welsh Office. It currently has control over only secondary legislation, or regulations, and the administration of the region. The power of the Welsh Assembly to make secondary legislation, moreover, is not general or uniform in nature. Rather, it applies only to certain (over 400) Westminster statutes, as specifically outlined in each of them (Jeffery and Wincott 2006, 6). All primary legislation remains a prerogative of Westminster, although the Government of Wales Act (1998) requires the secretary of state for Wales to consult with the Assembly about the UK government's legislative program. If, as some plausibly maintain, the ability to pass primary legislation is considered an essential criterion of autonomy, then Wales is not an autonomous region. In the 2006 Government of Wales Act, however, the UK parliament legislated to extend and generalize the Assembly's powers of secondary legislation. The Act also provided for the Assembly to have powers of primary legislation in specified fields, but only after this had been supported by a referendum in Wales.

Wales's relatively modest degree of self-government is linked to the fact that support for self-government there is markedly lower than in Scotland, since many among Wales's large English-speaking majority are skeptical. The Welsh rejected devolution in 1979 by 79.3 percent to 23.7 percent, a degree of opposition similar to that expressed in the northeast of England's 2003 referendum. Twenty years of Thatcherite government helped reduce enthusiasm for centralization, and the Welsh approved devolution in 1998, but by the narrowest of margins, 50.3 to 49.7 percent, on a low turnout of 50.1 percent. The government's margin of victory was linked, arguably, to the fact that it deliberately placed Scotland's referendum a week earlier, rather than at the same time, as in 1979, on the assumption that the expected affirmative vote in Scotland would facilitate a yes vote in Wales.

While Northern Ireland has an "assembly" like Wales, this is in practice a parliament with primary legislative powers, similar to Scotland's, and, indeed, to Northern Ireland's parliament between 1921 and 1972. The Northern Ireland Assembly enjoys jurisdiction over all matters not "reserved," or "excepted" to Westminster.[10] The Assembly sits in the same building as the Stormont parliament, but the latter was bicameral, whereas the Northern Ireland Assembly is unicameral.[11] The term "assembly" was first adopted by the UK government in 1973 to describe the legislature established under the Sunningdale Agreement, and was chosen to distinguish it from its Stormont predecessor, which had a very adversarial style and which behaved in a de facto independent manner with unacceptable, and eventually, from the perspective of Britain, deeply embarrassing consequences (Ward 2000, 119; Hadfield 1989, 119).[12] The term may also have appealed to nationalists precisely because it disassociated the new regime from the old one, and to unionists who were against substantial devolution for Northern Ireland and who preferred integration with Great Britain.

Northern Ireland's new autonomy arrangements are different from those in Scotland (or Wales), and from the Stormont period, in a number of important ways. First, under the Agreement, Northern Ireland does not just enjoy autonomy but is linked to the Irish Republic through a number of all-Ireland political institutions. The most important of these is the North-South Ministerial Council (NSMC), a body nominated by the Republic's government and the Northern Ireland co-premiers.[13] The Agreement also allows the Irish Republic's government access, through the British-Irish Intergovernmental Conference, to policy formulation on all matters not, or not yet, devolved to the Northern Ireland Assembly or the NSMC. This continues the arrangements first agreed to in the Anglo-Irish Agreement of 1985.

Second, the Northern Ireland Act, the UK statutory form of the Agreement, provides for the Assembly to seek jurisdiction over *any* reserved matter, where there is cross-community consent (O'Leary 1999, 1647). The Scotland Act or Government of Wales Act contains no similar provision. There is thus an explicit path for Northern Ireland, unlike Scotland and Wales, to extend its autonomy. While the Scottish parliament has control over policing and justice, unlike the Northern Ireland Assembly, the UK government has promised to transfer these powers to Belfast once there is a consensus among Northern Ireland's parties. The original draft of the Northern Ireland Act gave the Assembly revenue-raising powers, but these were taken out at the request of the local parties.

Third, under the Agreement, Westminster has formally conceded that Northern Ireland can secede from the United Kingdom to join a united Ireland, if its people, and the people of the Irish Republic, voting separately, agree to this. Scotland or Wales have no analogous formal right of secession, even if at least one British prime minister, John Major, is on record as saying that the Scots are free to go whenever they want to (Keating, 1996, 242). The words of prime ministers are not the same thing as law.[14]

Fourth, while the basis of Northern Ireland's autonomy in Westminster legislation makes it appear superficially similar to Scotland's, its autonomy, unlike that of Scotland, is also entrenched in an international treaty between the United Kingdom and the Republic of Ireland.[15] Moreover, the UK government, through the Agreement, has explicitly recognized the right of the people of Ireland to self-determination, and the Agreement was ratified not just by a referendum in Northern Ireland but also by a simultaneous referendum in the Irish Republic. There has been no similar explicit recognition of the Scottish people's right to self-determination. The proper understanding of Northern Ireland's Agreement is that the UK government and parliament cannot exercise power in Northern Ireland in a way that is inconsistent with the Agreement without breaking its treaty obligations and denying Irish national self-determination. This means that the relationship between the United Kingdom and Northern Ireland established by the Agreement is, properly speaking, that of a "federacy," a system of autonomy that cannot be unilaterally altered by the center alone. This is different from the arrangements in Scotland and Wales which are based on devolution (O'Leary 1999, 1646–47).[16]

This change was obscured by the actions of the UK government between 2000 and 2002, when it unilaterally suspended Northern Ireland's political institutions on four occasions. This, however, was a breach of the Agreement which the Irish government chose not to challenge because of the need to maintain good working relations with Britain and to avoid dangerously polarizing matters within Northern Ireland. Irish nationalists subsequently insisted, and the British government agreed, that the suspension power be repealed.[17]

These distinctive dimensions of Northern Ireland's autonomy arrangements are there at the behest of Irish nationalists, about 40 percent of Northern Ireland's population. They, unlike their Welsh and Scottish counterparts, see themselves as part of a national community that stretches beyond UK frontiers; hence the insistence on cross-border institutions and on a role for the Irish Republic's government in Northern Ireland. Between 1972 and 1998, even moderate Irish nationalists, represented by the Social Democratic and Labour Party, consistently rejected autonomy arrangements that were internal to the United Kingdom. More radical nationalists, represented by Sinn Fein and the Irish Republican Army (IRA), rejected any link with the United Kingdom and insisted on a British withdrawal and a united Ireland. They eventually compromised, accepting that a united Ireland could not be achieved without the consent of the people of the North and South voting separately, thus making an agreement with unionists possible. As a quid pro quo, republicans demanded the Agreement's provisions on Irish self-determination, and the maximum degree of freedom from British rule. The British government's decision in 2000 to unilaterally suspend the institutions aroused strong opposition from republicans, and, while it did not produce a resumption of armed conflict, the decision helped to prevent the IRA from decommissioning its weapons and Sinn Fein from recognizing Northern Ireland's new police service. It was only when London agreed in 2003 to remove its suspension power that progress became possible.

The academic literature on UK asymmetric autonomy has generally acknowledged the centrality of the cross-border dimensions of Northern Ireland's Agreement, but not so much the distinction between the status of Northern Ireland's autonomy and that of Scotland (or Wales).[18] Both features, however, were important. The first suggests that minorities with national kin on the other side of state frontiers may need to be treated differently from minorities wholly internal to the state. The second suggests that states may have some success extending devolution to minorities that are not seriously or violently alienated from the state. However, if they want to end militant secessionism, or reintegrate territories which have de facto seceded, and are unable to prevail militarily, they may, as in Northern Ireland, have to concede a "federacy."

The UK's new autonomy arrangements have given rise to an additional type of asymmetry, although technically one that could exist even if the powers and status granted to its different regions were perfectly uniform. This is an asymmetry in the design of political institutions across the state. Elections to the Scottish Parliament and Welsh Assembly are conducted on the basis of the "additional member system" of proportional representation (PR-AMS), similar to that used in Germany, rather than the single-member plurality system that is used for elections to the UK parliament. Scotland elects 73 members from single-member constituencies and an additional 56 from eight seven-member regions, while Wales elects 40 members from single-member constituencies and another 20 from four five-member constituencies. Each voter can vote in a single-member constituency and for a party list in the corresponding multimember regional constituency. The system delivers proportionality by privileging parties that are penalized in single-member constituencies by compensating them in the regional ballot.[19] While both electoral systems deliver more proportionality than Westminster's, they are not equally proportional. Scotland's electoral system, with its lower ratio of single-member to multimember seats and its larger number of seats per region, is more proportional than that of Wales.

The executive-formation process of Scotland and Wales is different from Westminster's in both minor and important ways. British government formation, by convention, is formed by the leader of the largest (usually the majority) party, who becomes prime minister and names the cabinet. In Scotland and Wales, executive formation has been codified, with the Scottish Parliament and Welsh Assembly electing their respective first ministers, who then appoint the rest of their executives (Ward 2000, 121–22). More important, while the single member plurality system used in Westminster elections usually produces single-party government, the proportional systems used in Scotland and Wales make coalitions more likely, although both have had single party *minority* governments since 1999. The Westminster electoral system invariably converts electoral minorities into governing "majorities," but majority governments in Scotland and Wales are likely to be based on electoral majorities.[20]

Northern Ireland's different internal institutional arrangements are tailored to its serious divisions. The electoral system used for the Assembly is the single transferable vote version of proportional representation (PR-STV), in eighteen six-member constituencies, resulting in 108 members of the legislative assembly (MLAs). This is a legacy of the 1920 Government of Ireland Act, when STV was picked to bolster the position of the unionist minority in Southern Ireland and the nationalist minority in Northern Ireland, and when it was regarded in the UK as the main alternative to single-member plurality. It has been used in the Irish Republic since 1921 and was used in Northern Ireland between 1921 and 1929, when it was changed to single-member plurality by the Unionist government eager to avoid the fragmentation of the Unionist party's vote (O'Leary and McGarry 1996, 121). PR-STV was "restored" in Northern Ireland by the British government after the abolition of Stormont in 1972 and was used for regional elections in Northern Ireland between 1973 and 1998. The choice of STV over PR-AMS in the Agreement is a result of this history, not, as some have suggested, because it delivers more proportionality.[21]

Northern Ireland's Agreement also mandated an inclusive or power-sharing executive. The government is led by first and deputy first ministers who, in spite of their titles, are co-premiers. Between 1998 and 2007, the decision-making rule for selecting these was a majority of the Assembly plus a concurrent majority of nationalist and unionist MLAs, which effectively meant unionist and nationalist co-premiers. Since 2007, the first minister is the nominee of the largest party from the largest designation ("nationalist," "unionist," or "other") while the deputy first minister is the nominee of the largest party in the second largest designation.[22] The rest of the cabinet is appointed according to the d'Hondt rule, and not by the first and deputy first ministers. This ensures that all parties that meet the quota established by the conjunction of the d'Hondt system and the limited number of ministries are entitled to seats in the executive. The effect, after the resumption of power sharing in March 2007, was that four parties, with 98 of the Assembly's 108 seats, received seats in government. D'Hondt also helps small parties entitled to executive positions to prevent large parties from monopolizing all of the most important portfolios (O'Leary et al. 2005).

The composition rules for Northern Ireland's executive are, therefore, more inclusive than Scotland's or Wales's, while both of the latter are, in turn, more inclusive than the conventions used at Westminster. Northern Ireland's rules are appropriate given the intensity of its divisions. If the Scottish, Welsh, or Westminster rules for executive composition were applied to Northern Ireland, the danger would arise of a minimum-winning coalition comprised exclusively of unionists, or a government that is restricted to nationalists in coalition with small centrist parties ("others"), or a cross-community coalition comprised of moderates. The first two possibilities would be potentially disastrous. Even the third would endanger peace and stability by excluding republicans and hard-line unionists (McGarry and O'Leary 2009b). When an executive of this last type was effectively mandated in the Sunningdale Agreement of 1973, it did nothing to resolve the violent conflict and collapsed after only five months (Wolff 2001). The Northern Ireland executive is different from Scotland's and Wales's in another way, which relates to the relatively deep alienation of Irish nationalists from the crown: its first ministers and executive are nominated by the parties and elected by the Assembly whereas the Scottish and Welsh first ministers are appointed by "Her Majesty" upon nomination by the Scottish parliament and Welsh Assembly. The rest of the Scottish and Welsh executive are appointed by the respective first ministers and serve "at her Majesty's pleasure."[23]

Northern Ireland's deep internal divisions required a number of other institutional arrangements that are missing from Scotland and Wales. The d'Hondt rule is also used for electing the chairmen and deputy chairmen of the Assembly's statutory committees, and for selecting the political representatives of the Policing Board, charged with holding the Police Service of Northern Ireland to account. While measures are passed in the Scottish parliament and Welsh Assembly by simple majority, key legislation in the Northern Ireland Assembly requires either a majority in the Assembly, plus a concurrent majority of nationalists and unionists, or a weighted majority of 60 percent in the Assembly, including at least 40 percent of both nationalists and unionists. In addition the Agreement made provision for a Northern Ireland Human Rights Commission, an Equality Commission, and a Civic Forum, the last to provide civic associations input into the region's governance. There are no analogous institutions in Scotland or Wales.

This asymmetry of intraregional institutional design shows the flexibility of autonomy arrangements: regional institutions can be tailored to cope not just with differential aspirations for autonomy, including aspirations for cross-border links, but also with different degrees of intraregional heterogeneity/division. This latter point provides an effective response to a key criticism of autonomy for nationalities: that it is unfair and results invariably in narrowly based and ethnocentric institutions which abuse minorities within regions (Nordlinger 1972; Wimmer 2003; Dalyell 1977, 293). The only previous UK example of regional political autonomy, Northern Ireland between 1921 and 1972, is often held up as the paradigmatic case of such abuse (Dalyell 1977, 293; Rose 1976).[24] Its experience was used by both British and Irish integrationists to argue that the region was a "failed entity" which should not be given autonomy, but which should be integrated into a centralized British or Irish state. However, the new arrangements in Northern Ireland show that the potential for minority abuse is not inextricably linked to autonomy, but is, rather, contingent on the design of the autonomous region's institutions. The same can be said, of course, for any territorial entity, including states themselves, which are just as likely (or unlikely) as autonomous regions to abuse minorities. In the case of the UK, the institutions of all the autonomous regions, and not just those of Northern Ireland, are more inclusive than the institutions of the center, although those of Northern Ireland are the most inclusive. The UK's asymmetric institutional design has another advantage: the diversity of institutional approaches allows experiments from which other parts of the state can draw lessons, such as on the merits/demerits of proportional representation and coalition government.

Assessing Asymmetry

Debate over asymmetric autonomy in the United Kingdom is usually divided into separate debates about Great Britain and Northern Ireland, reflecting the consensus among academics and politicians that the challenges are different in each case. In both places, critics have argued for a symmetric approach, whether based on centralization or decentralization. During the 1970s, some British critics of devolution to Scotland and Wales argued for a modest degree of symmetric (nonlegislative) devolution based on the English regions plus Scotland and Wales, or the English regions, Wales, and a number of Scottish regions (Crowther-Hunt and Peacock 1973; Dalyell 1977, 299-302). The Conservative Party, which governed the UK in 1979–97, preferred the centralized status quo for Great Britain, although it was prepared, albeit inconsistently, to support autonomy for Northern Ireland. Since devolution, a small number of politicians on the right, and the Campaign for an English Parliament, have argued for far-reaching symmetric decentralization with England as a single region. Politicians on the left, and the Campaign for English Regions, have generally rejected an English parliament, but have argued for symmetry, or greater symmetry, based on English regional assemblies.

For these critics, asymmetric autonomy has various flaws. Centralists and those who support a modest degree of symmetric decentralization worry that asymmetric autonomy, based on the nationality principle, accentuates national divisions and weakens overarching identities, and hence the union. The current arrangements, it is feared, give additional resources to Scottish and Welsh nationalists and augur increasing and polarizing intergovernmental conflict between London and Edinburgh if not between London and Cardiff.[25] Asymmetry is also seen as breaching values of equal citizenship, as it involves giving autonomy, or greater autonomy, to only certain parts of the state. The result is to deny a "voice" to other regions (in England), many of which have social and economic problems that are at least as serious as those of Scotland and Wales (Bogdanor 2003, 223).[26] English nationalists argue that the current arrangements breach notions of *national* equality, as the English are the only nation in the UK which lacks self-government.[27] Several of these critics point to what is an unfair and possibly untreatable consequence of asymmetry, the fact that Scottish (and Northern Irish) MPs in the Westminster parliament can, in principle, decide legislation that affects only England (and Wales) while English MPs have no reciprocal say over such matters in Scotland (and Northern Ireland). In the UK, this problem is known as the "West Lothian question," after the Scottish constituency of Tam Dalyell, an arch-critic of devolution, but it is an issue that also arose during the Irish Home Rule debates, and is relevant to other cases of asymmetric autonomy.

Asymmetry, then, is seen not only as strengthening nationalism in the periphery, but as promoting a variety of grievances in the English core (Crowther-Hunt and Peacock 1973, viii; Bogdanor 2003, 223). A number of critics have argued that these twin consequences will produce instability, followed by breakup, and have published several books to this effect.[28] Not everyone is sorry, with the Scottish Nationalist Party embracing the new arrangements precisely because they share this analysis. One academic critic has added that asymmetry is an affront to democratic accountability, as it has resulted in a "dog's breakfast" of institutions that citizens cannot comprehend.[29]

In Northern Ireland, unionist critics of its Agreement have argued that Northern Ireland should be treated the same as other parts of the United Kingdom. Some call for "integration," understood as a democratized version of "direct rule" from London in which Britain's main parties would contest elections in Northern Ireland, Northern Ireland would have its full (proportionate) complement of MPs at Westminster, and Northern Ireland legislation would be debated in Parliament in the same way as legislation affecting the rest of the UK, rather than being passed by "order in council." Unionist integrationists have also supported symmetric devolution "all round" on the basis of the Scottish model and, particularly, the Welsh model with its more limited autonomy. The Welsh model is considered attractive by unionist critics not just because it involves relatively modest devolution but also because, at least until 2006, administration in Wales was based on a quasi-municipal council or "corporate assembly" model of government, in which there was no cabinet or executive exercising collective responsibility. Wales's administrative officers were heads of Assembly committees and known as "Assembly secretaries" rather than as "ministers," while their leader was the "Assembly First Secretary."[30] The Welsh model had the advantage, from the critics' perspective, of ruling out cabinet-style power sharing with nationalists, and particularly with republicans, and of making administrative decisions subject to approval of the Assembly with its unionist majority.[31] As recently as 2004, the Democratic Unionist Party (DUP) proposed a "corporate assembly" model as a preferred alternative to "mandatory" power sharing with Sinn Fein (DUP 2004).

Unionist critics of the Agreement believe that a sui generis, or asymmetric, treatment of Northern Ireland is likely to destabilize the union, as it encourages Irish nationalists to believe that a united Ireland is possible. The Agreement is seen as a prize won by militant republicans and conceded by a UK government eager to avoid expensive attacks on Great Britain (Kennedy 1999). Such appeasement, it is argued, will lead to new and increased militancy, perhaps after a short respite. Unionist and other critics have spoken of a flawed or even a "failed" peace process (Peatling 2004). They have opposed the Agreement's focus on accommodating two national communities as divisive, and criticized both the Agreement's North-South institutions and its inclusive provisions for executive power sharing within Northern Ireland. The executive arrangements are seen as particularly unworkable as they bring together in the same government strong supporters and strong opponents of the union (Roche 2000; McCartney 2000).[32] It is feared that the resulting instability will be exploited by nationalists, while unionists prepared to share power are seen as complicit in the union's destruction.

The main problem with these criticisms of the UK's recently adopted asymmetric institutions is that the symmetric alternatives are likely to be even more problematic. In Great Britain, the Scots are strongly supportive of substantive autonomy. The Conservative Party, the only political party that opposed devolution during the 1997 UK election, failed to win a single seat in Scotland, and has since swung behind the new Scottish institutions in an attempt to retain its deposits in Scottish elections. Had the centralized and more symmetric status quo been maintained with respect to Scotland it is unlikely to have produced stability or strengthened the union.[33] It is more likely to have strengthened Scottish nationalists. It should be recalled, after all, that when the UK government refused to concede Home Rule to Ireland in the face of Irish public opinion, support shifted from home rulers to secessionists. The latter were able to mobilize their supporters without the benefit of autonomous institutions. When the Westminster election of 1918 produced a large majority of Irish MPs in favor of independence, they simply withdrew to form a separate parliament, and seceded three years later.[34]

Nor is symmetric *decentralization* a satisfactory answer for Great Britain. The Scots are more strongly supportive of autonomy than the Welsh, and both nationalities are much more autonomist than the English. Any conceivable model of symmetric decentralization would likely involve less autonomy than the Scots or the Welsh would be willing to accept, but more than the English want. Symmetric decentralization involving England as a single unit would be profoundly problematic for additional reasons already noted in this chapter, while symmetric decentralization involving the English regions would imply equating communities that do not regard themselves as nations with those that do. The comparative evidence from elsewhere, including Canada and Spain, suggests that the nationalities would balk at such equivalence. Even if some English regions were to seek their own assemblies, it is unlikely in any foreseeable scenario they all will do so, or that any will seek the same degree of autonomy as Scotland or Wales. Any future for Great Britain that reflects bottom-up sentiment is likely to be asymmetric.

This does not mean that asymmetry will produce stability or unity, although it is arguably more likely to do so than symmetry, given that it is more clearly in line with people's wishes.[35] Critics of the new arrangements are correct to argue that devolution gives resources to nationalists that they lacked previously. Scotland already had its own boundaries, flag, traditions, and sports teams, but it now also has its own government and parliament. This is likely to promote a greater focus on Scottish issues, and a "federalization" of British parties, civic associations, and interest groups. The use of PR in regional elections in Scotland has helped the Scottish National Party (SNP), which had low and dispersed levels of support, to win seats and make its voice heard. Regional elections have also, arguably, helped the SNP increase its support, as its program seems more relevant in Scottish than UK-wide elections.[36] It is possible that the stability that has existed during the first decade of devolution is a result not of devolution, or not just of devolution, but of the fact that the British Labour Party has dominated the UK government and the executives in Scotland and Wales. This has meant that intergovernmental relations have been a relatively benign intraparty affair. The UK government has generally had little difficulty cooperating with its peripheral counterparts in these circumstances, such as when dealing with the European Union or public finances. This, however, may represent a lull before the storm. Labour's hegemony in the periphery ended in 2007 when Scotland elected a SNP minority government. There is also the possibility of a Conservative government at Westminster in which, as in 1979–97, the Scots and Welsh will be weakly represented. It is unlikely that intergovernmental relations will be as amicable in the future as they were during devolution's first decade.

On the other hand, asymmetric devolution does not point inexorably to breakup. The autonomous institutions also constrain the SNP. PR in regional elections means that it is very difficult for the SNP to become a majority government, with control of the legislative agenda, including the holding of a referendum on secession and the shaping of the referendum question.[37] PR does not prevent the SNP from persuading a potential coalition partner to support its agenda, but it does raise the bar for the success of secession, and does so, moreover, without unfairness, unlike some of the disproportional electoral systems that are sometimes recommended by those for whom the priority is to hold states together (e.g., Horowitz 1991). The resources of government give the SNP the opportunity to promote secession, but there are also pressures on a governing party to make current arrangements work if it wishes to secure reelection, and this can undercut support for radical change.[38] While increased intergovernmental conflict is to be expected, this is something that occurs elsewhere without producing breakup. The evidence from other comparable Western democracies, including Canada (Quebec), Spain (Basque country, Catalunya), Finland (Aaland Islands) and Italy (South Tyrol), indicates that they have weathered intergovernmental conflict without falling apart, although Canada came close to doing so in 1995. These states have survived intact, in spite of having different parties in power at different levels, including nationalist parties at the regional level and unionist parties at the central or federal level. One reason for the success of autonomy in these cases is that the states involved are reasonably prosperous democracies, in which their minorities have nested identities; they identify with their regions and the state, and this in turn may be linked to the state's preparedness to concede genuine autonomy before relations have polarized. They are not analogous to the failed federations that have broken up in the communist and post-colonial world, the experience of which appears to overly influence the analysis of critics of autonomy (See McGarry and O'Leary 2005).

One way to reduce the danger of future instability is to address the West Lothian question. While survey data shows that the English are supportive of autonomy for Scotland and Wales, and are not concerned about the subsidization of those regions, there is some latent concern about the prospect of Scottish MPs deciding laws that affect only England (Curtice 2006, 129–30).[39] Relatedly, there is evidence—as when there was criticism of Tony Blair's appointment of John Reid, a Scottish MP, as UK minister for health in 2003—that the English are not keen on Scottish ministers running essentially English departments (BBC 2003).

Two possible answers to the West Lothian question can be dismissed at the outset, on the grounds that they are unwanted and unfair, respectively. The unwanted answer is symmetry, whether centralized or decentralized. The unfair answer is to *underrepresent* Scotland (or Northern Ireland) in the UK parliament on the grounds that this parliament is less relevant to them. The difficulty with underrepresenting Scotland is that the Scots (and Northern Irish) are entitled to be fully, that is, proportionately, represented when the UK parliament is discussing common matters. Reducing Scotland's representation on such matters would make it less likely that the central parliament would take Scotland's interests into account, and less likely that the Scots would identify with the UK.[40]

The most sensible answer to the West Lothian question is what has been called the "in and out" principle. Here, the asymmetrically autonomous region continues to be equitably represented in the common legislature, but its representatives vote only on common matters, abstaining on issues that are in the competence of their regional government, as Scottish nationalist MPs currently do (Keating 2001, 132). Asking Scottish MPs to abstain on English business would remove an English grievance without creating a Scottish one, as Scottish opinion is strongly supportive of such a step. Indeed the Scots in some polls are more likely to support barring Scottish MPs from English matters than the English themselves (Hazell 2006a, 14, 21, n. 11). Suggestions of this sort are usually objected to on the basis that it is difficult to separate bills in this way, or that bills involving expenditure outside the autonomous region necessarily have implications for expenditures within it (see Russell and Lodge 2006, 88; Bogdanor 2007). However, these are largely technical drafting and budgetary matters rather than insuperable obstacles. An apparently more profound criticism is that the "in and out" practice is difficult to reconcile with core parliamentary conventions of responsible and accountable government, whereby the executive must command a majority in the legislature and preside over a coherent legislative program. The concern here is that a government, comprised in the normal Westminster way from a minimum winning majority, could lose this majority when dealing with noncommon matters (matters that apply only to that part of the state outside the autonomous region). This need only pose a danger of government resignation, however, if the government insists on making these matters of confidence. The problem would not arise if the government simply refrained from imposing unpopular measures on nonautonomous regions—if it adopted a convention of winning majority support in nonautonomous regions on matters that were exclusive to such regions.

This leaves delicate questions relating to the composition of the UK government. The extension of the "in and out" principle to the United Kingdom's executive branch suggests that members of the common legislature from the asymmetrically autonomous region should, ordinarily, be given ministerial responsibility only for common matters. It is provocative and hardly necessary to appoint a Scottish MP as a minister of health or education in the UK government, when these portfolios are not concerned with Scotland. As the prime minister, and several other ministers, preside over both common and English- (and Wales-) only matters, a Scot can hardly be fairly ruled out of those positions; to do so would almost certainly guarantee the state's breakup.

Another way to stabilize the United Kingdom's new asymmetric arrangements would be to introduce a proportional electoral system for UK-wide elections that would reduce the convergence of nationality and party representation. Under the current system of single-member plurality, there is a reasonable prospect of the election of a Conservative government at the center that does not have representation, or much representation, in Scotland. Such a government is likely to be seen, and perhaps to behave, like an English government, with centrifugal effects. However, the Conservative Party's weakness in Scotland, like its strength in England, is exaggerated by single-member plurality.[41] PR at the UK level would reduce the Conservative Party's hold on English seats, while enhancing its representation in Scotland. Both effects would reduce its image as an "English" party. PR would additionally make it more difficult for the SNP to dominate Scotland's representation at Westminster than under current electoral arrangements. The SNP would be unable to emulate the Bloc Québecois, which has dominated Quebec's representation in Canada's federal parliament with only a plurality of the vote. PR would also almost certainly eliminate the prospect of one-party government at Westminster, and give rise to coalitions, based on a much broader level of support than one-party governments usually have. A consensual government of this type would be more like those within the United Kingdom's autonomous regions and more appropriate for the governance of a plurinational state.

In Northern Ireland, there is no evidence that the nationalist community, about 40 percent of the population, could be brought to embrace symmetric institutional arrangements. Even moderate, or "constitutional," nationalists in the Social Democratic and Labour Party (SDLP) have consistently rejected integration into the United Kingdom. A reasonable facsimile of this, direct rule from London, was the status quo between 1972 and 1998, and existed alongside violent conflict that cost more than 3,000 lives. The SDLP has also consistently rejected symmetric decentralization on the Scottish or Welsh models, arguing instead for maximum devolution combined with all-Ireland institutions. It has always insisted on executive power sharing, and during negotiations on the Agreement, pressed for an inclusive form of power sharing that would give seats to the republicans of Sinn Fein. This followed from the moderates' belief, based on the Sunningdale fiasco of 1974 and Sinn Fein's emergence as an electoral force, that an Agreement without republicans would be unstable, and not in the interests of nationalists, as it would weaken their presence in the executive. As a result, the only agreement possible in 1998, from the perspective of nationalists, was an asymmetric one, that included the central institutional features of the Agreement.

Contrary to the Agreement's critics, it has ushered in a palpably successful peace process. According to the Police Service of Northern Ireland, lethal political violence dropped from 509 killed in the nine years before the Agreement (1989–97) to 134 in the nine years after (1998–2006), a decline of three quarters (PSNI 2007). While 105 members of the security forces were killed in the earlier period, only five have been killed since, two of these in 1998. Since January 2003 there have been no civilian deaths from intercommunity violence.[42]

The war between the IRA and the British state is now over. The IRA in 2005 destroyed its arsenal and "disbanded its operational structures." Defections to dissident republican paramilitary organizations have been minimal. The recent resumption of power sharing in March 2007 was followed by statements from both major loyalist paramilitary organizations, that they had placed their weapons "beyond reach" (*Independent* 2007). The Agreement has resulted in demilitarization by the British Army—its return to barracks and a normal peacetime garrison (McKittrick 2007)—and in the construction of a new police service, more widely accepted than before. These facts hardly illustrate the flawed or failed peace process described by the Agreement's critics.[43]

Political stability has been less in evidence. The Agreement's institutions took nineteen months to establish and were suspended on four occasions after 2000. Post-Agreement elections have also resulted in a movement in electoral support from the moderate parties in each bloc toward radical parties, a trend described by the Agreement's critics as a "victory of the extremes" (Patterson 2005). As McGarry and O'Leary have shown, however, much of the political instability that marred progress after 2000 was caused by security-related controversies over demilitarization, decommissioning of paramilitary weapons, and policing reform, rather than by flaws in the design of the Agreement's political institutions (McGarry and O'Leary 2008). The movement of support to radical parties was also not as damaging as the critics alleged, as it took place alongside a clear moderation of the radical parties and an increased willingness on the part of each community to compromise.[44] These facts explain why the two radical parties were able, with reasonable enthusiasm, to reach an agreement on power sharing in early 2007, and why, in the Northern Ireland Assembly elections of March 2007, parties committed to power sharing won every seat and 93 percent of the vote. By contrast, the only party that unequivocally opposed the Agreement, the United Kingdom Unionist Party, which is closely associated with the criticisms on the Agreement outlined in this chapter, received a paltry 1.5 percent. These developments came as a surprise to the Agreement's critics.[45]

Like devolution to Scotland, Northern Ireland's new power-sharing deal may not succeed over the long term. However, it has advantages that its predecessors lacked. The deal has significant popular support. The security issues that destabilized the institutions between 1998 and 2007 have now largely been dealt with.[46] Both Sinn Fein and the DUP remain reasonably united behind the pact, although the latter has a new leader, Peter Robinson, who is less visibly enthusiastic than his predecessor, Ian

Paisley. Even if the DUP-Sinn Fein pact does not survive, the Agreement has a default option. The failure of power sharing will result in increased cooperation between the London and Dublin governments through the British-Irish Intergovernmental Conference, possibly combined with increased responsibilities for larger, more efficient local governments, particularly those prepared to accept power sharing. London and Dublin will make this default clear should the DUP, the newest convert to inclusive power sharing, consider collapsing the new accord. Even if future stability is not guaranteed, one of the Agreement's critics has pointed out that the region is currently "at its most stable . . . in a generation" (Shirlow 2007).

In sum, it can be argued that asymmetry has delivered institutions that have brought peace and consensus government to Northern Ireland, while accommodating the aspiration of the Scots and Welsh for autonomy. The new institutions are also broadly in line with what the English want, and adjustments can be made to accommodate concerns relating to the West Lothian question. While the new institutions do not guarantee stability or unity, the onus is on supporters of symmetry to show that their alternatives would do better.

Conclusion

The comparative utility of the UK experience with asymmetric autonomy may be doubted. The United Kingdom is, after all, a prosperous, liberal, and mature democracy, quite different from many of the states covered in this volume. However, its experience is broadly relevant in a number of respects. First, the UK is similar to several of these other states in that it has an asymmetric political sociology. The dominant national community, the English, do not seek autonomy and is largely content to be governed from the center, but there are nationalities that seek different degrees of autonomy. This is a pattern that exists elsewhere, in states like Moldova, Georgia, and Sri Lanka. In none of these states are symmetric prescriptions likely to be fruitful, whether based on centralization or decentralization. As in the UK, centralization is unlikely to satisfy the nationalities, while symmetric decentralization is unlikely to be preferred by the dominant nation. The UK experience suggests that asymmetry is the only way to give each of the state's communities broadly what they want.

Second, the United Kingdom has confronted a militant secessionist movement in Northern Ireland, which, in the view of British army commanders, could not be defeated militarily. The conflict has been ended, with no immediate prospect of resumption, by an Agreement tailored precisely to the needs of the region, rather than by "one size fits all" arrangements applied throughout the UK. The Agreement won the support of Irish nationalists, including militant Irish republicans, because it involved substantive, guaranteed autonomy, as well as cross-border links, internal power sharing, demilitarization, and security-sector reforms. A similar tailored approach, involving substantive and guaranteed autonomy, is likely to be needed in other secessionist struggles, including the de facto secessionist regions of Abkhazia, South Ossetia, Tamil Eelam, Transdniestria, and Nagorno Karabakh.

Third, the challenges facing the UK include those of a region, Northern Ireland, that has its own serious internal divisions, comparable to several other regions that are candidates for autonomy, including Tamil Eelam, Darfur, and Mindanao. Here, the UK experience offers lessons on both inappropriate and appropriate prescriptions. From 1921 to 1972, the UK allowed Northern Ireland to be governed under the same majoritarian institutions that were used at the central level to govern the rest of the state. This insistence on institutional (executive) symmetry across the UK had ultimately disastrous consequences, including, by the late 1960s, the complete alienation of the region's minority, the abolition of the regional government, and a low-level insurgency that lasted for a quarter of a century. This experience is often used, unfairly, to support the argument that autonomy arrangements in heterogeneous regions are inevitably unstable and unfair to local minorities, and that the proper alternative is centralization. Centralization, however, was not a realistic option for Northern Ireland, and has not worked in the other regions either. In the Good Friday Agreement, the UK government agreed, by contrast, to autonomy linked to institutions tailored to the needs of a divided region, including consociational power sharing and other measures for minority protection. These institutions have played an important role in bringing peace. In the case of internally divided regions, the UK experience suggests that autonomy is not equivalent to oppression of regional minorities, as long as it is remembered that the design of the region's institutions of government is as vital as autonomy itself.

On the other hand, the UK willingness to support asymmetry does not mean that the other states discussed in this volume will be similarly forthcoming. There are a number of factors that distinguish the UK. Its preparedness to accept asymmetric autonomy has been partly shaped by its history as a *union* state, which involved a long tradition of asymmetric arrangements within a centralized order. Its situation may be more analogous, therefore, to other union states, such as Spain, than to states with a Jacobin unitary tradition, including Turkey and Moldova. The latter are more likely to resist asymmetric autonomy, or indeed any kind of autonomy for nationalities.

The UK willingness to embrace asymmetric autonomy can partly be explained by the dominance of England and by its independent history and identity. England's strong sense of identity means that the English do not fear the breaking up of the state in the way that Castilians do, or as do the English speakers in what has been called the "rest of Canada." A lack of concern about secession helps to explain the state's preparedness to facilitate both asymmetry and autonomy.

The UK willingness to accommodate its minorities may also have been facilitated by the fact that it exists in a benign neighborhood, one which is tightly integrated into prestigious supranational organizations, like the European Union (EU) and the North Atlantic Treaty Organization (NATO). As an independent Scotland would be likely to join the EU and NATO, England would not be shut out of its current economic markets or faced by a military threat on its frontier. This makes secession, and hence autonomy, less threatening than it would otherwise be. Autonomy for the Celtic parts of the UK is also unthreatening because none of these regions is the satellite of, or aspires to join, a threatening neighbor.

These various factors make the UK situation unlike several of the cases where asymmetric autonomy is currently being mooted. Moldova, Georgia, Cyprus, and Sri Lanka either do not have union-state traditions or their dominant peoples do not have separate histories and identities. They all exist in threatening neighborhoods, where autonomy for their nationalities is usually seen as strengthening the position of neighboring enemy states. This helps to account for the protracted stalemate in each of these states. Even if asymmetric autonomy makes sense for each of them, sense may not prevail.

Notes

I thank the Social Science and Humanities Research Council of Canada for research funding. I would also like to thank Margaret Moore, Brendan O'Leary and Michael Keating for their helpful comments on an earlier draft of this chapter, and Mira Bachvarova for assisting with proofreading.

1. The Greater London Authority has responsibility for strategic policy coordination in transport, economic development, policing, and fire services. Outside these responsibilities, it is able only to define policy goals, which it must leave to London's various local authorities to implement.

2. Asked in 2003, "How much do you trust the UK government to work in the best long-term interest of England/Scotland/Wales," the numbers of English, Scots, and Welsh who selected "just about always" and "most of the time" were 53 percent, 21 percent, and 22 percent respectively (Curtice 2006, 133). Curtice did not ask Northern Ireland's nationalists what they thought of the UK government, but we can safely assume that their level of trust would be significantly lower that that of the Scottish or Welsh.

3. As Elkins and Sides show in a global study, majority communities are significantly more likely to identify with the state than minorities, and less likely to identify with their ethnic community (Elkins and Sides 2007, 697–98). For evidence that the English are more likely than the Scots or Welsh to prefer a British national identity, see Curtice 2006, 131–33.

4. Active support is limited to obscure organizations like the Campaign for an English Parliament, described by *The Guardian* as a "little-known group with a website, an address in Norfolk and a few romantic supporters led by an Anglo-Saxon bookseller, and to a few Tory backwoodsmen" (*Guardian* 1999).

5. As a report on devolution put it, "No significant group—whether demarcated by age, gender, social class, political affiliation, or local authority area, voted in favour" (ERSC 2006, 6).

6. Indeed, the government's backing of English regional assemblies offers support for what critics of autonomy wrongly hold to be generally true: that autonomous institutions are based on elite preferences rather than genuinely popular and deep-rooted sentiment.

7. Hazell, who supports English regional assemblies, rejects a federation in which England is a single unit, writing that "No federation can operate successfully where one of the units is so dominant" (Hazell 2006b, 224).

8. These have been identified by the Scottish parliament as including health, except for health services that have been reserved to Westminster, local government, housing, education and training, transport, law and order, sport, farming, fishing, forestry, the arts, the countryside, and economic development (cited in Ward 2000, 126).

9. Survey data from 1998 to 2003 shows that when Scottish voters were offered the option of independence, no devolution or a Scottish parliament (devolution), a consistent majority opted for a Scottish parliament. Support for Scottish independence ranged from 26 to 30 percent, while support for a Scottish parliament ranged from 52 to 60 percent (see ERSC 2006).

10. This distinction was used originally in the 1920 Government of Ireland Act. Reserved matters may be subsequently transferred.

11. Northern Ireland's parliament sat in Belfast in 1920–30 and at Stormont in 1930–72.

12. As a British government "green paper" put it, "It will be seen from the submissions of some of the parties that there is a view that any new legislature should not be called a Parliament. It is argued that the title and the adoption of elaborate Westminster procedures have not only been out of proportion to the real functions independently performed and to the size of population covered by them, so that these arrangements have led to what may be described as 'overgovernment,' but also have promoted a false view of 'Stormont sovereignty' which has been positively harmful" (Northern Ireland Office 1972).

13. It was agreed that it should meet in plenary twice a year, and in smaller groups to discuss specific sectors (say, agriculture or education) on a "regular and frequent basis." In addition, the Agreement provided for a number of cross-border or all-island "implementation" bodies. These eventually turned out to be six in number, and they were given the task of cooperating over inland waterways, food safety, trade and business development, special EU programs, the Irish language and Ulster Scots dialect, and aquaculture and marine matters.

14. The distinction is denied by one leading constitutional authority. Vernon Bogdanor writes: "Thus in both Northern Ireland and Scotland, it has come to be accepted that their constitutional status depends not only upon the decisions

of a supposedly sovereign parliament at Westminster but upon the wishes of their people" (Bogdanor 2003, 239). Bogdanor's view relies on collapsing the difference between explicit legal fact and convention. My colleague, Michael Keating, shares Bogdanor's view, and argues that convention (the prime minister's view regarding Scotland) is the same as law in the UK system. He believes, in fact, that Scotland's right of self-determination is more extensive than Northern Ireland's, because the latter stretches only to the right to join a united Ireland (personal communication).

15. Agreement between the government of the United Kingdom of Great Britain and Northern Ireland and the government of Ireland, available at British-Irish Council Web site, www1.british-irishcouncil.org/welcome/text.htm (accessed 15 September 2008).

16. For federacy and how it differs from "devolution," see McGarry and O'Leary 2009a.

17. McGarry and O'Leary have argued that the UK actions mean that such a repeal would be inadequate, as there is little to stop the UK government from behaving in a similar way in the future. For the Agreement to be fully implemented, it would be desirable to entrench it in a joint and justiciable protocol to a treaty of the EU. This is the sole obvious way in which it could be constitutionalized in the otherwise constitution-free UK system. This proposal would mean that a decision by Ireland or Britain unilaterally to suspend the institutions would be regarded as a breach of the treaty by the appropriate court (McGarry and O'Leary 2004, 219).

18. For an exception, see McLean and McMillan 2005, 9, 241. British scholars often point out that it is difficult to imagine circumstances, beyond those of a political emergency, in which the UK parliament would decide unilaterally to reduce, suspend, or rescind Scotland's or Wales's self-government, both of which have been ratified in popular referendums (Bogdanor 2003, 225–28). Indeed, one could get the impression from standard accounts of UK devolution, such as Bogdanor's, that Northern Ireland is the only part of the United Kingdom where Westminster is entitled to routinely exercise powers of unilateral intervention.

19. A party's regional vote total is divided by the number of single-member constituency seats its members won in the region, plus one. The party with the highest vote total then elects one "additional member," and its divisor is increased by one. The process is repeated with the next regional seat going to the party with the highest total. This is the same d'Hondt system that is used to allocate ministries in the Northern Ireland executive.

20. Scotland was governed by a Labour-Liberal Democrat coalition in 1999–2007, and has been governed by a SNP minority government since. Wales was governed by a Labour minority executive from 1999, a Labour-Liberal Democrat coalition in 2000–2003, a Labour government (with half the Assembly seats) in 2003–7, and a Labour-Plaid Cymru coalition since.

21. Jeffery and Wincott 2006, 7) write that PR-STV was adopted in Northern Ireland, as opposed to the PR-AMS system used in Scotland and Wales, to "produce the proportionality of electoral outcomes felt to be necessary for the legitimacy of government in a society deeply-divided between . . . nationalist and unionist communities." The problem with this is that PR-STV, ceteris paribus, is no more proportional than PR-AMS. PR-STV does have an advantage over PR-AMS in a divided society, in that it creates electoral incentives for political moderation by allowing for the possibility of cross-bloc voting during lower-preference votes, but there is no evidence that these advantages informed its selection.

22. St. Andrew's Agreement, Annex A, para. 9, North Ireland Office Web site, http://www.nio.gov.uk/st_andrews_agreement.pdf (accessed 15 September 2008). This revision was chosen to allow the Democratic Unionist Party to take the position of first minister without having to vote for Sinn Fein's nominee as deputy first minister. The wording also allowed for the possibility of a future first minister or deputy first minister being selected from the "others," something which was virtually impossible under the original selection rules.

23. See Northern Ireland Act 1998, secs. 16–21; Scotland Act 1998, secs. 44–47; and Government of Wales Act 2006, secs. 46–48.

24. Dalyell used the example of Northern Ireland between 1921 and 1972 to suggest that all parochial regional governments, including any future government based on Scotland, were likely to be illiberal in nature.

25. For a general comparative account of how autonomy strengthens minority nationalism by giving it new resources, see Roeder 2007.

26. Bogdanor warned that resentment in the English regions would lead them, particularly once devolution was up and running, to demand their own assemblies, with the northeast, seeking "an assembly which could compete with the Scottish parliament in bidding for funds from central government." Also see the comments by Hazel and Jeffery at BBC News Web site, http://news.bbc.co.uk/2/hi/uk_news/politics/7093198.stm (accessed 15 September 2008).

27. See Campaign for an English Parliament Web site, www.thecep.org.uk/wordpress (accessed 1 September 2008).

28. See Dalyell 1977. For similar arguments that Britain was doomed, see Marr 2000; Nairn 2000; Hitchens 1999 and Redwood 1999.

29. Alan Ward described the asymmetrical nature of the new arrangements as resulting in a bewilderingly complex "dog's breakfast" that was "incomprehensible to most citizens" and that would weaken the UK. By contrast, he argued, a symmetrical package of decentralization, either a "UK federation, or home rule all round," would "do a great deal to cement the regions into the union permanently" (Ward 2000, 135–36).

30. Government of Wales Act 1998, sec. 53.

31. As recently as 2003, the Democratic Unionist Party, Northern Ireland's largest party, expressed a preference for Welsh-style committee government over the d'Hondt form of power sharing in Northern Ireland's Agreement (see DUP 2004).

32. These arguments are closely related to the allegedly nonpartisan account of Rick Wilford and Robin Wilson, both of whom also believe that the Agreement's focus on binationalism is divisive, and that inclusive power sharing is unworkable (Wilford and Wilson 2006).

33. Matters would probably be even worse if the centralized status quo ante was reintroduced. It is one thing to deny autonomy, and an arguably even more serious matter to rescind it.

34. For a general argument that autonomy promotes breakup but centralized government does not, see Roeder 2007.

35. Norman Davies, dean of British historians, argued several years before devolution was implemented that the Union between England and Scotland would not survive to its tercentenary in 2007 (Davies 1999, 1053). Writing again after devolution, Davies thought that it would extend Britain's existence, albeit not for long (1053).

36. In every election to the Scottish parliament, the SNP has done better, and

in the 1999 and 2007 elections significantly better, than in the closest (immediately preceding) Westminster election. In the 1999 Scottish elections, the SNP won 28.7 percent of the constituency vote, compared to 21.94 percent in the 1997 UK elections. In the 2003 Scottish elections it won 23.77 percent compared to 20.1 percent in the 2001 UK elections. In the 2007 Scottish elections, it won 32.9 percent compared to 17.6 percent in the UK elections of 2005.

37. In the UK government's view holding a referendum on secession is beyond the powers of the Scottish parliament, but it would be difficult in practice for Westminster to prevent one.

38. Witness the dilemma of the Parti Québecois. Its success in promoting the French language while in government has arguably helped, paradoxically, to undercut support for secession by making Canada work.

39. In 1997, 23 and 25 percent of the English were against devolution to Scotland and Wales, respectively; by 2003 these figures had dropped 10 points to 13 percent and 15 percent (Curtice 2006, 130). What little support there is for English regional assemblies appears to be directed against London more than against Scotland and Wales. On the other hand, in 2000–2003, 57–64 percent of the English agreed or strongly agreed that Scottish MPs should not be allowed to vote on laws affecting only England (Curtice 2006, 123, 127; Hazell 2006b, 222–23).

40. Gladstone's first Irish Home Rule Bill had proposed that *no* Irish MP be allowed to sit in Westminster, even though Westminster would still have taxed Ireland, and had responsibility for foreign, defence, monetary policy, and so on. The proposal was intended to get the Irish out of Westminster, a key appeal for wavering Liberals, but it was nonetheless an unsustainable idea that would likely have given way quickly to dominion status, which is likely why many Irish home rulers supported it.

41. Similarly, SMP for UK elections also increases the prospects of Scottish nationalists dominating Scotland's representation in the UK parliament. The SNP could win a sizable majority of Scottish seats with a mere plurality of the vote, in much the same way that the Bloc Québecois has with respect to Quebec's seats in the Canadian parliament. An alleged virtue of SMP is that it produces broad-based parties throughout the state that divide on programmatic issues, but when party support is territorially concentrated, as in the UK, it can exacerbate centrifugal tendencies.

42. If data are taken from a longer time frame, the twelve years before and after the peace process began in 1994, the decline in violence is even more noteworthy: 909 people were killed between 1983 and 1994, but only 179 since 1994 (Police Service of Northern Ireland 2007).

43. There has also been a "peace dividend." A U.S. newspaper reported that Belfast's city center was "a showcase of prosperity" (*USA Today* 2007).

44. This argument is explained at length in McGarry and O'Leary 2008. Also see Mitchell, Evans, and O'Leary, forthcoming.

45. Three weeks before the DUP-Sinn Fein Pact, Conor Cruise O'Brien wrote that a deal was "not on," and "never was on" (O'Brien 2007). Kevin Myers wrote two days after the DUP-Sinn Fein Pact was announced that there was as much chance of the two parties resuming power sharing on the designated date of 8 May as of "Dana [the diminutive Irish female singer] becoming heavyweight wrestling champion of the world" (Myers 2007).

46. The last remaining significant obstacle is the transfer of policing and jus-

tice powers to the Northern Ireland Assembly, something on which nationalists and republicans insist.

References

BBC. 2003. Confusion reigns over cabinet shake-up. 13 June.

Bogdanor, V. 2007. Tory plan for an English Parliament will wreck the Union. *Guardian*, 4 November.

———. 2003. Asymmetric devolution: Toward a quasi-federal constitution? In *Developments in British politics*, ed. P. Dunleavy, A. Gamble, R. Heffernan, and G. Peele. London: Palgrave Macmillan. 222–41.

———. 1999. *Devolution in the United Kingdom.* Oxford: Oxford University Press.

Colley, L. 1992. *Britons: Forging the nation, 1707–1837.* New Haven, Conn.: Yale University Press.

Crowther-Hunt, L., and A. Peacock. 1973. *Memorandum of dissent by Lord Crowther-Hunt and Professor A. T. Peacock.* Kilbrandon Commission, *Report of the Royal Commission on the Constitution, 1969–73*, vol. 2. London: HMSO.

Curtice, J. 2006. What the people say, if anything. In *The English Question*, ed. R. Hazell. Manchester: Manchester University Press. 119–41.

Dalyell, T. 1977. *Devolution: The end of Britain?* London: Jonathan Cape.

Davies, N. 1999. *The Isles: A history.* New York: Oxford University Press.

Democratic Unionist Party (DUP). 2004. Devolution now: The DUP's concept for devolution. Paper presented to Prime Minister Tony Blair, 5 February. http://www.dup.org.uk.

Economic and Social Research Council (ERSC). 2006. *Devolution and Constitutional Change: A research programme of the Economic and Social Research Council.* Final Report, March. http://www.devolution.ac.uk/final_report.htm (accessed 15 September 2008).

Elkins, Z., and J. Sides. 2007. Can institutions build unity in multiethnic states? *American Political Science Review* 101, 4: 693–708.

Fukuyama, F. 2000. Don't do it Brittannia. *Prospect* 52.

The Guardian. 1999. Obscure campaigners for an English parliament unnerved by Conservative drum beating. 16 July.

Hadfield, B. 1989. *The Constitution of Northern Ireland.* Belfast: SLS Legal Publications.

Hale, H. 2004. Divided we stand: Institutional sources of ethnofederal state survival and collapse. *World Politics* 56, 2: 165–93.

Hazell, R. 2006a. Introduction: What is the English Question? In *The English Question*, ed. R. Hazell. Manchester: Manchester University Press. 1–23.

———. 2006b. Conclusion: What are the answers to the English Question? In *The English Question*, ed. R. Hazell. Manchester: Manchester University Press. 220-41.

Hitchens, P. 1999. *The abolition of Britain.* London: Quartet Books.

Horowitz, D. L. 2001. The Agreement: Clear, consociational and risky. In *Northern Ireland and the divided world: Post-Agreement Northern Ireland in comparative perspective*, ed. J. McGarry. Oxford: Oxford University Press: 89–108.

———. 1991. *A democratic South Africa? Constitutional engineering in a divided society.* Berkeley: University of California Press.

The Independent. 2007. UVF "deactivates" and agrees to put weapons "beyond reach." 4 May.

Jeffery, C., and D. Wincott. 2006. Devolution in the United Kingdom: Statehood and citizenship in transition. *Publius* 36, 1: 3–18.

Keating, M. 2006. From functional to political regionalism: England in comparative perspective. In *The English Question*, ed. R. Hazell. Manchester: Manchester University Press. 142–57.

———. 2001. *Plurinational democracy: Stateless nations in a post-sovereignty era.* Oxford: Oxford University Press.

———. 1996. *Nations against the state: The new politics of nationalism in Quebec, Catalonia and Scotland.* London: Macmillan.

Kennedy, D. 1999. Dash for agreement: Temporary accommodation or lasting settlement? *Fordham International Law Journal* 4, 22: 1440–46.

Kilbrandon Commission. 1973. *Report of the Royal Commission on the Constitution, 1969–73.* 2 vols. London: HMSO.

Marr, A. 2000. *The day Britain died.* London: Profile.

McCartney, R. 2000. Devolution is a sham. *The Observer*, 20 February.

McGarry, J. 2004. The politics of policing reform in Northern Ireland. In *The Northern Ireland Conflict: Consociational engagements*, ed. J. McGarry and B. O'Leary. New York: Oxford University Press: 371–402.

McGarry, J., and B. O'Leary. 2009a. Territorial pluralism: Its forms, flaws and virtues. In *Plurinational federalism and federations*, ed. F. Requejo. Barcelona: Institut d'Estudis Autonomics.

———. 2009b. Power-shared after death of thousands. In *Consociational theory: McGarry and O'Leary and the Northern Ireland conflict*, ed. R. Taylor. London: Routledge.

———. 2005. Federation as a method of ethnic conflict regulation. In *From power-sharing to democracy: Post-conflict institutions in ethnically divided societies*, ed. S. Noel. Montreal: McGill-Queen's University Press. 263–96.

———. 2004. Stabilising Northern Ireland's Agreement. *Political Quarterly* 3, 75: 213–25.

McKittrick, D. 2007. Northern Ireland: The longest tour of duty is over. *Independent*, 4 August.

McLean, I., and A. McMillan. 2005. *State of the union: Unionism and the alternatives in the United Kingdom since 1707.* Oxford: Oxford University Press.

Mitchell, P., G. Evans, and B. O'Leary. 2007. Extremist outbidding in ethnic party systems is not inevitable: Tribune parties in Northern Ireland. Paper available from authors.

Myers, K. 2007. This latest Northern deferral is part of the dance of deception. *Independent*, 27 March.

Nairn, T. 2000. *After Britain: New Labour and the return of Scotland.* London: Granta.

Nordlinger, E. 1972. *Conflict regulation in divided societies.* Cambridge, Mass.: Center for International Affairs, Harvard University.

Northern Ireland Office. 1972. *The future of Northern Ireland: A paper for discussion.* Green Paper. London: HMSO, 1972. Available through Conflict Archive on the Internet (CAIN). http://cain.ulst.ac.uk/hmso/nio1972.htm.

Northern Ireland Tourist Board (NITB). 2007. Fact-finder Japanese market. www.nitb.com/article.aspx?ArticleID=1271 (accessed 6 July 2007).

Oberschall, A., and L. Palmer. 2005. The failure of moderate politics: The case of Northern Ireland. In *Power-sharing: Institutional and social reform in divided societies*, ed. I. O'Flynn and D. Russell. London: Pluto: 77–99.

O'Brien, C. C. 2007. Planned Islam ban signals new Dutch intolerance. *Irish Independent*, 3 March.

O'Leary, B. 1999. The nature of the Agreement. *Fordham Journal of International Law* 22, 4: 1628–67.

———. 1989. The limits to coercive consociationalism. *Political Studies* 37, 4: 562–87.

O'Leary, B., B. Grofman, and J. Elklit. 2005. Divisor methods for sequential portfolio allocation in multi-party executive bodies: Evidence from Northern Ireland and Denmark. *American Journal of Political Science* 49, 1: 198–211.

O'Leary, B., and J. McGarry. 1996. *The politics of antagonism: Understanding Northern Ireland.* London: Athlone.

Patterson, H. 2005. What victory of the extremes means for all of us. *Irish Independent*, 7 May.

Peatling, G. K. 2004. *The Failure of the Northern Ireland Peace Process.* Dublin: Irish Academic Press.

Police Service of Northern Ireland (PSNI). 2007. Security statistics. http://www.psni.police.uk/index/ statistics_branch/pg_security_stats.htm (accessed 15 September 2008).

Redwood, J. 1999. *The death of Britain? The UK's Constitutional Crisis.* London: Palgrave Macmillan.

Republican Sinn Fein. 2007. No new era yet. *Blanket*, 26 March.

Roche, P. 2000. A Stormont without policy. *Belfast Telegraph*, 30 March.

Roeder, P. 2007. *Where nation states come from: Institutional change in the age of nationalism.* Princeton, N.J.: Princeton University Press.

Rokkan, S., and D. Urwin. 1982. Introduction: Centres and peripheries in Western Europe. In *The politics of territorial identity: Studies in European regionalism*, ed. S. Rokkan and D. Urwin. London: Sage for European Consortium for Political Research. 1-17.

Rose, R. 1976. On the priorities of citizenship in the Deep South and Northern Ireland. *Journal of Politics* 38, 2: 247–91.

Russell, M., and G. Lodge. 2006. "Governing England by Westminster." In *The English Question*, ed. R. Hazell. Manchester: Manchester University Press.

Sandford, M. 2006. Facts on the ground: The growth of institutional answers to the English Question in the regions. In *The English Question*, ed. R. Hazell. Manchester: Manchester University Press. 174–93.

Shirlow, P. 2007. Why it's going to take two to tango. *Belfast Telegraph*, 14 March.

Stevens, C. 2004. English regional government. In *Devolution and British politics*, ed. M. O'Neill. Harlow: Pearson. 251–68.

Sunday Times. 2005. Crime rate in the North "world's lowest," says UN. 18 September.

Taylor, R. 2006. The Belfast Agreement and the politics of consociationalism: A critique. *Political Quarterly* 77, 2: 217–26.

———. 2001. Northern Ireland: Consociation or social transformation. In *Northern Ireland and the divided world: Post-Agreement Northern Ireland in comparative perspective*, ed. J. McGarry. Oxford: Oxford University Press. 36–52.

The Times. 2007. Tough talk is losing its edge as Ulster's election trail goes cold. 1 March.

Trench, A., ed. 2007. *Devolution and power in the United Kingdom.* Manchester: Manchester University Press.

University of Ulster. 2007. Northern Ireland is the UK's regional hotspot for house prices rises, says a survey out today. 6 July.

USA Today. 2007. Peace (finally) at hand in Northern Ireland? 19 March.

Ward, A. 2000. Devolution: Labour's strange constitutional "design." In *The changing constitution,* ed. J. Jowell and D. Oliver. 4th ed. Oxford: Oxford University Press. 111–36.

Watts, R. 1999. *Comparing federal systems.* Montreal: McGill-Queen's University Press.

Wilford, R., and R. Wilson. 2006. From the Belfast Agreement to stable power-sharing. Paper presented at the PSA Territorial Politics Conference, Queen's University, Belfast, January.

Wimmer, A. 2003. Democracy and ethno-religious conflict in Iraq. *Survival* 45, 4: 111–34.

Wolff, S. 2001. Context and content: Sunningdale and Belfast compared. In *Aspects of the Belfast Agreement,* ed. R. Wilford. Oxford: Oxford University Press. 11–27.

Part II
Conflict Settlements

Chapter 7
Thinking About Asymmetry and Symmetry in the Remaking of Iraq

Brendan O'Leary

The English poet John Keats told us that

> Beauty is truth, truth beauty,—that is all
> Ye know on earth, and all ye need to know. ("Ode on a Grecian Urn")

Sadly, however, many psychologists tell us that we judge beauty by people's symmetry, not their truthfulness (Swami and Furnham 2007). The concept of symmetry, and its antonym asymmetry, contains both aesthetic and geometric ammunition. Symmetry suggests balanced form or balanced measure; asymmetry suggests the unbalanced, or the ill proportioned. Symmetry is also linked to the idea of correspondence: entities on opposite sides of a center, axis, dividing line, or mirror, symmetrically correspond.

Symmetry and asymmetry are now attached to the literature on territorial constitutional design. Within this literature asymmetrical entities suffer from the presumption that they are ill proportioned, imbalanced, and irregular. The reasonableness of that judgment is the subject of this book, and most of my coauthors question the negative appraisal of asymmetrical federations with solid arguments and empirically convincing observations. This chapter, in contrast, offers a skeptical scrutiny of the symmetry-versus-asymmetry debate. I argue that debate over symmetry and asymmetry cannot reasonably be confined to any one dimension of formal power; that the notions of symmetry and asymmetry themselves are typically not rigorously defined; and that their practical importance may be overrated. The chapter is not, however, an exercise in negativity: I try to put forth reasonable and operational conceptions of symmetry and asymmetry. But the suggestion will be made that all actual federations are asymmetrical in at least one respect. Therefore, perhaps, not too much weight should be attached to asymmetry per se in accounting for the success or otherwise of federations in resolving or regulating national, ethnic, linguistic, or religious conflict. It remains possible that the number and degrees of asymmetry may matter—though how, exactly, is not clear.

What definitely matters in the places deeply divided along the cleavages just mentioned is whether they are organized in pluralist federations; or whether they have consociational power-sharing arrangements. Pluralist federations are plurinational, decentralized, and consensual, whereas integrated federations are mononational, centralized, and majoritarian (O'Leary 2005b). A pluralist federation may not guarantee harmony, but it may help resolve or regulate national, ethnic, religious, or linguistic conflicts. Cross-community executive power sharing, proportionality, autonomy, and veto rights characterize full consociations. These can be contrasted with single-party winner-takes-all executives, majoritarian electoral rules, unitary and uniform centralization, and the absence of veto powers for any agent other than the governing majority (Lijphart 1977; O'Leary 2005a). Consociational arrangements also do not guarantee harmony but may help resolve or regulate national, ethnic, religious, or linguistic conflicts. A political "balance of power" may be vital to the effective workings of both pluralist federations and consociations. But such a political balance need not resemble aesthetic or geometric notions of symmetry, nor rest on formal constitutional symmetry. I shall suggest that both "symmetrical" and "asymmetrical" formulas can be used to help the pluralist and consociational medicine go down. But it is the medicine that matters, and the patient's willingness to complete the course prescribed. Whether the sugar crystals that coat the medicine are symmetrical or asymmetrical is irrelevant—unless the patient irrationally attaches great importance to them. The constitutional reconstruction of Iraq that is still underway will be used to illustrate these suggestions.

Symmetry in federal design is often used as a synonym for equality, and asymmetry is often treated as a synonym for unequal—or different. There are at least two forms of inequality that might take a federal system away from symmetry: inequality in the constitutional powers of the federated units (generally called regions below), *or* inequality in the extent to which the regions share power within the federal government. Let us call the first of these *asymmetrical powers,* and the second *asymmetrical shares.* We then have two different ways of measuring reductions in the degree of asymmetry in federations.

Definition A: *Asymmetry is reduced to the degree that the federated entities are equalized in their formal constitutional powers of self-government (powers).*
Definition B: *Asymmetry is reduced to the degree that the federated entities are equalized in their formal constitutional powers within the federal government (shares).*

It follows from these definitions that there are four types of federation, one symmetric (1) and three asymmetric (2.1–2.3):

1. In a *symmetric federation* regions enjoy equal self-government within their domains *and* share powers equally within the federal government (symmetrical powers *and* symmetrical shares).

2.1. In an *asymmetric federation* regions differ in their powers of self-government but share power equally within the federal government (asymmetrical powers and symmetrical shares).

2.2. In an *asymmetric federation* regions enjoy equal self-government within their domains but share power unequally within the federal government (symmetrical powers and asymmetrical shares).

2.3. In an *asymmetric federation* regions differ in their powers of self-government (some have more than others) and share power unequally within the federal government, (asymmetrical powers and asymmetrical shares).

Does this typology aid understanding? Consider the first modern federation, the United States of America. Its constitution was remade in Philadelphia in 1787 to replace the Articles of Confederation (Bailyn 1993; "Constitution" 1993; "Articles of Confederation" 1993). In the standard understanding of the U.S. Constitution each of the states has equal constitutional powers of self-government. Each is also entitled to two senators in the house of the federation (the Senate), who express the equal right to participate in the federal government. Each state also sends members to the house of the people (the House of Representatives) in proportion to its population at the last census (Art. 1.2), a principle of proportionate equality but a different representation principle from that (now) used to elect the Senate. The United States therefore has asymmetrical representation in its federal legislature because states with smaller and larger populations have the same number of representatives in the Senate. The equality of states in the Senate creates inequality in the voting power of individuals across different states, and therefore within the federation. The U.S. has one of highest degrees of asymmetry in the voting power of its citizens when one compares the value of a vote in the smallest state with that in the largest state (Stepan 1999, 2001). Sometimes this asymmetry is said to be balanced, because the equality of states in the Senate is balanced against the proportionality principle that represents federal citizens in the House. But in what sense is this so-called "balance" symmetrical? The principles do not weigh the same on any agreed measure. It is certainly a clash of principles, but there is no symmetry. They are incommensurable principles. One is a principle of parity, the other of proportionality. Only in rare cases will they have the same practical meanings. The US not only has two federal legislative bodies constructed on asymmetrical principles of representation; it also has two unequal federal legislative bodies, because the Senate has prerogatives over impeachment not shared by the House (Art. 1.3), and over the ratification of treaties, appointment of ambassadors and public officials, and court appointments (Art. 2.2). The federal legislative bodies are therefore asymmetrical in their powers. The founding modern federation, upon quick inspection, consequently does not conform to any simple conception of symmetry. The United States seems to be an example of asymmetric federation (2.2), symmetrical powers and asymmetrical shares. But even that is too quick a judgment.

The United States, as a sovereign political system, encompasses entities beyond the fifty states of the union, for example, "associated states" such as Puerto Rico, and the Indian Nations, which have treaty relations with the federal government, and the federal district of Washington, D.C., which has no representation in either chamber of Congress. These entities have powers of self-government, but they are different powers from those enjoyed by the states of the union. Within the federal government these entities possess no formal representative voting power, and therefore no formal power. These facts may suggest that the United States is an example of asymmetric federation (2.3), asymmetrical powers and asymmetrical shares. Some have called certain of these entities outside the union "federacies" (Elazar 1987). But this coding may in turn be challenged because (say some) the Indian territories and associated states are subordinate entities of the federal government, and are therefore neither members of the federation nor regions with a federal relationship with the federal government. That would still mean that there are territories within the U.S. political system that have asymmetrical shares. (Should the entire U.S. therefore be classified as a synthesis of an asymmetric federation and a colonial government, or a synthesis of an asymmetric federation and a union state?)

The structure of the U.S. federation, which has often shaped thinking on federations and federalism, therefore suggests immediate difficulties with easy notions of what constitutes symmetry and its opposite. Its history suggests even more difficulties. One of the U.S. operational principles of expansion was that all states should be created equal: for that reason, in 1784, Jefferson replied to a request by Congress that asked him how to apportion the land inherited from the British victory against France in 1763 by suggesting that it should be carved wherever possible into states having two degrees of height and four degrees of width (Stein 2008, 1–2). But that areal principle of symmetry was only partly respected in the making of new states, and is manifestly violated in the cases of California and Texas. The Constitution also tacitly rested on a principle of balance between the North and the South, between free and slaveholding states. This "principle" of balance was subsequently reformulated in the Missouri-Maine compromise of 1821, which lasted until the period immediately preceding the U.S. Civil War. Under this compromise new states were added to the union on a principle of balance: territories joined as new states in pairs, one free and one slave (Weingast 1998). This principle of "balanced" additions protected the Southern slaveholding states, which thereby enjoyed a self-sustaining veto in the Senate. The slaveholding states also remained overrepresented in the House because of the constitutional rule that counted noncitizens (slaves) as three-fifths of a person for the purposes of apportioning seats in the House of Representatives (Art. 1.2) (for an extended discussion of the importance of this rule in the prebellum United States see Wills 2003). A principle of symmetry (Missouri-Maine) protected an ugly bargain (between the free and the slaveholding states).

This past, especially of a federation that protected a distinct, autonomous, and hierarchical society (Southern slaveholding), has made many American constitutional lawyers and political scientists unwaveringly skeptical and sometimes hostile toward states' rights. That is why most of them today favor federal legal supremacy to protect individual human rights. It is also why they reject the electoral college, which does not give each citizen an equal chance of electing the president, and has many other flaws which can also be described as forms of asymmetrical voting power (Edwards 2004). A fluent expression of this entire outlook is Robert Dahl's *How Democratic Is the American Constitution?* (2001). Liberal Americans are, I suggest, culturally ill-prepared to consider that in other places regional rights, including regional judicial supremacy, and asymmetries of a different kind, might jointly serve to protect rather than damage historically disadvantaged minorities. The intellectual dominance of American public law and political science in the academic world partly encourages the widespread intellectual hostility toward multinational, decentralized, and consensual federations, especially if they embed consociational "quotas" and veto rights. But, what matters for our immediate purposes is that it is not easy to say whether either symmetry or asymmetry per se was responsible for the maintenance of slavery (and subsequently of racist discrimination) in the institutional history of the United States. The symmetrical powers of states, and the symmetrical principle for the addition of new states (the Missouri-Maine compromise) mattered. But so did the absence of a bill of rights for all persons with universal jurisdiction, and the asymmetrical shares of Southern states in representation in the Senate and House. Symmetrical and asymmetrical institutional principles combined to maintain the constitutionality of slavery until the crisis of the Civil War. It is difficult to claim that either the symmetries or the asymmetries were more important in protecting this organized injustice.

Belgium may be the most obvious functioning example of asymmetric federation (2.1), a federation that combines asymmetrical powers and symmetrical shares. Its three communities and its three territorial regions have different powers of self-government (Fitzmaurice 1996; Murphy 1995). Brussels in particular has fewer powers than either Flanders or Wallonia. But Belgium's two major constituent peoples enjoy equality within the federal government (to be more precise, they enjoy equality over the process of making amendments to the federal constitution). Asymmetric federation (Art. 2.1) also serves as a reasonable sketch of how the Parti Québecois, at least at some junctures, has wanted to reconstruct Canada (Young 1995; Iacovino this volume). It has sought equality between Québec and the Rest of Canada in a confederal government, but more extensive powers (and status) for Quebec compared with the nine provinces of "English Canada."

The intricate details of these U.S., Belgian, and Canadian examples, and their correct classifications within the typology at various junctures of their history, are not what fundamentally matter for this argument. It is enough that there appear to have been specimens of all three types of asymmetrical federation. What matters is to consider whether there have ever been *any* fully symmetrical federations. After all, any federation that has two federal legislative bodies will almost certainly have at least one asymmetry. Its house of the federation will differ from its house of the people (in the methods and district-magnitudes used to elect office holders, in their terms of offices, in their internal decision-rules, or in their legislative powers). The existence of any of these differences creates asymmetrical shares (either for regions or citizens in the federal legislature). In consequence, all actually existing federations are asymmetrical; after all, any federation, which would have two absolutely identical legislative bodies to represent its regions and its federal citizenry, would have one redundant body. So, it would appear that anyone who argues for (or against) a wholly symmetrical federation is wasting his or her breath. If all actually existing federations are asymmetrical then it may be the extent to which they are asymmetrical, and the dimensions along which they are asymmetrical, which are provoking controversy. Alternatively, symmetry and asymmetry are simply the rhetorical clothes in which the participants dress their arguments.

These considerations perhaps explain why, tacitly at least, most academic discussions of asymmetry in federations currently tend to focus on asymmetrical powers rather than asymmetrical shares, that is, on inequalities in constitutional powers between regions. For a good example, see the essay of my regular coauthor John McGarry in a recent issue of *Ethnopolitics* (McGarry 2007). All the constructive replies in the same journal share McGarry's premise (Hechter 2007; Rezvani 2007; Conversi 2007; Adeney 2007). But it is not obvious that this is the sole way we should proceed analytically. Political debates over powers are almost always likely to spill over into debates about the appropriateness of shares (and they do, including in the symposium I have just cited). Some, for example, argue that any asymmetry in powers should be compensated for by an asymmetry in shares. For example, if Quebec is to have more autonomy than Ontario, then, say some, it should have (correspondingly?) less power in the Ottawa federal government—though how this "corresponding" reduction would be measured and established presents a conundrum. The same questions arise in union states. Under the Government of Ireland Act of 1920 what became Northern Ireland had a mandatory reduction in the number of members elected to the Westminster parliament, allegedly to compensate for the fact that it was then the sole part of the United Kingdom to have a devolved parliament. (In fact, it seems more likely that British party leaders primarily wanted to quarantine Irish matters from affecting the smooth running of the Westminster parliament.) When devolution was granted to Scotland in 1997 a process was set in train to reduce Scotland's "overrepresentation" in the union parliament—though not to less than it would be if apportionment occurred solely on the size of its population. Any asymmetry in the powers of regions automatically generates asymmetry in the federal legislature.

A region with just one more exclusive power than all the other regions (or, differently put, with just one greater power of autonomy) establishes a conundrum in the federal legislature. *Either* the members from the special region vote on matters arising under that power when the federal legislature votes on this subject for other regions, *or* they do not. If they do, they have asymmetric shares: they vote on something affecting others, but the others have no right to vote on the region's governance of that power. If they do not, they also have asymmetric shares: they are excluded from participating in the full powers of the federal government. The so-called "West Lothian question" is an automatic consequence of any asymmetry in powers of self-government among regions, applying to both federations and union states. Only very small entities are likely to have little controversy attached to the issue of the relationship between asymmetrical powers and asymmetrical shares, because elected members from these entities are not likely to be pivotal in federal or union legislatures (at least if their members are elected by proportional representation).

These considerations suggest that it is impossible to seal off discussions of the symmetry or asymmetry of the powers of regions from symmetry or asymmetry in shares. But it remains wholly plausible to argue that powers and shares do not exhaust the subjects that arise under considerations of symmetry and asymmetry. After all, we might want to consider symmetries and asymmetries in status—to the extent that these can be differentiated from powers and shares. Are some regions named differently to others? Do some have titular nationalities, whereas others do not? We could, similarly, examine symmetries or asymmetries in recognition. Are some regions deemed "distinct societies," "nations," or the "homelands" of "historic nationalities"? We might also examine asymmetries in resources. Are some regions much less advantaged in natural or fiscal resources than others, and is this fact obscured by a formal symmetry in their constitutional powers? We might also examine asymmetries that occur in the incidence of federal burden-sharing (e.g., in the incidence of taxation) or benefit-sharing (e.g., in royalties from natural resources).

These considerations suggest the following additional possibilities in appraising possible reductions in asymmetry in federations:

Definition C: *Asymmetry is reduced in a federation (i) to the degree that the federated entities are equal in their titles, and modes of formal recognition; and (ii) to the degree that the regions are symbolically treated as cosovereign within the federation and within the international arena (status asymmetries).*
Definition D: *Asymmetry is reduced in a federation (i) to the degree that the federated entities are equal in population, area, or wealth; (ii) to the degree that the federated entities are collectively equal in resources to the federal government; and (iii) to the degree that each federated entity shares equally in the burdens and benefits of membership within the federation (resource asymmetries).*

Let us call these additional sources of inequalities within federations status and resource asymmetries respectively.[1]

These conceptual and comparative considerations lead to three conclusions. (1) There are no real-world symmetrical federations in shares and powers. (2) Asymmetries in the powers of regions automatically generate asymmetries in regional shares of power in the federal (or union) legislature. (3) A fuller account of asymmetries can be considered with respect to four concepts that can be expected to interrelate and overlap in complex ways: powers, shares, status, and resources. Can these abstract considerations inform understanding of the highly contested case of contemporary Iraq, which is still undergoing profound conflict, and which is undergoing unfinished and uncertain reengineering as a federation?

Before we can answer that question let me summarize Iraq's constitution-making process since the U.S. intervention of 2003. Briefly, its new constitution, ratified in 2005, has radically altered the Transitional Administrative Law (TAL) of 2004, which was negotiated under the direction of the administrator of an international occupation, Ambassador L. Paul Bremer III of the Coalition Provisional Authority. The TAL was a compromise between, on the one hand, the integrationist, centralizing, and majoritarian ambitions of the American-led Coalition Provisional Authority and many of the Sunni and liberal Arab Iraqis on the Iraqi Governing Council, and, on the other hand, the pluralist, decentralist, and consensual vision of a new Iraq sought by the Kurdistan Region (the full text is in Appendix 2 of O'Leary et al. 2005).

The TAL created the possibility that Arab Iraq would be federated on the basis of fourteen provinces in Arab Iraq, whereas Kurdistan would be a place apart, a "federacy" (for a full analysis of the TAL, see O'Leary 2005b). Kurdistan's primary objective in the negotiation of the TAL was to regularize its irregular status—which was that of an internationally and nationally unrecognized autonomous entity. It submitted a formal constitutional proposal to the negotiations and a statement of principles of federalism (the former is in Appendix 1 of O'Leary et al. 2005; the latter is in the possession of Dr. Khaled Salih). The former indicated Kurdistan's wish to be treated distinctly from Arab-dominated Iraq; the latter indicated its commitment to a pluralist, multinational, multiethnic, and consensual Iraqi federation.

Kurdistan's constitutional proposal sought the recognition of the Kurdistan Region with the full attributes of domestic statehood, that is, the formal recognition of all the powers that the region had exercised since Saddam Hussein's regime had quit the territory shortly after the first Gulf War. It sought continuity in its institutions and laws, and the primacy of Kurdistan's enactment of law, "except as related to matters within the exclusive competence of the Provisional Government of Iraq," and the supremacy of its laws within its territory (O'Leary et al. 2005, app. 1, Art. 1). It wanted full control over its own security, and to protect Iraq's borders where they are also the borders of the region (Art. 2); full ownership and control over its natural resources (Art. 3); full fiscal autonomy and the right to a proportionate share of federal revenues (Art. 4); and, last, but not least, the right of separate ratification of the Permanent Constitution through a popular referendum within Kurdistan. Kurdistan's negotiators did not formally propose in this particular text any alterations in the borders of the region, but they were prepared to accept any formulas that would enable substantive parts of the Kirkuk governorate and other "disputed territories" to join the region, before or in the Permanent Constitution, and they put forward constructive submissions in this vein (these are in my possession and of Dr. Khaled Salih and Ambassador Peter W. Galbraith).

Kurdistan's priorities in the negotiation of other provisions of the TAL were a federation that would protect substantive secularism, that is, limit Islam's role in public life, and one that would establish Kurdish as a full, official, and equal language of the federation. It sought power sharing, proportionality, and veto capacities in the workings of the provisional Iraqi federation-wide government, and these affected its proposed amendments to proposals on the powers of the prime minister and cabinet, the presidency, and on subsequent proposals on electoral arrangements.[2]

Many of Kurdistan's ambitions opposed the goals of the American and British administrators, and many of the Arabs on the Iraqi Governing Council, apart from those in the Supreme Council for the Islamic Revolution in Iraq (SCIRI). The CPA wanted to make the governorates (the eighteen provinces established under the Baathists) the building blocks of the federation rather than distinct, larger, and more powerful ethnic or religiously defined regions. They wanted the Kurdistan Region to be dissolved and to prevent the aggregation of any governorates into bigger regions, that is, to prevent what they called ethnic or religious or sectarian federalism. They wanted the subordination of all security forces to the federal authorities. They wanted the federal government to have full ownership, control, and management over natural resources, and strong fiscal powers. And most initially wanted an Iraq-wide ratification of the making of the Permanent Constitution through a simple majority approval process in a referendum.

The TAL: Powers, Shares, Status, and Resources in the TAL of 2004

The outcome was that under the TAL (Art. 53(A)), the Kurdistan Region was treated as an exception: "The Kurdistan Regional Government is recognized as the official government of the territories that were administered by that government . . . on March 19 2003." It was the sole recognized region; and its name was strikingly different from all the other federative entities. Kurdish became the second official language of Iraq and the official language of the region. Kurdistan's name refers to a titular nationality. Its etymology means "a place abounding with Kurds." The Baathists had previously recognized its autonomy, but the March 1970 agreement between Mulla Mustafa Barzani, the president of the Kurdistan Democratic Party (KDP), and Saddam, broke down in 1974. The governmental institutions of Kurdistan that were recognized included the Kurdistan *National* Assembly. No other federative entity in

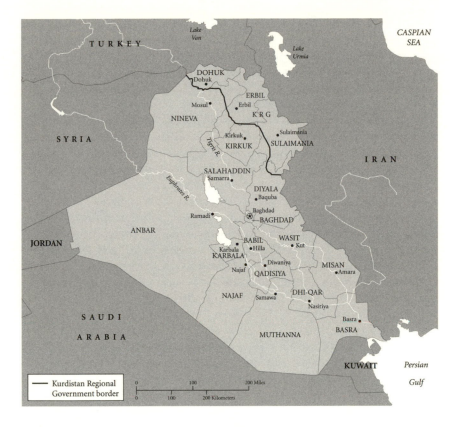

Map 1. The status quo: no symmetrical alignment of the boundaries of the Kurdistan region and existing governorates.

the TAL had such titular and status distinctions accorded to it. Kurdistan's provisional territorial delimitation also cut across several of the existing governorates (provinces), as we can see in Map 1.

Kurdistan's legal past was treated differently—its laws made since 1992 were in effect recognized, provided they were compatible with the TAL (Arts. 3; 54(A),(B)). It was entitled "to retain regional control over police forces and internal security" and it had "the right to impose taxes and fees" (Art. 54(A)). In resources the Kurdistan Region was assured a proportionate share of the revenues of the natural resources of Iraq, the management of which, "in consultation with the governments of the regions and the administrations of the governorates," was defined as an exclusive competence of the federal government (Art. 25(E)). Implicitly, as an area understood to be "unjustly deprived of these revenues by the previous regime," it was expected to receive more than its proportionate share for a period according to the same provision. Its powers and its status were therefore different to the eighteen governorates; and its competences to raise resources were also different. Its allocation of federal resources would be the same as other areas of Iraq, subject to the rectification of historic injustices.

What about shares in the powers of the federal legislature? In the transitional period, Iraq had a single-chamber constituent assembly, the Iraqi National Assembly, which functioned as a parliament under the TAL. In the absence of a second chamber it follows that no asymmetries flowed intrinsically from the existence of two chambers. Moreover, the Kurdistan Region and the governorates per se were not represented as districts in the transitional election arrangements for the Iraqi National Assembly. The elections took place under Iraq-wide list proportional representation. (There were three separate elections in January 2005, to the Iraqi National Assembly, to the KRG, and to the governorates, but each independently used list-PR in the entirety of the relevant jurisdiction.) In consequence, the voting power of an individual voter from Kurdistan (or of any Kurd) was identical to that of every other Iraqi for the election of the constituent assembly. So, Iraq under the TAL appears to be best classified as a case of "asymmetry in powers, but symmetry in shares," that is, in the typology above it fits best with the description of asymmetric federation (Art. 2.1).

Kurdistan was the sole federative entity in the TAL with the right to amend federal legislation in domains outside of the exclusive powers of the federal government (Art. 54(B)). This is clearly an asymmetrical power when contrasted with the governorates. But what about with respect to shares? We might consider this to be a moot point in classification. Kurdistan had no special status in the making of federal legislation, but it had the special power to modify (or veto) it in domains within its competence.

Contrary to what has often been asserted, Kurdistan's formal power to ratify the Permanent Constitution was not asymmetrical in any respect. Indeed, the KRG, as such, had no specific power over the making or ratification of the Constitution. Instead, the drafting power was granted to the transitional Iraqi National Assembly (Art. 60). The ratification power was granted to all citizens voting in a referendum *and* to the citizens of all eighteen governorates (provinces) (Art. 61 (C)). A majority of voters could reject the draft constitution, but so could any combination of three governorates, whose citizens voted "No" by two-thirds or more of the voters who turned out. A qualified majority was therefore required to ratify the Constitution: a majority of the voters in Iraq as a whole were required to approve it *and* sixteen provinces were required to endorse it, minimally at support levels of over one-third of their voters. Therefore, with respect to this important power of constitutional ratification, the sole region recognized under the TAL had no formal power whatever. The ratification power belonged symmetrically to the governorates: each governorate was equal in its pivotality over the making of the Constitution. But this power constituted an asymmetry among voters' powers, because voters in governorates with smaller populations had a higher chance of casting a pivotal vote. So in constitutional ratification we can choose to classify Iraq as symmetrical with respect to governorates or asymmetrical with respect to voters. And we could choose to say it was additionally asymmetrical because governorates rather than regions had ratification authority.

This analysis is, of course, purely formal. The de facto situation is different. Within the Kurdistan Region, two of Kurdistan's political parties, the KDP and the Patriotic Union of Kurdistan (PUK), organized in the Kurdistan Alliance, were able to mobilize overwhelming majorities within three governorates (Dohuk, Erbil, and Sulaimania), and a majority in one other (Kirkuk). So because the Kurdistan Alliance, organized throughout the KRG and beyond, could organize an effective "No" vote Kurdistan had de facto pivotality in the drafting of the Constitution, as some predicted might happen (Ekland et al. 2005).

Kurdistan was the sole region recognized as established, but the TAL did allow other regions to be formed (Art. 53(C)). They could be created through the aggregation of up to three of the existing governorates (though specific exclusions to this right were made in the cases of Baghdad and Kirkuk governorates). But obstacles were placed upon new region-formation, which, as it transpired, prevented any being formed during the transitional period before the making of the Permanent Constitution. Mechanisms of aggregation had to be proposed by the Iraqi interim government, and legislated by the National Assembly, and then approved in a referendum among the people of the relevant governorates (Art. 53(C)).

Powers, Shares, Status, and Resources in the Iraqi Constitution of 2005

The Permanent Constitution of Iraq was substantively negotiated in the summer of 2005. The elections of January 2005, boycotted by most Sunni Arab politicians and voters, left the Iraqi National Assembly dominated by the United Iraqi Alliance, a coalition of Shiite religious parties, and by the Kurdistan Alliance. The Shiite Arab negotiators were led by representatives of the Supreme Council for the Islamic Revolution in Iraq (SCIRI, and now the Iraqi Supreme Iraqi Council; ISCI). They cemented a constitutional pact with the Kurdistan Region, which was then ratified by four out of five of Iraq's voters, and by sixteen of the eighteen governorates in the referendum conducted on 15 October 2005. SCIRI and the Kurdistan Alliance shared a strong commitment to a decentralized federation, for which they drafted provisions. Most Sunni Arabs voted against the Constitution: they regarded as anathema the very possibility of region formation within Arab Iraq.

Under the Permanent Constitution some of the provisions of the TAL remained the same to the letter, or in substance, while others were decisively altered. Kurdistan remained provisionally distinctive in several respects. The Kurdish language remained one of the two official languages, and the official language of the region. Under Art. 117(1) Kurdistan was the sole federal region recognized when the Constitution came into force. The manner in which Kurdistan's borders could be modified was also implicitly distinctive and, similar to the provisions of the TAL, Art. 140 of the Constitution mandated executive arrangements for the implementation of Art. 58 of the TAL, which had foreseen procedures, including a referendum and border adjustments, to enable Kirkuk governorate (and other districts and subdistricts of disputed territories) to join the KRG. Art. 141 of the Iraqi Constitution also specifically provides for laws and contracts made by the KRG after 1992 to "remain in effect," unless they violate the Constitution, and, by implication, ratifies the legal status of the Peshmerga, who are the lawful army of Kurdistan under Law Number 5 of the Kurdistan National Assembly of 1992. Kurdistan now has the capacity to veto any unilateral change to its definition and powers by the federal government, a power that goes beyond its previous right to amend federal legislation. So, Kurdistan is, for now, a federacy: it has a federal relationship with the federal government that is not enjoyed by any other existing entity. In a federation, a federacy is normally culturally different from the other units in the federation, and may enjoy different powers to those units or choose to exercise the same powers in a strikingly different manner. The division of powers between a federacy and the federal government is entrenched, cannot be unilaterally altered by either side, and, to work, normally has to have established arbitration mechanisms to deal with difficulties that might arise between the federacy and the federal government. Ronald Watts, however, defines a federacy as an entity that exercises little influence over the actions of the federal government (Watts 2001, 27). But if so, Kurdistan is currently an exception to Watts's rule: so far, federal ministers from Kurdistan and a Kurdish president have been key players in the federal executive since 2005, and they have not confined their interests to Kurdistan's regional interests. That may change, but if they cease to play a major role in the federal government, that will be as likely to herald de facto or de jure secession as confirmation of Watts's conception of a federacy: the record of two-unit confederations or federations is wholly discouraging.

What changed between the TAL and the Constitution as regards powers, shares, status, and resources? First, under Art. 117(2), the Constitution strongly anticipated the formation of other regions, "This Constitution shall affirm new regions established in accordance with its provisions." An entire section, Section 5 of the 6 sections, is headed "Powers of the Regions." It has two chapters, one referring to regions, and the other to "governorates that are not incorporated in a region." The Council of Representatives created under the Constitution was mandated under Art. 118 to enact, within six months of its opening session, "executive procedures" to form regions "by a simple majority of the members present." It passed the relevant law in 2006 but postponed its operation until 2008. Compared with the TAL, region formation was clarified and eased. A referendum to facilitate the aggregation of governorates into a region can be triggered in one of two ways: either through a request by one-third of the council members of each of the relevant governorates, or a petition of one-tenth of the voters in each of the relevant governorates (Art. 119).

Second, regions were granted their own powers under Art. 121, each of which serves to make any new region resemble Kurdistan. All governmental powers aside from those exclusively belonging to the federal government may be exercised by the regions (Art. 121(1)). "In case of a contradiction between regional and national [read "federal"] legislation in respect to a matter outside the exclusive authorities of the federal government, the regional power shall have the right to amend the application of the national [read "federal"] legislation within that region" (Art. 121(2)). This provision clearly extends the power once held by the KRG under the TAL to all future regions. "Offices for the regions and governorates shall be established in embassies and diplomatic missions, in order to follow cultural, social and developmental affairs" (Art. 121(4)), a power which no federative entity explicitly enjoyed under the TAL. All regional governments are charged with responsibility for "internal security forces for the region" (Art. 121(5)). Each region, including Kurdistan, is mandated to adopt a constitution "of its own that defines the structure of powers of the region, its authorities, and the mechanisms for exercising such authorities," provided that it is consistent with the federal constitution (Art. 120).

Under the Permanent Constitution the Kurdistan Region therefore looks as if it became the norm for the definition of a region, not an exception, defining the standard and the scope of powers to which any other future region may aspire. But that is not quite precise. It is more accurate to say that the Kurdistan Region, as Kurdistan's negotiators sought it to be in the negotiations over the TAL, now became the norm for the definition of a region. That is because Kurdistan's powers were expanded, compared with both the federal government and the TAL. The federal government completely lost its exclusive powers over oil and gas, as we shall see, and its powers over security were formally confined to "national (federal) security policy."

The Permanent Constitution of 2005 potentially reduces the possibly striking asymmetry in the degree of self-government between the Kurdistan Region and other possible regions. The Constitution also sought to strengthen the existing governorates not organized in a region in Section 5 of the Constitution. It did this first by reducing the exclusive powers of the federal government. Second, it removed governorate councils from the control of federal ministries (Art. 122(5)), and mandated that they have independent finances (through a grant). Third, it permitted a federal law to enable governorates to delegate powers to the federal government, and vice versa (Art. 123), implicitly encouraging governorates to determine what degree of centralization should apply to them. So, although the governorates are plainly weaker entities than the regions (so there are asymmetrical powers), there is no constitutional impediment to them acquiring the powers of regions (either through region formation or through negotiations under Art. 123). So, it is possible to argue that any asymmetry in powers between regions and governorates will flow from a choice of the governorates that decide not to organize in regions. Baghdad governorate can become a region, but it may not merge with a region (Art. 124(3)). Outside of the (limited) exclusive powers of the federal government, regions and governorates (asymmetric entities in status) are free to establish different degrees of autonomy from, or cooperation with, the federal government. They can modify federal legislation, opt out of it, or veto it (within their units). This flexibility enables the evolution of asymmetric policies and practices amid the formal symmetry of powers among regions and the formal symmetry of powers among governorates not organized in or as regions.

What about shares of powers in the federal government? The constitutional process has left ambiguous the shares of power of regions and provinces within the federal government. That is not just because regions other than Kurdistan do not yet exist, and not just because the federation's second chamber and the federation's supreme court, and their powers, have not been established or institutionally specified. But unlike the TAL, a second chamber has to be created, so certain fresh asymmetries will inevitably flow from the formation of the Council of the Union (from its election procedures, its terms of office, and its powers). The new electoral law for the Council of Representatives has already created asymmetries. Using list proportional representation to elect the federal legislature across Iraq as whole, as occurred under the TAL, established a full symmetry of power among voters: a vote anywhere in Iraq had the same power of affecting outcomes. But the electoral law negotiated after the Permanent Constitution has altered matters. Iraq now has a two-tier list-PR system, applied first in the governorates and then in a secondary tier for Iraq as a whole. But the accidental (and bizarre) choice of a non-compensatory principle for the second tier has created some novel and insufficiently appreciated asymmetries. Compensation is applied in the secondary tier for disproportion within each governorate, but not across Iraq as a whole. In consequence, governorates in which there are lower turnouts in the vote will enjoy higher representation in the Council of Representatives than they would in a fully compensatory system. It is also an oddity that the weaker tier, governorates rather than regions, have become the electoral districts for the federal house of representatives—a very curious asymmetry in shares.

In the rules governing the formation and functioning of the federal executive in the transitional arrangements within the Permanent Constitution, and the subsequent permanent arrangements that are intended to replace them, lie important consequences for the implicit power of regions within the federal government. One of these is that the Permanent Constitution envisages a shift away from a three-person presidential council to a merely symbolic president. Without formally saying so, it was plain that the Presidency Council, elected by the Council of Representatives, would always have one place for a representative for Kurdistan. For that reason some Kurds (and some Sunni Arabs, for different reasons) may press to retain the Presidency Council, with its power of veto over federal legislation, beyond the transitional period.

As for matters of symmetry in status, we can say that any regions that form will be equal to Kurdistan in their names, titles, and forms of recognition. They will also have larger resources whenever they are formed through aggregation than the governorates which they incorporate. If Iraq were to be reframed around five regions (as advocated by Iraq's national security advisor Mowaffak al-Rubaie in 2008), then it is quite possible that such regions would have a rough symmetry in population and area, as seen in Map 2 (O'Leary 2009). By contrast, the Iraq of the TAL, in which Kurdistan was the sole region and Iraq was really a two-unit federation in which Kurdistan was a federacy and the rest of Arab Iraq had, for practical purposes, a unitary government, was highly asymmetrical in resources. A two-unit entity would have high inequalities in population, area, military, and fiscal resources. A three-region Iraq—in which a "Shi'astan" would outnumber both Kurdistan and any prospective "Sunnistan"—would also be highly asymmetrical in demography and area.

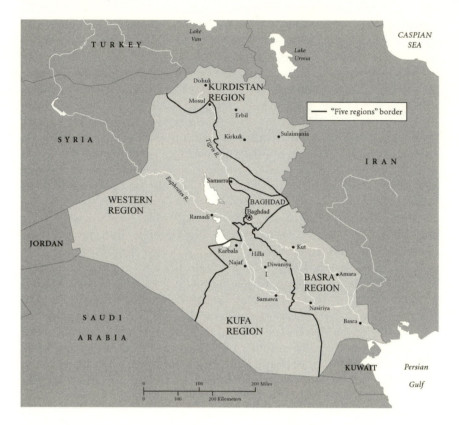

Map 2. Al Rubaie's plan for regions symmetrical in status, powers, and population size.

Al-Rubaie (2008) maintains that

> the political objectives of Iraq's three main communities are unrealizable within the framework of a unitary, centralized state. . . . The absence of any truly national parties and leadership that reach the Iraqi people exacerbates the problem. . . . Resolution can be achieved only through a system that incorporates regional federalism, with clear, mutually acceptable distributions of powers between the regions and the central government. . . . A key condition for success is that the balance of power should tip decisively to the regions on all matters that do not compromise the integrity of the state. . . . Iraq needs a period of time during which the Shiites and Kurds achieve political control over their destinies while the Sunni Arab community is secure from the feared tyranny of the majority.

While expressing flexibility on the exact territorial configuration of a federalized Iraq, he insists that it should permit the assignment of nearly all domestic powers to the regions, to be funded out of a percentage of oil revenue distributed on the basis of population. The federal government should be responsible only for essential central functions such as foreign policy (including interregional affairs), defense, fiscal and monetary policy, and banking.

In this crisply articulated vision he suggests that a regional and decentralized federation will better match religious, educational, and cultural policy preferences than could a central government, and that "a regional framework for economic policy would also fit better with traditional trade patterns and markets." He also foresees the exact territorial configuration of regions:

> Iraq's political geography suggests five likely federal units: A "Kurdistan province," including the current Kurdistan and surrounding areas; a "Western province," including Mosul and the upper Tigris and Euphrates valleys; a "Kufa province," built around the Middle Euphrates governorates; a "Basra province," including the lower Tigris and Euphrates valleys; and a "Baghdad province," built around Greater Baghdad, which may include parts of Diyala and Salahadin Governorates. The Kurdish region would be given special constitutional status as a recognized society and culture with a unique identity (similar to the Canadian province of Quebec).

Map 2 sketches what al-Rubaie's propositions would look like if implemented. These proposals show the considered reappraisal of Iraq by a leading Shiite intellectual and policy maker whose chief responsibility is security for the whole of Iraq. He will happily cede "surrounding areas" to Kurdistan (Kirkuk and the disputed territories), and grant it special status as a nation, as Quebec is now recognized in Canada. He wants to see his own community divided among three large regions (running from Baghdad and parts of Diyala downward). He contemplates a mixed central region in Greater Baghdad. He packages his proposal with a caution: "Iraq's constitution was ratified before its communities reached agreement on many vital issues, such as provincial powers." He therefore favors a referendum on a reformed constitution, but reformed around a regional federal consensus. That regionalism, he thinks, should be funded though a per capita allocation of oil revenues. Al-Rubaie's lucid federal vision provides an appropriate junction to consider the federalization of Iraq's natural resources.

The Constitution's provisions on natural resources are appropriate for a pluralist federation. They preclude no community from equitable treatment. Art. 111 declares that "oil and gas are owned by all the people of Iraq in all the regions and provinces." This article is *not* a subclause of Article 110, which specifies the exclusive powers of the federal government. That was deliberate, as a comparison with the relevant article

(Art. 25(E) in the TAL makes clear. This construction establishes that Art. 111 is subject to the supremacy of the law of any established region, which for the present simply means Kurdistan, but would include any future regions. A reading of Art. 111 as a requirement that oil and gas be exclusively owned by Iraqis, or exclusively governed through a single public corporation, may be read by a court to contradict Art. 112, which commends the "most advanced techniques of market principles and encouraging investment." Any reasonable court need not presume that Art. 111 prohibits foreign direct investment, or equity sharing, in which Iraqi governments (note the plural) would have a golden share. Therefore Art. 111 does not mandate the continuation of a centralized, vertically integrated industry. The other critical article, Art. 112, has two parts:

> (1) The federal government, with the producing governorates and regional governments, shall undertake the management of oil and gas extracted *from present fields*, provided that it distributes its revenues in a fair manner in proportion to the population distribution in all parts of the country, specifying an allotment for a specified period for the damaged regions which were unjustly deprived of them by the former regime, and the regions that were damaged afterwards in a way that ensures balanced development in different areas of the country, and this shall be regulated by a law.
> (2) The federal government, with the producing regional and governorate governments, shall *together* formulate the *necessary* strategic policies to develop the oil and gas wealth in a way that achieves the highest benefit to the Iraqi people using the most advanced techniques of market principles and encouraging investment. (my emphases)

These provisions are also subject to regional legal supremacy. Art. 112(1) affirms that the federal government's prescribed role is solely managerial. It does not require the form of a single public corporation. The managerial role is confined to currently exploited fields. Equally vital, the managerial role is shared with the respective regions and governorates where production takes place. The Arabic version subtly implies a lead role for federal management. This interpretation is not contested by Kurdistan, provided, of course, it is not abused. Art. 112(1) makes it mandatory to plan a per capita formula for the distribution of revenues from oil and gas production from currently exploited fields. So, Sunni Arabs and Sunni-Arab-dominated regions or governorates are not cut out of revenues from currently exploited fields. Far from it; no Iraqi is. At present, nearly all Iraq's oil and gas revenues flow from fields that were being exploited in 2005. However, the per capita formula, may, by statute, be modified by time-limited support for regions deprived under Saddam and "damaged after." Any allotment has to be time-limited, and it has to be consistent with a "balanced" development strategy. It would be unconstitutional for the Iraqi authorities to dwarf the per capita allocations by the allotment reparations. Sensible advice to the Sunni Arab community should focus on developing a statute that places a premium on the per capita revenue allocations, and that limits (or removes) the period of reparations, which are to apply to the regions that "were damaged." This clause was intended to cover southern governorates damaged under Saddam (during the Iran-Iraq War and after the Shiite Arab uprising) and Kurdistan (which did not gets its fair share of Iraq's revenues during between 1992 and 2003, and which was outside the grip of the regime from 1992).

Art. 112 is equally important because of what it does not say. Its complete silence on future (or unexploited in 2005) oil and gas fields removes any role for the federal government in their management, as well as over legislation. The injunction on future policy planning specified in Art. 112(2) has an important "together"—the Arabic version is equally clear on this. The "together" implies a full regional veto as regards the content of Article 112(2). The substance of Article 112(2) obligates regional and provincial governments to formulate necessary strategic policies together with the federal government. The necessary policies flow from Iraq's membership in the Organization of Petroleum Exporting Countries (OPEC). It would be odd if Iraq's regions were to develop completely different exploitation and pricing policies. Iraq's OPEC membership may necessitate regional (and producing provincial) agreements on production quotas. But necessity does not dictate a single vertically integrated oil or gas industry; and necessity does not require regions to link their new (or old) fields to existing Iraq-wide pipelines. Regions are free to have their own investment strategies, oil and gas industry infrastructures, and exploration strategies. Unquestionably, it was the intention of the negotiators to grant future supremacy in ownership and management to the regions (and governorates) over unexploited fields of oil and gas. Arts. 112(1) and (2) must be read together: the obligation to achieve the "highest benefit to the Iraqi people" is confined to policy as regards "present fields." Regions are not, by implication, required to make any federal-wide distribution of benefits from new fields of oil and gas. Nothing stops them from agreeing to that; but they are not obligated to do so. President Massoud Barzani of the Kurdistan Regional Government has, however, indicated his government's willingness to commit to such distributive arrangements, provided others (especially in the south and in Baghdad) do so.

The constitutional provisions governing oil and gas are consistent with the vision of a pluralist federation. They permit the federal government to work. There will be a sufficient revenue base, from present oil and gas fields, for a workable federal government. Iraq's present fields have long lives ahead of them. When regions develop outside Kurdistan, there will be a corresponding reduction in the necessary revenues for the federal government to execute its functions, especially if the regions exercise their constitutional right to monopolize internal security.

These arrangements are just and gradualist. There is a constitutional obligation to have per capita allocations of revenues from existing fields to all regions and governorates. There is a constitutional obligation to redress past misallocations. There will therefore be a slow adjustment from a time when all oil revenues from currently exploited fields fund all Iraq's governments to a time in which there will be an Iraq of its regions, with greater revenues from the to-be-exploited fields. This gradual shift will enable appropriate development strategies. The Constitution and likely future revenue shifts permit Iraqis to share all future revenues from regions. Given that they do not know, contrary to rumor, who stands to gain most from future regional revenues from presently unexploited or undiscovered fields, they may sensibly bind themselves to a distribution rule which benefits them all, whatever the geological and financial facts turn out to be. That is precisely what Kurdistan has proposed. The draft federal oil law negotiated by the federal government and the KRG in 2006, but not yet agreed to by Baghdad, respects this obligation. It is not true that Sunni Arab majority areas have no future prospects of oil and gas development. All three major communities predominate in some territory where there are good prospects of new fields. Baghdad, which should become a region itself, also straddles good prospects.

The "curse of oil" is indeed one of the major potential threats to the prospects of Iraq's successful democratization. For that very reason democrats should welcome the fact that the Constitution recognizes decentralization provisions over control and ownership of oil and natural gas, and the fact that Kurdistan's oil law and the draft federal oil law have state-of-the-art transparency provisions. Kurdistan's proposal, so far resisted by the Baghdad oil ministry, to process all revenue allocation through an internationally supervised trust, remains on the table.

The constitutional arrangements on natural resources may facilitate the settlement of the status of Kirkuk because they deliberately separate deciding the final territorial status of Kirkuk province from the question of the ownership, management, and revenues of the Kirkuk oilfield. Under Art. 112(1), the long-exploited Kirkuk oil field must be federally managed, in conjunction with *either* the Kurdistan Regional Government *or* Kirkuk province (*or* both), and the revenues distributed according to the per capita formula and a balanced development requirement. Therefore, the rest of Iraq does not lose its stake in Kirkuk's oilfield, whether it is in the KRG or not. The bargain of 2005 on natural resources was part of a coherent remaking of Iraq as a pluralist federation and it deserves a chance to work. The differences between the KRG and Baghdad, though not yet resolved, are not huge and may yet be bridged.

The Constitution of Iraq allows and encourages a highly pluralist, decentralized, and consensual federation. The *exclusive* powers of the federal government (Art. 110) are few: formulating foreign policy and diplomatic representation; negotiating, signing, and ratifying international agreements and treaties; negotiating signing, and ratifying debt policies and formulating foreign sovereign economic and trade policy; formulating and executing national security policy, including establishing and managing armed forces to secure the protection and guarantee the security of Iraq's borders, and to defend Iraq; formulating fiscal and customs policy; issuing currency; regulating commercial policy across regional and governorate boundaries in Iraq; drawing up the national budget of the state; formulating monetary policy; establishing and administering a central bank; regulating citizenship and the right to apply for political asylum; regulating broadcasting frequencies and mail; drawing up the general and investment budget bill; and planning policies relating to water sources from outside Iraq and guaranteeing the rate of water flow to Iraq and its just distribution inside Iraq in accordance with international law and conventions. And that is it. Where there is a regional government its writ is supreme in every other domain of politics. Amendments to the Constitution that would weaken regional powers are blocked unless the relevant region's parliament and people consent to them (Art. 126(4)).

Iraq has the features of a pluralist federation and of a liberal consociation —on paper (McGarry and O'Leary 2007). Pluralist federations and consociational arrangements require suitable internal and external support-structures. That Iraq lacks a community with a preponderant and cohesive majority that will rally behind just one list or party makes coalitional politics possible. The internal balance among the three major communities may also assist coalitional politics. As long as Shi'a and Sunni Arabs deeply distrust one another they are less likely regularly to join together to oppress Kurds. As long as Kurds cannot win independence because of implacable opposition from Turkey and Iran, they have a strategic interest in alliances with Arab parties and politicians who respect Kurdistan's autonomy. Most Kurds share the same branch of Islam with Sunni Arabs, though they support a different school of law in the Sunni tradition and are much less zealous. And most Kurds share with some leading Shiite Arabs an interest in building an Iraq of its regions rather than a recentralized Iraq. Their joint history as victims of Baathism makes them partial allies. The Sunni Arabs, displaced from power, have mostly learned that they are unlikely to win back power through guerrilla struggle or terrorist methods. They are in search of new political strategies.

Some have considered experimenting with alliances with the Sadrist Shiites, in the interest of promoting a recentralized Iraqi nation-state, and others, less religious, have looked toward secular Kurds and secular Shiites. These internal conditions make federal coalitional and consociational politics possible.

Externally, pluralist federations and consociations require regional powers or great powers to balance against each other, or to make agreements not to disturb the internal equilibrium that makes federal and consociational politics possible. The regional powers must practice self-restraint, avoiding interventions on behalf of their coethnics or coreligionists. Or, instead, the neighboring powers must be kept out by the threat-capacities of great powers. The critical question for Iraq's future is whether the United States and regional powers will support the external conditions necessary to give federal or consociational politics within Iraq a chance to stabilize. I have examined these issues at length in *How to Get Out of Iraq with Integrity* (O'Leary 2009). There I emphasize that the regionalization program of the Constitution—which recognizes and makes possible a bigger and therefore more powerful Kurdistan, and which allows the emergence of a big and powerful south or multiple souths, as well as powerful governorates—enables the internal regionalization of security. In the worst-case scenario, this shift has the possibility, eventually, to confine Sunni Arab violence to Sunni Arab-dominated territories, and areas at the edges of their heartlands. In the best-case scenario, in which Sunni Arabs take charge of their own security, within functioning provinces (or in a region or regions), the majority within each of the three major communities will be able to breathe easier and be less of an intrusive threat to the others.

The push toward regionalization, informal and formal, has regrettably not just been the result of logic, persuasion, reasoned discourse, and information about pluralist federations, but owes more to the territorial homogenization flowing from sectarian and ethnic expulsions, and "fear of the other."

The stalling and blocking of regionalization in Arab Iraq, registered clearly in the provincial elections of 2008, and hailed by centralizers, is certainly the product of a tacit alliance between Sunni and Shiite centralists, but it seems unlikely to endure. Voting patterns continued to show strong regionalism: Kurdistan's lists won throughout the disputed territories and Kurdistan's existing provinces and Kirkuk did not participate; Prime Minister Nouri al-Maliki's list was the plurality (but not the majority) winner in most Shiite majority governorates, but it did not win in one Sunni majority governorate. Iraq as I write is therefore poised at a critical juncture before the United States exits. In a benign scenario a pluralist federation will emerge, in which Kurdistan democratically incorporates the disputed territories and enjoys extensive self-government and control over the future exploitation of its natural resources. In this benign scenario in Arab Iraq provinces will become important as vehicles of local-security provision, and power sharing will operate in the federal government. In the malign scenario a recentralized Baghdad government, as at present, will ride roughshod over the Constitution, blocking the development of regional and provincial autonomy and preventing the implementation of Kurdistan's constitutional rights. That scenario will send Arab Iraq back to war with Kurdistan—and rekindle war within Arab Iraq (since a long-term positive-sum coalition government between Sunni and Shiite Arabs seems highly implausible).

At no juncture in writing *How to Get Out of Iraq with Integrity* did I consider that particular arguments or proposals about symmetry or asymmetry were likely to be of profound importance. That was not, I think, an oversight or the result of bias on my part. The balance of political power that is necessary to make Iraq work as a federation need not rest on any particular combinations of symmetry and asymmetry. Iraq will only function as a democracy if it combines pluralist federal and liberal consociational principles. The benign scenario can emerge as easily with regions (with symmetrical powers) throughout Iraq, or with one Kurdistan Region and governorates outside Kurdistan (asymmetrical entities in status with regions) becoming powerful entities in Arab Iraq. But it cannot emerge from a highly centralized Arab-dominated Iraq—that path has been tried and has always led to war, and there is no good reason to think that path has better future prospects. What matters for the benign scenario is preventing the recentralization of power in the Baghdad government (especially over security and natural resources). The full recentralization of power in the Baghdad government may well trigger a war with Kurdistan (over the disputed territories) and a politics of coup and countercoup among Sunni and Shiite leaders (over who holds power in Baghdad). In deciding whether the benign or the malign scenario will emerge, the use of the hard and soft power of the United States, and the policies of Iraq's neighbors, will be decisive, for good or ill. Discussions and proposals for symmetry and asymmetry, by comparison, will be sideshows. But if the practical formula for success becomes known as "a region for Kurdistan and provinces for Arabs," who would reasonably object?

Notes

1. There is at least one other possible variable for measuring symmetry or asymmetry in a federation. The suggestion is sometimes made that in a balanced

federation the powers of the regions are balanced against those of the federal government, while in an imbalanced federation power predominantly lies with either the regions or the federal government. The regions and the federal government may share constituent or co-sovereign power in making or amending the constitution, they may have co-sovereign powers in key functions; they may have shares in making legislation or its implementation; and they may share resources. But it is not all clear what this has to do with any idea of symmetry. To the extent that it has perhaps it is covered in my distinctions above (of powers, shares, status, and resources).

2. I drafted and was in attendance for the submission of Kurdistan's memorandum to the UN Electoral Assistance Unit on electoral arrangements in the spring of 2004, and was responsible for drafting Kurdistan's positions on electoral laws in the making of the permanent Constitution in the summer of 2005.

References

Adeney, K. 2007. Comment: The "necessity" of asymmetrical federalism? *Ethnopolitics* 6, 1: 117–20.

al-Rubaie, B. M. 2008. Federalism, not partition: A system devolving power to the regions is the route to a viable Iraq. *Washington Post*, 18 February, A19.

"The Articles of Confederation." 1993. In *The debate on the Constitution: Federalist and anti-federalist speeches, articles, and letters during the struggle over ratification*, pt. 1, ed. B. Bailyn. New York: Library of America.

Bailyn, B., ed. 1993. *The debate on the Constitution: Federalist and anti-federalist speeches, articles, and letters during the struggle over ratification*. Pt. 1. New York: Library of America.

"The Constitution." 1993. In *The debate on the Constitution: Federalist and anti-federalist speeches, articles and letters during the struggle over ratification*, pt. 1, ed. B. Bailyn. New York: Library of America

Conversi, D. 2007. Asymmetry in quasi-federal and unitary states. *Ethnopolitics* 6, 1: 121–24.

Dahl, R. A. 2001. *How democratic is the American Constitution?* New Haven, Conn.: Yale University Press.

Edwards, G. C., III. 2004. *Why the electoral college is bad for America*. New Haven, Conn.: Yale University Press.

Ekland, K., B. O'Leary, and P. R Williams. 2005. Negotiating a federation in Iraq. In *The future of Kurdistan in Iraq*, ed. B. O' Leary, J. McGarry, and K. Salih. Philadelphia: University of Pennsylvania Press. 116–42.

Elazar, D. 1987. *Exploring federalism*. Tuscaloosa: University of Alabama Press.

Fitzmaurice, J. 1996. *The politics of Belgium: A unique federalism*. Boulder, Colo.: Westview.

Hechter, M. 2007. Asymmetrical federal systems: Self-determination, cultural identity, and political and fiscal decentralization. *Ethnopolitics* 6, 1: 125–27.

Lijphart, A. 1977. *Democracy in plural societies: A comparative exploration*. New Haven, Conn.: Yale University Press.

McGarry, J. 2007. Asymmetry in federations, federacies, and unitary states. *Ethnopolitics* 6, 1: 105–16.

McGarry, J., and B. O'Leary. 2007. Iraq's Constitution of 2005: Liberal consociation as political prescription. *International Journal of Constitutional Law* 5, 4: 670–98.

Murphy, A. 1995. Belgium's regional divergence: Along the road to federalism. In *Federalism: The multiethnic challenge,* ed. G. Smith. London: Longman.

O'Leary, B. 2009. *How to get out of Iraq with integrity.* Philadelphia: University of Pennsylvania Press.

———. 2005a. Debating consociational politics: Normative and explanatory arguments. In *From power-sharing to democracy: Post-conflict institutions in ethnically divided societies,* ed. S. Noel. Montreal: McGill-Queens University Press.

———. 2005b. Power-sharing, pluralist federation, and federacy. In *The future of Kurdistan in Iraq,* ed. B. O'Leary, J. McGarry, and K. Salih. Philadelphia: University of Pennsylvania Press. 47-91.

O'Leary, B., J. McGarry, and K. Salih, eds. 2005. *The future of Kurdistan in Iraq.* Philadelphia: University of Pennsylvania Press.

Rezvani, D. A. 2007. Shaping the federacy research agenda. *Ethnopolitics* 6, 1: 129–31.

Stein, M. 2008. *How the states got their shapes.* New York: Smithsonian/Harper-Collins.

Stepan, A. 2001. Toward a new comparative politics of federalism, (multi)nationalism, and democracy: Beyond Rikerian federalism. In Stepan, *Arguing comparative politics.* Oxford: Oxford University Press.

———. 1999. Federalism and democracy: Beyond the U.S. model. *Journal of Democracy* 10, 4: 19–34.

Swami, V., and A. Furnham. 2007. *The psychology of physical attraction.* London: Psychology Press.

Watts, R. L. 2001. Models of federal power-sharing. *International Social Science Journal* (March): 23–32.

Weingast, B. R. 1998. Political stability and civil war: Institutions. Commitment, and American democracy. In *Analytical narratives,* ed. R. H. Bates, A. Grief, M. Levi, J.-L. Rosenthal, and B. R. Weingast. Princeton, N.J.: Princeton University Press.

Wills, G. 2003. *"Negro president": Jefferson and the slave power.* New York: Houghton Mifflin.

Young, R. A. 1995. *The secession of Quebec and the future of Canada.* Montreal: McGill-Queen's University Press.

Part III
Emerging Settlements

Chapter 8
The Case for Asymmetric Federalism in Georgia: A Missed Opportunity

Jonathan Wheatley

Let us first consider what we mean by federalism. By federalism I refer to the constitutional arrangements in place in federal political systems (Elazar 1987, 1993, 1994; Watts 1998), which include not only strict federations but a wider array of decentralized political systems such as confederacies, associated states, federacies, and constitutionally decentralized unions (Elazar 1987).

Federal political systems can express three main types of asymmetry, as described in the introduction of this book. First, states that are otherwise unitary can allow a special arrangement whereby one or more regions enjoy a special autonomous status. In this case, the autonomous unit and its autonomy are anomalous in comparison with the rest of the state. Generally, these units are defined as *federacies*, of which Finland and the Aaland Islands are an example. Second, constitutionally decentralized states that have a number of autonomous units can grant a higher level of autonomy to one or more such unit. Spain is an example of this form of asymmetry, as Catalunya has enhanced autonomy compared to the other autonomous units. Finally, we can have fully federal states that are asymmetric in terms of the authority the federation has over each federal subject. For example, matters that belong to the jurisdiction of the overall state in some federal subjects are the competence of the subject itself in others. Here a clear example is Canada, where Quebec has broader legislative power than other Canadian provinces.[1]

In addition to the more "classical" models of asymmetric federalism, we can also envisage cases that stretch the very notion of the federal state itself. Such cases include those in which a "satellite state" adheres loosely to a federation or constitutionally decentralized state as an associated state or as a joint member of a confederation but does not share sovereignty in any meaningful way. Puerto Rico's status as a "satellite" of the United States conforms to this model.

Historical Background to Territorial-Administrative Divisions in Georgia

From its inception, the Union of Soviet Socialist Republics was envisaged as a federal state based on the principles of asymmetric federalism that loosely conform to the third model described above. According to the Union Treaty of 30 December 1922 that established the USSR, the union was to be governed by its own federal government, although each top-level or union republic within the union, of which there were initially four (Russia, Ukraine, Byelorussia, and the Transcaucasian Soviet Federated Socialist Republic), was granted the formal right of secession. Other smaller regions that were deemed to "belong" to a particular nationality were given the status of "autonomous republic," "autonomous *oblast* (province)" or "national *okrug* (district)"—in descending order of autonomy—within a given union republic. These regions were typically established as "national homelands" for a particular national group. Each union republic was entitled to its own flag, its own language, its own administrative structure, and its own "official" culture. Autonomous provinces and autonomous republics were also granted most of these attributes but not the right to secede. By the end of the Second World War, the USSR incorporated fifty-three autonomous territorial units, including fifteen union republics. In reality, power rested with the Communist Party of the Soviet Union, with the centralized Committee of State Security (KGB), and with the all-union ministries. The autonomy of the various union and autonomous republics was therefore strictly limited and until the end of the 1980s, the notion of a union republic seceding was a theoretical possibility only.

The Georgian Soviet Socialist Republic contained three autonomous entities: the autonomous republics of Abkhazia and Adjara, and the autonomous province of South Ossetia. During the early years of Soviet rule, Georgia formed part of the Transcaucasian Soviet Federated Socialist Republic (TSFSR), together with Armenia and Azerbaijan. Within the TSFSR, Abkhazia had the rather vague status of a "contractual republic" that was associated with, but not subordinated to, Georgia until 1931, when Abkhazia was made an autonomous republic within Georgia. The other two entities were formally subordinated to Georgia from the outset. The TSFSR was formally dissolved in 1936.

While Abkhazia gained its autonomous status by virtue of the distinct ethnicity and language of its Abkhaz inhabitants, Adjara was granted the status of autonomous republic on the basis of the religious affiliation of a majority of its inhabitants. Having been a part of the Ottoman empire from the mid-seventeenth century until its incorporation into the Russian empire in 1878 after the Russian-Turkish War, many of its inhabitants were Muslim Georgians. Finally, South Ossetia had the lower status of an autonomous province because it was not the only homeland for the Ossetian population that made up a majority in the province. North Ossetia, on the other side of the Georgian-Russian border, was an autonomous republic within the Russian Federation and constituted the principal "national homeland" for the Ossetian people. Below the level of the autonomous units, Georgia is further subdivided into districts. Altogether there are sixty-nine districts in Georgia and six cities not subordinated to districts, including districts and cities within the autonomous entities.

The Conflicts in Abkhazia and South Ossetia

It is beyond the scope of this article to discuss the wars that led to the de facto succession of Abkhazia and South Ossetia in the early 1990s. Here I will merely outline the main facts that are relevant for their relationship, and that of Adjara, in relation to the rest of Georgia, and how this relationship was interpreted by the various sides. During the Soviet period, it is worth pointing out that Abkhazia repeatedly petitioned Moscow for the autonomous republic to be incorporated into the Russian Federation; these petitions were made in 1956, 1967, and 1978. In August 1990, the Supreme Soviet of Abkhazia adopted a declaration of state sovereignty and declared that the inclusion of Abkhazia within Georgia had no legal basis. In South Ossetia, a similar process was underway as the Soviet superstate began to collapse; in November 1989 the South Ossetian Supreme Soviet approved a decision to unite South Ossetia with the North Ossetian ASSR and declared South Ossetia to be an independent republic within the USSR in September 1990.

Open warfare began in South Ossetia in January 1991, a month after the Georgian government led by the newly elected "Round Table" bloc of the nationalist leader Zviad Gamsakhurdia annulled South Ossetia's status as an autonomous province, making it a part of Georgia like any other. The hostilities lasted for a year and a half until a joint peacekeeping force of Georgians, Russians, and Ossetians took control in July 1992. On the other hand, the Georgian side never attempted to abrogate the autonomous status of Abkhazia, not even during the period of armed conflict from August 1992 to September 1993.

Following the wars, the separatist authorities in the Abkhazian capital Sukhum(i) controlled all of Abkhazia, except for the narrow and remote Kodori Gorge. Similarly the South Ossetian separatists in Tskhinval(i) controlled most of the former autonomous province of South Ossetia, except for most of Akhalgori district and a few villages in Tskhinval(i) rural district (in the Liakhvi Gorge). Within the areas controlled by the separatists most Georgians were expelled; this applied most of all to Abkhazia, where massive population displacements saw more than 200,000 Georgians driven from their homes to find refuge in other parts of Georgia. Some Georgians in Abkhazia's southern district of Gal(i) remained, although periodic conflicts with the de facto authorities forced many of these inhabitants to leave too. The most serious incident occurred in May 1998, when the Abkhaz authorities drove most Georgians out of Gal(i), ostensibly as part of a fight against Georgian partisans. However, many returned and most of Gal(i) is now ethnically Georgian. Overall, the war dramatically altered the demographic balance of Abkhazia: in 1989 ethnic Georgians outnumbered Abkhaz by around two and a half to one (see below). In 2003, according to a survey by the de facto authorities in Sukhum/Sokhumi, the population of ethnic Georgians had fallen to 44,000 (down from 240,000 in 1989) and were now outnumbered by Abkhaz by more than two to one. Of those Georgians remaining, a large majority lived in the Gal(i) district.

Constitutional Provisions

The Georgian Constitution of 1995 does not specify the internal territorial-administrative arrangement of the Georgian state; Article 2.3 notes that it will be "determined by constitutional law on the basis of the authority demarcation principle effective over the whole territory of Georgia at such a time when there is full restoration of Georgian jurisdiction" (i.e., restoration of Georgia's territorial integrity after the reincorporation of Abkhazia and South Ossetia). Article 4.3, however, suggests that some kind of federal political system may be feasible in the long term, stating as it does that the parliament will consist of two chambers, a Senate and a Council of the republic, in which the Senate "will consist of members elected from Abkhazia, Adjara, and other territorial units of Georgia as well as five members appointed by the president." Two-chamber arrangements in which the interests of the constituent regions are represented in an upper house tend to be found in federal political systems. Today, however, the parliament of Georgia consists of just one chamber and the country remains a unitary state. The Constitution also specifically mentions the "Autonomous Republic of Abkhazia" and (following a 2000 amendment, see below) the "Autonomous Republic of Adjara." In contrast, it refers to "the former autonomous oblast of South Ossetia" (Art. 1).

At local level, power also remains highly centralized. Reforms that came into effect with local council elections in 1998 gave a limited degree of local self-government to districts (*olqebi*), towns and villages or communities of villages (*temebi*), but real power at local level came to rest with the district administrators (*gamgeblebi*), who were appointed by the president. Considerable authority also accrued to the provincial governors (*rtsmunebuli*). The post of governor was established by the then head of state, Eduard Shevardnadze, in 1994 to strengthen central control over the region, and each governor was in charge of one of the nine provinces (*mkhareebi*) of Georgia that lay outside the autonomous entities.[3] The high degree of centralization was not reflected in high levels of supervision on the part of the central authorities over the governors and district administrators; the latter were allowed to engage in corruption in return for their loyalty to the center.

Outside the breakaway territories, central control was weakest in the autonomous republic of Adjara. During Shevardnadze's period as head of state and (from 1995) president, no law was put into place to define the division of competences between the central authorities and the government of the autonomous republic. In practice, Adjara was controlled entirely by a local strongman, Aslan Abashidze, a former middle-ranking Soviet bureaucrat, who ruled the region as if it was his own personal fiefdom. However during the thirteen years of Abashidze's rule in Adjara (from 1991 to 2004), Adjara remained nominally loyal to Tbilisi and there was no public mood for separation. Abashidze did, however, gain an important concession from Shevardnadze in return for not standing against him in the 2000 presidential elections—the term "autonomous republic of Adjara" was enshrined in the Georgian Constitution (Art. 3.3) and Adjara was guaranteed a deputy speaker of the Georgian Parliament (Art. 55.1). It remained unclear, however, what this autonomy meant in practice.

Models for a Final Settlement in Abkhazia

The first rudimentary initiative at conflict resolution in Abkhazia was undertaken in 1991 by the government of president Zviad Gamsakhurdia. This initiative did not deal explicitly with the division of powers between the government of Abkhazia and the central government in Tbilisi, but restricted itself to the internal design of the autonomous republic. The initiative established a system of ethnic quotas for the Abkhaz parliament in order to answer fears by the ethnic Abkhazian elite that the Abkhaz would lose all influence, given their demographic disadvantage with respect to Georgians. A deal was struck in August 1991 between Gamsakhurdia and the Abkhaz leadership whereby electoral districts were to be demarcated according to ethnic principles so that each group would receive a fixed number of seats in the new 65-seat Abkhazian parliament. Thus the Georgian population (representing 45.7 percent of the population in 1989) would receive 26 seats, the Abkhaz (17.8 percent) would receive 28 seats, while the others (primarily Armenians—14.6 percent, and Russians—14.3 percent) would receive the remaining 11 seats. It was also determined that a two-thirds majority was required to take decisions on constitutional issues, thus preventing either of the two main groups from pushing through constitutional amendments without the consent of the others. However, this power-sharing arrangement was not to hold; in July 1992, the Supreme Soviet of Abkhazia passed by a simple minority a law reinstating a draft Abkhaz Constitution proposed in 1925 that declared that relations between the Georgian and Abkhazian republics were based on a union treaty and granted the Republic of Abkhazia the right to secede both from the Transcaucasian Federated Republic and from the USSR. This move, which effectively ignored the constitutional deal signed the year before, was one of the factors that precipitated the thirteen-month war for control over Abkhazia and the exodus of more than 200,000 Georgians, as well as representatives of other nationalities, from the territory of Abkhazia.

The next attempt at resolution of the conflict occurred after the end of the war. In April 1994 a Declaration on Measures for a Political Settlement of the Georgian/Abkhaz Conflict was signed by both Georgian and Abkhazian sides after several rounds of negotiations in Geneva, New York, and Moscow with the facilitation of the Russian Federation and with the participation of representatives of the Conference on Security and Cooperation in Europe (CSCE) and the United Nations High Commissioner for Refugees (UNHCR). As well as reaffirming an earlier commitment to a ceasefire, the Declaration stipulated that Abkhazia would have its own constitution, legislation, and state symbols, but the two parties would engage in joint action in the fields of foreign policy and foreign economic ties; border guard arrangements; customs; energy, transport, and communications; ecology and the elimination of the consequences of natural disasters; and human rights. Further details on division of competences were not elaborated. In principle, the Georgian side interpreted this declaration as favoring a federal political system, while the Abkhaz side interpreted "joint action" more loosely in terms of a loose confederation of sovereign states.

The idea of Abkhazia as part of a federation or as an associated state linked to Georgia was later taken up in mediation efforts launched by the UN at the end of the 1990s. In 2001, after lengthy consultations with the so-called "Group of Friends of the UN Secretary General on Georgia," Germany, France, the Russian Federation, the United Kingdom, and the United States, the UN special representative for Georgia, Dieter Boden, outlined a series of principles enshrined in an unpublished paper called "Basic Principles on the Distribution of Competencies Between Tbilisi and Sukhumi" and informally known as the "Boden Document," which, he hoped, would form the basis for negotiations towards a final settlement of the Georgian-Abkhaz conflict. These principles explicitly refer to the ideas sketched out in the 1994 Declaration and define Abkhazia as a sovereign entity within a sovereign state of Georgia. The Boden Document also determines equality between the government of the Georgian entity in Tbilisi and the government in the Abkhaz capital Sukhum/Sokhumi, declaring that while the latter would not be subordinate to the former, both would be subordinate to a federal constitution. It also declares that the government of the federated entity would have no right to infringe on the Constitution of Abkhazia, but at the same time neither of the subordinating entities could terminate or modify the Federal Agreement that unites the two without mutual agreement (Coppieters 2004). Because they do not determine how the various competences would be divided between the federal entity and the subordinate entities, the principles enshrined in the Boden Document leave open both the option of Abkhazia becoming a constituent member of a federation strictu sensu or of it becoming an associated sovereign state without the unilateral right to secede.

Generally, the Georgian side endorsed a settlement that was based on the principles of asymmetric federalism, although it was not clear whether this endorsement represented any more than empty rhetoric for the benefit of international and domestic consumers. President Eduard Shevardnadze explicitly mentioned the concept of asymmetric federalism as a solution to the impasse regarding the country's territorial integrity, but there were few signs that he was actively seeking a solution. The "frozen conflict" situation that became entrenched and institutionalized after the wars, both in Abkhazia and in South Ossetia, proved highly advantageous for criminal groupings that exploited the porous "border" between these enclaves and the rest of Georgia for the smuggling of contraband goods. Some of these groupings are believed to have had the protection of government officials who benefited financially from these activities (Shonia 2003; Kuhkianidze, Kupatadze, and Gotsiridze 2004). Despite the avowed intent of the Shevardnadze administration to return the breakaway territories to Georgian sovereignty, whether as part of a federation or otherwise, there were elements within his administration that preferred the status quo. As a result, there were few serious initiatives toward conflict resolution during the Shevardnadze period.

After mass demonstrations forced the resignation of President Eduard Shevardnadze on 23 November 2003 in the wake of flawed parliamentary elections, the new government led by Mikheil Saakashvili took a far more proactive stance than his predecessor on the need to restore the territorial integrity of Georgia. Greater emphasis was placed on the need for some kind of federal political system that would give real autonomy to Abkhazia.

Probably the most far-reaching effort by the Georgian side to bridge the huge divide in perceptions and expectations between Tbilisi and Sukhum/Sokhumi came as a result of a series of thirteen informal workshops held in Austria and Germany between February 2000 and May 2004 with the participation of intellectuals and politicians from both sides. The meetings were organized and managed by the Berlin-based Berghof Research Center and the British-based organization, Conciliation Resources. As a result of these workshops, in May 2004 a series of proposals on a possible settlement of the conflict was presented to the National Security Council of Georgia. The proposals were presented by Paata Zakareishvili, Konstantin Kublashvili, Archil Gegeshidze, David Bakradze, and Ivlaine Khaindrava, four of whom had participated in the workshops (all except Khaindrava). They recognize Abkhazia as a sovereign entity within Georgia's national borders. As in the case of the Boden Document, Tbilisi and Sukhum/Sokhumi would both be subject to an agreement governing the division of competences between the two constituent entities that neither could amend without consent from the other side. However, according to these proposals, most competences would rest with the constituent states with the federal state only having authority over foreign policy, defense, customs, and measures against organized crime remaining. Abkhazia would also have its own central bank and Abkhazian army conscripts would not be required to serve outside the territory of Abkhazia (Wolleh 2006).

It must be stressed, however, that these proposals were not official government proposals and two of the authors, Paata Zakareishvili and Ivlaine Khaindrava were members of the liberal-leaning Republican Party of Georgia, which went into opposition against Saakashvili's government at almost exactly the same time as the proposals were published. For this reason, little attention has since been paid to them by the Georgian government (see below).

In June 2006, the Georgian government itself set down a series of rather vaguely worded proposals that it hoped would form the basis for a road map toward a final settlement. This initiative was mainly the work of Irakli Alasania, President Saakashvili's advisor on issues of conflict resolution. As to the final status, Alasania's proposals simply stated that the Georgian side was ready to launch consultations to grant Abkhazia broad internal sovereignty based on principals of federalism and promised Abkhazia "dignified representation" in all branches of the Georgian government (Civil.Ge 2006). This last clause would seem to suggest a

federal political system that would stop short of Abkhazia's equal participation in a federation.

Obstacles to a Settlement

Progress toward a final settlement of the Georgian-Abkhaz conflict since
the end of the war and up to the events of August 2008 appeared to go
backward rather than forward. Although both sides endorsed the 1994
Declaration, no progress was made on fleshing out the principles enshrined within it, and on 3 October 1999 Abkhazia held a referendum
to adopt a constitution that had already been passed by the Supreme
Soviet of Abkhazia in 1994 and that envisaged full independence for
the republic. However, former residents of Abkhazia living as displaced
people in the rest of Georgia were unable to vote. Following this referendum, the Abkhaz side rejected all proposals of federation—or even
confederation—with Georgia, insisting on nothing less than full independence. Some elements of the Abkhaz leadership have since talked
of seeking associate status instead with the Russian Federation. Indeed,
in October 2001, the de facto president of Abkhazia, Vladislav Ardzinba,
gave an interview with the Russian newspaper *Nezavisimaya Gazeta* in
which he proposed that Abkhazia should be a subject of international
law with UN membership but should at the same time implement a common foreign and defense policy with Russia. Ardzinba also suggested
that Abkhazia should have a common currency and customs union with
Russia, and should guard its state border jointly with Russia (RFE/RL
2001). This view was not shared by all of the Abkhaz elite; other leaders,
most notably President Sergei Bagapsh and Prime Minister Alexander
Ankvab, then rejected the idea of a union with Russia. At the same time
they remained categorically opposed to any form of union with Georgia.

Gradually, Moscow's attitude also began to harden against the notion
of Abkhazia as part of a federation with Georgia. While publicly Russia
still recognized Georgia's territorial integrity, a subtle change of emphasis could be observed. Thus, in December 2002, Russia ignored a trade
embargo imposed in 1996 by the Commonwealth of Independent States
on Abkhazia at Georgia's insistence by reestablishing a rail link between
Sochi and Sukhum/Sokhumi. Also, in June 2002, the Russian Foreign
Ministry had begun granting Russian citizenship to citizens of Abkhazia
and South Ossetia. By 2006, an estimated 85 percent of inhabitants of
Abkhazia and South Ossetia were believed to hold Russian citizenship
(Yasmann 2006). This allowed Russia to take a more proactive stance by
insisting that its policy in Abkhazia was merely aimed at protecting its
own citizens.

Russia (albeit reluctantly) signed up to the Boden Document in 2001, and supported Security Council Resolution 1393 (January 2002), which welcomed and supported the finalization of the Document. However, in January 2006, after five successive six-monthly Security Council resolutions had been passed reiterating or stressing "strong support" for the document,[4] at Russian insistence Security Council Resolution 1656 restricted itself to a rather terse statement extending the term of the UN Observer Mission in Georgia to Abkhazia by two months (instead of the standard six months) and made no mention either of the Boden Document or of the "territorial integrity of Georgia within its internationally recognized borders," which previous resolutions had referred to. Although subsequent resolutions restored the reference to the "territorial integrity of Georgia within its internationally recognized borders" and reinserted a mention of the Boden document,[5] this mention was weaker than in earlier resolutions as the resolutions restricted themselves to "recalling" their "support" (instead of "strong support") for the Boden principles, while at the same time welcoming "additional ideas that the sides would be willing to offer with a view to conducting creatively and constructively a political dialogue under the aegis of the United Nations." In practice this meant that the Boden document was dead in the eyes of the Russian Federation.

The Russian and Abkhazian sides also started to point to parallels between the status of Abkhazia and that of Kosovo. In a press conference on 31 January 2006, Russian president Vladimir Putin asked, "If people believe that Kosovo can be granted full independence, why then should we deny it to Abkhazia and South Ossetia?" He stressed that he was not proposing that Russia should recognize Abkhazia and South Ossetia as independent states immediately, but added that "such a precedent does exist" (RFE/RL 2006). For his part, Abkhaz president Sergei Bagapsh launched a new initiative in May 2006 calling for negotiations between the Georgian and Abkhaz sides on the peaceful coexistence of Georgia and Abkhazia as independent states and on cooperation in fighting organized crime.[6] In July 2007 he stated that, despite Russia's objections to Kosovo's independence, "The fate of Kosovo . . . is already determined, which in turn means that our fate will also be determined in nearest future." He added that Abkhazia has "even more historical and legal grounds for independence than Kosovo" (Civil.Ge 2007a).

The notion of a common precedent for the recognition of Kosovo and Abkhazia is a controversial one. When the USSR and the Federal Republic of Yugoslavia disintegrated, the principle of preserving the territorial integrity of the moribund superstate was superseded on the grounds that the latter was already in a state of effective dissolution (in the case of Yugoslavia) or because of voluntary self-dissolution based on the principle of express self-determination (in the case of the USSR). The constituent republics of both the USSR and Yugoslavia were therefore given the right to self-determination. However, only full federal subjects were granted the right to secede, which at first glance would appear to exclude both Abkhazia and Kosovo. However, in both cases there is an ambiguity that both the Kosovan and Abkhazian sides use to argue that they were, in fact, full federal subjects. Under the 1974 Constitution of the Socialist Federal Republic of Yugoslavia, Kosovo enjoyed federal status as an autonomous province, although at the same time it was described as a constituent part of Serbia. Thus it somehow belonged to the "first tier" of federal subjects at the same time as belonging to the "second tier" as a territorial unit within Serbia. In the same way, the Abkhazian leadership and intellectuals argue that Abkhazia joined the USSR as a constituent republic within the Transcaucasian Federation and that its subordination to the Georgian Republic in 1931 was illegal.

The Kosovans base their claim to the right to secede on the grounds that the human rights of a large part of the population were systematically violated by the Belgrade authorities, most notably in 1998 and 1999. The Abkhaz authorities also point to violations of their human rights during the Georgian invasion of August 1992. However, beyond this point parallels on human rights abuses are far harder to draw. This is because of the systematic violation of human rights perpetrated by militias fighting on the Abkhazian side against the peaceful Georgian population of Abkhazia in the autumn of 1993 that resulted in the forced displacement of more than 200,000 Georgians from the region. While there was also a wave of revenge attacks on Serbian communities in Kosovo following the defeat of Serb forces by NATO in 1999, which also resulted in displacement of the population, the scale of these attacks was not comparable to those that occurred in Abkhazia. The scale of the displacement in Abkhazia means that while a majority of today's inhabitants of the enclave support independence, as evidenced by the 1999 referendum, it is highly unlikely that the prewar population would have done likewise, especially since only 17.8 percent of the population were ethnic Abkhaz. It is therefore very difficult to argue for Abkhazian independence on grounds of "popular will," and to grant independence is likely to be seen as rewarding ethnic cleansing, setting a dangerous precedent in the rest of the globe. In Kosovo, where approximately 90 percent of the population was ethnic Albanian before the war and mainly supported full independence, such arguments do not apply.

However, although the arguments for granting Abkhazia the right to self-determination are considerably weaker than those for granting the same right to Kosovo, the recognition of independence for Kosovo undermined the prospects for any settlement that defines Abkhazia as an integral part of Georgia. In particular, the recognition of Kosovo's independence by the United States and a number of European Union states was seen as an attempt to humiliate Russia, leading Russia to take a more muscular stance regarding Abkhazia and South Ossetia. The possibility of a federal-type settlement all but disappeared in August 2008 following the military conflict between Georgia and Russia over South Ossetia, when the Russian Federation recognized Abkhazia as an independent state. Given Russia's status as a permanent member of the UN Security Council, this is likely to mean that any discussions that involve federalism (asymmetric or otherwise) will be put on hold for the foreseeable future.

Models for a Final Settlement in South Ossetia

The South Ossetian case is different from the Abkhazian case in two key respects. First, a majority of those living on the territory of South Ossetia were Ossetian before the war broke out. According to the 1989 census, the population of the autonomous province of South Ossetia was almost 100,000, of whom 66.2 percent were Ossetians and 29 percent were Georgians. The proportion is probably similar today, despite a significant fall in the Ossetian population of Akhalgori (which, until hostilities broke out in August 2008 and Russian forces occupied the district, was integrated into "Georgia proper") and a corresponding decrease in the Georgian populations of those parts of South Ossetia that have been controlled by the de facto authorities.

Second, until 12 November 2006 South Ossetia had not formally declared independence. This is because most members of the de facto authorities in Tskhinval(i) did not see independence as a viable option. Most members of the elite support unification with North Ossetia in the Russian Federation, which implies some form of incorporation into Russia. During Georgia's abortive attempts in 2004 to pressurize the South Ossetian population into abandoning the de facto president, Eduard Kokoity, and integrate into Georgia, banners were visible in the streets of Tskhinval(i) bearing the caption "Putin—Our President." This opinion was not universal, as there are more radical elements who wanted unconditional independence. The latter view, however, was a minority one at the time.

Far fewer concrete proposals have been made as to the future status of South Ossetia in comparison with Abkhazia. Since the emergence of Kokoity as leader in 2001, the de facto authorities in Tskhinval(i) have rejected all proposals in which South Ossetia remains a part of Georgia. Although, his predecessor, Ludwig Chibirov, appeared somewhat more ready to compromise, no concrete proposals were drawn up. This was partly due to the attitude of the Georgian government, which, until 2004, refused to recognize South Ossetia as anything more than an ordinary territory of Georgia, preferring to use the term "Samachablo" (after a historic Georgian principality) or simply "Tskhinvali district." It was also due to the fact that certain Georgian officials appeared to profit from the "frozen conflict."

After Mikheil Saakashvili became president of Georgia in January 2004, the Georgian position became at the same time more aggressive and more compromising. On the one hand, the rhetoric against the de facto authorities became progressively more inflammatory as leading members of the Georgian government frequently referred to Kokoity as a criminal. On the other hand, Tbilisi was showing willingness to grant significant autonomy to the region of South Ossetia, and in 2004 Mikheil Saakashvili for the first time used the term "South Ossetia" in public statements to refer to the region.

The first substantive proposals from the Georgian side on how South Ossetia could be governed within a unified Georgia came in March 2005. According to the proposals, drawn up by the Georgian government, South Ossetia would be granted autonomous status as a territorial entity of Georgia. It would also have its own elected legislature and its own executive branch, the head of which would be elected by the population of the region. South Ossetia would also be represented in all branches of power (legislative, executive, and judicial) at national level, although the precise manner in which it would be represented would be left to a separate constitutional law. National security and defense, state border protection and customs, national currency and national taxation policies, as well as foreign policy, would be the remit of the Georgian national authorities. The South Ossetian authorities would have competence over education policy and Ossetian would have official status as a state language alongside Georgian within the territory of South Ossetia. South Ossetia would also be granted certain rights with regard to foreign trade relationships. There would be a three-year transition period for conflict resolution, during which time international organizations would monitor the implementation of the new status and a mixed Georgian-Ossetian police force would be established with the help of international organizations. Finally, the Georgian authorities would allow a simplified border regime from the South Ossetian population between South Ossetia and the Russian Federation (Civil.Ge 2005).

By late 2006, it appeared that the Georgian authorities were preparing to implement the sort of settlement outlined above without the approval of the de facto South Ossetian authorities. On 12 November 2006 presidential elections were held by the de facto authorities in Tskhinval(i) together with a referendum on the question: "Do you agree that the Republic of South Ossetia preserve its current status of an independent state and be recognized by the international community?" Kokoity was reelected with 98.1 percent of the vote and the motion on independence was approved with 99.9 percent, according to the figures provided by the de facto authorities. At the same time, an alternative election and referendum were held in those parts of South Ossetia still under Georgian administration, prepared by the Tbilisi-backed "Salvation Union of Ossetia," which had been established a few weeks earlier by some members of the former de facto South Ossetian government under Ludvig Chibirov (1996–2001) and by Ossetian activists living in other parts of Georgia. The alternative poll elected Dmitri Sanakoev, a former prime minister under Chibirov, as alternative de facto president of South Ossetia. The alternative referendum proposed the start of negotiations with Georgia on a federal arrangement for South Ossetia. Sanakoev had become Tbilisi's favored leader of South Ossetia.

In 2007, moves were afoot by the Georgian government to implement some kind of settlement, irrespective of the attitude of the de facto authorities. Parliament passed a resolution on 8 May 2007 to establish a provisional administrative-territorial unit on the territory of South Ossetia. It remained unclear what authority this unit would have, but in lieu of any settlement it would clearly only apply de facto to those (mainly Georgian) parts of South Ossetia that were not part of the breakaway region. The provisional administration was to be tasked with developing plans for the peaceful resolution of the conflict, together with international organizations and the Georgian government, and to carry out negotiations on defining the autonomous status of the region. A window was left open for the de facto authorities to participate in this process; during a speech on 23 April, Saakashvili suggested a five-point plan, whereby the Sanakoev administration and the Kokioty administration could combine to form a provisional government that would be allowed to appoint deputy ministers of internal affairs, finance, economics, education and science, healthcare and social protection, culture, justice, agriculture, and environment, who would be responsible for issues relating to the region (Civil.Ge 2007b).

Despite this window, it was made clear that the participation of the de facto authorities was not a prerequisite for a settlement. On 10 May, Saakashvili appointed Sanakoev as head of the new South Ossetian provisional administrative entity. In July, the Georgian government established a state commission, chaired by Georgian prime minister Zurab Noghaideli, that would work on conflict resolutions issues and would work toward defining a final status for South Ossetia. Although Sanakoev was represented in the state committee, de facto authorities did not participate.

In the end, military confrontation undermined all prospects for a peaceful settlement in South Ossetia based on some kind of federal solution. Already in the summer of 2004, Georgian law enforcement agencies moved in to close Tskhinval(i)'s Ergneti market, ostensibly to crack down on "contraband." This led to nearly two months of sporadic fighting between the Georgian and Ossetian sides and undermined Ossetian support for any kind of solution in which South Ossetia would be affiliated with the Georgian state. The coup de grace was delivered in August 2008, when Georgian forces briefly entered Tskhinval(i) before being repulsed by Russian troops. This in turn led to Russia's recognition of South Ossetia as an independent state (although given the large number of Russian troops on South Ossetian sides this move is probably better understood as de facto annexation of South Ossetia) and put an end to all negotiations.

Adjara

Following the removal of Aslan Abashidze from power in May 2004 as a result of peaceful protests, the Georgian government sought to establish full control over the region. For the first time a law defining the competences of the government of the Autonomous Republic of Adjara was passed and signed into law on 5 July 2004. The law defines a thirty-member elected Supreme Council of Adjara, elected in part by proportional representation (eighteen seats) and in part directly through single-mandate constituencies (twelve seats). In July 2008, a new law was passed reducing the total number of deputies to eighteen (twelve elected by proportional representation and six in single-mandate constituencies). The Supreme Council is led by a head of government who has been proposed by the president of Georgia and approved by the Supreme Council itself. The president of Georgia is given the power to dissolve the Supreme Council and the Adjaran Cabinet of Ministers, while both the head of the Supreme Council and the parliament of Georgia are able to veto legislation passed by the council. Critics referred to the arrangement as "nominal autonomy." Certainly the arrangement provided few incentives for Abkhazia and South Ossetia to consider any form autonomy arrangement within Georgia, due to the fear that they may be granted similarly limited powers.

The Prospects for Asymmetric Federalism in Georgia: A Missed Opportunity

Theoretically, asymmetric federalism in Georgia could have involved any one of a large number of arrangements that provide different levels of competences to different regions. Under such arrangements federal law would be applied differentially to a number of different territorial units of Georgia. For example, Georgia could be established as a federation consisting of twelve federal units: the nine *mkhareebi*, Adjara, South Ossetia, and Abkhazia. Under such a system, the nine *mkhareebi* and Adjara could be given relatively limited competences, such as control of education and cultural policies, and be mainly subject to federal law, while Abkhazia and South Ossetia could be given wide-ranging competences in most if not all spheres, except defense, foreign policy, and border control. A variation on this model would be to give Abkhazia a somewhat higher degree of autonomy than South Ossetia, as was the case during the Soviet period. Another possible variation on this theme would be to give Adjara slightly more competences than the nine *mkhareebi*. All these variants would conform to the second or third model of asymmetric federalism identified in the beginning of this chapter.

However, such models are unlikely to be implemented in Georgia. First of all, after the wars for secession in the early 1990s, which are seen by many as an unwelcome consequence of Soviet-style "asymmetric federalism," the Georgian government is highly unlikely at present to cede extra powers to the *mkhareebi*, which have not, so far, enjoyed any autonomous status. In particularly there is a constant fear on the part of Georgian policy makers and the general public alike that if autonomy were ceded to Kvemo Kartli and Samtskhe-Javaketi, where the Azeri and Armenian national minorities are concentrated (45.1 percent of Kvemo Kartli's population is Azeri, while 54.6 percent of Samtskhe-Javakheti's population is Armenian according to the 2002 census), this would provide a pretext for Armenian and Azeri separatist groups to agitate for unification with host states Azerbaijan and Armenia. For this reason, federalism of any kind—especially if it involves *further* decentralization—is seen by many Georgians as a dangerous step.

Far more important, however, events on the ground have moved faster than the search for a settlement. The military conflict between Russia and Georgia over South Ossetia led to Russia's recognition of both Abkhazia and South Ossetia, effectively precluding all prospects for a federalist solution in which the two breakaway regions could take part in some kind of federation or confederation together with the rest of Georgia.

It appears that there was indeed a window of opportunity in the mid-1990s for some kind of settlement based on asymmetric federalism, but at the time of this writing that window is closed. As mentioned above, even the de facto Abkhaz authorities endorsed the 1994 "Declaration," albeit on the understanding that it envisaged a confederal rather than a federal-type solution. However, following the 1999 referendum in Abkhazia any such settlement appeared more and more unlikely. Prospects diminished still further following the decision to grant citizens of Abkhazia and South Ossetia Russian passports. Today, in the aftermath of a military confrontation between Russia and Georgia, the conflicting "national projects" of the two countries and the growing symbolic importance of the conflicts in Abkhazia and South Ossetia to the national pride of the two countries, the perspective for any federal-type solution that includes either of the two breakaway republics looks extremely dim.

Notes

1. Similarly, Sabah and Sarawak have wider powers of jurisdiction than other parts of the federation of Malaysia.
2. For the most part, Georgian place names end with the letter "i," while neither Abkhaz nor Ossetian place names do so. Here both forms of spelling will be indicated.
3. Mtskheta-Mtianeti, Shida Kartli, Kvemo Kartli, Kakheti, Samegrelo and Zemo Svaneti, Racha-Lechkumi and Kvemo Svaneti, Guria, Imereti, and Samtskhe-Javaketi.
4. UN Security Council SRes1494 (30 July 2003); SRes 1524 (30 January 2004); SRes 1554 (29 July 2004); SRes 1582 (28 January 2005); SRes. 1615 (29 July 2005), http://www.un.org/documents/scres.htm (accessed 1 September 2008).
5. Namely, SRes. 1666 (31 March 2006); SRes. 1716 (13 October 2006); SRes. 1752 (13 April 2007); SRes. 1781 (15 October 2007), http://www.un.org/documents/scres.htm (accessed 1 September 2008).
6. Known as the "Key to the future," this unpublished May 2006 position paper contained the Abkhaz de facto government's proposals for a comprehensive resolution of the conflict.

References

Civil.Ge. 2007a. Abkhaz leader speaks of Sanakoev, Kosovo case. 31 July. http://www.civil.ge/eng/article.php?id=15523 (accessed 1 September 2008).

_____. 2007b. Saakashvili offers cooperation within new administration of South Ossetia. 23 April. http://www.civil.ge/eng/article.php?id=14997 (accessed 1 September 2008).

_____.2006. Tbilisi unveils principles of Abkhazia peace plan. 9 June. Civil.Ge, Daily News Online, <www.civil.ge/eng/article.php?id=12789 (accessed 1 September 2008).

_____. 2005. Tbilisi unveils document on South Ossetia status. 24 March. http://www.civil.ge/eng/article.php?id=9425 (accessed 1 September 2008).

Coppieters, B. 2004. The Georgian-Abkhaz conflict. *Journal on Ethnopolitics and Minority Issues in Europe* 1: chap. 5.

Elazar, D., ed. 1994. *Federal systems of the world.* 2nd ed. Harlow: Longman.

_____.1993. International and comparative federalism. *Political Science and Politics* 26, 2: 190–95.

_____.1987. *Exploring federalism.* Tuscaloosa: University of Alabama Press.

Kukhianidze, A., A. Kupatadze, and R. Gotsiridze. 2004. *Smuggling through Abkhazia and Tskhinvali region of Georgia.* Tbilisi: Transnational Crime and Corruption Centre.

Radio Free Europe/Radio Liberty (RFE/RL). 2006. Russia: Putin calls for "universal principles" to settle frozen conflicts. 1 February. http://www.rferl.org/content/article/1065315.html (accessed 1 September 2008).

———. 2001. How does Abkhazia envisage its future relationship with Russia. *Caucasus Report* 4, 3 (29 October). http://www.rferl.org/content/article/1341917.html (accessed 1 September 2008).

Shonia, T. 2003. *Kriminalnyi oazis Tsvietiot v zonie Gruzino-Abkhazkogo konflikta.* Panorama 1, Institute for War and Peace Reporting, www.iwpr.net (accessed 1 September 2008).

Watts, R. 1998. Federalism, federal political systems, and federations. *Annual Review of Political Science* 1: 117–37.

Wolleh, O. 2006. *A difficult encounter: The informal Georgian Abkhazian dialogue process.* Berghof report 12. Berlin: Berghof Research Center for Constructive Conflict Management.

Yasmann, V. 2006. Independence votes popular in the Kremlin. *Radio Free Europe/Radio Liberty.* 15 September. http://www.rferl.org/content/article/1071365.html (accessed 1 September 2008).

Chapter 9
Gagauz Autonomy in Moldova: The Real and the Virtual in Post-Soviet State Design

Oleh Protsyk

Various efforts to assess the effects of autonomy arrangements on the prospects of achieving stability and democracy in ethnically heterogeneous societies receive a lot of attention in the literature.[1] The Gagauzian autonomy illustrates some of the key challenges of elaborating and implementing autonomy provisions in the context of fledgling democratic institutions and the weak system of rule of law. Although the Gagauz autonomy is often considered a rare case of successful conflict transformation in post-Soviet space, the actual implementation of autonomy provisions has been a highly contested issue. The terms of the autonomy deal—the framework of rules and provisions that central authorities and Gagauz elites agreed upon in 1994—have not elicited political actors' compliance with the written letter of the law to the extent that the legal literature on autonomy usually assumes.

This chapter provides an analysis of the terms of, and reasons for, the Gagauz autonomy agreement. Its main focus, however, is on how the implementation process led to the establishment of an autonomy regime whose functioning is far from the model envisioned in the founding documents of the Gagauz autonomy. It examines strategies employed by the central government and autonomy authorities in implementation struggles and discusses outcomes produced by the interaction of these strategies. This analysis increases our leverage for explaining successes in securing stability and democracy without falling into the trap of attributing them simply to the formal introduction of an autonomy arrangement.

The discussion pays close attention to the context in which political struggle over implementation of autonomy provisions takes place. Characteristics of the domestic political and legal environment affect the choices available to political actors and shape their strategies. For the purposes of this chapter, key characteristics of the domestic environment include the autonomous region's economic vulnerability, prevalence of neopatrimonial political practices, and weakness of the rule-of-law tradition in Moldova. The latter two characteristics set the Gagauz case and many others in the developing world apart from territorial autonomy in developed Western democracies. The latter cases provide much of the inspiration for normative writing on autonomy, but the utility of autonomy principles for the former cases is of central concern for the situation we are considering.[2]

The chapter starts with a review of the context and legal provisions of the 1994 agreement on the establishment of Gagauz autonomy and how this agreement was translated into specific norms and practices. These norms and practices, which dramatically limited the scope of the autonomy that many believe the 1994 settlement envisioned, are presented as a product of asymmetric power bargaining between political actors operating in a weak rule-of-law environment. Finally, the chapter examines how this process of defining and narrowing the actual scope of autonomy affected the behavior of elites and their commitment to the region's democratization and nonconflictual relations with the center.

Terms of the Gagauz Autonomy Deal: Definitional Vagueness and Its Consequences

In Markku Suksi's volume on autonomy arrangements, published by the leading publishing house in international law, the Gagauz autonomy is classified as a "full-fledged" autonomy arrangement, in the same category as full European autonomies in Italy, Spain, Portugal, and the Aaland Islands (Suksi 1998). Suksi distinguishes "autonomies proper" from other autonomy-like arrangements in Europe that lack exclusive law-making powers, de jure or de facto. In another authoritative document, a Venice Commission opinion on amendments to the status of the Gagauz autonomy stated that "the extent of the powers conferred on the Gagauzian autonomous institutions is very striking" (Venice Commission 2002a).

What these accounts fail to acknowledge is a level of conceptual and definitional vagueness in some of the main provisions of the autonomy's founding document, the 1994 Law on Special Legal Status of Gagauzia. Especially with regard to the key question of distribution of competences, the document provides very little guidance on the powers that belong to the central or autonomy government and how these governments should go about deciding where authority and responsibility reside on matters of policy and governance. The agreement to establish a territorial autonomy for the Gagauz minority in Moldova was a product of intense negotiations that followed the period of ethnopolitical mobilization in the early 1990s. Competing claims for sovereignty, public protests, and even small-scale violence between civil and paramilitary groups claiming to represent the interests of the titular group and the Gagauz minority characterized the period of Soviet disintegration and establishment of the independent Moldovan state (King 1997; Crowther 1998; Neukirch 2002). Autonomy settlement thus became a response to an acute need to regulate ethnopolitical conflict in order to prevent its further escalation.[3]

The Law on Special Legal Status of Gagauzia outlined the key provisions of the autonomy status. The law was passed by the Moldovan parliament after a period of negotiations between the central authorities and the Gagauz representatives, which also involved international mediation (Järve 2008; Webster 2005). The international community applauded the fact that a compromise had been achieved, and a number of observers praised the 1994 law for providing a solid foundation for ethnic tension deescalation and a crucial mechanism for meeting the Gagauz minority community needs under the general framework of the Moldovan state (Kolstø 2002; Roper 2001; Thompson 1998). As one of the analysts noted, the Gagauz case is the only case in central and eastern Europe and the former Soviet Union where de jure autonomy status was granted to an ethnic group (Järve 2008).

The key points of the 1994 law addressed the issues of drawing the administrative boundaries of the Gagauz autonomy, establishing its legislative and executive authorities and the scope of their powers, specifying procedures for minority representation on the central level, and decision-making rights to the legislative assembly in a wide range of policy areas.[4] Specific choices with respect to each of these key aspects of autonomy arrangement have contributed to a distinct profile of the Gagauz autonomy in a formal legal sense.

Art. 5 of the law stated that Gagauzia is composed of localities where Gagauzians make up more than 50 percent of the population, and an option for holding a referendum on joining the Gagauz autonomy for communities with less than 50 percent Gagauz. Some general characteristics of an autonomy established on the basis of this and other provisions of the 1994 law are outlined in Table 1.

The law provided general parameters for the SMD system of election to the Gagauz legislative assembly and included a provision on direct popular election for the head of the executive government, governor (*bashkan*) of Gagauzia. The law did not envision special norms for Gagauz representation in the national parliament but provided quite specific guarantees for the executive representation. The governor of Gagauzia is a member ex officio of the Moldovan cabinet. The heads

TABLE 1. Profile of Autonomous Territorial Unit of Gagauzia (Gagauz-Yeri)

Status	Autonomous Territorial unit (23.04.1994)
Capital	Comrat
Population	155.646 (4.6% of total population of Moldova, excluding Transnistria).
Official languages	Gagauz, Moldovan, Russian
Governor	Formuzal Michael Macar (2006–present)
Chairman of the People's Assembly	Stepan Esir
Area	1.830 km² (707 mi²)
Density	85/km²
Administrative divisions	1 municipality (Comrat), 2 cities (Ceadir-Lunga, Vulcanesti), 23 communes (29 settlements). Gagauzia is structured in three districts: Comrat, Ceadir-Lunga, and Vulcanesti.
Ethnic composition (percent)	Gagauz (85.7), Moldovan (8.1), Bulgarians (5), Russian (2.4),Ukrainian (2.3)
Ethnic population by native language (percent)	Gagauz (92.3), Russian (5.84), Moldovan (0.86), Ukrainian (0.41), Romanian (0.22), Bulgarian (0.21)
Religion (percent)	Orthodox (93), Baptist (1.62), Roman Catholic (0.06), other (5.32)
Economy	Agro-industrial sector (cereals, crops, viticulture and wine making, animal breeding, tobacco). More than 5,000 enterprises registered (agricultural, processing, textiles, ready-made clothes), 14 wineries, more than 450 small businesses. A Free Economic Zone, Valcanes, is based in Gagauzia.
GNI per capita Moldova ($)	930
Currency	Moldovan leu (MDL)

Sources: National Bureau of Statistics, 2004 census results, http://www.statistica.md/recensamint.php; World Bank (Moldova Data Profile), http://devdata.worldbank.org/external/CPProfile.asp?PTYPE=CP&CODE=MDA

of departments of the Executive Committee, the autonomy's executive body, can be made members of executive boards of national ministries at the governor's request. The heads of the Gagauzian departments of justice, internal affairs, and security, the head of the procurator's office and the chairman of the appeals court are ex officio members of the respective national ministries and other government institutions.

The law also listed policy competencies of the Gagauz autonomy in various substantive areas. Art. 18 stipulated that the autonomy forms its budget from all types of payments by the national and autonomy legislations. Art. 12 granted the legislative assembly the power to make decisions in areas as diverse as science, culture, and education on the one hand, and economy and environment on the other. Neither Art. 12 nor any other article in the autonomy statute provided details on what type of decision-making rights in relation to each specific policy area were envisioned.

While the 1994 law is structurally generally similar to autonomy laws adopted elsewhere, it is much shorter. Table 2 compares the general characteristics of the 1994 law with the 1972 autonomy statute for South Tyrol, a frequently cited example of successful autonomy in Europe. As this comparison demonstrates, the terms of the South Tyrol law are more detailed than those of the 1994 Gagauzia status law in almost every provision. Although the count of words and statute articles that is the basis for the content analysis presented in Table 2 is no substitute for substantive legal analysis of individual provisions, the magnitude of the difference in volume is telling. For example, the articles describing institutions of legislative and executive government in the South Tyrol statute are four times larger than the articles dealing with the same issues in the Gagauzia law. The differences in the size of articles dealing with policy competencies are even more dramatic, with the South Tyrol statute containing approximately nine times more text than the Gagauzian one.

The issue of competencies proved to be an especially controversial topic in the process of implementation of the 1994 law in Gagauzia. These controversies were, to a significant extent, "programmed in" at the stage of drafting the autonomy statue. A minimalist approach to the content of drafted provisions, which obviously made negotiations easier at the time of drafting, resulted in a lack of any specifications regarding what authority in a given policy area means or how decision-making in that particular area was distributed between the central and autonomy governments. The choices made at the stage of drafting the law postponed the conflict to the post-agreement phase.

The wording of Article 12 and especially section 2, which simply lists different policy areas in which the Gagauz autonomy has competences, has generated some of the most lasting disagreements between central and autonomy government. Table 3 gives exact wordings of some competency provisions from Art. 12, sec. 2 and compares them with the provisions for the same policy areas in the 1972 South Tyrol statute. This comparison further underscores the point about how little substantial content on issues of policy competence is provided by the Gagauzian statute law. Art. 17 of the Gagauz statute provides some details on what the autonomy authorities can actually do, but this article is framed explicitly in terms of responsibilities of the executive, not the legislative body.

Table 2. Number and Size of Articles in Autonomy Statutes by Category

	Law on Special Status of Gagauzia (1994)	Special Autonomy Statute for South Tyrol (1972)
General provisions	No. of words: 301 Total no. of articles: 5 Arts. 1–2; Arts. 4–6	No. of words: 209 Total no. of articles: 3 Arts. 1–3
Use of languages	No. of words: 53 Total no. of Articles: 1 Art. 13	No. of words: 374 Total no. of articles: 4 Arts. 99–102
Distribution of policy competencies	No. of words: 338 Total no. of articles: 1 Art. 12 (not incl. points 4, 5, 6)	No. of words: 2,992 Total no. of articles: 12 Chapter II: Functions of the Region (Arts. 4–7; 354 words) Chapter III: Functions of the Province (Arts. 8–15; 1,481 words) Chapter IV: Provisions Common to the Region and the Provinces (Arts. 16–23; 1,157 words)
Main legislative and executive autonomy bodies	No. of words: 1,064 Total no. of articles: 9 Arts. 7–11; Arts. 14–17	No. of words: 4,090 Total no. of articles: 34 Chapter I: Organs of the Regions (Arts. 24–46) (2,009 words) Chapter II: Organs of the Province (Arts. 47–54; 2,081 words)
Approval and promulgation of laws	No. of words: 123 Total no. of articles: 1 Art. 13	No. of words: 518 Total no. of articles: 6 Arts. 55-60
Finance	No. of words: 76 Total no. of articles: 1 Art. 18	No. of words: 1,567 Total no. of articles: 18 Arts. 69–86
Jurisdictional organs	N. of Words: 267 Total N. of Articles: 3 Arts. 20-22	No. of Words: 618 Total no. of articles: 7 Arts. 90–96
Constitutional Court	No. of words: 100 Total no. of articles: 2 sub-paragraphs Art. 12 points 4, 5	No. of words: 263 Total no. of articles: 2 Arts. 97–98
National security and internal affairs	No. of Words: 267 Total no. of articles: 2 Arts. 23–24	No. of words: 265 Total no. of articles: 2 Arts. 87-88
Change and amendments	No. of words: 31 Total no. of articles: 1 Art. 27	No. of words: 249 Total no. of articles: 3 Arts. 103–105

Sources: "Law on the Special Legal Status of Gagauzia," 23.12.1994; "Special Statute for the Region of Trentino Alto Adige," 31.08.1972. The 1972 South Tyrol Statute also contains the following sections with no comparable equivalent in the 1994 Gagauzia Law: "Local Government Bodies," "Public Property and Estate of the Region and Provinces," "Lists of personnel employed in State Offices in the Province of Bolzano."

Law on the Special Status of Gagauzia	Special Autonomy Statute for South Tyrol
- Gagauzia is an autonomous territorial unit, with a special status as a form of self-determination of the Gagauzes, which constitutes an integral part of the Republic of Moldova. - The People's Assembly of Gagauzia shall pass local laws in the following areas:	- Trentino Alto Adige, comprising the territory of the Provinces of Trento and Bolzano, constitutes an autonomous region, with legal status, within the political structure of the Italian Republic, one and indivisible, on the basis of the principles of the Constitution and according to the present Statute.
Science, culture, and education	Province: - Protection and preservation of historic, artistic and popular heritage* - Local customs and traditions and cultural institutions (libraries, academies, institutes, museums) at provincial level; local artistic, cultural, educational events and activities; in the Province of Bolzano, also through media of radio and television, but without power to set up radio and television stations* - Nursery schools* - School welfare in regard to educational sectors in which Provinces have legislative competence* - Vocational training* - Primary and secondary education (middle schools, classical, scientific, teacher-training, technical, further education, artistic secondary schools) **
Local financial, budgetary, and tax activities	Region: - Regulation of land and agricultural credit institutions, savings banks and rural banks, regional credit organizations** - Revenue from mortgage taxes collected on property situated in its territory shall be assigned to the Region. Specific quotas of state tax revenue collected in the territory of the Region shall also be assigned to the Region (see Art. 69) - To the extent that foreign trade is subject to the limitations and approval of the State, the Region shall have power to authorize such trade within limits to be established by agreement between Government and Region. In the case of foreign trade based on quotas that affect the economy of the Region, the latter shall be assigned part of the import and export quota, to be fixed by agreement between Government and Region.

Province:
- Regulation of smallholdings in accordance with Art. 847 of Civil Code; regulation of "entailed farms" and family holdings governed by ancient statutes or customs*
- Provinces may authorize opening and transfer of branches of local, provincial, or regional credit institutions, following consultation with Ministry of the Treasury.
- Unless general rules on economic planning provide for a different system of financing, the Ministry of Industry . . . shall assign to the Provinces of Trento and Bolzano quotas of the annual allocations contained in the state budget for the implementation of state laws to finance increases in industrial activity. The quotas shall be fixed. . . . Should the State intervene with its own funds in the provinces of Trento and Bolzano in order to carry out special national school building plans, these funds shall be used in agreement with the Provinces.
- The Province of Bolzano shall use its own funding allocated for welfare, social, and cultural purposes in direct proportion to the extent of each linguistic group and with reference to the needs of this group, except in the case of extraordinary events requiring immediate intervention for special requirements.
- The Province of Trento shall ensure the allocation of funding to an appropriate extent in order to promote the protection and the cultural, social and economic development of the Ladin, Mocheni, and Cimbrian populations resident in its territory, taking into account their size and specific needs.

The income from tax collected on electrical energy consumed in their respective territories shall be assigned to the Provinces.
- 9/10 of the annual rent established by law and payable for concessions of large-scale diversions of public water in the Province, granted or to be granted for whatever purpose, shall be assigned by the State to the Province.
- Provinces may impose levies and taxes on tourism.
- Provinces shall be assigned specific quotas of the yield from the tax revenues of the state collected in their respective territories (see Art. 75).

Region and Province:
- The Region and the Provinces may, by law, levy their own taxes in conformity with the taxation

	system of the state in matters of their respective competence.
	- The Region and the Provinces may issue internal loans on their own guarantee for an amount not exceeding their normal income in order to provide for investments in works of a permanent character.
	- The Region and the Provinces shall collaborate in the assessment of state taxes on the income of bodies with fiscal residence in their respective territories.
	- The Region, Provinces, and Communes shall have their own budget for the financial year, which shall coincide with the calendar year (for more details see Art. 84).
Economy and ecology	Province:
	- Protection of the countryside*
	- Artisan activities*
	- Mines, including mineral and thermal waters, quarries, and peat bogs*
	- Hunting and fishing*
	- Alpine pastures and parks for protection of flora and fauna*
	- Tourism and the hotel industry, including guides, alpine bearers, ski instructors, and ski schools*
	- Agriculture, forests and forestry personnel, cattle and fish breeding, plant pathology institutes, agricultural consortia and experimental stations, hail protection services, land reclamation*
	- Third, fourth, and fifth category water works*
	- Commerce**
	- Commercial businesses, without prejudice to requirements of state laws for obtaining licenses, supervisory powers of the state for reasons of public safety, and power of the Ministry of the Interior in accordance with national legislation the provisions adopted in the matter, however definitive. Ordinary appeals procedure against such action shall take place within the framework of the provincial autonomy**
	- Increase in industrial production**
	- Use of public waters, except for large-scale diversions for hydroelectric purposes**
	- With regard to concessions for large-scale diversions for hydroelectric purposes and extension to their term, territorially competent Provinces shall have the power to present their observations and objections at any time before the publication of the final decision by the Higher Council for Public Works.

TABLE 3. Comparative Table on Wording of Selected Competences (*continued*)

- The Provinces shall also have the right to appeal to the Higher Courts for Public Waters against decrees granting concessions or extensions

Sources: "Law on the Special Legal Status of Gagauzia," 23.12.1994; "Special Statute for the Region of Trentino Alto Adige," 31.08.1972.
* Estimates of exclusive competences; **estimates of shared competences. Competences were not affected by the following legal amendments and changes: "Autonomous Territorial Unit of Gagauzia," Art. 111 (25.07.2003); Constitution of Republic of Moldova; "Modified Text of the Constitution of the Trentino Alto Adige and the Provinces of Trento and bolzano," 18.10.200.

For example, the Art. 12 provision that the Gagauz assembly shall pass local laws on "local financial, budgetary, and tax activities" is interpreted by central government authorities as the right to lower local taxes and choose which local taxes to collect within the autonomy. The list of local taxes is regulated by the national legislation and is applicable to all local public administration units in the country. The Gagauz autonomy in this legal framework is just one local public administration unit.

In retrospect, the choice to leave the description and division of competencies unspecified and blurred has been highly consequential. By granting what appears on paper to be vast policy competences, the 1994 law raised the minority group's expectation about the actual scope of powers the autonomy obtained. The central state actors interpreted the vagueness of the provision as an invitation to specify the scope of autonomy competencies through legislative acts at the national level. This initial choice of the drafting provisions also contributed to weakening the autonomy's powers of self-government in ways that are touched on in the next section of this chapter.

Responses to "Salami Tactics" of Reducing the Scope of Autonomy

In game theory "salami tactics" refers to devices to reduce the other player's threat of actions in the way that salami is cut—one slice at a time (Dixit and Skeath 1999). The development of a legal framework for the Moldovan state in the period after 1994 was motivated by numerous factors, many of which had no relation to the autonomy. Yet the proliferation of laws, cabinet orders, and resolutions had the effect of shrinking the policy space for Gaguaz self-government. New normative acts passed by the national parliament and executive bodies in the period after 1994 routinely ignored the special status of Gagauzia. As the Gaguazians frequently point out, national legal development produced hundreds of acts that regulate societal relations throughout the country without any consideration for the special status of Gagauzia (Järve 2008).

The very weak sense of obligation or commitment on the part of central state actors to grant substantive policy competencies to the autonomy can be seen as partly rooted in the weakness of rule-of-law tradition in the post-communist world. The Gagauzian side claims that such obligations result from the central government's agreement to the 1994 autonomy statute. The very idea of contractual relations with the autonomy unit seems to be an uneasy concept for the central government. The Venice Commission recommendation—to specify in constitutional amendments that not only the autonomy unit but also the central government has the right to appeal autonomy decisions to the Constitutional Court—did not receive support among national lawmakers (Venice Commission 2002b). The lawmakers chose instead to specify in a revised version of Article 111 that control over conformity with national legislation on Gagauzian autonomy territory is exercised by the Moldovan cabinet. Overall, the actions of the central government indicate that it interprets its commitments as limited to recognizing the right of the autonomy to form its legislative and executive institutions, not its right to legislate independently of central authorities in policy areas listed in the statute.

This is reflected, for example, in bargaining over fiscal competencies. Since 2004 the central government has agreed to the autonomy requests that certain types of national taxes such as VAT and excise duties remain in the autonomy's budget. At the same time, the central government enacted a policy of reducing central budget transfers to the autonomy in proportion to the tax revenues kept by the autonomy on the basis of the 2004 agreement. The "equalization" principle, which means distribution of financial resources in accordance with population size of administrative units, is frequently evoked by the central government as justification for this policy (Osoian 2007).

The salami-slicing effect here refers to the inability of the Gagauz side to mount any credible opposition to this gradual encroachment on what the autonomy representatives believe are their self-government rights. No single legal act passed by the national level authorities was strong enough to allow ethnic minority entrepreneurs to mobilize public support in the autonomy and threaten the center with the possibility of new confrontation. In the view of minority representatives, every new piece of national legislation that ignored a special status of autonomy implied further encroachment on their autonomy rights and put additional curbs on the power of autonomy.

Autonomy authorities tried several strategies to reverse this trend. They included appeals to the constitutional court, efforts to introduce amendments to the national constitution, attempts to raise the status of the 1994 law, and initiatives to establish a new agreement between the central government and autonomy about the distribution of competences or individual pieces of national legislation. None of these strategies have so far proved successful in producing results that autonomy authorities would have liked to see.

The 1994 law referred legal disputes that arise between the autonomy and the central government to Moldova's Constitutional Court. There have been six appeals by the autonomy's legislative assembly to the Court. One of these appeals was later recalled by the Gagauz authorities; the Court rejected the other five on various technical grounds. Given the serious shortcomings in how appeals were prepared by the Gagauzian side, it would not be justified to attribute rejections to some negative predisposition on the part of the Court (Zaporozhan 2007). This record, however, has had a negative effect on autonomy representatives' confidence in the ability of the Court to address their grievances.

A strategy to introduce changes to the Moldovan Constitution resulted in modifications of two constitutional articles. Since the 1994 Law on Special Status was passed after the adoption of the Constitution, the Gagauzian authorities pushed for constitutional amendments to entrench autonomy status and strengthen its powers. While the goal of entrenching status was achieved by the adoption of the "Autonomous Territorial Unit of Gagauzia" (Art. 111) in 2003, the content of this article as well as the mention of the autonomy in Art. 110 did little to strengthen the autonomy's claims for greater control over its own affairs. The only substantive addition to its powers—the right of legislative initiative in the national parliament (Art. 72)—had few practical consequences, given that such an initiative requires the support of a legislative majority to become a national law. To date, no autonomy initiative has been supported by the national parliament.

Two other initiatives—raising the status of the 1994 law and concluding a new agreement between the central government and autonomy about the distribution of competences—were motivated by a desire to work around the developments in the national legal framework.[5] The autonomy authorities have slowly realized that a gradual encroachment on autonomy status, manifested in their view in the proliferation of national legal acts applied to the entire territory of the country, could not be reversed by appealing to the central authorities to make amendments to hundreds of pieces of recent legislation. Raising the status of the autonomy law or concluding a treaty in addition to the existing law was meant to surpass this reality by exempting the autonomy from the framework provisions in certain policy areas mentioned in the 1994 autonomy law. As should already be obvious, these initiatives found little support in central government institutions.

Not being able to raise the status of the law, the Gagauz authorities resisted any attempts to change it. Amending the law has been advocated by the central government authorities on the grounds that the Moldovan legal framework has evolved very significantly since the passage of the 1994 law, and there are a growing number of contradictions between the national legislation and the autonomy statute. The Gagauz side, on the other hand, sees the law as a crucial guarantee of the region's special status and is suspicious of any attempts to modify it.

Attempts by the Gagauz authorities to secure amendments to the key pieces of national legislation to provide some space for autonomous decision making in certain policy areas also proved unsuccessful. To illustrate the Gagauz authorities' preferences for autonomous decision making in policy areas, Table 4 lists draft amendments (and summarizes their key provisions) prepared by the autonomy authorities for consideration by the national parliament in the aftermath of the 2001 national parliamentary elections. The elections were won overwhelmingly by the Moldovan Communist Party, which positioned itself as the most minority-friendly among the major national parties.[6] As the table indicates, the autonomy authorities identified as their priority the introduction of changes in the fiscal code and laws on budgetary system and budgetary process, licensing business activity, local public administration and the status of local public officials, administrative-territorial organization, political parties, and other areas of economic and political life. None of these autonomy initiatives found support in the national government controlled by the Communist Party. The party, whose share of votes in Gagauzia went down dramatically in the next parliamentary elections in 2005, nevertheless retained its status as a governing party at the national level.

Another strategy for reversing the trend to reducing the scope of autonomy—noncompliance with national legal acts—has also been explored by the Gagauz side. Noncompliance combined with autonomy regulations unilaterally issued by the Gagauz authorities created many contradictions in the legal order, a basis for serious concern among legal practitioners across the country.[7] Noncompliance, however, has a sporadic nature and, for reasons outlined in the next section of this chapter, does not amount to organized and systematic resistance to the central government. It is, however, rationalized by autonomy actors as a response to what is perceived as fundamental reneging by the central government on its previous commitments with regard to the status of the Gagauz autonomy.[8]

TABLE 4. Draft Amendments to the National Legislation Proposed by Gagauz Authorities, 2001

Field	Law	Summary of proposed amendment
Budget and finance	Fiscal code	To introduce, besides the two existing categories of taxes (national and local), a new type of "taxes of autonomous-territorial unit"
	Law on budgetary system and process	To establish a new budgetary category (besides the existing state and local budgets): "budget of autonomous-territorial unit," and to clarify the sources of income for this budget. To allow the approval of this budget with a deficit
Public utilities	Law on electrical utilities	To establish a strong control on switching off the electrical utilities by electricity providers
Business activity	Laws on licensing business activity	To provide the executive authorities of the Gagauz autonomy with a right to issue licenses in areas of business activity currently regulated by national ministries
Government and administration	Law on status of local public officials	To exclude the members of the People's Assembly of the Administrative Territorial Unit (ATU) of Gagauzia from the list of officials whose status is regulated by this law
	Law on local public administration	To exclude provisions regarding the ATU Gagauzia from this law. To ensure that the national cabinet does not unilaterally appoint its representative (prefect) in the autonomy as it does in second-level administrative-territorial units (*judets*) and Chisinau municipality
	Law on administrative-territorial organization	To allow Gagauz authorities to regulate administrative-territorial organization inside the autonomy
Law enforcement	Law on Office of Prosecutor	To elevate the status of the prosecutor's office in Gagauzia. To ensure that prosecutors appointed by the General Prosecutor of the Republic of Moldova in the autonomy are appointed only if their candidature is preliminarily agreed on with autonomy authorities
Property and privatization	Law on environmental protection	To clarify autonomy's competences over control and exploration of natural resources

Table 4. Draft Amendments to the National Legislation Proposed (*continued*)

	Law on property	To clarify autonomy's competences over control of public property
	Law on public property of administrative-territorial units	To ensure autonomy's right to regulate privatization process on territory of autonomy
	Land code	To allow autonomy authorities to regulate (by issuing "local laws") land issues, such as changing status of land, prices for buying/selling land
Government and administration	Law on parties and other sociopolitical organizations	To allow citizens living in the autonomy to form regional political parties and other sociopolitical organizations. To provide autonomy's justice department with powers to register political organizations and regulate their activities
	Electoral code	To provide Gagauz electoral bodies with a greater degree of control over electoral process and local referendums

Source: Draft laws presented by the Gagauz autonomy authorities at the OSCE-sponsored seminar "Chisinau-Comrat: relations between the centre and the region in fiscal-budgetary, state property and legislative adaptation fields," OSCE Mission, Chisinau, 11–12 December 2001.

Explaining Stability and Democracy Records

The effects of autonomy on securing interethnic peace and democracy, as noted in the introductory section of this chapter, are central concerns for the literature on power sharing. Detailed examination of the Gagauzian case suggests that emerging patterns of stability and democracy could not be attributed exclusively or primarily to the effects of formal institutional arrangements. These patterns are better explained by examining the interplay of formal and informal rules and practices that shape relations between the center and autonomy and have profound effects on political dynamics inside the autonomy.

Informal mechanisms of control are ubiquitous under the weak rule-of-law system.[9] A large volume of literature on informal institutions, norms, and rules in states with weak legal systems testifies to the significance of problems faced by post-Soviet states (McMann 2006; Galligan and Kurkchiyan 2003; Hale 2003; Darden 2001). Informal rules and norms relevant to this specific discussion of the functioning of an autonomous regime include subordination of the judiciary branch to the executive branch of government, selective use of law enforcement, and arbitrary application of administrative norms and regulations by government bureaucracies.

The center and the autonomy have managed to avoid serious confrontation since the 1994 autonomy settlement was achieved. This means there have been no widespread violence, sustained mass protests, or riots. It does not, however, imply that relations between the center and autonomy have been cordial and mutually satisfactory. The underlying tensions surfaced from time to time, manifesting in occasional noncompliance with national legislation, sporadic public actions, radical political statements, and symbolic gestures. Thus, for example, in August 2001 Moldovan mass media reported on festivities celebrating the eleventh anniversary of the attempt to proclaim Gagauzia's sovereignty. The speaker of the autonomy's legislative assembly allegedly claimed in his speech during the event that if the Moldovan authorities failed to adjust national legislation to accommodate Gagauz laws, the Gagauz authorities would have to reactivate the 1990 declaration of independence and set up their own state structures (Järve 2008).

The absence of serious confrontation, despite growing disillusionment on the part of the Gagauz establishment with how the autonomy functions, has to be explained. As literature on intragroup dynamics suggests, accounting for the behavior of a minority elite can be a starting point for such an explanation.[10] A review of minority elite action in the Gagauz case suggests that, overall, the elite avoided mobilizing the autonomy population in its efforts to win concessions from the central government. While the rhetoric has escalated at times, the Gagauz elite have not been willing to risk open conflict with the center over the status of autonomy.[11]

The Gagauzian incumbent governor's story is telling in this respect. The 2006 elections saw a race between incumbent governor Gheorghii Tabunshchik, supported by the central government, and Mikhail Formuzal, a leading opposition figure who severely criticized Tabunshchik for his conformist stand. After winning the election, Formuzal chose to scale down his rhetoric and adopt a reconciliatory stand toward the central government. This accommodationist approach was due in part to a realization of the counterproductivity of escalating tensions with the center, whose increasing assertiveness under the Communist Party-led government reflected growing consolidation of the Moldovan state. While in many respects this state remains very weak, its affairs are no longer in complete disarray, as was the case at the beginning of 1990s, when the Gagauz minority leaders faced the weak institutions of the newly emerged state torn by ethnopolitical conflicts.

The accommodating stand of autonomy elites in the Gagauz case is partly explained by the high level of the region's economic dependence on the center. The underdeveloped character of the region's economy is illustrated by the fact that only about half the budget is covered by its own fiscal and nonfiscal income. The rest comes from deductions from state taxes and direct transfers from the national budget. In 2005, for example, the deductions from state taxes accounted for 30 percent of autonomy budget and national budget transfers for 21 percent (Osoian 2007).

The central government also exercises a high level of discretion in budget transfers. Moldovan experts on economy often decry the lack of formalized procedures for making decisions about transfers (Ionita 2006). The discretionary nature of this decision making increases the central government's leverage over local governments across the country as well as over the Gagauz leadership. The latter can be denied a fair share of transfers in case of political tensions with the center. In 2007, for example, Governor Formuzal claimed that 90 million MDL of transfers from the draft law on the state budget for 2008 did not meet the autonomy's real needs. The calculations offered by autonomy authorities were 49 million MDL higher. There was 13 million less than necessary for education; another 2.7 million for cultural programs, and so on (Nesterova 2007).

While the final transfers for Gagauzia in the 2008 budget were raised to 105 million MDL, this example illustrates one type of risk that political confrontation with the center creates for the autonomy leadership. Inability to secure sufficient financial inflows from the national center can undermine autonomy leadership support at home vis-à-vis other elite groups competing for control of the autonomy government.

The autonomy leadership's unwillingness to take a more radical stand in demanding greater scope for self-government is also a product of other forms of informal pressure exercised by the central government. As already mentioned, informal practices such as subordination of the judiciary to the executive branch and selective law enforcement are important tools of social control in post-communist states. Two of the three governors of the Gagauzian autonomy has since the establishment of the autonomy in 1994 faced criminal charges by central government-controlled prosecutors for mishandling their duties (primarily, corruption). Dmitri Kroiter, elected governor in 1999, resigned in 2002 under pressure from the central government.[12] Mikhail Formuzal was subject to many criminal charges, brought against him when he was in opposition and still outstanding when he became governor.

Overall, the autonomy elites face a credible threat to their tenure in various offices (and criminal charges brought against them through legal mechanisms of the central state), if the Gagauz autonomy is disrupted, and if their actions depart too far from the preferences of the central authorities.[13] Thus, mechanisms of coercion and cooptive control rather than power sharing might better explain the observed patterns of stability in center-autonomy relations after the 1990–92 confrontation period.[14]

Conclusion

Traditional conceptions of law see legal documents such as the Gagauz autonomy statute as structuring relations between the center and the autonomy on principles of obedience, obligation, and compliance with the provisions of the law. In transitional post-communist societies as well as in much of the developing world, the applicability of these principles to the behavior of all types of political and societal actors cannot be taken for granted. In other words, the autonomous causal efficacy of a law should not be assumed to follow its mere passage.

The Gagauzian experience with autonomy nevertheless provides several lessons for the drafters of autonomy provisions. First, having too general and poorly specified provisions on distribution of competencies in the autonomy's founding documents contributes in the long run to undermining the position of the autonomy, especially if power differentials between majority and minority are great. Second, territorial autonomy provisions are not likely to become a preferred choice for accommodating minority demands in the post-Soviet space, with the possible exception of a few already frozen conflicts. Territorial autonomy arrangements were possible in circumstances of extreme central state weakness, the case in the early years of transition from communism. The recovery of the central state, in either democratic or authoritarian form, makes central authorities increasingly unwilling to cede control over territory through institutionalization of autonomy.

The above findings can be read as contradicting some of the recent literature claims that state strength is an important condition for successful implementation of power-sharing agreements (Rothchild and Roeder 2005). State strength is defined in terms of the effectiveness of central government, and administrative bureaucracy might expand without any benefits for autonomy government. In the Gagauz case, the growing tax-collecting and service-delivery capacities of the Moldovan state contributed little to empowering an autonomy that continued to exist primarily on paper. Power-sharing literature would benefit from more detailed and systematic specification of the conditions of the relationships it hypothesizes.

For social scientists, the Gagauz experience also highlights the importance of considering informal mechanisms of subordination and control when trying to explain patterns of order and stability in multiethnic societies. The current strand of power-sharing literature seems to pay little attention to earlier theorizing on the role of control in governing multiethnic societies. This literature and our understanding of societal stability in culturally diverse societies outside the Western world would benefit from further research on the interplay between formal and informal institutions in shaping the dynamics of majority-minority relations and regulating ethnopolitical conflicts.

Notes

1. The most recent accounts include Roeder 2007; Norris 2007; Rothchild and Roeder 2005; Weller and Wolff 2005; Wimmer et al. 2004.

2. Factors such as the level of international involvement or the intensity of the preceding conflict also play some role in explaining implementation outcomes in the case of Gagauz autonomy. These issues are not addressed here because they have been already examined elsewhere (Järve 2008; Neukirch 2002).

3. For a widely used taxonomy of macropolitical forms of ethnic conflict regulation, see McGarry and O'Leary 1993.

4. Law on the Special Legal Status of Gagauzia, no. 344-XIII, 23 December 1994, Chisinau, Moldova.

5. The Moldovan constitutional system envisions three types of laws: constitutional, organic, and ordinary. The 1994 autonomy law has a status of ordinary law by which amendments can be introduced by the three-fifths majority of national parliament (Art. 111).

6. On the positioning of Moldovan political parties on minority issues see Protsyk et al. 2008.

7. Author interviews with the officials of legal departments of national parliament and Gagauzian assembly, March 2007.

8. In September 2001 the legislative assembly of Gagauzia adopted a resolution stating that the political leadership of Moldova "deliberately does not implement" the resolution of the Moldovan parliament of 23 December 1994. On the Implementation of the Law on the Special Status of Gagauzia, see Jarve 2008, 39.

9. For a discussion of the rule-of-law concept see, for example, Maravall and Przeworski 2003; and Czarnota et al. 2005.

10. Elite behavior is a crucial element in explaining intergroup accommodation in a classical version of power-sharing theory. For a critical evaluation of different accounts of elite motivation in seeking intergroup accommodation see Lustick 1979.

11. The most pronounced escalation of relations between central authorities and governor took place at the beginning of 2002. The conflict, however, was a result of the attempt by the recently elected central government to orchestrate a campaign against the governor with the goal of dismissing him by a popular referendum of confidence. Thus, the governor's confrontational stand was

a reaction against the new central government's attempt to install a more loyal candidate (Järve 2008).

12. For an account of the Gagauz autonomy's political evolution, see Botan 2007.

13. Similar types of charges were made against the speaker of the Gagauz legislative assembly in 2002 (Järve 2008).

14. On control as a mean of ethnic conflict regulation see McGarry and O'Leary 1993; Lustick 1979, 1987.

References

Botan, I. 2007. The recent elections in Gagauzia and their eventual consequences. Report written for ECMI Project Enhancing the Gagauzian Autonomy 2006 (funded by Zivik/German MFA). January.

Crowther, W. 1998. Ethnic politics and the post-communist transition in Moldova. *Nationalities Papers* 16, 1 (March): 147–64.

Czarnota, A., M. Krygier, and W. Sadurski. 2005. *Rethinking the rule of law after communism.* Budapest: Central European University Press.

Darden, K. A. 2001. Blackmail as a tool of state domination: Ukraine under Kuchma. *East European Constitutional Review* 10, 2–3: 33–45.

Dixit, A., and S. Skeath. 1999. *Games of strategy.* New York: Norton.

Galligan, D. J., and M. Kurkchiyan. 2003. *Law and informal practices: The post-communist experience.* Oxford: Oxford University Press

Hale, H. E. 2003. Explaining machine politics in Russia regions: Economy, ethnicity, and legacy. *Post Soviet Affairs* 19, 3: 228–63.

Ionita, V. 2006. Cadrul general al finanĭelor publice locale. In IDIS "Viitorul" *Descentralizarea: Elementele unui model.* Chisinau: Editura TISH: 103–19.

Järve, P. 2008. Gagauzia and Moldova: Experiences in power sharing. In *Settling self-determination disputes: Complex power-sharing in theory and practice,* ed. M. Weller and B. Metzger. Leiden: Brill.

King, C. 1997. Minorities policy in the post-Soviet republics: The case of Gagauzia. *Ethnic and Racial Studies* 20, 4: 738–56.

Kolstø, P. 2002. *National integration and violent conflict in post-Soviet societies: The cases of Estonia and Moldova.* Lanham, Md.: Rowman and Littlefield.

Lustick, I. 1987. Israeli state-building in the West Bank and Gaza Strip: Theory and practice. *International Organisation* 41, 1: 151–71.

———. 1979. Stability in deeply divided societies: Consociationalism versus control. *World Politics* 31: 325–44.

Maravall, J. M., and A. Przeworski. 2003. *Democracy and the rule of law.* Cambridge: Cambridge University Press.

McGarry J., and B. O'Leary. 1993. *The politics of ethnic conflict regulation: Case studies of protracted ethnic conflicts.* London: Routledge.

McMann, K. 2006. *Economic autonomy and democracy.* New York: Cambridge University Press.

Nesterova, O. 2007. Meditsinskii polis za poltseny. *Logoss-Press* 35 (723), 28 September.

Neukirch, C. 2002. Autonomy and conflict-transformation: The Gagauz territorial autonomy in the Republic of Moldova. In *Minority Governance in Europe,* ed. K. Gal. Budapest: Open Society Institute.

Norris, P. 2007. *Driving democracy: Do power-sharing regimes work?* New York: Cambridge University Press.

Osoian, I. 2007. Financial autonomy of Gagauzia. Report, European Centre for Minority Issues, Flensburg, December.

Protsyk, O., I. Bucataru, and A. Volentir. 2008. *Party competition in Moldova: Ideology, organization, and approaches to ethno-territorial conflicts.* Chisinau: Moldova State University.

Roeder, P. G. 2007. *Where nation-states come from: Institutional change in the age of nationalism.* Princeton, N.J.: Princeton University Press.

Roeder, P. G., and D. Rothchild. 2005. *Sustainable peace: Power and democracy after civil wars.* Ithaca, N.Y.: Cornell University Press.

Roper, S. D. 2001. Regionalism in Moldova: The case of Transnistria and Gagauzia. *Regional and Federal Studies* 11, 3: 101–22.

Rothchild, D., and P. G. Roeder. 2005. Power sharing as an impediment to peace and democracy. In *Sustainable peace: Power and democracy after civil wars,* ed. P. G. Roeder and D. Rothchild. Ithaca, N.Y.: Cornell University Press.

Suksi, M. 1998. *Autonomy: Applications and implications.* The Hague: Kluwer Law International.

Thompson, P. 1998. The Gagauz in Moldova and their road to autonomy. In *Managing diversity in plural society: Minorities, migration and nation-building in post-communist Europe,* ed. M. Opalski. Ottawa: Forum Eastern Europe.

Venice Commission. 2002a. Consolidated opinion on the law on modification and addition in the Constitution of the Republic of Moldova in particular concerning the status of Gagauzia. Opinion 191/2001, CDL-AD (21 August) 20. Strasbourg Council of Europe, 21 August.

———. 2002b. Draft consolidated opinion on the law on modification and addition in the Constitution of the Republic of Moldova in particular concerning the status of Gagauzia. CDL (2002) 040. Council of Europe: Strasbourg. 4 March.

Webster, J. A. 2005. Model for Europe? An evaluation of Moldova's autonomy for the Gagauz. Paper presented at 2005 World Convention of the Association for the Study of Nationalities, 14–16 April, New York.

Weller, M., and S. Wolff. 2005. *Autonomy, self-governance, and conflict resolution. Innovative approaches to institutional design in divided societies.* New York: Routledge, 2005.

Wimmer, A., R. Goldstone, D. Horowitz, U. Joras, and U. Schetter. 2004. *Facing ethnic conflicts: Toward a new realism.* Lanham, Md.: Rowman and Littlefield.

Zaporozhan, V. 2007. Prava obrashnia konstituzioni CYD. Training. European Centre for Minority Issues, Comrat, 14 March.

Chapter 10

Asymmetric Autonomy and Power Sharing for Sri Lanka: A Political Solution to Ethnic Conflict?

Kristina Eichhorst

Sri Lanka's Ethnic Conflict: The Difficult Search for a Political Solution

Sri Lanka's twenty-five-year-old civil war between the Sinhalese-dominated government of Sri Lanka (GOSL) and the Tamil guerrilla organization Liberation Tigers of Tamil Eelam (LTTE) is essentially secessionist. Since 1983, the LTTE has been fighting for its own Tamil homeland, the so-called "Tamil Eelam." By the beginning of 2008, this war left 70,000 people dead. Although there have been numerous initiatives over the years to find a political solution to the conflict, none of these have been successful so far. A reminder of how difficult it is to end the violent hostilities has been the breakdown of a Norwegian-brokered ceasefire that lasted for nearly four years but ended de facto in 2005–6 with renewed and intensified fighting. On 2 January 2008 the ceasefire agreement was finally abrogated officially by the GOSL.

Concurrently, however, a new peace initiative was initiated, aimed at a political solution via constitutional reforms based on a broad consensus among all relevant political and ethnic groups. To reach such a consensus, an All Party Conference was summoned; in June 2006, its delegates appointed an All Party Representative Committee (APRC) to work on a constitutional proposal for a lasting political solution. The committee was assisted by a multiethnic panel of constitutional law experts (the Expert Panel). In December 2006, however, four different reports were issued, reflecting differing opinions within the Expert Panel. Moreover, Sri Lanka's biggest opposition party had withdrawn from the whole process and the LTTE's political wing, the Tamil National Alliance (TNA), was never included. Nevertheless, fourteen different parties were represented continuously in the APRC, including the Eelam People's Democratic Party, the Sri Lanka Muslim Congress, the Ceylon Workers Congress, and the Buddhist radical nationalist National Heritage Party (Jathika Hela Urumaya; JHU). Moreover, a broad majority of the panel members, including the Tamil and Muslim members, reached consensus and agreed on a so-called "majority report." It suggested far-reaching power-sharing arrangements and asymmetric autonomy provisions. For more than a year, the report's content and the question of its implementation were debated intensely in Sri Lankan political circles.

Since the country's political elites tried to build a consensus among all ethnic communities, this new peace initiative was called "a glimmer of hope" (Liyanage and Sinnathamby 2007) within Sri Lanka's intricate conflict. Moreover, the report's approach—power-sharing and asymmetric autonomy provisions—appeared particularly promising. Nevertheless, it raised two basic issues. First, could the majority report meet the specific needs of Sri Lanka's deeply divided society? Was its design sophisticated enough to accommodate the claims of ethnic minorities, most notably the Tamil community but also the Muslim minority, while maintaining the territorial unity of the state? Second, given the three deviant proposals and the withdrawal of the opposition party as well as the general and widespread antipathy toward the concept of autonomy within the Sinhala community, the question remained whether implementation of the majority report, requiring a constitutional reform and hence a two-thirds majority in parliament, was realistic and practicable. In other words, did the APRC-process and its majority report represent the long-sought political solution to Sri Lanka's ethnic conflict?

Sri Lanka: A Deeply Divided Society

When answering the first questions on design, the complex structure of the country's society should be taken into account: Sri Lanka is a "deeply divided society" (Lijphart 2004, 96). The tiny island of only 65,000 sq km with an estimated population of 20 million includes a multitude of different ethnic groups. In terms of language, religion, country of origin, and/or caste these groups can be classified broadly as Sinhalese, (Sri Lankan) Tamils, Indian Tamils, Muslims, and "others." However, the term "deeply divided" does not refer simply to numbers; it also points to both perceived and de facto intensity of the various cleavages between different groups. Obviously, the most important in this regard is that between the Tamil minority and the Sinhalese majority, the latter representing approximately 80 percent of the population.[1]

Although the source of this conflict can be traced back to the British colonial period, it became politically relevant only after Sri Lanka's independence in 1948 (Wickramasinghe 1995). Sinhalese politicians, committed to the idea of a Sinhalese nation-state, soon dominated the decision-making process of the newly independent country and worked to entrench their vision of the state. The result was political marginalization of the Tamil community. Conflicts arose around central issues, notably language rights, education, and land. Massive discrimination of the Tamil minority led to increased alienation from the state.

Nevertheless, during the first decades of independence the Sinhalese-Tamil conflict remained strictly nonviolent in character and demands for self-determination were neither widespread nor vehement. Until the early 1970s, mainstream Tamil politicians were rigidly committed to the territorial integrity of the Sri Lankan state. British-educated and state-conscious, they numbered themselves among the leading political elite of the country. As such, they were confident of resolving outstanding issues within the state polity.

During the early 1970s, however, it became increasingly apparent that it was impossible to enforce Tamil interests within existing political structures. Thus, in 1976, Tamil politicians ended their consensus-oriented strategy and issued the Vaddukoddai Resolution, claiming an independent Tamil state. On the basis of this resolution the dominant Tamil party (Tamil United Liberation Front, TULF) won a landslide in the country's parliamentary elections, becoming the biggest opposition party in Sri Lanka. To date, this electoral victory is regarded by Tamil politicians as a popular mandate to negotiate Tamil independence. The conflict, initially issue-related, became predominantly territorial (Matthews 1982, 1123–24).

While the moderate Tamil elite refrained from violence, and would probably have refrained from secession had federal reforms been implemented, other more radical and militant Tamil actors soon emerged. They advocated an independent Tamil homeland and were determined to enforce their claims with violence. Increased polarization of the Sinhalese and Tamil communities led to the weakening of moderate Tamil parties and to the growing influence of radical actors. Violent intraethnic competition broke out among militant Tamil groups, for leadership of the Tamil community, from which the LTTE emerged victorious. Intraethnic violence was also directed against moderate Tamil politicians who frequently became, and remain, victims of deadly assaults. With the

LTTE rising to supremacy within the Tamil community, the conflict became secessionist in essence and violent in nature (Singer 1996).

In 1983, after severe anti-Tamil riots in Colombo the steady escalation of conflict led to full-scale civil war. Ever since, the Sri Lankan Armed Forces (SLAF) and the LTTE have been engaged in intense fighting, interrupted only by short periods of ceasefire. Numerous military successes and setbacks on both sides, as well as the fruitless intervention of an Indian Peacekeeping Force (IPKF) in the 1980s, suggest the impossibility of ending the conflict by military means. Yet, the long history of attempts to find a political solution indicates that the probability of ending the conflict by political means is only marginally better.

Sri Lanka's State Design: A History of Failed Attempts to Devolution

Following numerous attempts to reform the unitary structure and to implement some form of autonomy, the Indian government sought to end the conflict by force under a United Nations mandate while simultaneously pushing for enforcement of the Indo-Sri Lanka Accord of 1987. Following the Indo-Sri Lanka Accord, the Constitution was amended in 1987 (the Thirteenth Amendment), which established the envisaged system of provincial councils.[2] The provinces became the unit of devolution with a chief minister and a provincial council to be elected every five years and a governor appointed by the president. Legislative powers were to be divided between the center and the provinces respectively via a "reserved list" and a "provincial list," while a "concurrent list" defined shared powers, albeit with supreme authority residing in the parliament. The latter construction was a common trait of the whole system. Provincial competences were not only limited but conditional, since their exercise depended on the governor, who was dependent on the president. Moreover, the parliament was authorized, by a two-thirds majority, to curtail the powers of the provincial list (which it did). Finally, the provinces were not granted financial autonomy and had limited financial resources of their own.

However, a lack of political will on the part of the Sri Lankan president Ramasinghe Premadasa led to a withdrawal of Indian troops in 1989–90. Fighting between the LTTE and the SLAF in the Northeast resumed and the NEPC was dissolved. Since the north and east were de facto controlled by the LTTE, all policy and procedures remained ineffective.

After the debacle of the Indian intervention, new attempts were made to solve the conflict by political means, the most important being the far-reaching devolution proposals presented by the governing Sri Lanka Freedom Party (SLFP)/People's Alliance (PA) in 1995.[3] However, even these popular measures were ultimately unsuccessful, and by the turn of the century the country's administrative and political structures remained inherently unitary with only minor concessions to the provinces.

A New Approach to Peace Building in Sri Lanka: International Engagement

Given this long history of failed attempts to find a national solution to Sri Lanka's conflict, outside mediation was sought. In 2000, Norway was formally invited by Sri Lanka's president, Chandrika Bandaranaike Kumaratunga (SLFP/PA), and the LTTE to act as facilitators for the peace process in the country. This approach was continued by Sri Lanka's new president, Ranil Wrickemasinghe (United National Party; UNP). At first, it appeared successful. In February 2002 both parties to the conflict signed a ceasefire agreement (CfA) in order to lay the foundation for negotiations on a long-lasting political solution. The Sri Lanka Monitoring Mission (SLMM) was established, consisting of members from Norway, Denmark, Sweden, Finland, and Iceland, to monitor the CfA and to mediate between both actors. Between September 2002 and March 2003, six rounds of negotiations between the GOSL and the LTTE took place in which substantial progress seemed to be made. In December 2002, negotiations in Oslo led to agreement by both parties "to explore a political solution founded on the principle of internal self-determination based on a federal structure within a united Sri Lanka" (RMFAN 2002). Although this declaration caused a stir internationally, the Oslo Declaration was only a nonbinding expression of intent without any concrete proposals on how this federal structure should work (Eichhorst 2003).

In the following months, the GOSL, assisted by Norway, prepared a draft institutional mechanism to set up an interim administration in the Northeast (GOSL 2003). Released in July 2003, it was summarily rejected by the LTTE, which, in April 2003, had withdrawn from the formal peace talks with the GOSL. Notwithstanding its withdrawal, in October 2003, the LTTE delivered its own proposal for a so-called "Interim Self-Governing Authority" (ISGA) (LTTE 2003). Both the GOSL and the LTTE drafts were solely provisional, to be followed by a comprehensive constitutional framework for a lasting political solution. They contained neither an overall institutional design for the whole country nor defined center-provincial relations, and were limited to internal administration of the Northeast.

Basically, both drafts proposed the establishment of some kind of administrative or self-governing body. However, the powers ascribed to the body by the two drafts indicated fundamental differences. The GOSL draft allowed its Provisional Administrative Council (Council) to exercise and perform "such powers and functions as are at present being exercised and performed by the Government in respect of regional administration . . . including rehabilitation, reconstruction and resettlement" (GOSL 2003). It excluded the areas of police and security, land, and revenue. The LTTE proposal, by contrast, accredited the ISGA with "powers in relation to resettlement, rehabilitation, reconstruction, and development, including improvement and upgrading of existing services and facilities . . . , raising revenue including imposition of taxes, revenue, levies and duties, law and order, and over land" (LTTE 2003, Art. 9.1). As a matter of course, the area of police and security (or "law and order") was particularly disputed since neither side was willing to leave these matters to the other. For the LTTE, it would have meant renouncing force, while for the GOSL it would have been tantamount to abandoning its claim to sovereignty in the Northeast.[4]

Another major dispute arose over the body's composition. While both the GOSL and the LTTE proposals ensured an absolute majority of LTTE appointees in the body,[5] GOSL insisted on implementing some form of power sharing and minority protection. This resulted from the substantial size of the Sinhalese and Muslim communities living in the areas concerned. In particular, the Muslim community in the hard-fought east had, over the years, been caught in the crossfire of Sri Lanka's civil war (ICG 2007a). Hence, an administrative mechanism had to incorporate Tamil and Sinhalese as well as Muslim concerns. For this purpose, two proposals were made: alternative A envisaged "two chairpersons, one representing the LTTE and the other the GOSL elected by and from amongst the members of the Council. Each chairperson shall have the right to veto any proposal brought before the Council" (GOSL 2003); alternative B foresaw only one chairperson elected from among the members of the Council (i.e., in all likelihood an LTTE appointee). An additional provision required that "any decision of the Council, which affects either the Muslim or the Sinhala community can only be made valid if the decision is supported by a majority of the Members of the Council and a majority of the representatives of the Muslim or the Sinhala communities as the case may be."

The GOSL approach was summarily rejected by the LTTE. The LTTE's own proposal did not contain any power-sharing provisions or minority-protection mechanisms; in fact, it would have enshrined the LTTE's autarchy over the Northeast.[6] Thus, the LTTE's ISGA proposal was neither acceptable to the GOSL nor to the Sinhala and Muslim communities in the Northeast. Following mutual rejection of the two drafts, negotiations ground to a halt. During the following months, both sides consistently and frequently violated the ceasefire agreement, a situation that came to be known as "no peace, no war" (Eichhorst 2006). In February 2006, the

SLMM tried to revive the CfA by launching another round of negotiations in Geneva. These diplomatic efforts were not successful, however, and did not stop the conflict from reescalating into full-scale civil war. Responsibility for this deterioration was, in large measure, attributed to Sri Lanka's new president, Mahinda Rajapakse (SLFP/PA), elected in November 2005. He had forged a coalition with two Sinhala nationalist parties, the JVP (Janata Vimukthi Peramuna; People's Liberation Front, a Marxist party) and the JHU, both critical of the CfA. In the following months, he took a tough stance on the peace process. His basic strategy seemed to be military defeat of the LTTE, accompanied by severe human rights abuses (ICG 2007b).

At the same time, however, Rajapakse summoned the All Party Conference to reach a consensus on a political solution and, in June 2006, fostered the establishment of the APRC and its Expert Panel.[7] Ultimately, he did not appear committed to the political approach but demonstrated a significant "lack of enthusiasm" (ICG 2007b, ii). This did not stop the APRC Expert Panel from working on a proposal for constitutional reform that resulted in the above-mentioned majority report.

The Majority Report and Its Possible Impact on the Overall State

The majority report (also entitled "Report of Subcommittee A," hereinafter RSCA) is only one of four different reports issued by members of the Expert Panel in December 2006.[8] In addition, a fifth proposal emerged later when the chairperson of the APRC, Minister Tissa Vitharana, presented a discussion paper aimed at a compromise. Nevertheless, the RSCA had been endorsed by eleven of seventeen members, including all members representing ethnic minorities, and it has been approved by many analysts in the Tamil community. Furthermore, the RSCA comprehensive institutional framework was widely publicized in the media and attracted interest not only from politicians but also from researchers and peace activists. For more than a year, therefore, the majority report represented the central document on proposals for constitutional reform and, as such, the basis for discussion of a political solution for Sri Lanka's ethnic conflict (Liyanage 2007).

The RSCA's Overall State Construction

Due to the historic misconception that "federal" implies "secessionist," and in view of the long history of secessionist aspirations, the question of which official term was to describe the Sri Lankan state structure was a delicate one (Fleiner 2007). For this reason, the RSCA deliberately avoided the use of distinctive expressions. The current term "unitary" was left out; instead, it described Sri Lanka as "one, free, sovereign and independent State . . . consisting of institutions of the Centre and of the Provinces" (Art. 2.2).

However, the RSAC's content appears federal in all but name. The RSCA proposes a trilevel organization of government, with national, provincial and local tiers.[9] To achieve provincial representation in the national legislature, it advises the establishment of a second chamber of parliament, a classic trait of federal systems. All legislation "may be initiated" in the second chamber with the exception of money bills. Moreover, paragraph 5.1(c) stipulates that the second chamber shall "have a distinct role to play in the national legislature" and could act "as an inbuilt mechanism against . . . legislation that may have an adverse effect in the Provinces."

Regarding the distribution of powers between the center and the provinces, the RSCA proposes a national list, a provincial list, and a concurrent list, the last consisting of minimal subjects and functions to avoid conflict between the center and the provinces. Rather, the RSCA intended to explicitly define and effect the distribution of powers between the center and the provinces (Art. 7.2).[10] Most important, however, were constitutional safeguards for provincial powers; that is, amendments would apply to a province only after passage in Parliament and approval by the relevant provincial legislature (Art. 19.1).

However, certain aspects of the overall state structure envisaged remained unclear. The RSCA was silent as to how the membership of the second chamber should be distributed among the provinces. Equal representation among all provinces might not be possible since the chamber's size would be 60, which is not divisible by 9 or 8 (depending on how the issue of the Northeast (de-)merger is resolved). This is important, since it determines central representation of provinces. It allows for built-in mechanisms to enhance integration of minorities, for example, by asymmetric representation, that is, by granting those provinces that are dominated by minorities a disproportionately higher number of seats in the second chamber. How this question will be resolved remains to be seen.

Another shortcoming is the RSCA's lack of detail on the legislative process and on the second chamber's legislative role. It is doubtful whether the lower house has the power to modify legislative drafts of the upper house. It is also unclear whether the phrase "may be initiated" is rigid or permits the lower house to initiate legislation. In both cases it is important to know whether the second chamber can veto modifications or initiatives of the lower house. Hence, a question mark hangs over the RSCA's federal character, since it is not clear how extensive the legislative influence of the upper house would be: would the second chamber really have an impact on the national legislative process or could it be bypassed by the lower house and remain a mere representative but powerless body? This is another decisive aspect regarding the integrative impact of the proposed second chamber.

Several aspects of the state's overall construction have not been mentioned thus far. Notably, the internal structure of the provincial system of government has not been specified. The most important aspect here would be the relationship between a provincial governor and its chief minister, and gubernatorial powers. The powerful office of provincial governor has previously been a major obstacle to substantial devolution in Sri Lanka, and a delineation of competences would be decisive for implementation of autonomy in Sri Lanka.

Notwithstanding these uncertainties, the RSCA unequivocally expresses the intention to "generate a sense of participation by the Provinces in the legislative and executive decision making at the Centre" (Art. 11.1), which suggests that the RSCA desires an influential role for the upper house and an essentially federal system. This is supported by the proposal to establish a council of chief ministers of the provinces to be chaired by the president for effective coordination between both levels of government as well as a quarterly conference of the chief secretaries chaired by the secretary to the president (Arts. 11.2, 3), a mechanism that would resemble the Canadian Prime Ministers' Conference. In sum, the RSCA seems to intend a federal system, but leaves open some important questions.

Asymmetrical Elements of the RSCA

The RSCA's autonomy provisions contain two broad areas of asymmetry: one regarding the Northeast, the other the Indian Tamils in the central uphill region.

With respect to the asymmetrical provisions for the Northeast, the RSCA refers explicitly to the "historical fact that the Tamil people had been agitating for self-rule over a period of time and [that] the present conflict has its origins in that agitation" (Art. 7.6). Against this background, the RSCA recommends that all subjects and functions belonging to the concurrent list be assigned to the Northeast provincial list. For the Northeast, the center would have no powers for framework legislation in terms of devolved subjects. This is meant to "act as a safeguard against possible intrusions by the Centre" (Art. 7.6). Furthermore, this clear-cut division of competences could reduce conflict between the center and the region over their respective powers.

The RSCA's asymmetrical provisions are intended to be temporary: "The above mechanism provides for asymmetry at the beginning but with all Provinces having the opportunity to ultimately take over all subjects and functions in the Concurrent List, resulting in symmetry" (Art. 7.7). Consequently, every province has the right to negotiate with the center over the transfer of subjects or functions of the concurrent list to its own provincial list. The RSCA's asymmetrical approach toward the Northeast seems tentative. First, the asymmetrical provisions are not prominent within the document but mentioned in passing. Second, there is no exclusivity to the Northeast, since any province can attain this status over time. This hesitancy can be explained by opposition anticipated from the Sinhala nationalist parties. Nevertheless, its impact can be decisive, since its design is intended to avoid conflict between the center and the Northeast and to grant the latter special recognition, at least initially.

Concerning asymmetrical elements for the Indian Tamil community, the RSCA's approach is twofold: first, it envisages the establishment of an Autonomous Zonal Council (AZC) within specified regions in the central uphill country with a territorial focus on Nuwara Eliya District in the Central Province, where Tamils of Indian origin live in substantial numbers (Art. 12). The AZC, whose main task shall be "to address the concerns" of the Indian Tamils, shall be assigned the powers of the specified administrative divisions and shall receive further competences for listed subjects, such as Tamil middle schools, agricultural development, and cultural affairs. Nevertheless, it was made clear that although the AZC shall be equipped with its own budget and the power to make bylaws, it will not be sovereign but will be subordinated to the Central Province legislature.

The second approach is nonterritorial and proposes the establishment of an Indian Tamil Cultural Council (ITCC) "to effectively contribute to the economic, social and cultural advancement of that community" (Art. 12.1). The ITCC, which shall be provided with annual government grants, shall consist of all members of parliament and provincial councilors belonging to the Indian Origin Tamil Community. Alongside five members appointed by the president, the members of the ITCC shall act as a consultative body to the AZC. This proposal derives from the fact that Indian Tamils live in substantial numbers in provinces other than the Central Province but do not have absolute majorities in those areas. Thus, the ITCC aims to advance their interests nationwide regardless of their place of residence.

In sum, the scope of the AZC and ITCC provisions seems limited. The appointment of the ITCC members by the president and the financial dependence on government grants represent significant constraints on its autonomy. Furthermore, the provisions leave unaddressed questions regarding the modalities of appointment for AZC members. Yet, in the face of the long history of neglected Indian Tamil grievances and political aspirations, the AZC and ITCC represent a decisive move forward. Both institutions will be supplementary to the possibilities for self-government granted by the devolution of powers to the provinces, to which Indian Tamils—at least in the Central Province—have access.

Managing Asymmetry: A Settlement for the Northeast

The most delicate part of the RSCA is in chapter 6, "Unit of Devolution." Although it is stipulated that the units of devolution shall be Sri Lankas provinces (a "nonethnic" criterion), it is acknowledged that "factors such as ethnicity and language could not be excluded in all situations and that there may have to be exceptions in order to address security and other concerns of communities. We are of the view that, ideally, such exceptions should be limited in time and that, ultimately, ethnicity should not be the sole criterion for the establishment of units. This should not, however, preclude special arrangements being put in place to address such concerns" (Art. 6.4).[11]

The following "arrangements" and "exceptions" apply explicitly to the special situation in the areas of the Northeast to which these provisions are limited—territorially as well as temporally. According to the RSCA they are intended to resolve the persistent dispute over the (de-)merger of the Northeast.

Finding a solution to the question of the Northeast (de-)merger is a basic requirement for any devolutionary project in Sri Lanka. From the outset of the country's civil war, the merger has been fundamental for all Sri Lankan Tamils, regardless of their political affiliation (Hariharan 2006). Its importance is reflected in its incorporation within the Indo-Sri Lanka Agreement of 1987, and remains evident in international (especially Indian) pressure against any demerger of the Northeast. However, in October 2006 the Supreme Court judged that the merger of the Northern and Eastern Provinces in 1988 had been invalid due to unfulfilled constitutional preconditions. With this ruling, the issue once again became extremely relevant.

To reach a consensus on the issue of the geographical, administrative, and political design of the Northeast, the RSCA proposes four alternative models. Model A (Art. 6.10(A)) envisages a single (merged) Northeast Province with two internally autonomous Sinhala and Muslim units, provided with legislative and executive powers relating to certain subjects such as law and order, education, and culture. Additionally, the possibility of introducing a double majority is mentioned as a safeguard for minority interests. Although it is not explained in detail, the term "double majority" in this context apparently refers to the requirement that legislative decisions must have both a majority in parliament and a majority of the members of parliament belonging to ethnic minorities (Muslim and Sinhalese minorities in this case). The critical point of model A is that neither Sinhalese nor Muslims settle in territorial contiguity. Their autonomous units would have to consist of a territorially contiguous base unit attached to noncontiguous enclaves. Thus it is acknowledged that this "attachment of enclaves may give rise to practical issues" such as administration and security.

Model B (Art. 6.10(B)) proposes a basic restructuring of the Northeast into three units, with a Muslim, Tamil, and Sinhala majority respectively. The use of the term "unit," however, seems euphemistic, since it entails the establishment of three ethnically defined provinces. Moreover, the noncontiguous settlement of the communities, in particular of the Sinhalese, would once again pose problems. Two suggestions have been made in this regard: either the Sinhalese unit would be essentially noncontiguous, or the Sinhalese majority areas would be attached to adjoining provinces. The Muslim majority unit, as in Model A, would consist of a contiguous base unit and noncontiguous enclaves. The remainder would be a noncontiguous Tamil majority unit. However, the issue of "economic viability of such a unit may arise." This applies in particular to irrigation schemes, which "would become inter-Provincial schemes." [12]

Model C (Art 6.10(C)) envisages an interim merger of the Northeast with an interim provincial legislature and government for a period of ten years with a referendum to be conducted at the end of this period. In addition, and in accordance with model A, the possibility of Muslim and Sinhalese autonomous units and double majority provisions are suggested. However, as with A, practical issues may arise from the establishment of autonomous units.

Finally, Model D (Art. 6.10(D)) recommends adhering to the demerger of the Northeast. The two provinces would have an Apex Council for coordination on matters of common interest. However, Tamil approval of this proposal seems unrealistic due to the historic importance of the Northeast merger to the Tamil community.

It had clearly not been possible for members of the Expert Panel to agree to a single proposal; instead, they proposed four different models. These differences within the group of RSCA supporters (let alone the three dissenting reports from the remainder of the panel) reflect the intricacy of the issue. The task of reaching a consensus on structure of the Northeast among political parties and within larger Sri Lankan society will be a difficult one.

Distribution of Powers

Regarding the distribution of power, the RSCA does not provide a detailed list of subjects and functions belonging to the national, provincial and concurrent lists but explicitly leaves this issue to recommendations at a later stage (Art. 7.8). However, in the chapter regarding fiscal devolution, the text refers to the Constitution Bill 2000, whose enumeration of subjects and functions, "eliminates much of the ambiguity that is present in the Thirteenth Amendment" (Art. 9.3a). This seems to recommend the bill as a possible model for distribution of powers, though it is not clearly articulated.[13] Moreover, the RSCA makes general suggestions regarding the distribution of powers; for example, subjects "which are necessary to ensure the sovereignty, territorial integrity and economic unity of Sri Lanka shall be reserved to the Centre" (Art. 7.3). According to the RSCA, this includes inter alia defense, national security, and maritime zones. While this will evoke fierce opposition from the LTTE, it is (according to international standards) quite common to leave subjects of national relevance to the center.

The areas of public order and the exercise of police powers will be devolved to the provinces, while Colombo City and its environs will be reserved for the central government. The same applies to "carefully demarcated strategic institutions/installations . . . for the purposes of Defence/National Security" (Art. 10.3), that is, the so-called "high security zones," which may cause conflict, since many encompass land seized from people now internally displaced (see below).

Somewhat problematic is the general stipulation directed at subjects not mentioned specifically in any list. In this case, only subjects that are ancillary to subjects or functions included in the provincial list shall be categorized as provincial matters. All other subjects not explicitly listed shall be deemed an item of the national list. This provision could be used by the center to accrue as much competence as possible simply by not regulating the assignment of specific issues to any list. The failure to define these matters would be a deficiency of the RSCA and could weaken the whole devolutionary project.

Governance Issues

The RSCA is characterized by its comprehensive approach. In addition to providing for asymmetric autonomy, it also deals with a wide range of governance issues. The most important one in this respect is the provision for power sharing at the center.

Power Sharing at the Center

The RSCA acknowledges that "the crisis in the Sri Lankan polity has arisen because . . . the numerically smaller ethnic groups have not had their due share of State power" (Art. 1.1). For this reason, it recommends recognizing the right of every community "to its due share of

State power including the right to due representation in institutions of government" (Art. 2.4). To this end, the RSCA develops a form of genuine power sharing between different communities that, according to the document, does not follow any particular model but meets the specific needs of pluralist Sri Lankan society.[14] Several RSCA stipulations aim at implementing power-sharing mechanisms.

First, it recommends establishing two vice-presidents "who shall belong to two different communities distinct to that of the President" (Art. 5.1b). It can be expected that this will result in a Tamil and a Muslim vice-president alongside a Sinhalese president. However, the RSCA does not define vice-presidential competences, or influence on presidential political decision making. Moreover, it deliberately does not decide the question of direct or indirect elections for vice-president. This is of utmost importance, since a direct election would assign the office much greater political weight than an indirect election. A directly elected vice-president would have a greater impact on the president's decision making than an indirectly elected vice-president. Consequently, the regulation of this issue will determine whether the vice-presidents will have a real impact or whether the office is merely a symbolic gesture. Thus, the regulation of this issue will be decisive for implementation of power sharing at the presidential level. In any event, the value of a symbolic gesture should not be underestimated.

Second, the RSCA proposes that "the Cabinet of Ministers should, in principle, reflect the pluralistic character and also be representative of the Provinces of Sri Lanka" (Art. 5.1h). No further details on terms or representative quotas are mapped. Once again, these issues are left to further proposals in a subsequent report. The specific regulation of this matter will be particularly important. Current experience shows that Tamils already are part of the government—for example, the late foreign minister Lakshman Kardigarmar, who was assassinated by the LTTE in 2005. However, these Tamil politicians are often members of the SLFP or the UNP. As such, they are not recognized as Tamil representatives or advocates of Tamil interests by a significant portion of the Tamil population (although they often are, or at least try to be). It is worth considering whether representation in the cabinet of ministers should be according to party affiliation rather than to an ethnicity.

Third, executive-power sharing is also envisaged at the provincial level, albeit with reservation. The RSCA explicitly refers to the risk that "a Provincial executive could become [a] breeding ground for corruption when there is no official opposition" (Art. 5.2a). Therefore, the RSCA recommends a time limit and built-in mechanisms for transparency.[15]

Fourth, provincial representation is recommended for the Constitutional Council, renamed the High Posts Commission (HPC) (Arts. 3.6,

5.1b). Apparently, the duties of the HPC will remain the same, namely, to recommend to the president persons for appointment as the chairman or member of several official commissions. In the event that these persons are appointed by the president, the HPC must approve them. At present, according to the Seventeenth Amendment of the Sri Lankan Constitution, the current Council's membership already reflects to some extent the diversity of the parliamentary parties. With the provinces to be represented in the future HPC, its membership would be more comprehensive. Since several provinces, such as the Central Province and the Northeast, will likely be dominated by Sri Lanka's ethnic minorities, this regulation implies enhanced guarantees for representation of minorities in the HPC. Furthermore, this will affect representation of minorities in the official commissions mentioned above. Additionally, the RSCA proposes that the HPC recommends and approves the members of the Constitutional Court (to be established, see below) and the courts of appeal. It provides explicitly that judicial officers should "reflect the pluralistic character of the Sri Lankan people" (Arts. 3.3, 8.1). A similar provision is made regarding the National and Provincial Public Service Commissions that shall be established to determine the cadres of their respective public services (Art. 14.8, 14.9). Moreover, on a more general basis, the RSCA provides that "there shall be equitable representation of the different ethnic communities of Sri Lanka in the public services" (Art. 14.12). Since Tamil representation in the public services had become a serious issue in connection with the implementation of "Sinhala Only" legislation, this provision is of extraordinary relevance.

All things considered, the RSCA's authors clearly intended to establish power sharing in a comprehensive way. However, the outcome will depend on various regulations still to be specified. If the RSCA were accepted as the official blueprint for a political solution to Sri Lanka's conflict, it would remain uncertain whether de facto implementation of power sharing in Sri Lanka would succeed.

Human Rights

Since the RSCA recognizes that minorities were sidelined and alienated from the state, it places considerable emphasis on group rights. It recommends constitutionally enshrining "the right of every constituent people to develop its own language, to develop and promote its culture and to preserve its history" (Art. 2.4). To this end the RSCA suggests "a comprehensive Bill of Rights that guarantees not only civil and political rights but also group, social, economic, cultural and children's rights" (Art. 15.1). As possible models, the RSCA refers to the South African Constitution as well as to the 2000 Draft Constitution for Sri Lanka and to the far-reaching stipulations for minority protection in Section 29(2) of the Soulbury Constitution.

To ensure effective enforcement of the Bill of Rights, the RSCA advocates "adequate machinery" (Art. 15.2), consisting of the Supreme Court, the national and provincial courts of appeal (both have a fundamental rights jurisdiction), the National Human Rights Commission, and possible further provincial human rights mechanisms. Moreover, the RSCA approves the establishment of a constitutional court outside the hierarchy of courts to adjudicate constitutional matters, including the proposed bill of rights. As mentioned above, its members shall be appointed by the president on the recommendation of the HPC and should reflect the pluralistic character of the Sri Lankan people (Art. 3.3). The Constitutional Court shall "have the power to strike down Central and Provincial legislation which is violative of the Constitution" (Art. 3.4).

Overall, the RSCA proposals attempt to lay out a comprehensive human rights framework for Sri Lanka. In view of the Sri Lankan conflict, its human rights crisis and national and international appeals for an effective human rights regime under international oversight, the RSCA's stipulations become even more important. However, their impact is contingent on implementation, notably, on effective law enforcement, human rights education within the police and the armed forces, disciplined enforcement in both instructions of human rights principles, an enhanced overall security situation and, ultimately, an end to civil war.

Managing Sri Lanka's Ethnic Diversity

The RSCA is dedicated to the management of Sri Lanka's ethnic diversity. Of greatest significance is the dual approach of asymmetric autonomy and power-sharing mechanisms. The RSCA's human rights regime also accentuates group rights. In addition, further stipulations aim at managing the country's ethnic diversity. First, the RSCA recommends that the Constitution stipulates that the state shall "preserve and advance a Sri Lankan identity, recognizing the multiethnic, multilingual, multireligious and multicultural character of the Sri Lankan society" (Art. 2.3). Based on this assumption, the RSCA suggests that "clearly defined affirmative action" (Art. 15.3) be considered with regard to disadvantaged communities. According to the RSCA, these measures should be time-bound and periodically reviewed. However, the RSCA does not specify the communities to which the term "disadvantaged" should apply, leaving room for serious dispute as to who is deserving of affirmative action.

Regarding management of ethnic diversity, one of the major unresolved questions is language, an issue of extraordinary relevance to the Sri Lankan conflict. Therefore, the RSCA urges the effective implementation of the language provisions (chapter 4) of the present Constitution (Art. 16.1). Accordingly, Sinhala and Tamil shall be the official languages of Sri Lanka. In addition, every person has the right to communicate in Sinhala, Tamil, or English with government officials. To date, neither provision has been fully implemented.[16] The RSCA attributed this to a lack of Tamil-speaking staff and an absence of constitutional clarity, and requires that the constitution's language provisions elaborate in detail the rights and claims of every person. While the RSCA often leaves details to later reports, it is very specific with regard to language rights. No less than fifteen paragraphs are dedicated to the comprehensive, all-encompassing implementation of language rights. Moreover, the RSCA states that "in order to facilitate better communication among the communities and to promote national integration, Sinhala, Tamil and English languages shall be made compulsory subjects at the GCE (O/L) examination" (Art. 16.4n).[17]

Further recommendations for enhancement of Sri Lanka's interethnic relations are made in the annex to the RSCA, notably concerning confidence building, relief, and rehabilitation. The RSCA points specifically to the large number of abductions, disappearances, and extrajudicial killings as a "matter of deep concern of the Tamil Community" (Annex to the Report, Art. 2.1).[18] Hence, the RSCA demands protection of the human rights of all people regardless of their ethnic affiliation. To avoid further communal clashes, special recommendations are made regarding the ethnic mixture of police personnel in multiethnic areas. Moreover, the ethnic imbalance in the police and armed forces should be adjusted to address dominance of the Sinhala community in both services.

In view of the huge number of internally displaced persons (IDPs) the RSCA recommends their rapid resettlement. In addition, "their personal safety and security should be guaranteed and compensation paid for the dislocation caused" (Annex to the Report, Art. 3.1). Similar recommendations are made regarding the government's "high security zones," lands that have been taken over by the armed forces, notably in the Jaffna Peninsula, causing the displacement of more than 65,000 people. The RSCA advises the government to release these lands when possible and, otherwise, to pay compensation to the persons dispossessed. Whether this will be politically enforceable remains to be seen.

Resource Issues: Land

The aforementioned measures for relief and rehabilitation were aimed at resolving central resource issues, namely, disputes over land that arose as a consequence of Sri Lanka's violent conflict. However, land was an issue in Sri Lanka long before the outbreak of the civil war (Kearney 1987–

88). These issues were connected with massive government-sponsored Sinhalese settlements, most in the 1970s, in "areas Tamils considered to be part of their traditional homeland" (De Votta 2000, 61). Hence, the RSCA deals specifically with this issue in a separate chapter.

The RSCA determines that all land currently controlled or used by the central government shall remain in its possession. All other land is assigned to the provincial governments. Provisions are made for the center and the provinces to negotiate the transfer of land required for the exercise of functions or subjects of the national or provincial list, respectively. In each case, approval by both the center and the provinces is obligatory (Art. 17.3, 17.4). For the resolution of further disputes over land, the RSCA advises the establishment of a National Land Commission (NLC) consisting of members of the center and the provinces in equal shares and representing the major communities (Art. 17.5). The NLC's main task should be to formulate national land-use policy and to monitor land use and compliance with relevant laws. The NLC should also be responsible for possible allocation of allotments to displaced residents. The selection of the residents shall be the responsibility of the provinces (Art. 17.9).

However, it remains questionable whether this would have a profound impact on the issue of land dispute. After all, the NLC is a mechanism not a solution. It remains to be seen whether NLC members would be able to agree on these issues.

Fiscal Devolution and Center: Province Fiscal Relations

At present, the allocation of funds from the annual budget to the provinces is entirely the preserve of the central government. Against this background, the RSCA concludes that the current "expenditure responsibilities and revenue powers result in a large provincial fiscal gap making Provinces overly dependent upon the Centre" (Art. 9.2). To abrogate this dependency, the RSCA strictly recommends redesigning fiscal and financial arrangements and delineating provincial expenditure responsibilities vis-à-vis the center. Regarding provincial income, the RSCA advises implementing "a combination of own sources of revenue and revenue sharing" (Art. 9.3 b) in order to make adequate revenue available to the provinces.[19] Furthermore, the RSCA pleads for equalization grants to be established for provinces to provide public services at least to a minimum national standard.

According to the RSCA, the main institutional pillar of the new fiscal framework is to be the Finance Commission (FC), with members appointed by the president on the recommendation of the HPC. The FC's main duty is to mediate in central—provincial disputes, especially to "exercise checks and balances on the Centre and become an effective agent of equity" (Art. 9.4). The RSCA's remarks underscore apprehension that central fiscal dominance could reevolve and undermine effective devolution by spending in areas of provincial competence. Therefore, the FC is charged with reporting overlap in expenditure, "as this is a serious issue" (Art. 9.5). Supplementary to the FC, a Finance Ministers Forum (FMF) is to be constituted to provide for consultation on fiscal and financial matters to mediate between center and provinces (Art. 9.6).

It is thus clear that the RSCA intends to provide for a comprehensive fiscal framework that would ensure the implementation of effective fiscal devolution in Sri Lanka. However, as long as provincial fiscal resources are not explicitly listed, it remains unclear how far-reaching provincial fiscal autonomy will be.

Dispute Settlement

The RSCA provides for the supremacy of the Sri Lankan Constitution and recommends that all actions of the center and the provinces be subject to judicial review. Thus the ultimate authority for dispute settlement is assigned to the Constitutional Court. This is not synonymous with a central role in dispute settlement; in fact, several provisions of the RSCA suggest that appeals to the Constitutional Court shall occur only as a last resort.

One example is the RSCA recommendation of "a mechanism for the resolution of disputes that may arise between the Centre and the Provinces or among the Provinces" (Art. 18.1). According to the RSCA, disputes shall be settled initially through informal discussions. If these discussions prove ineffective, the RSCA proposes three further steps: first, mediation by the Council of Chief Ministers chaired by the president; second, arbitration by a tribunal appointed by the second chamber, and; finally, reference to the Constitutional Court. In several other recommendations, the RSCA assigns to the Constitutional Court the attribute of a court of last resort. The FC and the FMF are two examples: their establishment and design signify the RSCA's intention to create consensus-building institutions and mechanisms that resolve disagreements before they evolve into serious conflicts. The same applies to the RSCA's array of various official commissions, such as the HPC, the National and Public Services Commissions, and the NLC. All of these are tasked with reaching consensus before serious quarrels arise.

Besides the general precautions for possible disputes, the RSCA makes specific comments on the risk of secession and demands "in-built mechanisms to discourage secessionist tendencies" (Art. 4.1). To this end, it recommends constitutional provisions prohibiting a provincial legislature or provincial government from promoting or advocating in any way the separation of any province or part thereof from the state. Moreover, the RSCA recommends constitutionally defining central emergency powers to be applied in the event of an "armed insurrection, grave internal disturbances or any act . . . which presents a clear and present danger to the unity, territorial integrity and sovereignty of the Republic" (Art. 4.3 a). These emergency powers shall enable the president to deploy armed forces, to assume the powers of the respective province, and "in an extreme situation" to dissolve the provincial legislature (Arts. 4.3 a, b, c). The exercise of presidential emergency powers shall be subject to parliamentary and judicial control (Art. 4.4). Once again, the Constitutional Court becomes the court of last resort for dispute settlement.

Conclusion

A concluding assessment of the RSCA's merits and shortcomings is difficult. Obviously, the RSCA's authors were well-intentioned. The envisaged system of far-reaching autonomy and power sharing would be most suitable for Sri Lanka's deeply divided society. However, the RSCA remains inexplicit on some basic issues, notably, in relation to devolution and asymmetric autonomy.

The RSCA Devolution and Asymmetric Autonomy Provisions: Adequate?

The RSCA's imprecision becomes apparent in its provision regarding the internal structure of provincial polities and the relationship between the gubernatorial office and the office of a provincial chief minister. Imprecision is also reflected in the RSCA stipulations concerning the distribution of second-chamber seats among the provinces, and the legislative powers of both chambers and the provinces, to mention a few. This imprecision poses a serious problem. Although the provisions of the RSCA intimate that a federal system is intended in all but name, the stipulations *not* made by the RSCA leave room for substantial dilution of the federal design.[20] Nevertheless, the intentionally far-reaching system is a positive and adequate approach to the Sri Lankan problem, and probably the only way to reach a political solution to the country's ethnic conflict. While the RSCA leaves room for dilution of its approach, it also allows for substantial devolution to be implemented and, if implemented, protected, for example by embodying safeguards for provincial powers.

Moreover, imprecision is not apparent in the RSCA's asymmetric autonomy provisions. Their phrasing is clear-cut and reasoned. At first sight, the two paragraphs on asymmetric autonomy for the Northeast seem quite restricted. However, by not applying the concurrent list to the region they offer a great de facto advantage. The effect is not only wider autonomy of self-government (depending on the issues included in the concurrent list) but an additional safeguard against intervention by the center, which might otherwise try to undermine provincial autonomy through excessive use of its framework legislation powers. Though the offer to the remaining provinces to negotiate the distribution of the concurrent list restricts the symbolic value of this regulation, it might cleverly avert massive opposition to asymmetry by Sinhala nationalists.

A further positive aspect concerns the asymmetric autonomy for the Indian Tamils. Also limited in scope, it represents recognition of the Indian Tamils as part of the Sri Lankan people whose claims are recognized and taken seriously. The combination of territorial and nonterritorial autonomy is, moreover, a sophisticated solution to the problem of the community's partly noncontiguous settlement. This time, the Indian Tamils' growing discontent has been anticipated at an early stage and RSCA supporters are determined to avoid developments akin to those of the Sri Lankan Tamil community.

Although the RSCA occasionally lacks clarity, it presents the most far-reaching approach to devolution in Sri Lanka's constitutional debate to date. In particular, the combination of federal intent and asymmetric autonomy represents a significant improvement on previous proposals.

Monodimensional or Complex?

The first chapter of the RSCA states explicitly that it pursues "an approach, which is double-pronged, i.e. Provincial institutions and local authorities will be set up as institutions of Government through which all communities can within the respective areas of authority, exercise power and develop their own areas. All communities will also share power at the Centre, thereby integrating them into the body politic and strengthening national integration" (Art 1.5).

This dual implementation of both autonomy and power sharing is the RSCA's most relevant merit. Its authors made allowances for community autonomy, while simultaneously trying to avoid alienation from the state through centralized power-sharing mechanisms. This is done in two ways: first, by embodying explicit power-sharing provisions in the RSCA and, second, by recommending a second chamber guaranteeing the involvement of the provinces in central decision making: "The concept of Provinces sharing power at the Centre was viewed as a possible mechanism that would generate a sense of participation by the Provinces in legislative and executive design making at the Centre, and would in turn weaken the tendency toward separation" (Art. 11.1). The effectiveness of these provisions depends on their implementation by the second chamber, notably regarding legislative veto over the lower house.

The power-sharing provisions also have some shortcomings. They are silent on exactly how the cabinet shall reflect the country's ethnic diversity. Nevertheless, they represent major progress in the debate on constitutional reform, since, for the first time in Sri Lankan history, they recommend official embodiment of power-sharing provisions in the Constitution. Moreover, although the envisaged office of vice-president may be solely representative, symbols are of the utmost importance in ethnic conflicts, and this stipulation and its potential impact should not be underestimated. With this dual approach the RSCA provides for a complex and sophisticated framework that combines autonomy while simultaneously integrating provinces at the center.

Chances of Implementation

This broadly positive assessment of the RSCA's contents is at odds with negative assessments of its chances for implementation, following the release of the final report of the APRC in January 2008. Under massive political pressure from President Rajapakse, who declared that any proposal should be in line with the Constitution, the APRC issued a report that contained a simple commitment to de facto implementation of the Thirteenth Amendment. The four-page document did not contain any of the far-reaching autonomy and power-sharing provisions of the RSCA. After 63 meetings over eighteen months, the result of the APRC process was a commitment to revive the failed Thirteenth Amendment, which could have been implemented during the last twenty years without any further consultations or negotiations. Political observers called it a "pathetic farce" (Saravanamuttu 2008).

However, this shattering result was expected. From the beginning, the RSCA's chances for implementation were slim due to Sri Lanka's intricate political circumstances, notably the intra-Sinhalese conflicts within the Sri Lankan polity, reflected and partially caused by Sri Lanka's party system. President Rajapakse earned much public support among Sinhalese voters through his political reputation as a hardliner, which clashed with the RSCA's moderate and reconciling approach to which public opposition in the south had been immense. To expect Rajapakse to approve the RSCA was far from realistic. Moreover, his party (SLFP) is politically dependent on the radical JHU and JVP, generating political constraints that would not have permitted comprehensive implementation of the content. The UNP also signaled its opposition to the RSCA. Thus, there would have been not enough support in parliament for the

RSCA, let alone a two-thirds majority to amend the Constitution. Watering down was thus expected.

Apart from the intra-Sinhalese conflicts, opposition within the Tamil community was also anticipated. While moderate Tamil politicians, researchers, and peace activists approved the RSCA in great numbers, opposition was voiced by members of the Tamil National Alliance, such as Gajendrakumar Ponnambalam, who rejected the devolutionary approach of the RSCA. Additional aspects of the RSCA caused further resistance, especially by the LTTE itself in relation to the proposed embodiment of safeguards against secession as well as to proposals for the Northeast. However, the most provocative stipulation of the RSCA in this respect can be found in the annex, which suggests initiating "a genuine peace process and decommissioning of arms by the LTTE" (Annex to the Report, Art. 4.2). With this stipulation, the RSCA's fate, viewed from an LTTE perspective, was sealed.

In conclusion, although the RSCA might be a good blueprint, it will not form the basis for the long-sought political solution to Sri Lanka's ethnic conflict. The implementation of the Thirteenth Amendment will not have a conflict-regulating impact on the country, and the failure of the APRC process has been another lost opportunity.

However, the likely impact of the RSCA on the Sri Lankan debate over constitutional reform and devolution should not be underestimated. Although its chances of implementation have vanished, it has dominated national debate for over a year. Its proposals on devolution have been the most far-reaching to date, and the idea of implementing power sharing at the center is entirely new to Sri Lanka. Even if their time has not yet come, these ideas will greatly influence further debate in Sri Lanka and possibly guide future proposals to a more far-reaching "federalist" direction.

Notes

I would like to thank D. Muttukrishna Sarvananthan, to whom I am grateful for providing me with information and documents on the current political and scientific debates in Sri Lanka. I would also like to thank Professor Dr. Edward Keynes for comments and advice.

1. The last proper census was conducted in 1981, shortly before the outbreak of Sri Lanka's civil war. Although there was a census in 2001, it is of limited use since it was not undertaken in the wartorn regions of the Northeast. This helps explain the significant variations in the data set. Data from 1981 and 2001 respectively (%): Sinhalese 73.9/82; Sri Lankan Tamils 12.7/4.3; Indian Tamils 5.5/5.1; Sri Lankan Moors (Muslims) 7.1/7.9; others 0.8/0.7 (DCS 2007).

2. The Thirteenth Amendment also stipulated Tamil as an official language of Sri Lanka.

3. The PA is a party alliance formed by the SLFP in the early 1990s with two Marxist left parties.

4. Moreover, the proposal stipulated that the "ISGA shall have control over the marine and offshore resources of the adjacent seas and the power to regulate access thereto" (LTTE 2003, 18). This stipulation would have enshrined the LTTE right to keep marine military capabilities and control the Northeast coast.

5. Hence, both proposals neglected dissenting Tamil voices and hereby confirmed the LTTE claim to sole representation—a bitter setback for moderate Tamil politicians, journalists, researchers, and peace activists.

6. Though it did include statements vis-à-vis the protection of human rights and the prohibition against discrimination, it did not issue guarantees regarding these warranties.

7. Moreover, in October 2006, Rajapakse and Wrickemasinghe signed a Memorandum of Understanding, in which they agreed on closer cooperation in order to find a political solution. The Memorandum was dissolved in January 2007, after the crossover of 18 parliamentarians from UNP to SLFP.

8. A printed version of the full text of the majority report can be found in the Appendix of Liyanage and Sinnathamby 2007. The following analysis is based on this document. Since its release further meetings of the Expert Panel have taken place. Possible changes that have been negotiated during these sessions cannot be considered since they have not been made public. Four members of the Expert Panel supported the dissenting minority report (Report of Subcommittee B, RSCB) and two members submitted a separate report each.

9. Local authorities, though, would not have legislative power but would only be empowered to make bylaws. The main intention of these local governments is to allow the people to control their own localities and their living environment (Art. 13.1, 2).

10. A clear distinction of areas of responsibility also holds true for the judiciary. Both the center and the provinces shall have their own judicial systems (Art. 8.1).

11. These comments seem to reflect on the scientific dispute among researchers about how to construct a federal unit regarding its ethnic composition. Further details on this issue can be found in Horowitz 2000, 613–28.

12. For example, the water supply to the eastern town of Trincomalee would be from outside the Province. In 2006, the occupation and closing of sluice gates by the LTTE shutting Sinhalese farmers off from water supply provoked fierce fighting between the SLAF and the LTTE. This underscores the need to regulate such issues.

13. The Constitution Bill 2000 in its second schedule contains two lists, a reserved (national) list and a regional list. Both lists in a very comprehensive and equitable way enumerate the subjects and functions belonging to the national and provincial sphere respectively. The full text of the Constitution 2000 Bill can be found in Somasundram 2000.

14. "Power sharing denotes the participation of representatives of all significant communal groups in political decision making, especially at the executive level" (Lijphart 2004, 97).

15. These comments clearly reflect the current critique on models of power sharing regarding their assumed liability to corruption and nepotism.

16. For example, 56.7 percent of the people in Colombo are Tamil-speaking; however, less than 1 percent of the staff are Tamil-literate. Kandy city is 25.7 percent Tamil-speaking, but none of the 60 staff working in the Registrars Office are Tamil-literate (Annex to the Report, Art. 1.5).

17. It is acknowledged that this has to be done in a staggered manner in view of resource constraints. To solve this problem the RSCA demands "immediate steps" (Annex to the Report, Art. 1.4) in order to provide for Tamil-literate staff in the government offices.

18. In 2006, 400 complaints of disappearances from Jaffna District alone were issued to Sri Lanka's Human Rights Commission.

19. Once again, the RSCA refers to the Constitution Bill 2000. If this is meant to follow the scheme of the Constitution Bill 2000, this would assign the following resources to the provinces: excise duties, taxes on wholesale and retail sales, taxes on sales and income not otherwise provided for, and items in the Provincial List.

20. After the RSCA was published, further meetings of the Expert Panel took place. Hence, it is possible that some of the imprecise stipulations have been improved already.

References

Department of Census and Statistics (DCS). 2007. Percentage distribution of population by ethnic group and district, census 1981, 2001. Department of Census and Statistics, Sri Lanka.

De Silva, K. M. 1981. *A history of Sri Lanka.* Delhi: Oxford University Press.

De Votta, N. 2000. Control democracy, institutional decay, and the quest for Eelam: Explaining ethnic conflict in Sri Lanka. *Pacific Affairs* 73, 1: 55–76.

Edrisinha, R. 1998. Trying times: Constitutional attempts to resolve armed conflict in Sri Lanka. In *Accord: Demanding sacrifice: War and negotiation in Sri Lanka.* London: Accord.

Eichhorst, K. 2006. "No peace, but war?" Das Scheitern des Friedensprozesses in Sri Lanka. *Internationale Politik* 61, 7: 100–107.

———. 2005. *Ethnisch-separatistische Konflikte in Kanada, Spanien und Sri Lanka: Möglichkeiten und Grenzen institutioneller Konfliktregelungen.* Kieler Schriften zur Politischen Wissenschaft 15. Frankfurt am Main: Peter Lang.

———. 2003. Der Bürgerkrieg in Sri Lanka: „Institutional engineering" als Lösungsansatz für ethnische Konflikte. In *Kieler Analysen zur Sicherheitspolitik*, ed. Institute for Security Policy at the University of Kiel (ISUK). Kiel: ISUK.

Fleiner, T. 2007. Ethno-nationalist demands as contemporary phenomenon: Structural challenges for modern constitutions. In *A glimmer of hope: A new phase in constitutional reforms in Sri Lanka*, ed. S. Liyanage and M. Sinnathamby. Colombo: South Asia Peace Institute.

Gopal, K. 2000. *Nationalism in Sri Lanka.* Delhi: Kalinga.

Government of Sri Lanka (GOSL). 2003. Provisional administrative structure for the northern and eastern provinces. Proposal for discussion. Peace in Sri Lanka Web site, www.peaceinsrilanka.org/peace2005/ Insidepage/Proposals/docs/GOSL%20Proposal.doc (accessed 1 September 2008).

Hariharan, R. 2006. *Sri Lanka: Northeast de-merger—at what cost?* Update 107. New Delhi: South Asia Analysis Group.

Horowitz, D. L. 2000. *Ethnic groups in conflict.* 2nd ed. Berkeley: University of California Press.

Hubbell, L. K. 1987. The devolution of power in Sri Lanka: A solution to the separatist movement? *Asian Survey* 27, 11: 1176–87.

International Crisis Group (ICG). 2007a. Sri Lanka's Muslims: Caught in the crossfire. *Asia Report* 134. Colombo/Brussels: ICG.

————. 2007b. Sri Lanka: Sinhala nationalism and the elusive southern consensus. *Asia Report* 141. Colombo/Brussels: ICG.

Jeyaraj, D. B. S. 2007. Constitutional reform for the Republic of Sri Lanka. In *A glimmer of hope: A new phase in constitutional reforms in Sri Lanka*, ed. S. Liyanage and M. Sinnathamby. Colombo: South Asia Peace Institute.

Kearney, R. N. 1987–88. Territorial elements of Tamil separatism in Sri Lanka. *Pacific Affairs* 60, 4: 561–77.

Liberation Tigers of Tamil Eelam (LTTE). 2003. The proposal by the Liberation Tigers of Tamil Eelam on behalf of the Tamil people for an agreement to establish an interim self-governing authority for the northeast of the island of Sri Lanka. Peace in Sri Lanka Web site, www.peaceinsrilanka.org/insidepages/proposals/proposals.asp (accessed 1 September 2008).

Lijphart, A. 2004. Constitutional design for deeply divided societies. *Journal of Democracy* 15, 2: 96–109.

Liyanage, S. 2007. Introduction. In *A glimmer of hope: A new phase in constitutional reforms in Sri Lanka*, ed. S. Liyanage and M. Sinnathamby. Colombo: South Asia Peace Institute.

Liyanage, S., and Sinnathamby, M., eds. 2007. *A glimmer of hope: A new phase in constitutional reforms in Sri Lanka*. Colombo: South Asia Peace Institute.

Manogaran, C. 1987. *Ethnic conflict and reconciliation in Sri Lanka*. Honolulu: University of Hawaii Press.

Matthews, B. 1982. District development councils in Sri Lanka. *Asian Survey* 22, 11: 1117–34.

Oberst, R. C. 1988. Federalism and ethnic conflict in Sri Lanka. *Publius* 18, 3: 175–93.

Royal Ministry of Foreign Affairs of Norway (RMFAN). 2002. Parties have decided parties to explore a political solution founded on the principle of internal self-determination based on a federal structure within a united Sri Lanka. Statement of the Royal Norwegian Government. Oslo: Royal Ministry of Foreign Affairs, 5 December.

Saravanamuttu, P. 2008. APRC: The year of the rat has begun. *Groundviews*, 31 January. www.groundviews.org/2008/01/30/aprc-the-year-of-the-rat-has-begun/#more-717 (accessed 1 September).

Shastri, A. 1992. Sri Lanka's provincial council system: A solution to the ethnic problem? *Asian Survey* 32, 8: 723–43.

Singer, M. R. 1996. Sri Lanka's ethnic conflict: Have bombs shattered hopes for peace? *Asian Survey* 36, 11: 1146–55.

Somasundram, M., ed. 2000. *Constitution 2000: Parliamentary debates (3, 7, 8 August)*. Colombo: Ethnic Affairs and National Integration Division of the Ministry of Justice, Constitutional Affairs, Ethnic Affairs, and National Integration.

Wickramasinghe, N. 1995. *Ethnic politics in colonial Sri Lanka, 1927–1947*. 2nd ed. New Delhi: Vikas.

Wilson, A. J. 2000. *Sri Lankan Tamil nationalism: Its origins and development in the nineteenth and twentieth centuries*. London: Hurst.

Chapter 11

Puntland's Declaration of Autonomy and Somaliland's Secession: Two Quests for Self-Governance in a Failed State

Janina Dill

During the 1990s the Democratic Republic of Somalia (Somalia) became notorious for what has become an increasingly common phenomenon of the post-Cold War international order: the prolonged and seemingly permanent absence of an effective government, or state failure. A UN peace-building mission and countless internationally sponsored peace conferences failed to pacify the country and to pave the way for the reconstruction of state structures. International diplomacy and a continuous inflow of foreign aid have produced, and so far sustained, a Transitional Federal Government (TFG), which presides over a perpetual civil war of ever proliferating factions, as well as continuing economic and social decline. Remarkably, however, the north of the country has escaped this fate.

At about the same time that the south descended into chaos, two territories in the north began a process of establishing self-governance. After unilaterally declaring independence from Somalia in 1991, the self-declared Republic of Somaliland (hereafter, Somaliland) evolved from a crippled, anarchic, and impoverished province into a relatively peaceful democracy showing signs of economic recovery (Bradbury 1997). The Puntland State of Somalia (hereafter, Puntland) to its east has never sought legal separation from the south. But since it declared autonomy in 1998, it has achieved first results in institution building (UNCHAS 2006).

Meanwhile, the international community remains focused on state reconstruction in the south and largely oblivious to the success of Somaliland and Puntland.[1] Throughout more than a dozen different peace initiatives the territorial integrity of a united Somalia has never been questioned. Somalia, though now synonymous with the permanent absence of effective government,[2] continues to be a sovereign member of the United Nations. Under the premise of Somalia's continued territorial integrity and international legal sovereignty, Puntland's nascent government structures coupled with its commitment to a united Somalia have at times been considered a possible building block for the reconstruction of a Somali state,[3] while the secession of Somaliland has consistently been branded a stumbling block to Somali reconciliation.

Beyond this superficial assessment, the international community has shown little willingness to inquire closely enough into the situation in the north to be able to explore the potential as well as to define a possible threat that de facto independence or regional autonomy might present for the rebuilding of a peaceful Somali state. Little attention is paid to the fact that Somaliland has evolved toward a functioning democracy, the only example in the Horn of Africa. Even fewer international actors have seriously inquired into the viability of regional self-governance in Puntland. Puntland's case of a federal unit waiting for the center to become fit to assume its role is one of a kind. Somaliland presents a unique case of self-reliant state building. To this day, neither Puntland nor Somaliland has been systematically assessed by the international community regarding their respective impact on Somalia.

This chapter will compare Puntland's declaration of autonomy and Somaliland's secession as two alternative ways to pursue self-governance in response to state failure. Since these two territories face the same regional context and share many cultural and political characteristics, their different success in establishing self-governance can be at least partly attributed to the different paths they have embarked on after parting ways with Somalia. In addition to the viability of their respective governance structures, the impact both territories have on the internationally managed efforts to rebuild Somalia has important implications for the widely held belief that territorial autonomy can be a means of pacification and regional self-government a building block for central statehood. Puntland and Somaliland thus present the rare opportunity to study the integrative or disintegrative forces of regional autonomy compared to its alternative, outright secession, in two similar cases.[4]

The aim of this chapter is twofold: first, to examine (from the point of view of the territories seeking self-government) whether regional autonomy or secession is more conducive to the establishment of an effective polity; and, second, to discuss whether secession and regional autonomy present a chance for the reconstruction of a failed state or whether they prove to be further disintegrative. After a brief sketch of the history of Somali statehood I will describe the emergence of Puntland and Somaliland. I will then explore to what extent autonomy and de facto independence, respectively, have determined Puntland's and Somaliland's uneven success in establishing self-governance. Lastly, I will enquire into the impact which both territories have had on the Somali peace process and discuss the implications, for territorial autonomy arrangements, of Puntland's fate as an autonomous region in a failed state.

Somaliland's Quest for Independence and Puntland's Pursuit of Autonomy as Responses to Somalia's State Failure

Somalia used to be an exceptional state in Sub-Saharan Africa in that it was an ethnically homogeneous entity (Simmler 1999, 98; Jacquin-Berdal 2002, 142). Yet, significant diversity stems from the fact that the Somali population is divided into six clan-families.[5] Throughout its history, Somali statehood has never been congruent with the homeland of these six clan-families, which is due to the colonial division of the area inhabited by Somalis into several distinct administrative entities. As a result, statehood as a form of political organization was experienced in radically distinct ways by the different sectors of the Somali population (Bradbury 1997, 5). While British rule in the north allowed for the preservation of traditional structures of self-governance (Prunier 1998, 225), Italian colonialism in the south resulted in the erosion of traditional forms of political organization and centralized colonial administration (Schoiswohl 2004, 143). These different developmental trajectories created an important fault line in the Somali population (Drysdale 1994, 123ff.).

As colonial domination drew to a close, however, a Somali nationalist movement emerged and the former British Somaliland united with the former Italian colony to form the Republic of Somalia on 1 July 1960. A common theme in all accounts of this unification is the haste and lack of preparation with which it was carried out. An Act of Union that was supposed to be adopted by the legislative assemblies in both northern and southern Somaliland never came into existence (Adam 1994, 23). While dubious in law, unification in fact took the form of a merger heavily privileging the south (Huliaras 2002, 158). The integration of the judicial and administrative systems, merging of two different currencies, and bridging of two administrative languages were effected in ways that disadvantaged the north (Contini 1969, 11ff.).

As a result, dissatisfaction with the unequal marriage surfaced almost immediately. The population of the former British Somaliland boycotted the referendum on the Constitution in June 1961 (Brons 1994, 10ff.), and in the same year British-educated army officers unsuccessfully launched a military coup against the government (ICG 2006, 5). Disappointed hopes that Somalia would be allowed to merge with the NFD and French Somaliland to thereby create a "Greater Somalia" resulted in further discontent.

The seizure of power by General Mohammed Siad Barre and the subsequent establishment of an autocratic centralized regime marked the end of Somali unity. Barre systematically favored loyal southern clans while severely discriminating against the majority clan-family in the north, the Isaaq (Brons 1994, 12). In response to Barre's dictatorial rule, several armed opposition movements emerged. In the former British Somaliland the Isaaq established the Somali National Movement (SNM). In retaliation to SNM activity, government forces killed some 40,000 people, most of whom were Isaaq civilians (Africa Watch 1990, 31). Initially, the SNM had differentiated between its goal of ousting Barre and its continued commitment to a united Somalia. Yet, in the course of fighting, in view of the magnitude of atrocities committed by a regime that many identified with the postcolonial state of Somalia as such, many Isaaq started to believe that the true aim of the struggle was independence (Bryden 2004, 23).

In the vacuum of power that followed Barre's flight from Mogadishu on 26 January 1991, order broke down completely (Mohammed 1997, 49) as the remaining state institutions crumbled. The first of many attempts to establish a transitional government alienated the SNM as protagonists of the Barre regime were invited to participate in the negotiations. This prompted the SNM to hold a separate peace conference in Burko. What was originally an attempt to organize the rebuilding of the region ended with a declaration of independence (Bryden 2004, 24), as "angry crowds" staged demonstrations demanding separation from the south (Brons 1994, 19). Somaliland declared its independence within the borders of the former British protectorate on 10 May 1991. It was thus the failure of north-south integration and of interclan power sharing that prompted the secession of Somaliland, or as Somaliland's official version states, the reestablishment of the independence of the former colonial entity Somaliland (Jacquin-Berdal 2002, 142).

Throughout this postcolonial struggle Puntland did not emerge as an entity with political agency until the second half of the 1990s. The opposition movement against Barre most active in the northeastern provinces, which during colonialism were mostly under Italian rule and today constitute Puntland, was the Somali Salvation Democratic Front (SSDF). Contrary to Somaliland, the region of Puntland is inhabited by clans from a single clan-family, the Darood clans. The SSDF was their opposition movement against the Barre regime and Puntland is best described as a Darood homeland. Contrary to Somaliland, in Puntland "clan agreement [thus] preceded any territorial definition" (Battera 2000).

By the end of the 1990s, reestablishment of a central Somali govern-

ment became increasingly less likely and the former opposition movements, splitting up into ever smaller militias, sought to consolidate their
territorial power bases, which began to serve as important bargaining
assets in the internationally sponsored peace process. Puntland was thus
not the only emerging entity;[6] however, it was the most successful and
the most viable because its initial withdrawal from the ongoing struggle in the south and its geographical distance to Mogadishu provided
space for a regional peace initiative and for structures of regional self-
governance to take root.

The quest for self-governance in both territories is ultimately a response to the failure of a Somali-wide reconciliation.[7] But why did the
two entities choose different paths to self-governance when they did opt
to (in Puntland's case partly) disentangle their fate from Somalia?

Three factors help explain why Somaliland severed ties with the south
earlier and more radically than Puntland. First, in contrast to Puntland,
Somaliland has a history as a distinct entity. This provides an important
reference point for the political identification of its population (Höhne
2006). People in Somaliland in fact refer to themselves as "Somalilanders"
(Höhne 2006, 401). Second, Somaliland's population, especially the majority clan-family of the Isaaq, was severely victimized under the Barre
regime. On the contrary, members of Puntland's Darood clan-family, in
spite of its later opposition to the regime, were not systematically dis-
criminated against. Finally, parts of the Darood live in the south. Puntland is consequently less likely to perceive its fate as disconnected from
southern Somalia (Höhne 2006, 410).

Puntland's Regional Autonomy and Somaliland's De Facto Independence: A Difference in Degree or Kind for Self-Governance?

I will now turn to the first decade of Puntland's autonomy and the first
seventeen years of Somaliland's de facto independence to explore to
what extent they have allowed for successful self-governance. To this end
I will compare, first, the results of the two endeavors to establish effective
self-governing entities, and second, their respective relationships with
Somalia resulting from the different paths they have chosen. Finally, I
will discuss a possible connection between the two variables.

The Success of Self-Governance in Somaliland and Puntland

In a series of clan-conferences after the declaration of independence
Somaliland forged a new "social contract . . . in stages" (Hussein 1997,
111). The second clan conference resulted in the adoption of the
Borama National Charter of Somaliland, which came into effect in May

1993 after being approved by 150 nominated representatives from different clans and communities. Article 5 stipulated that the charter should be replaced by a constitution legitimized in a public referendum. The 1997 Interim Constitution, which was first approved by elders at a clan conference, was adopted with an overwhelming majority through public referendum in 2001. Since the Constitution designates Somaliland as "a sovereign and independent country" (Art. 1), many inhabitants of Somaliland casting their vote perceived this act as a referendum on independence (Baldo, 2006, 7).

Before the referendum Somaliland had faced two armed power struggles among political opponents backed by rival clans. Both were solved through extensive brokerage by clan elders and broadly participatory clan conferences. The Constitution called for decentralization through elections to local councils so as to give effect to the Isaaq's pledge not to dominate other groups, and for direct presidential elections,[8] which were both held after its entry into force. The process of establishing legitimate governance structures was finalized with elections to the legislature's lower house in 2005.[9] Somaliland's upper house assembles nonelected clan elders, so that traditional structures of conflict resolution and inter-clan communication are integrated into formal governance structures (Constitution 2001, Arts. 57ff.).

The population of the northeast, now Puntland, held its first clan conference in 1994. However, power struggles within the SSDF hampered regional agreement. When four years later the Darood met again, they adopted the Charter of Puntland State of Somalia, which declared the region an autonomous state within Somalia. The SSDF was disbanded and its leader, Abdullahi Yusuf, became the first president of the autonomous region Puntland.

While the declaration of autonomy signified, at least in the short run, the abandoning of a national Somali peace process and the prioritization of regional pacification (Mattei 1999, 7), Art. 1(4) of the charter committed Puntland to recreate Somalia as a federal state. The particulars of this recreation and procedures for a federalization were not specified (Battera 2000, 4) and are only marginally more elaborate in a constitution that was adopted in 2001. This constitution foresees that the president is elected by the House of Representatives (Art. 61(10)). Its sixty-six deputies are meant to be elected directly by universal suffrage (Art. 59(2)). While Puntland does not have a bicameral system like Somaliland, the role of the elders is constitutionally recognized as mediators for conflict resolution (Art. 101(5)), though they are not allowed to be part of a political organization or a formal political body (Art. 101 (3)).[10]

Puntland's path after declaring autonomy strikingly resembles Somaliland's after secession. However, neither Puntland's Constitution nor its House of Representatives have obtained the legitimacy that their counterparts in Somaliland have gained through democratic elections and a constitutional referendum. Though Puntland's Constitution foresees both, there has been no constitutional referendum and the currently appointed representatives in the legislative assembly have not been legitimized through general elections (Farah 2002, 7ff.). Puntland's presidents, in turn, have relied on military power to sustain themselves. Between 2001 and 2004 the consolidation of the newly established institutions was held back by armed clashes when President Yusuf refused to step down after a clan conference had nominated a political rival to replace him in 2001. Puntland's descent into a "clan dictatorship" (Hagmann and Höhne 2007) was averted when Yusuf was elected president of Somalia in 2004 during the peace and reconciliation conference held in Kenya at the time.

Likewise, decentralization and *local* self-governance in Puntland have not proven as effective as in Somaliland. Although the current president, General Mahamud Muse Hersi, who was elected by parliament in 2005, introduced district councils that allow different clans and subclans to share power with the government (AllAfrica 2007), he frequently interferes with the councils' work. In December 2007 he dissolved the parliament so that Puntland would be governed primarily by presidential orders.

Overall, Puntland's public administration is "embryonic" (Hagmann and Höhne 2007, 22), its legitimacy shaky. Contrary to Somaliland's postsecession development, Puntland's pursuit of self-governance through autonomy has not resulted in functioning constitutional mechanisms for the transfer of executive and legislative power. Puntland has failed to establish a decentralization scheme that allows for intercommunal power sharing, a parliament that is legitimized through elections, and a government that is not dependent on military power (Menkhaus 2002, 38; Battera 2004, 9). Partly as a result of its more consolidated governance structures, Somaliland's internal security situation is better than Puntland's (Farah and Lewis 1997, 362).

In both territories the positive effects of demobilization and pacification are mitigated by the armed clash in the contested border regions of Sool and Sanaag (Höhne 2007). Moreover, neither Somaliland's authorities nor their counterparts in Puntland have a monopoly over the use of force in the classical sense. Firearms are omnipresent in Somali households and the population relies heavily on family, clan, and other communal structures for their protection. Local politicians and elders generally solve conflicts and disputes, filling in for official courts and the nascent central police forces (Hagmann and Höhne 2007, 22ff.).

Though similar in both territories, this decentralized order works better in Somaliland. This is primarily due, not to the slightly different constitutional role of elders and customary dispute settlement mechanisms, but rather to the fact that in Somaliland traditional structures were systematically revitalized upon the declaration of independence as a precondition for peace on a territory inhabited by very heterogeneous clans and groups (Menkhaus 2004).

Internal security provides an environment conducive to business and entrepreneurship and has led to first signs of economic recovery in Somaliland. Puntland, on the contrary, "has teetered for years on the edge of bankruptcy" (Höhne 2007, 4) and has recently struggled with hyperinflation. Neither Somaliland's nor Puntland's authorities have the capacity or budget to provide basic public goods and state services (UNCTS 2007, 4). However, in Somaliland business and civil society have partly filled the place of the state, providing universities, hospitals, electricity, telephone services, roads, airlines, and even safety (Sorens and Wantchekon 2000, 9). As a result Somaliland does better regarding most human-development indicators.[11]

In conclusion, Somaliland is stronger than Puntland according to three closely related indicators for the success of self-governance: it has more legitimate governance structures with functioning constitutional mechanisms for the sharing and transfer of power, it has maintained relative internal security, and it is economically more stable, thus providing better for the fulfillment of basic human needs such as food, health, and education.

The Orientation of Self-Governance: Somaliland's and Puntland's Status and Their Stance Toward the International Effort to Rebuild Somalia

Since its declaration of independence, Somaliland has consistently boycotted the factional reconciliation efforts organized by the international community for Somalia (Farah 2002, 2). The international community, in turn, has shunned the breakaway republic, refusing to recognize it. After international donors and governmental organizations initially merely called on the government to participate in the peace conferences for Somalia,[12] more recently the Intergovernmental Authority on Development and the African Union have established low-key working relations with Somaliland's authorities (Huliaras 2002, 174). Numerous NGOs and UN agencies are also active in Somaliland now. While some countries have received representatives from Somaliland (Jacquin-Berdal 2002, 196), it has, to date, rather strained relations and little contact with the TFG.

Somaliland's status as a nonrecognized, de facto independent entity and the resulting initial absence of external aid have long been perceived as an impediment to its consolidation. Yet, as a result most achievements in the rebuilding of the state are attributable to local actors, and the governance structures now established are truly rooted in Somaliland's society. In this reading, Somaliland's international isolation and its consistent refusal to participate in international efforts to rebuild Somalia have helped produce more viable structures of self-governance (Terlinden and Debiel 2003, 2).

Puntland's authorities have displayed a less coherent approach to southern politics. Before 1998 the SSDF took part in factional reconciliation conferences in the south. The first government of Puntland, however, stayed clear of negotiations until in 2000 a delegation went to Djibouti, where a peace conference was about to begin, but left the scene before having attended negotiations and officially rejected the initiative (Farah 2002, 13). Since the stalled peace process was relaunched in 2002 in Kenya, Puntland has been an active participant and a staunch supporter of the TFG, which emerged as a result of it in 2004 (PDRC 2005, 16).

As a consequence of Puntland's participation in the internationally sponsored peace process, the international community has treated Puntland mainly as an asset for state reconstruction. The United Nations Development Programme (UNDP) works with Puntland (GPS 2007a), and the region has received attention from the World Bank, something that Somaliland has long been denied. Moreover, relations with Somalia are generally good. In January 2008, upon a visit to Puntland the president of the TFG and former president of Puntland, Abdullahi Yusuf, thanked Puntland for its "support to the cause of Somalia as a nation" (GPS 2008a).

This paints the picture of a substate entity working toward the consolidation of the central government and waiting to take its place below it. In reality the picture is much more complicated. Puntland clearly strives to appear as committed to the international community's effort to rebuild a Somali state and to differentiate itself from the "spoiler" Somaliland, a strategy that ensures access to international funds and positions in the central government. On the other hand, Puntland's leaders jealously protect their region's autonomy against interference from the south. In March 2008 Puntland's government issued a policy statement, which aptly expressed its strategy of walking on the fence between vows of unity and affirmations of autonomy and even independence.

> The essence of the [government] stands for three essential policy engagements namely (1) to save Puntland territory and waters from the hostilities created by the absence of central government and confrontations of political factions serving negative interests (2) to be part of the pursuit to restore a Somali central authority based on a federal system, the only system that

would prevent totalitarianism and dismemberment and (3) to cooperate with the international community to find a solution to the Somali crisis in general and to support the reconstruction and development in Puntland in particular. (GPS 2008b)

Notwithstanding the explicit backing of the TFG, the statement draws attention to its significant shortcomings, and suggests that the power asymmetry which is usually expected to exist between a central government and a federal unit is reversed in this case.

(1) Puntland will not, under any circumstances, accept a central government of totalitarian nature. . . . (2) Puntland does not and will not recognize a central government solution of Somalia via the concepts of conquest of European colonial powers which were replaced by the Act of Union of the Somali Republic and the constitution of that Republic approved in a national referendum in 1961 and (3) until such times an all inclusive federal constitution is effected and state governments, convias nced of the sharing of power and resources, are instituted, Puntland's support of the TFG should not be interpreted in any manner that Puntland is part of the TFG—Puntland shall remain *independent* for its laws, policies and interests. (GPS 2008b; emphasis added)

Puntland's oscillation between dictating conditions for support and affirming commitment to what will ultimately be subordination finds its most condensed expression in President Hersi's 2007 announcement that "Puntland will always protect its territorial integrity," while it "will continue to manage its own affairs as part of a future Federal Somali Government."[13]

This in fact ambivalent relationship is paralleled by a rather equivocal legal situation. Since Puntland and Somalia have never entered into a power-sharing agreement or federal treaty their legal relationship can only be inferred from a combined reading of their current constitutions. Puntland's 2001 Constitution (revised in 2007) provides in Article 3 (1) that "Puntland State is part of Somalia; it is her duty to contribute to the establishment and protect a Somali Government based on the Federal System." Article 3 (3) adds that "pending the completion of the Federal Constitution approved by a popular referendum, Puntland State shall have the status of an independent State." Federalization is thus postponed to an uncertain future event in the Somali peace process. However if a constitutional referendum was held in the south, federalization would follow automatically and would not require express consent on the part of Puntland. This legally unusual affirmation of independence, pending a constitutional referendum constituting a federal state that does not yet exist, almost puts Puntland on a similar footing with Somaliland: the legal limbo of self-declared de facto independence.

Despite this automatism of federalization the distribution of competences in a future federation is not specified; the Constitution merely says in Article 3 (2) that "the powers that Puntland State shall cede to the Federal Government of Somalia and the rights that will be preserved shall be determined through negotiation." This is plausible in the light of the fact that this is not an agreement *between* Somalia and Puntland but a constitution containing a unilateral declaration of commitment to federal incorporation.

Nevertheless Puntland's Constitution spells out a procedure for harmonization with a federal constitution in Article 135: "the House of Representatives will set up a special Committee, composed by members of all the political factions to review the present Constitution in order to determine if there are discrepancies and/or contradictions between the two constitutions. . . . If such discrepancies or contradictions exist, the Special Committee will reform this Constitution in order to harmonize it with the texts of the Federal Constitution, taking into account the *primacy* of the Federal Constitution over the Puntland State Constitution" (emphasis added).

In 2009 the transitional period was extended until 2011. This makes Puntland's granting of primacy to it appear rather bold; Somalia's constitutional process was scheduled to finish in 2009. The Transitional Federal Charter of 2004 indeed commits the "Transitional Federal Government of the Somali Republic [to] hav[ing] a decentralized system of administration based on federalism" (Art. 11(1)). But whereas Puntland's Constitution foresees negotiations between the center and the regions, Somalia's transitional charter already includes two annexed schedules detailing a distribution of competences between the center and the regions. Powers that are meant to be federal are, among others, foreign affairs, defense, and finances (Annex). Though classical federal powers, these are currently the most important sources of power for Puntland's governing elites.

While the obstacles to the realization of a federal state, which would clarify the legal situation between Somalia and Puntland, lie first and foremost with Somalia, the largely unresolved question of power sharing suggests that it is by no means certain that Puntland would simply take its place as a substate unit if a federal constitution was approved by referendum. A first writing on the wall for conflict was Puntland's reaction to the TFG's complaint about its signing of an international treaty with Yemen regarding fishing rights. The Minister of Fisheries asserted "the authority to sign deals with 'foreign partners' and that 'Puntland owns its coastal resources'" (Weinstein 2007a). This draws attention to another likely point of contention. Somalia's current constitution envisages that natural resources will be administered at the federal level. However, in 2005 Puntland signed an agreement with Australian Range Resources,

Ltd., to explore its territory for oil and minerals (Africa Online 2008). It is doubtful that Puntland's strongmen will easily give up control of these sources of revenue, especially in light of the absence of a wealth-sharing mechanism in the current federal charter. The TFG has already protested against the exploration deal.

But does the fact that Puntland's autonomy, and hence its relations with Somalia, is ambivalent in fact and ambiguous in law represent the cause of its shortfall vis-à-vis Somaliland regarding the establishment of effective and legitimate self-governance?

The Link Between Status and Success: The Pitfalls of Territorial Autonomy in a Failed State

Both entities are de facto independent, since Somalia lacks the capacity to intervene in either. De jure, neither of them enjoys internationally recognized sovereignty. The only difference between them that arose as an immediate consequence of Somaliland declaring independence and Puntland declaring autonomy was their relation with Somalia, and by implication with the international community engaged in the Somali peace process.

Even at first glance, Puntland's problems seem to be intimately connected with its involvement with Somalia. Puntland's militias have not only taken an active military role in the south to fight the Islamic Courts Movement in 2006 but in the ongoing factional fighting (Hagmann and Höhne 2007, 24), claiming that armed southern militias spill over into its territory (GPS 2008b). The government of Puntland is quick to point to "external" security threats as the main reason for its failure to meet many of its good governance goals. Correspondingly, the priority on the government's agenda is rolling back Somaliland in the west and strengthening Puntland's security toward the south. The implementation of the government reform program and democratization only come third and fourth on the agenda.

Though the detrimental effect of Puntland's involvement in armed hostilities is plausible, it is not at the origin of Puntland's slacking consolidation. Rather, its armed meddling with southern factions is part of the larger problem that is Puntland's stake in the Somali peace process, which in turn is a direct consequence of its specific status of an autonomous federal unit in waiting. It appears that the link between the distinctive ways in which the two entities pursue self-governance and their relative success is that Puntland's trajectory of self-governance is necessarily oriented toward Somalia; Somaliland's development as a self-governing entity to the contrary is centered on itself. This can be explained by taking a step back to look again at the difference in the constitutional setup of self-governance in the two entities.

The above comparison suggested that Somaliland's stronger bicameral legislature as well as its more prominent traditional structures of dispute settlement have been more conducive to the establishment of effective government, internal security, and economic recovery. However, this is not what causes Puntland's elites to be much more reluctant to pass on power, to allow for elections, and to rule in accordance with their constitutional mandates than their counterparts in Somaliland. After all, Puntland's constitution foresees universal elections for the House of Representatives, and the effectiveness of Somaliland's clan conferences and elders' mediation is more the result of a commitment to using these traditional structures in order to preserve the intercommunal peace than of their constitutional role. The precise legal features of Somaliland's and Puntland's versions of self-governance are relevant for the question of their success in self-governance only in that they suggest something about its orientation.

Ugo Mattei argues that in many African states the process of constitution making has proven more important than the written outcome, since it is during the constitutional negotiations that a social contract and future allegiance to the polity are forged through the hammering out of intercommunal power sharing, access to resources and positions (Mattei 1999, 2). Kenneth Menkhaus describes Somaliland as the product of such an attempt to achieve peaceful relations and equal access to power and privilege among the clans present on the territory (Menkhaus 2004, 22). This is manifest in the strong decentralization scheme and empowerment of the elders.

Though Puntland's is the more homogeneous society, internal disagreement right at the beginning showed the necessity of brokering an intercommunal peace there as well, but in the "ethno-state" (Menkhaus 2004, 22). Puntland elites did not share and later transfer power in such a way as to ensure regional peace. The purpose of Puntland's declaration of autonomy, it should be recalled, was to consolidate the territorial power base for the SSDF in order to protect it against interference by other factions involved in the central peace process and in turn to use it as an asset for participation therein.[14] Puntland's trajectory of self-governance, that is, the pursuit of autonomy, is in accordance with this purpose. It is oriented toward the central state.

To appreciate the implications of this we have to take into account how Somalis have historically experienced central statehood under colonialism, especially during the Barre era: "For Somalis, the state is an instrument of accumulation and domination, enriching and empowering those who control it and exploiting and harassing the rest" (Mbugua 2004, 28). The Republic of Somalia was a case par excellence of the exploitation of state power for elite gain, clientalism, and failed power sharing (Mbugua 2004, 28). International initiatives to restore Somalia have inadvertently perpetuated this concept of statehood. Power sharing among factions, warlords, clans, and other actors managing to get a seat at the negotiation table has become an internationally sponsored and therefore perpetual exercise (Sorens and Wantchekon 2000, 8). Positions in the various transitional national governments come with access to funds and foreign aid (14). This keeps the stakes high and allows warlords and clan militias to cover their costs, thereby perpetuating not only the negotiations but also the civil war.

Gaining power in Puntland is gaining a ticket to this process, as was manifest when the first president of Puntland switched to the position of president of the TFG. Self-governance in Puntland has thus become a mirror image of the central power struggle. The influence on the national peace process conferred by holding an office in Puntland raises the stakes of keeping that office, thereby fueling competition and political rivalry and diminishing elite interest in good governance at home (Menkhaus 2004, 24). At the same time the political fate of Puntland's political leaders no longer depends primarily on how successful leaders are in promoting regional prosperity.

On the contrary, Somaliland's lack of external funds and the unavailability of national office and influence at the center as a goal for elites have meant that the ultimate purpose of self-governance lies in Somaliland's consolidation. On this trajectory of self-governance, which is oriented to the stabilization of independence, the question of power sharing has truly been transferred to a lower level, inspiring genuine interclan cooperation and thus allowing for the consolidation of self-governance.

In conclusion, the most important variable determining why Puntland is less successful than Somaliland is its trajectory of self-governance: autonomy is necessarily oriented toward a central state. As the purpose of self-governance becomes to partake in an internationally sponsored, protracted peace process, power sharing and intercommunal peace at home are neglected, elites are less inclined to submit their political fate to elections, and the autonomous region stays invested in the often armed struggle for central power.

Puntland's and Somaliland's Impact on Somalia: Regional Autonomy as a Means of State Building?

In light of the finding that autonomy is less successful than de facto independence regarding the establishment of effective and legitimate self-governance, we can now revisit our intuitions that an autonomous Puntland striving to serve as a building block for a federal Somalia has an integrative impact on Somali statehood, while Somaliland's secession has acted as a centrifugal factor. In this context I will also discuss the implications of Puntland's case for the concept of territorial autonomy in general.

The international community has long acted as if these intuitions were correct. Puntland mostly enjoyed the unquestioned status of a building block and Somaliland has only recently and reluctantly been allowed on the international stage. In reality, however, Somaliland's declaration of independence had no significant impact on the peace process in the south. If Somaliland were to be internationally recognized, the only effect would probably be that Somalia would lose between a fourth and a third of its population and one-fifth of its territory on the official world map.[15] It is the comparison with Puntland that debunks the myths of the detrimental effect that Somaliland's independence has on Somalia, which are two of the most widely accepted reasons cited against granting it recognition. The first assumption is that the participation of a relatively effective regional entity in the peace process can be the nucleus or a building block for successful central state-building. Puntland's example shows, not only that it is difficult to extrapolate from regional successes in power sharing to the center, but that regional self-governance is much less successful when it is overshadowed by the central peace process. Second, contrary to widely held beliefs, Somaliland's declaration of independence has not served as a signal to ever smaller substate units to likewise attempt secession. One could of course argue that this is because Somaliland has been unsuccessful in obtaining international recognition. In fact, in spite of its recent success in attracting foreign donors and its increasing activity in international relations, coupled with its considerable success in terms of consolidation and prosperity, Somaliland has not served as a model for other regions. Again the comparison with Puntland suggests that factors such as political identity and history create different matrices for the decision between national unity and independence for different communities.

Puntland's own influence on Somalia has been neither integrative nor disintegrative. Puntland has never been a building block in the way that those who invented the concept envisaged.[16] Of course there has never been a systematic attempt to build similar autonomous regional entities throughout Somalia. Somalia has come to be equated with the area around Mogadishu, its reconstruction with the establishment of a central government. Moreover, the concept that an autonomous region can serve as a block to rebuild failed central statehood is fundamentally challenged by the observation that self-governance in Puntland is negatively affected by its involvement in the central peace process.

On the other hand, as participation in the Somali peace process has been extraordinarily attractive for Puntland's elites, its autonomy has not proven disintegrative in the sense of serving as a stepping stone to secession.[17]

Puntland's autonomy and Somaliland's de facto independence have neither exerted a measurable disintegrative pressure nor had a discernable positive impact on Somalia—at the same time, Somaliland's path has brought enormous benefits to the population of Somaliland. The lack of effective government in Somalia is not due to a temporarily challenged monopoly of the use of force. Somalia's situation has been characterized by the total and persistent absence of any effective authority since 1990 (Zartmann and Deng 1991, 5), which renders Somalia the epitome of state failure (Thürer 1999). Four years after its establishment, the TFG controls less than 20 percent of the country (Weinstein 2007b). It is hard to imagine that anything happening in a region like Puntland or Somaliland could affect a state-building effort that has not yet reached beyond Mogadishu.

This suggests that only limited generalizations can be drawn from the results of this case study. Somalia's corroded statehood and the protracted peace process are crucial to the finding that Puntland as an autonomous region has faced more problems in establishing regional self-governance than the secessionist Somaliland, and that neither autonomy nor secession prove significantly disintegrative or integrative. We will not find many cases of declared autonomy vis-à-vis a central government that is in fact absent. However, Puntland's fate as an autonomous region in a failed state serves as a cautionary tale for autonomy arrangements in general, which have come to enjoy the status of a panacea to protect the rights of territorially defined groups while at the same time preserving the cohesiveness of heterogeneous societies.

The case of Puntland draws attention to the fact that, rather counterintuitively, autonomy can also be threatened by *dysfunctional* central statehood, albeit in a different way. If the central government is weak, challenged or absent autonomy does not allow for effective and legitimate self-governance, thus losing its pacifying impact on the region and its integrative potential for the central state.

Ultimately territorial autonomy or self-governance is meant to *empower* a region or substate entity through a mechanism for transferring power from the center to the region. If this power asymmetry is amiss, there is a danger that any achievement at the regional level is jeopardized by the struggle for central power. Autonomy, in order to allow for the establishment and consolidation of effective self-governance thus presupposes an effective center that is capable of delineating its own affairs from the autonomous region. The comparison between Somaliland and Puntland shows that autonomy is only a shield behind which self-governance can flourish if this is upheld by a central government.

Notes

I am grateful to Dr. Iqbal Jhazbhay, Ulrike Dill, and Dr. Federico Battera for their help in the acquisition of documents, and to Nicolas Lamp for his insightful comments.

1. For an account of the difference in UN assistance to the south and the north, see Hussein 1997.

2. The "Somalization" of a civil war has become shorthand for a course of conflict that leads to destruction of state institutions and permanent absence of effective government (Robin 2003, 20).

3. For a comprehensive analysis of the so-called building-block-approach, see Bryden 1999.

4. For the methodological background, see George and Bennet 2005.

5. According to Lewis 1998, the Somalis define their social position according to a lineage system based on clan families, further divided into clans, subclans, and extended families.

6. "Separate civil administrations also emerged in parts of central and southern Somalia, such as Hiraan, Jowhar and the Juba Valley" (UNCTS 2007, 3); cf. also Menkhaus 2004.

7. Puntland emphasizes this in the official account of its history (PDRC 2005, 10).

8. According to Article 83 the president is directly elected jointly with the vice-president.

9. For a detailed account of the four elections, see ICG 2003.

10. "In order to protect the dignity and impartiality of the traditional leaders it is forbidden for them to participate in political association and parties."

11. Puntland was adversely affected by the tsunami that hit its coastline in December 2004; as a result many of the biggest obstacles to development, such as lack of roads and insufficient food supplies, affect Puntland even more (UNCHAS 2006).

12. In his 28 February 2007 report the secretary general puts Somaliland in quotation marks and merely notes its refusal to participate in the latest federal initiative. Report of the Secretary General on the Situation in Somalia, 28 February 2007, S/2007/115, at 4.

13. President Mohamuud Muuse Hersi on occasion of the opening of the nineteenth session of the parliament of Puntland. Quoted in GPS 2007b.

14. Menkhaus observed that "the key variable in whether regional administrations are likely to yield co-existence and power-sharing, rather than ethnic hegemony, appears to depend on the primary purpose which regional polities serve" (2004, 23).

15. One-third of the Somali population live in Puntland, which, at 212,510 km^2, is slightly bigger than Somaliland (137, 600 km^2) (WFP 2007; ICG 2006).

16. The "building-block" approach was first advocated by the Special Representative to Secretary-General Boutros Ghali, Mohamed Sahnoun, in 1992. He proposed to work separately with four entities, Somaliland, the SSDF, and two rival factions controlling different parts of the south. He resigned as a result of

the UN lack of commitment to the concept and focus on the central government (Bryden 1999).

17. The recent disagreement over the management of natural resources between the TFG and Puntland's government in view of the prospect of considerable rents from oil drilling could be interpreted as an indication that this might change in the future.

References

Adam, H. M. 1994. Formation and recognition of new states: Somaliland in contrast to Eritrea. *Review of African Political Economy* 59: 21–38.

Africa Online. 2008. *Range resources confirms its exploration activities in Puntland.* 27 March.

Africa Watch. 1990. *Somalia: A government at war with its own people.* New York: Africa Watch.

AllAfrica. 2007. Somalia: Puntland president rules by decree, not democracy. 9 December. http://allafrica.com/stories/200712100587.html (accessed 11 July 2009).

Battera, F. 2004. State and democracy-building in sub-Saharan Africa: the case of Somaliland. A comparative perspective. *Global Jurist Forum* 4, 1: 1–21.

———. 2000. Remarks on the 1998 Charter of Puntland State of Somalia. United Nations Development Office for Somalia, www.somaliawatch.org/archive-jun02/020707602.htm (accessed 1 September 2008).

Bradbury, M. 1997. *Somaliland.* CIIR Country Report 1997. London: Catholic Institute for International Relations.

Brons, M. 1994. *Somaliland: Zwei Jahre nach der Unabhängigkeitserklärung.* Hamburg: Arbeiten aus dem Institut für Afrikakunde.

Bryden, M. 2004. Somalia and Somaliland: Envisioning a dialogue on the question of Somali unity. *African Security Review* 13, 2: 23–33.

———.1999. New hope for Somalia? The building-block approach. *Review of African Political Economy* 26, 79: 134–40.

Contini, P. 1969. *The Somali republic: An experiment in legal integration.* London: Franck Cass.

Drysdale, J. 1994. *Whatever happened to Somalia?* London: Haan.

Farah, A. Y. 2002. *African conflicts, their management, resolution and post conflict reconstruction.* Addis Ababa: United Nations.

Farah, A. Y., and I. M. Lewis. 1997. Making peace in Somaliland. *Cahiers d'Études Africaines* 146, 37-2: 349–77.

Geiß, R. 2003. *"Failed states": Die normative Erfassung gescheiterter Staaten.* Berlin: Duncker and Humblot.

George, A. L., and A. Bennet. 2005. *Case studies and theory development in the social sciences.* Cambridge, Mass.: MIT Press.

Government of the Puntland State of Somalia (GPS). 2008a. The President of the TFG makes an official visit to Puntland. 18 January. http://www.puntland-govt.com/en/currentissues/information/current_issues_more.php?id=368 (accessed 11 July 2009)

———. 2008b. Puntland government policy statement. 22 March. http://www.somalitalk.com/oil/plpolicy.html (accessed 9 July 2009).

———.2007a. UNDP Puntland review. 12 December. http://www.puntlandgovt.com/en/currentissues/information/current_issues_more.php?id=580 (accessed 9 July 2009).

————. 2007b. President opens the 19th Session of the Puntland Parliament. 3 November. http://www.puntlandgovt.com/en/currentissues/information/current_issues_more.php?id=512 (accessed 9 July 2009).

Hagmann, T., and M. V. Höhne. 2007. Failed state or failed debate? Multiple Somali political orders within and beyond the nation-state. *Politorbis* 42: 20–26.

Höhne, M. V. 2007. *Puntland and Somaliland clashing in northern Somalia: Who cuts the Gordian Knot?* Social Science Research Council, http://hornofafrica.ssrc.org/Hoehne/index.html (accessed 1 September 2008).

————. 2006. Political identity, emerging state structures and conflict in northern Somalia. *Journal of Modern African Studies* 44, 3: 397–411.

Huliaras, A. 2002. The viability of Somaliland: internal constraints and regional geopolitics. *Journal of Contemporary African Studies* 20, 2: 157–82.

Hussein, S. 1997. Somalia: A destroyed country and a defeated nation. In *Mending rips in the sky: Options for Somali communities in the 21st century*, ed. H. M. Adam and R. Ford. Lawrenceville, N.J.: Red Sea Press.

Baldo, Suliman. 2006. Somaliland: The other Somalia with no war. *The Nation*, Nairobi, 30 June.

International Crisis Group (ICG). 2006. Somaliland: Time for African Union leadership. *Africa Report* 110.

————. 2003. Somaliland: Democratisation and its discontents. *Africa Report* 66.

Jacquin-Berdal, D. 2002. *Nationalism and ethnicity in the Horn of Africa: A critique of the ethnic interpretation*. Lewiston, N.Y.: Edwin Mellen.

Lewis, I. M. 1998. *A pastoral democracy: A study of pastoralism and politics among the Northern Somali of the Horn of Africa*. Hamburg: Lit.

Mattei, U. 1999. Patterns in African constitution making. *Cardozo Law Bulletin*, www.jus.unitn.it/cardozo/Review/Constitutional/Mattei-1999/Patterns.html (accessed 1 September 2008).

Mbugua, K. 2004. Prospects for peace and state re-building in Somalia. *Conflict Trends* 1: 25–31.

Menkhaus, K. J. 2004. *Somalia: State collapse and the threat of terrorism*. Oxford: Oxford University Press.

————. 2002. *Evaluation of the war-torn societies project in Puntland*. Ottawa: International Development Research Center.

Ministry of Planning and Statistics Puntland State of Somalia (MPSPS). 2003. Puntland facts and figures, www.puntlandchamberofcommerce.com/downloads/PuntlandFigures.pdf (accessed 1 September 2008).

Mohammed, H. M. 1997. Somalia: Between self-determination and chaos. In *Mending rips in the sky: Options for Somali communities in the 21st century*, ed. H. M. Adam and R. Ford. Lawrenceville, N.J.: Red Sea Press. 49–65.

Prunier, G. 1998. Somaliland goes it alone. *Current History* 97, 619: 225–53.

Puntland Development Research Centre (PDRC). 2005. *Traditional multi-stakeholder dialogue on structures in local government for local development*. Garowe: PDRC. http://info.worldbank.org/etools/docs/library/153066/somaliapuntland.pdf (accessed 1 September 2008).

Schoiswohl, M. 2004. *Status and (human rights) obligations of non-recognized de facto regimes in international law: The case of "Somaliland"; The resurrection of Somaliland against all international "odds"; State collapse, secession, non-recognition and human rights*. Leiden: Nijhoff.

Simmler, C. 1999. *Das uti possidetis-Prinzip: Zur Grenzziehung zwischen neu entstandenen Staaten*. Berlin: Duncker and Humblot.

Sorens, P. J., and L. Wantchekon. 2000. *Social order without the state: The case of Somalia.* New Haven, Conn.: Yale Center for International and Area Studies.

Terlinden, U., and T. Debiel. 2003. Somaliland: Building government bottom-up. *ZEF News* 14, 2: 1–2.

Thürer, D. 1999. Der "zerfallene Staat" und das Völkerrecht. *Die Friedens-Warte* 74, 3: 275–305.

UN Country Team Somalia (UNCTS). 2007. *UN transition plan for Somalia, 2008–2009.* Internal Displacement Monitoring Centre, www.internal-displacement. org/8025708F004CE90B/ httpCountry_ NewDocuments? ReadForm&countr y=Somalia&count=10000 (accessed 1 September 2008).

UN Office for the Coordination of Humanitarian Affairs Somalia (UNCHAS). 2006. *Puntland.* Nairobi: UNCHAS.

———. 2005. *Overview of humanitarian environment in Somaliland.* Nairobi: UNCHAS.

Weinstein, M. A. 2007a. The "Puntland State of Somalia" comes into play. *Power and Interest News Report,* 2 August.

———. 2007b. Somalia's new reality: A strategic overview. *Power and Interest News Report,* 27 December.

World Food Programme (WFP). 2007. *Puntland: Food security and vulnerability assessment.* Nairobi: WFP Somalia.

Zartmann, W., and F. M. Deng. 1991. Introduction. In *Conflict resolution in Africa,* ed. W. Zartmann and F. M. Deng. Washington, D.C.: Brookings Institution.

Conclusion

Marc Weller

Asymmetric autonomy remains the tool of choice in the settlement of ethno-political and self-determination conflicts. Given the diverse challenges posed by ethnic diversity to existing states, it is not surprising that the flexibility offered by asymmetrical designs makes this a tempting option. There are, however, a number of general points that can be observed on the basis of the case study review conducted by this project.

General issues

First, it has been argued by Brendan O'Leary that all instances of autonomous governance, even in the framework of what appears to be an entirely symmetrical federal structure, are essentially asymmetrical. Size of territory, population, relative economic strength, amount of fiscal transfers to and from the center, and many other issues will render any system of devolved governance asymmetrical in some way. The truth of this assertion is undeniable. After all, the question of whether a system is symmetrical depends on what symmetry is measured against.

An example is furnished by representation of federal units in an upper chamber. If one considers the legal equality of each federal unit as the starting point for the analysis, then assigning a similar number of representatives from each unit to the senate would appear symmetrical. If, on the other hand, the starting point is the right of each individual within the overall state to be represented at equal value then such a solution might appear asymmetrical, given the variance in population numbers among the federal units. Hence, the concept of asymmetrical settlement nevertheless retains its value when considered as a principal means of analyzing the de jure construction of a state. On this basis, one might then add considerations of the de facto situation in which the respective units find themselves, adding an even more complex understanding of asymmetry in practice.

Second, but related, one may note the existence of a rather bewildering array of asymmetrical settlements. Although this adds complexity to the four basic types of asymmetry noted in the introduction to this volume, it should not discourage analysis or classification of asymmetrical approaches to state construction. Different ethno-political composition, diverse historical experience, and the strength of commitment of the entity to self-governance or even independence make tailor-made solutions essential. Nevertheless, it remains useful to bear in mind the major types of asymmetrical solution that may be applied.

At times, only one entity will exhibit the features requiring a bespoke arrangement within a state, and a federacy-type arrangement might ensue. In other instances, one state might note significant divergences among the distinct entities it contains. John McGarry's review of the relatively stable case of the United Kingdom has furnished one such example. Northern Ireland was addressed by way of an advanced autonomy self-determination settlement, combined with strong power-sharing mechanisms, on the basis of an international treaty. Scotland has obtained a federacy status, both in terms of its institutional establishment and in terms of the competences exercised by its institutions. Devolution has been more limited for Wales. There are also special provisions for other regions, such as Greater London. England, on the other hand, remains under the direct control of the center. As McGarry has argued, this diversity is both necessary and reasonable, in view of the varying levels of demands for self-governance posed by the regions. Complexity in such an instance is not necessarily problematic. It may not be easy to administer, but if it meets the wishes of the respective populations it can work.

There is, however, one other type of complexity that does bear significant risk. This concerns instances of peace settlements in pieces. The best example of this is furnished by Sudan—a case we have addressed in a previous book and which has therefore not been revisited here. In that instance, a whole series of peace settlements were concluded over time for different regions. This included the so-called Comprehensive Peace Agreement (CPA) in the south, the Eastern Peace Agreement, and a proposed settlement for Darfur. The CPA also contains special elements addressing individual federal units enjoying special status, and the capital city area Khartum. While each settlement might conceivably have been able to function by itself, little or no regard seems to have been paid to the question of how the succession of arrangements would operate together. The situation is made even more difficult due to the fact that the north-south settlement is a transitory one, potentially leading to the independence of the south.

One way of attempting to avoid complexity running wild is exemplified by the Russian Federation. Based on previous Soviet practice, Russia has attempted to limit the variety of options available by establishing distinctive types of autonomous governance that may be applied in different circumstances. In the rather more chaotic days of postcommunist transition, such relative uniformity was undermined by a host of separate, bilateral arrangements. Now that Moscow has recovered its tools of attraction and control, a somewhat controversial movement toward recentralization and greater uniformity is afoot.

A third major finding in relation to asymmetrical autonomy settlements is the principle of variable geometry. Its flexibility is threefold: it can offer the option of establishing additional autonomies at a later stage, it can make room for local self-determination in establishing the boundaries of autonomous units, and it can offer the possibility of enhancing autonomous competences in due course.

In a number of the cases reviewed, autonomy is posited as a dynamic option that can be developed over time. In the case of Iraq, for instance, the constitution remains open to territories other than the Kurdish region to claim autonomy. Proposals for a Sri Lanka settlement would also allow other entities to emulate the status foreseen for the Northeast.

In the second place, the territorial definition of the region entitled to claim autonomy is also flexible. While, previously, there appears to have been an expectation that autonomous entities would be established within previously existing local or regional (provincial) administrative boundaries, this emphasis on the *uti possidetis* doctrine even in an internal context is being progressively undermined. A number of settlements offer local populations the possibility of opting into, or out of, newly established autonomous units. In addition to the cases of Mali and Gagauzia addressed in this book, one might note the settlements of Mindanao/Philippines or Southern Sudan in this context.

There is also a third element of dynamism. This relates to the flexibility in assigning competences to the autonomous entity. Increasingly, residual authority is assigned to the autonomy, which can consequently expand its jurisdictional remit over time. Other means of introducing flexibility include the open formulation of legal competences, which assigns them to the layer of authority best placed to exercise them. Northern Ireland, as opposed to Scotland and Wales, has the power to extend its jurisdiction to cover even "reserved" matters, provided such an action is supported by both communities.

Another approach is to allow the autonomous unit to expand its jurisdiction as its effectiveness increases. In the settlement suggested for Sri Lanka, all provinces would, over time, claim the bulk of competences that are principally concurrent. Similarly, the case of South Africa provides for the gradual taking over of shared competences as circumstances in the individual provinces permit.

In addition to these general points, a number of more specific observations can be made.

Implementation Issues

The first of these specific areas of interest concerns the issue of assigning competences just noted. In some instances of settlement, competences are assigned in a very general way, making it impossible to implement the settlement reached. In Gagauzia, the very expansive competences were subsequently scaled back via a central law on administration of the autonomy, and there has been persistent competition between the central government and the autonomy to fill the jurisdictional space left open by the agreed autonomy statute. Central government attempts to render the autonomy "consistent" with the overall constitution, which is code for undermining the essence of autonomous decision making and replacing it with decentralization. After all, if the autonomy was established as an asymmetrical settlement, then it is unlikely to be consistent with constitutional provisions that apply in relation to the state overall, or to other regions.

The delicate nature of asymmetrical arrangements is also usefully illustrated in the case of Hong Kong. There, a tremendous imbalance in legal and factual power exists between the center and the autonomy. Indeed, the very notion of a huge central state run by a one-party system does not augur well for the maintenance of asymmetrical autonomy arrangements. Indeed, as argued by Johannes Chan, China has been rigorous in insisting on its sovereignty and the supremacy of its legal order. However, in practice, its overwhelming interest in maintaining Hong Kong as a lucrative hub of economic activity has led to a relatively stable modus vivendi.

In other cases, the balancing of competences has been achieved through formal legal institutions. In fact, such mechanisms can even be found in the more classical examples. In relation to the Aaland Islands, the Finnish Ministry of Justice ratifies regionally made law. A joint Finnish-Aaland Islands Delegation (composed of two representatives from the center and two from the islands) offers an opinion on whether or not such an act has been adopted in accordance with the delegation of competences. If an excess of power is found to exist, the matter is checked by the Supreme Court before the Finnish presidency can exercise its prerogative of annulling the act in whole or in part.

Of course, relations between autonomous units, or between them and the center, are also often subject to elaborate power-sharing mechanisms. Again, this is not entirely new. In South Tyrol there have been provisions for guaranteed representation in the legislative assembly, governmental participation, and for the rotation of high executive office. There are also modest blocking powers. In the autonomous legislature, the minority can be out-voted, but it can take the matter to the constitutional court if it is opposed by two-thirds of the deputies from an ethnic group. Hard veto (each group voting separately and in favor) is in place for certain budgetary issues.

On the other hand, the case of Bosnia and Herzegovina, not addressed in this volume, has shown the risk of excessive consociationalism, particularly if made manifest by ethnic vetos and blocking powers. Once such mechanisms have been established as part of a postconflict settlement, it is very difficult to remove them as part of a transition of the relevant society to "normal life." In international settlement practice, the Bosnia and Herzegovina, experience has been taken into account. Instead of simple veto mechanisms, incentives for intergroup cooperation are increasingly built into settlements. Moreover, the areas of so-called "vital interests" of communities to which a veto may relate are more carefully circumscribed. Vetoes are coming to be replaced by an objection procedure, involving attempts of mediation and compromise and, if that fails, resolution through judicial, rather than political, means. The evolution of approaches in this respect can be easily detected when considering the flow of Balkan settlements, starting with Bosnia and Herzegovina, the Rambouillet draft, the Ohrid agreement on Macedonia, the Kosovo Framework Constitution, and finally the Ahtisaari Comprehensive Proposal on the Future Status of Kosovo, as implemented in Kosovo's new 2008 constitution.

Another important issue concerns the relations between an asymmetrical autonomy and the center. Monodimensional autonomy would simply grant powers of independent decision making to the region (although within the overall legal order of the state). However, if the autonomy is meant to function within the state, it is necessary to regulate its interaction with the state powers to which it is still subject. For instance, asymmetrical autonomy arrangements tend to neglect questions of application of central competences on their territory through federal agencies or their equivalent. In other instances, the exercise of federal functions may be conducted through local agencies, either directly or by way of decentralized administration. In the latter case, it is interesting to note that devolution does not exclude simultaneous application of decentralization to the autonomous entity.

Often, a new autonomy will be hesitant to discuss the administration of central competences on its territory. At times, there might be interest at least in addressing the reverse side of the coin—the representation of the asymmetric entity in the central institutions of the state. For instance, the Kurdish region has achieved a key role for itself within the organs

of Iraqi central government. Such arrangements may include the assignment of reserved seats in the legislature, or mechanisms for enhanced
(disproportionate) representation in it. There may also be powers of
legislative initiative assigned to regions that might otherwise not enjoy
them. Governmental posts may be reserved for the autonomy, including
in some instances the positions of vice-president or deputy prime minister (where the president or prime minister does not happen to represent
the autonomy). In other instances, the government will at least establish
contact offices for the autonomy at the center, to give it immediate and
high-level access. The South Tyrol Standing Commission in the office of
the Italian prime minister serves as an example.

Asymmetrical autonomy is thus often connected with some level of
power sharing. However, an additional element of state construction
may be required: entitlements of groups and individuals. Human and
minority rights would be guaranteed within the autonomy, and such arrangements would ordinarily entail access to human rights enforcement
beyond regional courts. The importance of this issue is aptly demonstrated by human rights practice, or lack of it, in the Srpska entity within
Bosnia and Herzegovina, or for any proposed settlement for Sri Lanka.

While the overall state will normally feature a common level of human
rights entitlement, the autonomy may come under well-founded pressure to offer additional rights to groups that now find themselves in a
nondominant position within the autonomous territory. This can take
the form of minority rights, including provisions for full and effective
equality for all. Such provisions may also extend to equal provision of
public services, as in relation to public housing in South Tyrol. There
may also be a need to secure the cultural identity of minorities through
special provision for minority languages and their official use, for minority cultural activities and education.

An additional special feature of asymmetrical autonomies concerns
foreign-affairs powers. The Aaland Islands can participate in treaty making and can even propose the launching of international negotiations.
Moreover, treaties affecting Aaland Island competences apply only after
consent from the island assembly; treaty provisions inconsistent with the
1991 Autonomy Act can only take effect with the support of a two-thirds
majority. There are also special exemptions from EU treaties and certain
supranational decisions. Moreover, the islands enjoy representation in
some intergovernmental bodies, such as the Nordic Council.

Hong Kong also enjoys a special international legal role, including a relative international legal personality. It has inherited treaty obligations and
benefits and can continue to participate in certain international bodies.

It has to be admitted, however, that these cases are somewhat unique.
A more widespread practice would be to allow asymmetrical autonomies

to conclude executive agreements relating to their areas of competence, and to generate arrangements for cross-border cooperation with other regions.

Where asymmetrical autonomy has been granted, it is often assumed that the autonomous entity will have the right to establish its own statute or constitution, provided it remains within the bounds of its authority. The central state would not, normally, be entitled to revoke or change this instrument, or the terms of the autonomy settlement, without the consent of the entity. Entrenchment of this commitment can be problematic, however. It is not always possible to reflect the newly achieved autonomy in the constitution. After all, the very reason for adopting asymmetry in the first place might have been to avoid change to the overall constitutional structure. However, in cases where formal constitutional (or international) entrenchment is difficult, there is room for back-tracking by central authorities, ostensibly in the name of ensuring constitutional consistency throughout the state. Indeed, even where constitutional amendments have been possible, subsequent revision may occur, as attempted by the Moldovan authorities in relation to Gagauzia. There, the autonomy law has the status of an organic law (i.e., one of constitutional standing) and a constitutional amendment was adopted, which at least referred to the new arrangement. However, this did not stop the central authorities from campaigning to reduce asymmetrical autonomy to local governance as exercised elsewhere in the territory.

Where conflicts of competence arise, or disputes about the extent of powers granted, a strong and neutral dispute-settlement mechanism would ordinarily be expected. However, especially with regard to asymmetrical autonomies, this may be problematic. A general purpose constitutional court may well be dominated by representatives who lack enthusiasm for, or interest in, the maintenance of the autonomy, or access to the court may be restricted.

This concern raises the wider issue of the potential problems and pitfalls of asymmetry.

Problematic Areas

First, it is sometimes argued at the conceptual level that asymmetry implies inequality. Hence, it is to be rejected. However, the principle of equality does not require that all situations be treated in exactly the same way. Instead, it requires only that similar situations be addressed similarly, while different circumstances require a more diverse approach. Nevertheless, in some of the cases reviewed here, the central authorities, and perhaps also the majority population, have argued against special provision for special regions. In Canada, asymmetry exists but it has been disguised. In Mali, the case of the Tuareq has been addressed under the guise of a general program of decentralization.

There is a similar tendency in relation to Sri Lanka. The proposed arrangements for the Northeast are potentially applicable to all provinces, that is, it can be argued that no asymmetry has been granted. Indeed, while the extensive Expert Panel proposal addresses many of the problems of asymmetrical state design identified here, the government has retreated to a far simpler solution. Such a solution, based on the presumption that any settlement must be accommodated within existing constitutional structures, will remain unacceptable to the Northeast. This refusal to engage on the basis of a balanced, overall plan may result in the continuation of prolonged and mutually damaging stalemate. Of course, besides the costs of continued conflict, there are additional risks. This fact has now been borne out by the recent events in Georgia and the territories of Abkhazia and South Ossetia. There, the failure to engage with the conflict through an expansive autonomy settlement has permitted reignition of the conflict. This has led to a de facto situation that challenges the doctrine of territorial integrity but that is nevertheless unlikely to be reversed.

Set against this hesitancy on the part of some governments to embrace wide-ranging asymmetrical autonomy, it is worth pointing out that the most well-established, classical ethnic settlements (Aaland Islands, South Tyrol) comprise asymmetrical solutions that have worked well in practice. But one must also note that even these early settlements are complex; they are not focused simply on granting autonomous powers of self-governance and leaving it at that. As noted, asymmetrical state design needs to be balanced by integrative tools or power sharing, by human-rights and minority-rights provisions, and by other means. Otherwise they may lose the transformative function intended. Instead of consolidating the unity of the state in the long term, they may contribute to its disintegration.

At times, there can be a strong incentive against a detailed, balanced settlement and, in such cases, an asymmetrical autonomy arrangement may present a convenient way of merely renaming the existing situation as a settlement. Such a situation can result in cases of armed conflict where de facto control of a region, obtained by secessionist groups through the use of force, cannot be challenged. Termination of the conflict is traded for recognition and legitimation of the exercise of such authority. However, settlements of this kind may be deficient in several aspects:

- The autonomous entity may not be sufficiently bound into the central state structure to retain an incentive to ensure the continued success of the overall state.

- The central state may not enjoy sufficient effectiveness in relation to the asymmetrical entity to exercise whatever state-wide competences may have been assigned to it in a settlement.
- There may be insufficient provision for the continued economic and fiscal integration of the state and for wealth-sharing.
- It may not be possible to ensure that the asymmetrical entity embraces the democratic practices to which it might have committed itself at the time of a settlement.
- The central state, but also international agencies, may not have the capacity to protect and promote human, and especially minority, rights in relation to either entity.
- The assignment of asymmetrical status to one entity may trigger campaigns and even insurgencies in favor of a similar status by other entities within the state.
- An asymmetrical design provides for separate legislative, administrative, and judicial competences and institutions for the formerly secessionist entity. However, as the central state does not transform itself into a "federal subject" itself, it lacks institutions that focus in their competence and activities exclusively on the area outside of the asymmetrically federal or autonomous territory.

Asymmetry is therefore not likely to offer a simple solution to difficult circumstances. It is in itself a challenging and complex concept. However, if asymmetrical autonomy designs are developed in a way that takes account of the complexities of the underlying conflicts, and are combined with other tools of state construction, they do offer a way out of otherwise unresolvable conflicts.

Of course, this does not mean that asymmetry can be the answer to all possible cases of ethnic or self-determination conflicts. Just as asymmetry comes in many guises, according to the specifics of the situation, autonomy is itself just one settlement option that will only be appropriate in certain circumstances. At the lower end of the spectrum, decentralization, enhanced local self-governance through the state, and improved provisions for human and minority rights may suffice. At the high end, recent practice ranging from Sudan to Bougainville and now Kosovo suggests that there are instances where integration is not the answer. Instead, secession may need to be offered as an option. However, even and especially in those kinds of cases, asymmetric autonomy will generally be deployed as a means of assuring a stable interim period, after which a change in status may be contemplated.

Contributors

Bill Bowring is Professor of Law at Birkbeck, University of London and is a practicing English barrister (mainly in the European Court of Human Rights). He founded and was the first director of the Human Rights and Social Justice Research Institute, and founder and now chair of the European Human Rights Advocacy Centre (EHRAC). He is also founder of the LLM in Human Rights at London Metropolitan University. He has published widely in English and Russian on law reform and human rights, as well as international law.

Johannes Chan, SC, is Professor and Dean of the Faculty of Law at the University of Hong Kong. His research areas include human rights, constitutional, and administrative law. He has published widely in these fields and is the first Honorary Senior Counsel in Hong Kong.

Janina Dill is a D.Phil. candidate at the University of Oxford, researching the effectiveness of international humanitarian law. She holds an MPhil in International Relations with Distinction from the University of Cambridge and a B.A. in International Relations with Honours from the Technical University Dresden.

Kristina Eichhorst has been a member of Team Asia at the Konrad Adenauer Foundation since April 2009. She was a researcher at Kiel University from 2001 to 2009, focusing on ethnic conflict in general and specializing in the Sri Lankan conflict.

Raffaele Iacovino holds a Ph.D. in the Department of Political Science at McGill University. A native of Montreal, his research interests lie in Canadian and Quebec politics, more specifically in the study of federalism, citizenship, and the politics of immigration/integration. Prior to his present position, he was a postdoctoral fellow with the Canada Research Chair on Democracy and Sovereignty (Chair, Geneviève Nootens), at the Université du Québec à Chicoutimi. He is co-author (with

Alain-G. Gagnon) of *Federalism, Citizenship and Quebec: Debating Multi-nationalism.*

Coel Kirkby's doctoral thesis traces the idea of "native" segregation in Canada and South Africa in the closing decades of the British Empire. While at the Community Law Centre at the University of the Western Cape, he assisted the South African government's diplomatic mission to the Democratic Republic of Congo.

John McGarry is Professor and Canada Research Chair in Nationalism and Democracy in the Department of Political Studies at Queen's University, Kingston, Ontario. During 2008-9, he served as Senior Adviser on Power-Sharing to the Mediation Support Unit of the United Nations. He is editor, coeditor, and coauthor of several books, including *European Integration and the Nationalities Question, The Future of Kurdistan in Iraq* (with Brendan O'Leary and Khaled Salih, available from the University of Pennsylvania Press), and *The Northern Ireland Conflict: Consociational Engagements* (2004). He has published in journals such as *Ethnic and Racial Studies, Ethnopolitics, Government and Opposition, Nationalism and Ethnic Politics, Nations and Nationalism, Parliamentary Affairs,* and *Political Studies.*

Christina Murray is Professor of Human Rights and Constitutional Law at the University of Cape Town. Between 1994 and 1996 she served on a Panel of Experts elected to advise the South African Constitutional Assembly and in 2009 she was elected by the Kenyan Parliament to serve on a Committee of Experts established to redraft the Kenyan Constitution. Her main research interests are constitution-making and constitutional design, devolution of powers, and women's rights.

Katherine Nobbs is Research Associate and Legal Adviser at the European Centre for Minority Issues, and Managing Editor of the *European Yearbook of Minority Issues.* She holds an MPhil in International Relations with Distinction from the University of Cambridge, a Graduate Diploma in Law with Commendation from the College of Law, Bloomsbury, and a First Class BA in Politics from the University of Nottingham. Her publications include *The Protection of Minorities in the Wider Europe* (ed., with Marc Weller and Denika Blacklock).

Brendan O'Leary, B.A. (Oxon), Ph.D. (LSE), is Lauder Professor of Political Science and Director of the Penn Program in Ethnic Conflict at the University of Pennsylvania. Recent authored and edited books include *How to Get Out of Iraq with Integrity, Terror, Insurgency and the State: Ending Protracted Conflicts* (with Marianne Heiber and John Tirman), *The Future of Kurdistan in Iraq* (with John McGarry and Khaled Salih), all available from the University of Pennsylvania Press); *The Northern Ireland Conflict: Consociational Engagements*; and *Right-Sizing the State: The Politics of Moving Borders*. He has acted as a constitutional and political adviser to governments, parties and international organizations on and in Northern Ireland, Somalia, Kwa-Zulu Natal, Nepal, and Kurdistan, and currently serves as a Power Sharing Expert for the Mediation Support Unit of the United Nations Department of Political Affairs.

Oleh Protsyk is Senior Research Associate at the European Centre for Minority Issues, Flensburg, Germany. His research interests include ethnic conflict regulation, representation and political parties, and executive-legislative relations. Recent articles have appeared in the *European Journal of Political Research, Post-Soviet Affairs*, and *Political Studies*.

Marc Weller is Reader in International Law at the University of Cambridge, and a Fellow of the Lauterpacht Research Centre for International Law and Hughes Hall. He is also Director of the Carnegie Project on Resolving Self-Determination Disputes Through Complex Power-sharing, and of the Cambridge Rockefeller Project on Restoring an International Consensus of the Rules Governing the Use of Force. His writings focus mainly on conflict management, international law, and minority rights. He has acted as legal advisor to several governments and organizations, and has been a member of international peace processes. Dr. Weller is also former Director of the European Centre for Minority Issues in Flensburg, Germany.

Jonathan Wheatley is Senior Research Associate at the Centre for Direct Democracy, University in Zurich, former Research Associate at the European Centre for Minority Issues, and former Research Fellow at the Osteuropa Institut, Free University Berlin. His publications include working papers for the European Centre for Minority Issues on regional integration in the two regions of Georgia, and *Georgia from National Awakening to Rose Revolution: Delayed Transition in the former Soviet Union*.

Stefan Wolff is Professor of Political Science at the University of Nottingham, where he also directs the Centre for International Crisis Management and Conflict Resolution. He holds an MPhil in Political Theory from Magdalene College, Cambridge, and a PhD in Political Science from the London School of Economics. He has written extensively on ethnic conflict and conflict resolution. Published works include *Ethnic Conflict: A Global Perspective*, *Self-Determination, Conflict Resolution and Autonomy* (with Marc Weller); and *The Ethnopolitical Encyclopaedia of Europe* (with Karl Cordell). He is also the founding editor of the journal *Ethnopolitics*.

Index